BEAUTIFUL CIRCUITS

BEAUTIFUL CIRCUITS

Modernism and the Mediated Life

MARK GOBLE

COLUMBIA UNIVERSITY PRESS   NEW YORK

Columbia University Press

Publishers Since 1893

New York   Chichester, West Sussex

Copyright © 2010 Columbia University Press

All rights reserved

Library of Congress Cataloging-in-Publication Data

Goble, Mark.

Beautiful circuits : modernism and the mediated life/Mark Goble.

p.   cm.

Includes bibliographical references and index.

ISBN 978-0-231-14670-8 (cloth : alk. paper) — ISBN 978-0-231-51840-6 (e-book)

1. Mass media and literature—United States.   2. American literature—20th century—History and criticism.   3. Mass media and culture—United States.   4. Interpersonal communication—Technological innovations—Social aspects—United States.   5. Social interaction—Technological innovations—United States.   I. Title.

P96.L5G63   2010

302.230973—dc22

2009053416

Columbia University Press books are printed on permanent and durable acid-free paper.

This book is printed on paper with recycled content.

Printed in the United States of America

c 10 9 8 7 6 5 4 3 2 1

References to Internet Web sites (URLs) were accurate at the time of writing. Neither the author nor Columbia University Press is responsible for URLs that may have expired or changed since the manuscript was prepared.

For Elisa Tamarkin

Contents

Contents

Illustrations

Acknowledgments

It is a hard thing to know that this book's first expression of gratitude is for someone who cannot read it: like so many others, I owe much to the intelligence and enthusiasm of Jay Fliegelman, who possessed the genius for taking so much pleasure in his students' work that it was simply impossible for them not to keep on doing it. His gifts were abundant, and they were taken from us too soon. There was not a book or object he could not bring to scintillating, complicated life, and though the chapters that follow have little to say on any of the subjects his own scholarship transformed, I know for certain that they would not have been written without him. The guidance and teaching that filled my years as a graduate student at Stanford continue to surprise and educate me. David Halliburton saw this project in its earliest incarnations and enlarged its prospects with his deep originality and commitment to eccentricity. Albert Gelpi made sure that no matter how far I wandered, I always came back to my texts and the traditions that informed them. Marjorie Perloff's energy and exacting sensibility convinced me that the reading we do as critics often does more justice when, as Frank O'Hara might say, "you just go on your nerve." Scott Bukatman arrived in the nick of time and made it possible for me to break some rules that I otherwise would have followed to no good end.

I was very fortunate to spend six years in the English Department at the University of California, Irvine, where my colleagues made this a better book by way of their kindness, friendship, and advice. Jerome Christensen was gracious as a chair and exemplary as an intellectual; Rodrigo Lazo, Jayne Lewis, James McMichael, Steven Mailloux, James Steintrager, Brook Thomas, Irene Tucker, and the late Richard Kroll were smart and spirited in their support. Michael Szalay made me own up to being a modernist after all, and Robert Folkenflik put the right book in my hands when I needed it most. Other friends and fellow Americanists made Los Angeles a secretly terrific place to be an academic, and I am truly lucky to be so indebted to such a group: Joe Dimuo, Paul Gilmore, Greg Jackson, Cathy Jurca, Chris Looby, Sianne Ngai, Sharon Oster, and especially Mark McGurl. Members of the Americanist Research Colloquium at UCLA generously read portions of this book and offered valuable suggestions, and members of the Southern California Americanist Group helped to clarify its purpose and prose with their impeccable camaraderie over the years. I am also grateful for lively responses from participants at meetings of the Digital Cultures Project and the Transliteracies Project, both housed at the University of California, Santa Barbara.

Early encouragement from Mary Kinzie, Carl Smith, Wendy Wall, and the late Robert Wiebe helped put everything in motion, along with the support of Helen Deutsch, whose later friendship became another reason to love LA. Moving north, I was welcomed to the University of California, Berkeley, by Stephen Best, Mitchell Breitwieser, Ian Duncan, Dorothy Hale, Colleen Lye, Kent Puckett, Samuel Otter, and Scott Saul, new colleagues whose immediate generosity and goodwill has been more appreciated than they probably realize. I would also like to thank a far-flung network of friends and colleagues who have been the best of interlocutors with their comments, criticisms, and general resourcefulness: Rachel Adams, Sara Blair, Marshall Brown, Stuart Burrows, Jay Clayton, Kevin Dettmar, Betsy Erkkila, Vivian Folkenflik, Jonathan Freedman, Eric Hayot, Alan Liu, Mark Maslan, Alexander Nemerov, Diana Paulin, Chris Spilker, Pamela Thurschwell, Cecelia Ticchi, William Warner, Kenneth Warren, Mark Wolleager, and especially Sandy Zipp, who is always fated to come at the end of a list like this even when he merits higher billing. Peter Coviello has been a true friend for more than twenty years, and I have come to count, in equal measure, on his exuberant intellect and the intelligence of his exuberance.

Funding from UC Irvine's Humanities Center and UC Berkeley's Committee on Research made it possible for this work to take its final shape. I am grateful to librarians and archivists at the University of California, Santa Barbara, the Huntington Library in Pasadena, and the Gallery Archives of the National Gallery of Art in Washington, D.C., for their assistance with resources and illustrations. The estates of Cecil Beaton, Walker Evans, Rube Goldberg, Man Ray, and Norman Rockwell were kind enough to grant me permission to publish images in this book. My special thanks to Chris Jordan and Ed Ruscha for their help in acquiring reproductions of their works, and for letting me include them here. Portions of chapter 1 and chapter 2 first appeared, respectively, in *ELH* 74, no. 2 (Summer 2007) and *Modern Language Quarterly* 62, no. 2 (June 2001), and I would like to thank Marshall Brown and the anonymous readers and editorial staffs at both journals.

I am altogether indebted to Philip Leventhal at Columbia University Press, who has been a remarkably insightful and patient editor, and who, along with Anne McCoy, Avni Majithia, Michael Simon, and the indispensable copy editor Jan McInroy, improved this book in countless ways. The anonymous readers at the press provided invaluable engagements with every aspect of the text and helped me sharpen both its argument and style; having the chance to revisit the book in light of their responses was one of the privileges of this process.

I come from a small family, so the encompassing love of my parents, Ben and Cary Goble, has been the largest of gifts. I am thankful for everything that Civia Tamarkin, Michael Cohen, Ira Levin, and Michelle Levin have done for me since I have been a part of their families, and I am honored to remember Bob Tamarkin for everything he did in the years I was fortunate enough to know him. All the rest—this book and whatever else I've managed to do right—is thanks to Elisa Tamarkin. The integrity of her love and brilliance has given me so much more than I ever thought it possible to receive. Without her, I could connect nothing with nothing.

BEAUTIFUL CIRCUITS

INTRODUCTION
"Communications Now Are Love"

Only communications can communicate.

NIKLAS LUHMANN

Only an art can define its media.

STANLEY CAVELL

Apparently literature had seen its better days by 1964, so Karl Shapiro asks that we observe "the Funeral of Poetry." We are welcome to send condolences at our convenience; attendance at the memorial is optional:

> A man appears at the corner of the street; I prepare myself for hospitality. Man or angel, welcome! But I am afraid and double-lock the door. On the occasion of the death of a political party, I send an epitaph by Western Union. I didn't go to the funeral of poetry. I stayed home and watched it on television. Moon in the bottom of the Steuben glass, sun nesting in New Mexican deserts—the primitive Christian communicated with a dirty big toe. He drew a fish in the dust.[1]

The last lines give religious coloring to Shapiro's mordant resignation in the face of new technologies that have rendered his vocation ready for this scene of loss; instead of offering "hospitality" to the "man or angel," Shapiro closes himself off and retreats inside his house. "Poems of a Jew," to recall the title of his 1958 collection, cannot hope to beat the power of the Word made flesh, which here seems just as immanent in the latest form of high technology (television) as it already was in the "primitive" toe-drawn fish that signals the profound devotion to visual representation and iconography that distinguishes Christianity.

"The Incarnation," writes media historian and Jesuit Walter Ong in 1967, "is an event not only in the objective world but also in the history of communication."[2] For Ong, the "highly visualist sensorium of technological cultures" is a residue of "Christian revelation" and its prolific iconographies. His argument is resonant with one made by Marshall McLuhan, who suggests that early Christian woodcuts, with their "low degree of data about objects," demand a high degree of viewer "participation" simply to make sense of them; thus, in the woodcuts' low-resolution imagery, we see the advent, so to speak, of television.[3] The resonance with McLuhan is no coincidence: Ong's master's thesis on Victorian poetry was directed by McLuhan, who was himself a Catholic convert long before becoming one of the twentieth century's most entertaining intellectuals—famous in the 1960s and 1970s for popularizing media studies in lecture halls, on campuses, and on *Laugh-In* ("What are you doin', Marshall McLuhan?" asks Goldie Hawn in a bikini).[4] In letters from the 1930s describing his conversion, McLuhan was already celebrating "communion" not only as a "spiritual act" but as a media event that must be seen and heard; he developed his theory about how media alter sensory perceptions as a correlative to the model of consciousness he found in Thomas Aquinas.[5] In a letter to Ong in 1953, McLuhan told his former student that "we need somebody to do a Thomist Theory of Communication," and by 1961 he let Ong know that he himself was rising to the occasion.[6] His growing interest in "the hypnotic aspect of *all* media" had inspired his return to Aquinas's model of the *sensus communis*, because, he tells Ong, the late-twentieth-century phenomenon of "participation mystique" is essentially its second coming. But McLuhan's best sellers of the 1960s call scant attention to these religious influences, and the pop graphics, models in miniskirts, and ad-speak of a book like *The Medium Is the Massage* (1967) do much to mask whatever pieties informed his life's devotion to communication. Still, his dream of media remains all-powerful, if not divine: "All media work us over completely. They are so pervasive in their personal, political, aesthetic, psychological, moral, ethical, and social consequences that they leave no part of us untouched, unaffected, unaltered."[7]

In 1948 McLuhan met another student (and another Catholic convert) who cared deeply for poetry, Hugh Kenner, whom he later introduced to Ezra Pound. Thus began one of the careers that made modernism as we know it from the latter half of the twentieth century. Kenner acknowledged the gesture by dedicating his first book on modernism, *The Poetry of Ezra Pound* (1951), to McLuhan with a line from Pound's Canto 3: "A catalogue, his jewels of conversation." Appearing in the wake of Pound's Bollingen Prize in 1949, Kenner's work confirmed the significance of modernism in even its most historically contentious modes, and by the time of *The Pound Era* (1971), the critical idiom that was the product of his preferences had flourished, if not more accurately "winged and propagated," as Kenner himself described the radiance of his modernist exemplar's light—but not without debt to McLuhan.[8] Kenner thanks his former mentor at the beginning of the book "for getting me in touch with Ezra Pound in the first place," but *The Pound Era* is a far more complicated tribute to McLuhan and his conceptualizing, epoch-defining zeal. For Kenner, Pound's writings, like McLuhan's media, "work over us completely" and leave no aspect of the world "unaltered"; Pound's poetry is "a patterned integrity accessible to the mind," and while it all too often, even for Kenner, tends to verbalize on matters better left alone, we admire its "mysterium in fragments" and know that there is "magical power in the tatter of a poem."[9]

McLuhan's influence on Kenner marks only one of many genealogies to which we owe the modernism passed down to us from the first generation of critics who canonized its major figures and traditions. But there is no mistaking that their relationship connects modernism's culture and aesthetics to a faith in communication, which is not something we always think it wanted. We expect to see modernism figured as antagonistic to the straightforward delivery of messages or in light of such familiar complaints as Kenner's that the "cow-at-a-billboard gaze attuned to neon signs and headlines" represents a blindness to "the singular purity of motive that underlies the comprehension of *any* poetry."[10] I am not interested in proving (again) that modernism positively thrived alongside mass communications, nor that it achieved many of its innovations by appropriating and importing new technologies while transmuting their appeal to something finer and more rare. This book is about how modernism itself desired communication and the many forms it took, not just as a response to the power of media technologies in the twentieth century but as a way of insisting that this power was already modernism's own. The experience of communication, as John Durham Peters writes, often looks less like a rational exchange of information and more like "belonging to a social body via an expressive act that requires no response or recognition."[11] Peters does not describe the only style in which modernism might be considered to communicate; but this is the kind of communication that Shapiro, for one, indulges despite himself by passively receiving word of poetry's demise in isolation. He stays home to watch the funeral on television, which is precisely how its effects are felt most deeply.

Shapiro was no great fan of modernism, but his real animus in "The Funeral of Poetry" is directed at a cause of death that implicates McLuhan, and the impulse to communicate more generally. Thus Shapiro starts: "The password of the twentieth century: Communications (as if we had to invent them)" (15). It is not hard to imagine such a pronouncement coming unironically from McLuhan, "the Dr. Spock of pop culture" or "the guru of the boob tube"—two nicknames gleefully reproduced by *Playboy* when it interviewed him—much less the profane promoter of high technology claimed by *Wired* magazine as a "patron saint."[12] McLuhan's *Understanding Media*, which first appeared in 1964, offered little consolation for "those who panic about the threat of the new media and about the revolution we are forging, vaster in scope than that of Gutenberg."[13]

Of course, Shapiro's mocking in 1964 also strikes a chord because it reminds us that the previous decades marked, according to Peters, "the single grandest moment in the century's confrontation with communication."[14] The study of both modernism and communications, we might say, emerged almost simultaneously as twentieth-century preoccupations and flourished as conglomerating triumphs of the postwar university in the United States. In this respect, I. A. Richards's offering of "A Theory of Communication" in his *Principles of Criticism* (1926) not only represents a crucial early moment in this shared history but also turns on a fine point of terminology whose many implications shape this book: "Although it is as a communicator that it is most profitable to consider the artist, it is by no means true that he commonly looks upon himself in this light."[15] New Criticism helped to enshrine what Richards describes as the paradoxical relationship between the "desire actually to communicate," which authors often do not have, and the "desire to produce something with communicative efficacy," which they do (28). T. S. Eliot captures this double logic best in "Tradition and the Individual Talent," where he criticizes any poetry that is an "expression of personality" and instead imagines the writer as an obscure, conductive medium who vanishes in a show of highly channeled sensibility, emotion, and technique. "It is in this depersonalization," writes Eliot, "that art may be said to approach the condition of science. I therefore invite you to consider, as a suggestive analogy, the action which takes place when a bit of finely filiated platinum is introduced into a chamber containing oxygen and sulphur dioxide."[16] In the resulting flash, the modern artist who might otherwise desire communication is consumed so that his work of art, if the reader is similarly reactive, might communicate more powerfully. The protocols of impersonality are just one of many innovations that help to teach us, as Mark Wollaeger has brilliantly shown, that "in some fundamental sense much of modernism can be read as an attempt to clear a space . . . for more authentic modes of communication."[17]

But communication did not attain its status as a twentieth-century "password" until cybernetics and information theory began to circulate widely in both academic circles and the public sphere. Again, Richards is prescient: "Communication," he writes in 1926, "takes place when one mind so acts upon its environment that another mind is influenced, and in that other mind an experience occurs which is like the experience in this first mind, and is caused in part by that experience" (177). This finely calibrated account of feedback loops, redundancy, and materiality—a mind needs an "environment" to influence other minds—signals almost all the crucial emphases of postwar cybernetics *avant la lettre*. Norbert Wiener's *Cybernetics: or Control and Communication in the Animal and the Machine* (1948), which is widely hailed for coining the term in its modern usage, draws on Richards for its most fundamental lesson that "any organism is held together . . . by the possession of means for the acquisition, use, retention, and transmission of information."[18] Warren Weaver, writing in *The Mathematical Theory of Communication*, defines communication in a similarly expansive mode, including "all of the procedures by which one mind may affect another," and so encompassing "not only written and oral speech, but also music, the pictorial arts, the theatre, the ballet, and in fact all human behavior."[19] When phrased with such leveling banality, the point of Shapiro's joke at the expense of "communications" seems rather apt ("as if we had to invent them"), which is not to discount the staggering influence of midcentury cybernetics that remains an essential context for understanding contemporary post-humanism in philosophy, biology, computer science, and literary theory.[20] In *Communication: The Social Matrix of Psychiatry* (1951), Jurgen Ruesch and Gregory Bateson argue that modern means of communication inevitably "will accelerate the dissemination of information to such an extent that in the not too distant future we can expect that no individual or group will be able to escape such influences for long."[21] Someday, we will all be always in communication.

For Shapiro, this future is already here, and "The Funeral of Poetry" marks one small aspect of the changes that have come:

> The password of the twentieth century: Communications (as if we had to invent them). Animals and cannibals have communications; birds and bees and even a few human creatures, called artists (generally held to be insane). But the bulk of humanity had to invent Communications. The Romans had the best roads in the world, but had nothing to communicate over them except other Romans. Americans have conquered world-time and world-space and chat with the four corners of the earth at breakfast and have nothing to communicate except other Americans. The Russians communicate other Russians to the moon. The entire solar system is in the hands of cartoonists. (15)

Even as he captures the exuberance of postwar cybernetic discourse ("Animals and cannibals have communications"), Shapiro invokes the long history of communications as a term used to describe the physical movement of things and people. Over the course of the nineteenth century, we learn from James W. Carey, this more material and transitive sense of communication faded from common use as first the telegraph and then the telephone provided spectacular new experiences of the comparatively ephemeral and instantaneous transmission of information across great distances.[22] In this respect, it seems only appropriate that Shapiro here displays an attitude toward technology that echoes Thoreau's famous skepticism in *Walden* about the telegraph ("We are in great haste to construct a magnetic telegraph from Maine to Texas; but Maine and Texas, it may be, have nothing important to communicate").[23] But Thoreau's antipathy looks timid next to Shapiro's unrelenting anger about communications, which finally produces a weird vision of the Holocaust and nuclear annihilation by way of a young girl's entirely absorbing fascination with technology:

> I am sitting in the kitchen in Nebraska and watching a shrouded woman amble down the market in Karachi. She is going to get her morning smallpox shot. It's cold and mental love they want. It's the mystic sexuality of Communications. The girl hugs the hi-fi speaker to her belly: It pours in

her openings like gravy. Money was love. Power was love. Communications now are love. In the spring Hitler arises. This is the time of trampling. My japanned birds in the radioactive snow are calling. (15–16)

I have no ready answer for the connection that Shapiro insinuates between a girl with a new hi-fi and Hitler's springtime, nor do I think that anything he imagines for us in "The Funeral of Poetry" should have him feeling so alarmed. A mysterious "they" wants "cold and mental love" instead of some more familiar affection; "Americans have conquered world-time" and degraded global culture with a rapaciousness that seems Roman in its imperializing scope; there is smallpox in Karachi, and Karl Shapiro, at home in Nebraska, is made to know it. That "cartoonists" have seized the "solar system" does not make their work the moral equivalent of *Triumph of the Will*. In all this worrying about mass culture and its mediums, Shapiro flaunts a patently modernist disregard for modernity itself, and especially for the degraded forms of amusement and entertainment that come to take the place, according to an old complaint, of art and literature as such. Clement Greenberg, writing in "Avant-garde and Kitsch," complains that the danger of "synthetic art" is that "it provides vicarious experience for the insensitive with far greater immediacy" than serious aesthetic objects.[24] Perhaps Shapiro was more the proper modernist than he let on, for he exhibits his own version of the "reaction formation," as Andreas Huyssen terms it, that orients the modernist aesthetic around a "paranoid view of mass culture" and the imperative to abstain "from the pleasure of trying to please a larger audience, suppressing everything that might be threatening to the rigorous demands of being modern and at the edge of time."[25] For Huyssen and many other recent critics, Shapiro's decision to embody everything he dreads about a culture killing poetry in the figure of a girl and her "communications" would seem not just conventional but overdetermined. Modernism, when it deigns to communicate at all, should do so with great difficulty and ambivalence; meaning should be hard-earned and always at risk of being lost to the opacity of an arcane reference, a daunting show of style or syntax, or a novel turn of phrase; new locutions and techniques must estrange us from the languages of everyday perception and experience and reveal a defamiliarized aesthetic that is more richly felt for being so overtly challenging.

This book is not an argument with such shopworn understandings of high modernism so much as it is an attempt to take modernist aesthetics seriously for all the ways in which they gratify and indulge their mediums and materialities of communication. The chapters that follow trace a modernism that is often indistinguishable from "McLuhanism" in its attraction to an impossible erotics that would treat the telephone as a sex object, or have a young girl rapturously hold stereo to body so that "her openings" might be filled with whatever form of information it pours out. It is this "mystic sexuality of Communications" that U.S. modernism puts to work in the first decades of the twentieth century and, in so doing, gives us anticipations of a world that offers still more delirious and visceral experiences of technology—experiences of the sort that new media theorists, including Katherine Hayles, Mark Hansen, Lev Manovich, and Brian Massumi, have described as central to the practices of digital art and contemporary computer culture.[26] But modernism, as I describe it here, also represents an archive of responses to technology that reflect a set of historical commitments to *mediums* that are not just remote from how we talk about *media* now but are provocatively outdated. I am content to let modernism remain on its own side of what McLuhan would call "the resonant interval of interface," a curious term he offers to describe the bonds between phenomena that, no matter how close, are predicated on the recognition of discontinuity.[27]

Or put differently, much of the newness that is attributed to new media art and culture is understood to render obsolete the sense of modernism and medium specificity (modernism *as* medium specificity) championed most notably by Clement Greenberg. "It quickly emerged," writes Greenberg in his 1960 essay "Modernist Painting," "that the unique and proper area of competence of each art coincided with all that was unique in the nature of its medium."[28] Identifying modernism with a commitment to the physical constraints and artistic conventions of individual mediums—so that to engage with their materiality is not just to discover but to delimit their ideal realms of practice and technique—Greenberg's arguments remain a point of departure for many writers seeking to understand the forms of multimedia, or new media art that follow modernism proper. Thus when Rosalind Krauss suggests that we are now in a "post-medium condition," she all but admits that what she means to say is "post-Greenberg."[29] And for Hansen, even this is not saying enough: Krauss's "reconceptualization of the medium" remains incapable of "grasping the *aesthetic* newness of new media art" because this art is designed to address the body "as a selective processor of information" whose "medial interfaces" displace and transform the very material limits of the art object with which traditional notions of the medium contend. New media art is defined by "its resistance to capture by now dated, historical forms of art and media criticism."[30] The very notion of the "medium" and its aesthetic epistemology is no more bleeding edge than Betamax.

When modernism's impulses toward an expanded field of sensory effects are referenced in new media studies, they are used to help define the period by its peculiar ethnology of mediums—which cannot survive their contact with, and colonization by, the delirious monoculture of the digital. No one argues this position with more swagger than Friedrich Kittler:

> The general digitization of channels and information erases the differences among individual media. Sound and image, voice and text are reduced to surface effects, known to consumers as interface. Sense and the senses turn into eyewash. Their media-produced glamour will survive for an interim as a by-product of strategic programs. Inside the computers themselves everything becomes a number: quantity without image, sound, or voice.[31]

This is what has happened to the "surrogate sensualities" that "so-called Man," to invoke Kittler's telling post-human coinage, once experienced as the specific effects of mediums (14). When Lev Manovich calls the computer our "universal media machine" and suggests that "all cultural categories and concepts" may be "substituted, on the level of meaning and/or language by new ones that derive from the computer's ontology, epistemology, and pragmatics," he assumes much the same position toward the aesthetics of "old" media as Kittler, though avoiding his cyberpunk machismo.[32] For Jay David Bolter and Richard Grusin, "no medium today, and certainly no single media event, seems to do its cultural work in isolation from other media, any more than it works in isolation from other social and economic forces," which suggests that we have never had mediums at all, at least not with the concentrated "purity" demanded by Greenberg's brand of modernism.[33] And so Bolter and Grusin are happy to define a medium as "that which remediates" or adapts a prior form of media in order to communicate (98). In more than merely spirit, this central insight strikingly recalls McLuhan, who first observes in *Understanding Media* that "the 'content' of any medium is always another medium."[34] However useful modernism's medium fetish—with all its recursive formalisms and untenable injunctions—may be as a first principle toward a media ecology, I would argue that it is more than just a symptom of the period's historical imagination that now seems like a mistake. When new media critics dispense with its aesthetics of medium specificity, what remains of modernism is a concern with the thematics of high technology, which cannot move past a formalism designed to rarefy and obscure the social and political significance of technology itself. Modernism, in a perverse play on Greenberg, seems most memorable today when the emphasis on its own medium is "transferred to subject matter" and treated as another sign of the "difficulties people faced in adjusting to new technologies and a changing ethos."[35]

These issues, not surprisingly, look different from the perspective of recent work on technology within a resurgent modernist studies, where modernism's immersion in a culture of new inventions and experiences of communication argues powerfully for its relevance. "That there should be some significant relation between aesthetic modernism and new media," Michael North observes, "seems true almost by definition. Modernism, after all, stakes its initial claim to fame on new modes and new methods, innovations so drastic they seem not just to change the old arts but to invent new and unrecognizable ones."[36] Yet understanding just what modernism can still teach us about the history and culture of media technology has meant, at least in practice, pushing aside the same aesthetics of medium specificity against which so many critics and theorists of new media define their projects. I have little desire to revisit arguments about how artists best acknowledged painting's flatness, nor much interest in celebrating the twelve-tone scale's aspirations to pure sound or in demonstrating the extent to which texts began to treat the contours of language as an obsessive preoccupation. But such rigorously formalist assessments of early-twentieth-century art and literature, which nobody has much championed for years, still manage to inform a model of modernism that persists as an object of skepticism and disfavor in modernist studies: an aesthetic of pristine self-regard and hypertrophied opacity that denies the historical conditions and politics of the period and assumes that the work of art should never permit itself merely to communicate with its audience. Writing in 1991's *Radical Artifice*—before either modernist or media studies were enjoying their current "new" formations—Marjorie Perloff had already signaled that reckoning with avant-garde aesthetics in "the age of media" meant dispensing with "modernist elitism" and "lingering Greenbergian notions of modern art . . . as the preservation of the purity of media, genre, and convention in the face of capitalist commercialism."[37] Werner Sollors speaks for what has emerged as a new conventional wisdom on modernism that sees it "merely as a set of stylistic conventions."[38] Indeed, the most compelling recent investigations of modernism—including work attuned to everything from the economics of literary professionalism to the influence of anthropology, from queer theory to class politics—effectively proceed from what Douglas Mao and Rebecca L. Walkowitz describe as the translation of modernism "from an evaluative and stylistic designation to a neutral and temporal one."[39] My chapters do not reflect a nostalgia for the modernism of Greenberg, much less Kenner, but they do proceed from a belief that there is reason to revisit what it meant for so many writers and artists to surrender to their medium at a moment when new practices of communication were making the experience of technology itself an occasion for aesthetic experiment and historical reflection.

◊

"Money was love. Power was love. Communications now are love." The words encode a familiar history of modernity in the nineteenth and twentieth centuries, and evoke the economic, artistic, intellectual, and psychological transformations associated with an increasingly pervasive culture of information. While this story is perhaps no longer told with the same breathless enthusiasm that marked so much discourse about the new economy and its media in the 1990s, we are still invited, on a regular basis, to "the funeral of poetry." Or books. Or reading.[40] At the height of the dot-com cultural bubble, Sven Birkerts worried about "the death of literature" and morbidly observed that "although significant works still get written, it is harder than ever for them to get published; or, once published, distributed; or once distributed, sold; or once sold, read."[41] But this is not the worst of it: Birkerts's "core fear is that we are, as a culture, as a species, becoming shallower. . . . Fingers tap keys, oceans of fact and sensation get downloaded, are dissolved through the nervous system. Bottomless wells of data are accessed and manipulated, everything at circuit speed. Gone the rock in the field, the broken hoe, the grueling distances" (229). This mix of neo-Luddite posturing and existential dread speaks to the overt millennialism of much new media culture; it speaks just as powerfully to the strategic blindness patterning such forms of Western anti-modernism, as I am sure that many of us could find, without much trouble, some rocky fields being worked with broken hoes at no great grueling distance from our home. Birkerts's figurative excess makes him an easy mark, but it also yields a vivid picture of the mediated life, which this book explores as a historical phenomenon, as central to the early twentieth century as to a later culture of new media. I am interested not only in the possibilities of a prior version of a "vast lateral connectedness" that threatens to supplant relations based on depth and mutual transparency but also in the way that modernist expression wants to wire bodies into circuits with all manner of machines. I pay close attention to scenes of communication where intimacy appears indistinguishable from the exchange of information, where simple conversation seems to require a daunting degree of technical proficiency, and where a network of transmitted feelings provides a model for almost any category of social definition or any representation of sexuality, class, or race. This is a book about relationships made possible *by* technology that are experienced as equally satisfying, if not more intense and affecting, as relationships *with* technology. In modernism, these relationships depend on the materiality of mediums; in new media culture, bodies and information want to meet on their own terms, and too much attention to the platform only gets in the way.

Put differently, when I read of "oceans of fact and sensation [getting] downloaded," I do not hear language that suggests a shallower, less desirable alternative to some more immediate or visceral experience; instead I hear echoes of a modernist attraction to the aesthetics of communication that contemporary media culture helps us to describe and reappraise. I am drawn to works that are themselves attracted to the "pure eroticism of *technique*" that Alan Liu has comprehensively examined—versions of the "technical feeling or feeling for the technical" that he identifies as "twentieth-century cool."[42] But I am just as interested in the significance of such technological desires for our sense of a historical period that remains distinctly different from our own. Thus while it is possible, for example, to understand Shapiro's rapturous image of communications oozing into bodies as mere precursor to the sorts of circuitry of flesh and media that defines the sensibility of cyberpunk—think of William Gibson's Case in *Neuromancer* "jacking" into his Ono-Sendai deck—these later fantasies of technology cannot explain why Gertrude Stein treats her telephone like a sex object in the 1930s or why telegrams are at least a kind of love for Henry James.

The pleasures of communication that Stein and James pursue are no less at stake for many other figures that I treat below. Thomas Foster has written that one of cyberpunk's most crucial contributions to the varieties of posthumanism, broadly construed, that shape the cultural matrix of new media studies is a "generalization of fetishism to include sexual investments in technology."[43] From the chocolate-grinder "bride" stripped bare by her "bachelors" in Duchamp's "Large Glass" to the robot "Maria" in Fritz Lang's *Metropolis*, we find anticipations of Foster's "technofetishistic" turn across a range of modernisms, both avant-garde and popular. That said, the particular pleasures of technology that I am after in U.S. culture of the early twentieth century do not necessarily figure as precursors to the world of "teledildonics" and other extreme examples of computer-aided sexualities that first emerged in such forums as *Future Sex* magazine and that still garner the occasional mention in *Wired* or on blogs like Gizmodo and Boing Boing.[44] Long before USB-enabled "Virtual-Holes" or Bluetooth "Hug Shirts," the text itself, as Roland Barthes reminds us, was both a medium and technology that operated at the heart of an elaborate network of sexual fantasy and implication. "The text itself is a fetish object," writes Barthes, "and *this fetish desires me.*"[45] Indeed, the special erotics of reading modernism—in its allusive difficulty, formal excess, and informatic density—pays tribute to the "whole disposition of invisible screens, selective baffles" that Barthes adores, along with the "vocabulary, references, [and] readability" that communicate to us the supremely flattering proposition that "the text chooses me." In *S/Z*, Barthes offers a somewhat more technically precise formulation of these pleasures. For while the subject matter of literature may often fixate on the *"idyllic"* communication "which unites two partners sheltered from any 'noise' (in the cybernetic sense of the word)," the text itself must function "like a telephone network gone haywire, the lines are simultaneously twisted and routed according to a whole new system of splicings, of which the reader is the ultimate beneficiary."[46] It is hard to say which seems more dated, Barthes's antiquated switchboard metaphor or his poststructuralist exuberance for "the flux of reading" in its indulgent slowness and self-regard. All the same, I take seriously his insistence that the pleasures of "readerly writing" are not simply the product of some ineffable experience of signifiers loosed from history and convention. "This noise is not confused, massive, unnamable," as Barthes insists; it is a "clear noise" that is capable of registering an occasionally dramatic amount of meaning and information. And like this book, or so I hope, it is "made up of connections."

I return to U.S. culture in the years from the turn of the twentieth century to World War II as a period when the once new media of the telegraph, telephone, phonograph, and cinema were becoming as pervasive and commonplace as television and computers seem to us today. I am especially interested in what happens when we think about modernism as a moment of "ubiquitous communication," a term adapted from computer science and product design, and evoking the complex ways technologies seem to vanish as they become more incorporated into our lives and as we come to assume their inevitable presence. So Adam Greenfield predicts a future where "ubiquitous computing" will materialize "a vision of processing power so distributed throughout the environment that computers per se effectively disappear."[47] He sees a "diverse ecology of devices and platforms, most of which have nothing to do with 'computers' as we've understood them," and the resulting technological experience will be a distributed phenomenon "where the power and meaning we ascribe to it are more a property of the network than of any single node, and that network is effectively invisible. It permeates places and pursuits that we've never thought of in technical terms" (16). I cannot assess the likelihood of such a future—networked microchips in every home appliance, clothes connected to the Internet, buildings tracking metadata placed on sensors in our shoes—but I find it strangely appropriate as a fantasy that can be retrofitted to describe a world entirely immersed in the technicalities of communication. At the risk of what Lisa Gitelman calls the "temporal asymmetry" of media archaeologies that simply juxtapose the present and the past—that trade on "formally" compelling connections instead of narratively coherent histories—I suggest that the acculturation to the "old" technologies of modernism's epoch depended on protocols of interaction and mutual understanding that turned on something like a sense of "distributed" communications, which is to say, a sense that any form of contact, however visceral or close, could be experienced as somehow "mediated," remote, or artificially sustained.[48]

◊

"Is the use one medium makes of another the clearest testimony to its nature?"[49] McLuhan's question captures with beautiful economy the internally split perspective of this book: I am interested primarily in literary modernism and its particular medium-specific tactics, values, and conventions in a culture of communications; and yet literary modernism's medium aesthetic is best tracked in works that are themselves acutely fascinated with the diversity of technologies that populate an early-twentieth-century media ecology. McLuhan is here amplifying one of the most cited passages from *Understanding Media*, a book that anatomizes a vast range of technologies he calls "media"—the spoken word, the written word, and print, but also clothing, clocks, the bicycle, and weapons— even as it renders each of them identical to one another by virtue of the fact, "characteristic of all media," that "the 'content' of any medium is always another medium."[50] Reduced still further, no doubt for maximum communicability, this argument stood behind McLuhan's pervasive axiom that "the medium is the message," which later bled into its more physical and carnal sequel, "the medium is the massage." Both of these pronouncements are generally amenable to, if not unconsciously in communication with, claims that Greenberg would make on behalf of modernism throughout his long career. Greenberg, to be sure, would have bristled at McLuhan's genius for turning aesthetic philosophy into kitschy taglines, but in early pieces such as 1940's "Towards a New Laocoön," he especially argued for a formalism in terms that are perhaps less antic than McLuhan's but no less sloganeering. "The arts, then, have been hunted back to their mediums, and there they have been isolated, concentrated, and defined," Greenberg observes, as if his own polemic is just a description of what has happened. "It is by virtue of its medium that each art is unique and strictly itself. To restore the identity of an art the opacity of its medium must be emphasized" (32). And as the arts attain their respective modes of "purity"—Greenberg's much-contested term that he himself ventures first in scare quotes, as if warming slowly to its potential for provocation—their "message" will become more powerfully their "massage." "Pure painting and pure sculpture," he writes, "seek above all else to affect the spectator physically. In poetry . . . it is decided that the medium is essentially psychological and sub- or supra-logical. The poem is to aim at the general consciousness of the reader, not simply his intelligence" (33).

McLuhan offered one of his few extended treatments of literary modernism in "Joyce, Mallarmé, and the Press," which appeared in the auspicious pages of the *Sewanee Review* in 1953. Though finally a celebration of *Ulysses* for its capacious multimedia aesthetic—it was Kenner, in fact, who encouraged McLuhan's turn to Joyce just as McLuhan was guiding Kenner to Pound—the essay starts with a brief account of communications history, from Plato to the present, that can be readily transposed into Greenberg's language of aesthetic differentiation and restricted competence. "Every medium is a unique art form," McLuhan writes, "which gives salience to one set of human possibilities at the expense of another set."[51] Much of the appeal of *Ulysses*, at least for McLuhan, rests on the novel's ability to embrace and reproduce so many mediums—orality, writing, print, newspaper, spectroscope, cinematic montage, and more—that its reader is effectively overcompensated for the "expense" in human possibility that comes with the commitment to "a unique art form" like the novel. For Greenberg, it is more important to keep each medium unique, no matter the expense: whatever a particular art may stand to lose when "hunted" to its native habitat and there entrenched within its singular domain of sensation and technique, the achievements of modernism prove that the sacrifice is worth the cost. "The arts lie safe now, each within its 'legitimate' boundaries, and free trade has been replaced by autarchy" (32).

From Michael Fried and Stanley Cavell, to Rosalind Krauss, T. J. Clark, Thierry de Duve, and Caroline A. Jones, there is little about Greenberg's modernism that has not been otherwise debated, championed, or savaged by art historians and critics from the 1960s to the present.[52] That literary critics have had less reason to return to Greenberg is in part a simple reflection that he chose to make his arguments on behalf of painting and sculpture, aside from the occasional nod to poetry. And as "purely" formalist definitions of modernism have yielded to more historically responsive understandings of the period, with renewed attention to both the stylistic range and the thematic richness of "modernisms" in the plural, the limitations of medium specificity have never been so obvious. Then, too, a literary critic must also suffer Greenberg's hostility to "literature's corrupting influence," by which he means the stress on "subject matter" from which art must "escape" for its "salvation from society" (33). Again, the scare quotes tell us most of what we need to know, and this imperative, according to Greenberg, is felt most fully just where we might expect: in poetry, which must go to special lengths to guarantee that "the content of the poem is what it does to the reader, not what it communicates." His silence about prose and novels would seem to confirm that these mediums are condemned to remain "literature" no matter how strenuously and self-consciously they reflect on their forms.[53]

I rehearse this familiar litany of formalisms because the works that are my primary concern below—the late novels of Henry James, Stein's autobiographical writings of the 1930s, narratives about race and music by James Weldon Johnson and F. Scott Fitzgerald, poems by William Carlos Williams and George Oppen, James Agee and Walker Evans's *Let Us Now Praise Famous Men*—manifest a shared commitment to the more sensuous and visceral experiences of other mediums that communicate somehow outside the competence of verbal expression, or, in more contemporary terms, in excess of its narrow bandwidth. These works and figures do not address the status of other mediums and technologies in a funereal tone, however, nor do they look out at a world of modern media with much fear or melancholy. It is a series of specifically literary encounters with technology that I trace in these pages, which is to say, encounters with works of literature that think it is their "nature" to make use of the expanded field of aesthetic possibility associated with modern media. The range of materials I consider shows the historical implications that follow on what Fredric Jameson once called, when postmodernism was in vogue, "the process whereby the traditional fine arts are *mediatized*" and thus "come to consciousness of themselves as various media within a mediatic system in which their own internal production also constitutes a symbolic message and the taking of a position on the status of the medium in question."[54] I would date this phenomenon to an earlier moment in a long epoch of modernity—a moment to which Jameson himself has lately returned—and suggest that it is even more important for how we understand the many forms of modernism that are proximate to its peculiar "teleology," which "read change as innovation" in order to "transcode the latter in terms of technique and of the technical developments within the medium itself."[55]

At the same time, there is something grim about the modernism described by Jameson, and though I am wary of the nostalgia for bygone avant-gardes or the McLuhanist devotion to whatever once was new, I would hope this book pays tribute to some of the better forms of thinking about—and thinking in—mediums from the first decades of the twentieth century. It is, after all, the seriousness with which the brand of modernism I explore treated questions about mediums that recommends it to us now. A modernist commitment to—even when it seems a pure infatuation with—the idea of the medium need not be an impoverished aesthetic reifying an expired formalism and repudiating, in advance, those histories that have returned to modernism with a rightful vengeance. I take inspiration from de Duve's attempt to push at the limits of modernism's concept of the medium from *within* its sometimes tortured logics and contradictory fantasies. Against those who would contend that "the search for the identity of the medium cleanses it of any alterity"—and we could certainly attribute such a view to Jameson and countless others, even if the chosen terms for what is "cleansed" might differ—de Duve insists that the medium "is the site of otherness as such."[56] Or put differently, to the degree to which we acknowledge that certain forms of modernist expression do, after all, reveal a distinctive tropism toward ever more elaborate and self-conscious experiences of the mediums they embody and desire, we should not worry that in returning to such matters we will sacrifice a more historical and political knowledge of the period, which is itself so newly won. We can learn from Kenner's insight that modernism's infamous "difficulty" and "obscurity" marked one path by which twentieth-century literature "evolved parallel technologies of its own," but we can also choose to part company with his cramped canon of central figures and cherished values.[57]

It is more than possible to trace the medium-specific fantasies and feelings that patterned modernism's culture, and at the same time to understand these moments as evidence of historical response instead of formalist evasion. I am frankly not inclined to take "the medium is the message" to mean there is no message, despite the long tradition of McLuhan's critics, starting with Kenneth Burke, who insisted that he said exactly this. Indeed, when Burke responded to McLuhan in 1966, he argued that for all the catchphrases that made *Understanding Media* so popular, McLuhan would have been well served by closer attention to Gottfried Lessing's original *Laocoön* (the same work of comparative aesthetics that served as one of Greenberg's points of departure in "Towards a Newer Laocoön"). "Under Lessing's guidance, with regard to *directly* communicative media and their tie-in with particular forms, or artistic modes," Burke instructs, "McLuhan could have systematically asked himself *just what kind of content* is favored by the peculiar nature of a given medium."[58] No doubt Burke would have found more troubling still the work of Friedrich Kittler, among the most influential of contemporary media theorists and perhaps the most unabashed in laying claim to McLuhan's epigrammatic style and categorical abandon. "What counts," writes Kittler of technological media, "are not the messages or the content with which they equip so-called souls for the duration of a technological era, but rather (and in strict accordance with McLuhan) their circuits, the very schematism of perceptibility."[59] What Kittler draws from McLuhan, and then amplifies with a rigor foreign to McLuhan's habits of thinking and writing, is a sense that modern mediums are forms that constrain their contents more than we might be willing to admit. In all of Kittler's post-humanist aggression against the very notion of "so-called Man," we witness a logic that banishes, as its first assumption, the vision of communicative agency that Burke wants to retain in stressing "how expert practitioners of a given medium may resort to the kind of contents that the given medium is best equipped to exploit" (416). "Contents" thus precede their mediums in this view, and we select the forms that we decide will best carry our messages to their intended receivers with the least noise and interference. Burke circumscribes the notion of the medium in a fashion that effectively invokes the infamous "conduit metaphor," which, as linguists have long argued, sustains a model of communications as the exchange of discrete meanings transported, as if the equivalent of objects, through neutral, arbitrary channels.[60] However, when McLuhan writes of media "*as forms*, as modes ever creating new assumptions and hence new objectives," he is arguing instead that it is impossible to isolate and distinguish among motives, messages, and materialities of communication.[61] My sympathies for Burke notwithstanding, the figures that are my concern show, though not without occasional reluctance, an attitude toward technology captured best by Kittler in a formulation that pays homage to McLuhan: "Media determine our situation, which—in spite of or because of it—deserves a description."[62]

Or as Kenner puts it, describing modernism's epoch, "Technology tended to engulf people gradually, coercing behavior they were not aware of."[63] This book is finally not about technology as a historical determinant, nor about its perceived ability to coerce behaviors that would otherwise remain inoperative. The mediated life of modern U.S. culture takes shape as a network of desires for more intimate, material, and affecting relations with technology. Still, modernism's language of medium aesthetics is an index to the power and appeal of such desires, and an example of what they look like in action. It is not just that many forms of desire were in communication with technology in the first decades of the twentieth century, but that technology itself gives shape and character to experiences of sexuality, racial identity, class, and history, each of which in turn expresses something of what it means to love the media of modernity, to believe they make love possible, and even, at times, to wonder if they love us back.

◊

My first two chapters focus on communications and trace how an everyday reliance on technology helped to pattern an acutely eroticized formalism that registers as a signature aesthetic of the modern. Constellated in turn around the telegraph and the telephone, these chapters are about technologies that, to borrow from Rosalind Krauss, "have *no* aesthetic lineage" behind them at the turn of the twentieth century.[64] Krauss says this specifically of the slide-tapes and photo-panels that contemporary artist James Coleman uses in many of his installation pieces; thus Coleman exploits material forms "taken from the commercial world of advertising or promotion," each of which "is so singular a support that to adopt it as a medium is immediately to put a kind of aesthetic patent on it" (8). Insofar as both the telegraph and the telephone played crucial roles in what economic historians refer to as the control revolution that brings to modern corporations a new emphasis on information, speed, and knowledge work, my attention to the erotic possibilities of these technologies discovers a version of the friction Krauss observes in Coleman's attempt to make art out of mediums whose very presence testifies to the tendency of the market to rationalize and condition all forms of expression.

Chapter 1 pursues the relationship between sexuality and technology in texts fascinated by the coded languages, practices, and cultural iconographies of the telegraph. I am interested in the way that Henry James's late novels—in particular *The Ambassadors* and *The Golden Bowl*—demonstrate not only how any relationship in James can become subject to an extravagance of mediation but also how his dedication to "the idea of connectibility" draws him to the world of the telegraph as he seeks to experiment with the stylistic innovations that mark his "major phase." We see in James how an aesthetic devotion to another medium may lead not to an attempt to reproduce its limits and conceits but rather to an understanding of how literary form itself might better reflect the felt intensities of modern communication. If James, in other words, wants his fiction to provide "different sorts and degrees of the communicable thrill," it is striking that his own stylistic prodigality—"his magnificent and masterly *indirectness*"—travesties a telegraphic economy of verbal efficiency, even as his novels fixate on the inscrutable pleasures of mediated communication.

I take my point of departure from Ella Cheever Thayer's 1880 novel *Wired Love*, a book that features protagonists who opt to undertake a curiously mediated romance: two telegraph operators, having fallen in love on the job, continue their courtship over a "private wire" between rooms in the boardinghouse where they both live. Thayer's melodrama makes clear that modern technologies of communication inspired their own versions of sexual experience, where the carnality of desire became largely the aftereffect of a medium's materiality. This is a calculus of sexuality and technology that we find as well in popular accounts of long-distance romances appearing in such compilations as *Lightning Flashes and Electric Dashes* and other fiction aimed at practicing telegraphers who were able to read the passages of Morse code that featured prominently in the narratives themselves. James's "In the Cage" gives us a memorable portrait of one such telegrapher, whose love-struck fantasies of intimacy with the upper classes turn out to depend entirely on her irrelevance to the social network she makes possible. But it is in James's subsequent novels, with their famous difficulty and obscurity, where the erotics of communication assume an ornate texture and abstraction as part of his self-conscious project to modernize his own narrative conventions.

I broaden this discussion of mediated sexuality in chapter 2, which looks at how Gertrude Stein's autobiographical writings of the 1930s project the consequences of her surprising popularity and celebrity onto a curious series of moments involving telephones, dogs, and movie stars. Even more than James's later novels, Stein's texts require us to confront what J. M. Bernstein calls "the demandingness of modernist works," which at once threatens to alienate the audience by relentlessly challenging all conventions of form and meaning while also aspiring to "extreme intimacy," as he puts it, "because the model of perfect communication between just two, unsupported by convention, are [*sic*] the silent exchanges between lovers."[65] What would seem, in quite strong contrast, to distinguish *The Autobiography of Alice B. Toklas* and its sequel, *Everybody's Autobiography*, is their shared interest in the extreme publicity that comes with fame, which Stein understands as both a form of noise that threatens to overwhelm her writerly identity and voice and, oddly enough, a distinctive and altogether class-specific means of securing intimacy amid a maximum of scrutiny and interference. In this respect, I suggest that Stein depicts a world of constant motion and communication that almost perfectly reproduces the modernity captured by MGM's 1932 blockbuster *Grand Hotel*—as both feature film and commercial product. Both Stein's avant-garde autobiographies and Irving Thalberg's showcase entertainment are distinguished by their reliance on cameo appearances—by the proliferation of big names and brief performances—that capture the speed and instantaneousness with which connections are recognized, experienced, and exploited in the modern world. The telephone is the plot device that enables much of the noise and name-dropping in *Everybody's Autobiography* and *Grand Hotel*; as McLuhan notes, "one of the most startling consequences of the telephone was its introduction of a 'seamless web' of interlaced patterns" as a regular feature of any social enterprise.[66] The telephone, he adds, is "an intensely personal form that ignores the claim" of privacy and inaccessible interiorities of every kind.[67] Thus, refusing to communicate, whether in the form of Stein's experimental language or in Garbo's wanting "to be alone," emerges as a modernist technique of reticence that makes keeping something *to* oneself the same as making a spectacle *of* oneself.

Chapters 3 and 4 are concerned with "recordings" in the context of U.S. modernism, and they focus on projects determined to restore more direct, immediate forms of contact—between writers and readers, past and present, African American and Anglo-American—even as they pursue increasingly involved commitments to the materiality and purely sensuous aspects of their mediums. These chapters address questions of medium specificity and its politics among works that, to varying degrees, aspire to embody crucial aspects of a modernist tradition at its most self-conscious and doctrinaire. Thus in chapter 3 I chart the ways in which modernism's famous aspirations to what Walter Pater calls "the condition of music" become, in texts interested in the possibilities of communication between black and white Americans, a means for imagining the experience of recorded sound as a vicarious experience of race. In works such as James Weldon Johnson's *The Autobiography of an Ex-Coloured Man* and Ralph Ellison's essay "Living with Music," notions of "instrumentality" are enlisted to contemplate the effects of treating black bodies as mere machines for making music; alongside period representations of the phonograph and the player piano, as well as Theodor Adorno's pugnacious writings on jazz, Johnson and Ellison help to illustrate just why a kind of racial unconscious patterns a U.S. culture of recorded sound. Why should the sound of music made by machines echo with the histories of slavery and segregation? And why should F. Scott Fitzgerald's *Tender Is the Night*, a compulsively musical novel only marginally interested in African Americans, feature an even more encrypted network of associations between recording mediums and fantasies of race and sex? It is not simply the fact that Fitzgerald's "lyricism" marks one of U.S. modernism's most extreme examples of the period's romance with musical aesthetics; it is also that his narratives are themselves pervaded by a sense that writing itself requires a "soundtrack" to communicate its meanings. From his relentless referencing of popular song as background noise to his insertion of his own lyrics as uncanny forms of narrative information, Fitzgerald demonstrates that the literary aspiration to more "musical conditions" is also an occasion to dream of a more immediate, more material experience of form that finally relies on race to constitute and embody its aesthetic.

I conclude with a chapter about the medium fetish for photography in the 1930s, in particular what emerges as a new archival sensibility that is attracted to modern media precisely because they hold out the promise that new technologies will make for better history. Photography's complicated claim to materiality—which has shaped criticism of the medium from Walter Benjamin to Stanley Cavell—provides the basis for a series of modernist experiments in historiography, each of which imagines that the best way to experience something like communication with the past is to dispose of the actual stuff of history in favor of a perfect archive—total, efficient, and mechanically "objective." This is an argument that Lewis Mumford ventures at length in 1934's *Technics and Civilization*, but a similar emphasis on the perceived materiality of the photograph inflects a wide range of poetry, painting, and documentary expression in the period. I look at how the desire for a perfectly mediated history patterns a diverse cross section of projects concerned to reproduce a visceral experience of the past: The Index of American Design, a massive cataloging of American material culture undertaken by the WPA; poems by William Carlos Williams and George Oppen; James Agee and Walker Evans's *Let Us Now Praise Famous Men*; and Charles Sheeler's images of the restoration efforts at Colonial Williamsburg, itself a spectacle of historicist virtuality and immersion. And so I end by examining what history itself looks like when it is powerfully communicated by way of a modernity that is technically superimposed and entirely circuitous. My final chapter, then, reflects on the relationship between the renewed practice of historicism and the ubiquity of still newer technologies of the archive—whose mediating textures, I suggest, are palpable in much of literary criticism's anxious attachment to the materiality of the past. Since photography represents figures as the exemplary medium for making history "modern" in the 1930s, the book ends with a discussion of contemporary photographer Chris Jordan's pictures of high-tech detritus—images of discarded cell phones, circuit boards, and other "e-waste" by the innumerable ton—all testifying to the degree to which our own media culture will leave behind a record that will survive long after we have fallen in love with other, newer forms of technology.

◊

I owe my title to Henry James and his preface to the New York Edition of *The American*. This text is well known for its description of what exactly "romance" means for James, a matter of great importance to his retrospective appreciation of—and apprehension about—this early novel, which was among the most extensively revised of any of the works in the New York Edition. The novel required such involved attention, James argues, because when he read it again, so many years later, it stood revealed to him as an "affront to verisimilitude" in the basic structure of its plot.⁶⁹ This is because the story of how the "American," Christopher Newman, having suffered mightily at the hands of the aristocratic Bellegardes in Paris, "should at the right moment find them in his power" and thus leaves the reader to face "the question of the utilisation of that knowledge," which is potentially the means for his revenge. The situation, in its elaborate contrivance and vivid symbolism, now strikes James as signaling that *The American* proceeds under "the emblazoned flag of romance," so he confesses that "the thing is consistently, consummately—and I would fain really make bold to say charmingly—romantic; and all without intention, presumption, hesitation, contrition." At first, the romantic aesthetic of the novel seems the product of its concocted settings, which glow with "the great Paris harmony" yet permit no real "transfusion of the immense overhanging presence" of the city as James knew it for himself (1059). But he then changes his mind and identifies the romantic character of *The American* as resulting from a kind of transmitted "presence" in the novel after all:

> I suggest not that the strange and the far are at all necessarily romantic: they happened to be simply the unknown, which is a quite different matter. The real represents to my perception the things we cannot possibly *not* know, sooner or later, in one way or another; it being but one of the accidents of our hampered state, and one of the incidents of their quantity and number, that particular instances have not yet come our way. The romantic stands, on the other hand, for the things that, with all the faculties in the world, all the wealth and all the courage and all the wit and all the adventure, we never *can* directly know; the things that reach us only through the *beautiful circuit* and subterfuge of our thought and our desire.
>
> (1062–1063; emphasis added)

Romance, then, suggests a pervasive epistemology of indirection and extension; it at once compliments and confronts the pressures of a "real" world we cannot avoid perceiving. What James defines as romance is really not defined at all so much as it is associated with the inescapably mediated and "circuitous" workings of desire itself. But our inability to know the "things" of romance in a direct and transparent fashion does not lessen their value nor render their effects trivial or immaterial. James makes no obvious reference to any medium here, but as we shall see in chapter 1, his late novels are marked by a devotion to a staggering variety of "circuits" between characters that fixate on media technologies to dramatize and figure what might be called the romance of modern life, which becomes oddly equivalent to the romance of reading James's fiction. It is around the aesthetic experiences made possible by these mediums that something as inscrutable as communication—which James is more than willing to mystify to suit his ends—takes on deliberate form and shape, perhaps not quite so messy as Shapiro's "gravy" but nevertheless a matter of great feeling, intrigue, and sexualized intimation. "The relations that connect experiences themselves," writes William James, not too long after his brother offered his theory of romance, "must themselves be experienced relations, and any kind of relation experienced must be accounted as 'real' as anything else in the system."[69] The idiom in which Henry James's novels account for the reality of connection, as we will see, reflects a remarkable investment in the connection to technology itself.

The sociologist Charles Horton Cooley was among the first to argue that communications, in the technical sense, should be considered a distinctive force, with its own determining logic, in the shape of everyday experience. "And when we come to the modern era, especially," Cooley writes in 1909, "we can understand nothing rightly unless we perceive the manner in which the revolution has made a new world for us."[70] By "revolution," Cooley means the combined effects of such inventions as the telegraph and telephone not only on how we communicate but also on how *much* we do so. "It is not too much to say that these changes," he continues, "are the basis, from a mechanical standpoint, of nearly everything that is characteristic in the psychology of modern life" (81). In this we hear anticipations of McLuhan, both in Cooley's emphasis on the relays between technologies and human beings and in his periodizing zeal and certainty. There is ample evidence here to back up Jameson's propositions that "the trope of modernity bears a libidinal charge" and that it is "the operator of a unique kind of intellectual excitement not normally associated with other forms of conceptuality."[71] Our ongoing fascination with new media technologies, even if it has receded from the high pitch and hysteria it reached at the close of the twentieth century, suggests that at least some of the energies that Jameson describes have long outlasted modernism, even as a latent affect for the avant-garde saturates our desire for sleeker cell phones, faster processors, smoother interfaces, greater memory, and more elegant operating systems. Modernism encouraged a unique structure of feeling toward the technologies of art and literature—in all the specificity of their material aesthetics—which survives and flourishes as a feeling for technology in general. But, as Jameson reminds us, "if everything means something else, then so does technology."[72] And if media now are love, we should know why.

Part One
Communications

1
PLEASURE AT A DISTANCE
IN HENRY JAMES AND OTHERS

The telegram I take as a kiss, which makes it taste good,

makes for pleasure, pride, and conceit.

FRANZ KAFKA, *LETTERS TO FELICE*

Impossible impossible impossible if you knew what it costs me to say so you can count

however at the regular rates ask Miss Robbins to share your regret I mean mine.

HENRY JAMES, TELEGRAM TO MRS. HUGH BELL

"The Idea of Connectibility"

What Henry James remembers of his arrival in England in the spring of 1869 would hardly seem appropriate for the first moments marking his celebrated "conquest of London."[1] James offers us, in the opening pages of *The Middle Years*, an image of the young American—"It was," he writes, "impossible to have been younger"—all but overwhelmed and victimized by every detail, every circumstance, and all the "immediate intensities of appreciation."[2] The "reacting small organism" that James figures himself at twenty-six shares much in common with so many of his most famous characters, from Christopher Newman to Isabel Archer to Lambert Strether, who likewise find themselves in the same breath exhilarated and compelled into "whatever inevitable submissions" Europe may demand. But I am less interested in this familiar and altogether Jamesian confusion between the "treasures of susceptibility" and the spoils of "conquest" than I am in the tantalizing logic of perception that he erects upon the particulars he recalls. There is, for instance, an especially rich muffin James has with tea that tastes not only of a "dab of marmalade" but also of "the damp and darksome light washed in from the steep, black, bricky street [he has disembarked in Liverpool], the crackle of the British 'sea-coal' fire, . . . the rustle of the thick, stiff, loudly unfolded and refolded 'Times,' the incomparable truth to type of the waiter, truth to history, to literature, to poetry, to Dickens, to

Thackeray, positively to Smollett and to Hogarth, to every connection that could help me to appropriate him and his setting, an arrangement of things hanging together with a romantic rightness that had the force of a revelation."

The charm of this passage is considerable, and James is thoroughly on display here as a master of both rarefied irony and baroque elaboration—two signatures of the style that we have long associated with the "major phase." I use this last phrase with as little inflection as possible, wanting neither to glorify nor to castigate the kind of writing that James produces from the later 1890s until the end of his career; but this construct of F. O. Matthiessen and an earlier generation of critics remains more than serviceable to the extent to which it focuses our attention on the moment when James starts dictating his fiction and thus engages, however reluctantly, with the full modernity of language and its technologies at the turn of the century.[3] I am after other effects of media in the work of Henry James, effects decidedly more fugitive than those emerging from the network of dictation and typewriter that describes his scene of writing after 1897. Thus I start where there is no technology to be found—just a muffin that symbolizes England with such extravagance that James is prompted to make a more theoretical reflection:

> To what end appropriation became thus eager and romance thus easy one could have asked one's self only if the idea of connectibility as stretching away and away hadn't of a sudden taken on such a wealth of suggestion; it represented at once a chain stretching off to heaven knew where, but far into one's future at least, one's possibilities of life, and every link and pulse of which it was going accordingly to be indispensable, besides being delightful and wonderful, to recognise.

This sentence features a kind of metaphor that James shows an increasing fondness for in the latter stages of his career, as he tries harder and harder to capture abstract and—some might say—arcane procedures of consciousness in tropes that are meticulous in their commonplace materiality. I am thinking of several instances in *A Small Boy and Others* where the arabesque loopings and leaps of James's memory are figured as if the products of such simple actions as squeezing a sponge or reaching into a bag, but one could as easily find examples in almost any of the New York Edition prefaces, or in almost any of the fiction from *What Maisie Knew* and later. And in many of these cases, I believe a careful reading would reveal something much like what we discover here: that the very attempt to figure the freedom and provisionality of experience yields the image of an object we would associate with containment (sponges, bags, and structures of every sort, i.e., the famous "house of fiction" from the preface to *The Portrait of a Lady* or Maggie's "pagoda" in *The Golden Bowl*) or, as we see here, with bondage. James wants to account for the tiny miracles of metonymy that can make an English muffin redolent of England. But he cannot really "question" these operations because—experience being reducible to nothing save experience—investigating this "romance" of "appropriation" is conditioned on "romance" *not* engendering a "wealth of suggestion," on consciousness itself *not* remaining open and improvisational, which is all to say that James's most treasured ideology of experience must be proven false to pose such questions in the first place. We know that experience is truly irreducible because the "idea of connectibility" is realized as an endless "chain" whose every link James can—and what is more, absolutely must—scrutinize and ponder. There is a twofold muddling of signifier and signified, or if you will, of medium and message. First, a muffin becomes improbably suggestive of everything from the smells of Liverpool to the writings of Smollett; then, in attempting to explain this "romance" of association, James must figuratively "chain" himself to the "idea of connectibility" as a means of proving that one's own experiences are answerable to no other logic save that of their relentlessly suggestive circuitry of reference and signification.

The fantasy of connection in my first epigraph—"The telegram," Kafka writes in 1912 to Felice Bauer, "I take as a kiss"—looks straightforward by comparison. But as Bernhard Siegert has demonstrated, the communication that went back and forth between Kafka and his fiancée, who worked for a leading German manufacturer of office machines, was tortuous and belabored in its modernity, with Kafka timing his every dispatch against the mail collection and delivery schedules of Prague and Berlin respectively, sending some letters "express" so they would arrive before other letters written earlier and tracking the speed of telegrams to ensure their optimal effect within his ongoing assault of standard mails.[4] James's telegram to Mrs. Hugh Bell is tortuous and belabored in its own right, and on a level that we might well expect of James—the level, that is, of style. Even in the roughly thirty words that are my second epigraph, James repeats himself ("Impossible impossible impossible") in a travesty of formal economy ("if you knew what it costs") only to leave us puzzling over narrative perspective and point of view ("ask Miss Robbins to share your regret I mean mine"). This is communication that takes a certain satisfaction in refusing to communicate, or at least in making communication difficult, with a finely calibrated treachery to its apparent clarity. Is it "impossible" for James to specify the nature of his "regret" or "impossible impossible" for him to "share" in that of Mrs. Bell? Mrs. Bell would surely know the "regular rates," and therefore be in a position to tally "what it costs" for James to send his message, which is to say, I would assume, that James's "costs" are merely rhetorical and not some cryptic confession that he is of a class that can't afford to send a telegram when the occasion demands it, or even when it doesn't. For all that James, in telling the story of a relationship between a nameless information worker and the aristocratic Captain Everard in "In the Cage," sympathetically assumes the place of the poor telegrapher, it is worth recalling that the vast majority of James's own society, like Everard's, "belonged supremely to the class that wired everything, even their expensive feelings."[5] James may not have enjoyed the success he wanted late in his career, but sending telegrams, at least, was one pleasure of modern life he could afford.

"In the Cage" signals a particular intensification in the way James renders some of his most intimate fascinations as powerfully technologized by the modern world. "This was neither more nor less," writes James of what his nameless telegrapher comes to feel, "than the queer extension of her experience" (845). Since almost all of James's characters are subjected to one form of "extension" or another—epistemological, psychological, moral, erotic—the story's telegraphic milieu and decidedly down-market setting in a grocery (pervaded by "the presence of hams, cheese, dried fish, soap, varnish, paraffin, and other solids and fluids") do not so much break new ground for James as extend some of his familiar preoccupations to a different class of "reacting organism" (835). But it is only in the past twenty years or so, judging from the impressive range of critics who have looked at "In the Cage," that we have come to recognize that James also produced one of the first fictions of an information economy. Indeed, as Katherine Hayles puts it, "James writes what may be called the prequel to the story of information in the twentieth century."[6] And nowhere is he more prescient than in his exquisitely frustrating choice to have the narrative turn on a sequence of numbers ("Make it seven nine four nine six one") first sent by Lady Bradeen, then lost, and finally recovered by the telegrapher herself in a feat of memory that marks at once the depths of her sympathy for Captain Everard and also the sheer inhumanity that he demands of her. We come to learn—though never exactly how or why—that these numbers seal the fate of

Captain Everard and force him to marry Lady Bradeen, forever putting paid to any romantic fantasies the telegrapher had entertained about her favorite customer. She is an avid reader, after all, of "borrowed novels, very greasy . . . in fine print and all about fine folks" (835). For Richard Menke, the telegrapher's inability to grasp the irony of this "disparity between her reading material and its materiality" is just the first of many errors she will commit, for all her sense of what James calls her "mastery and power" and for all the data in "her small retentive brain."[7]

While James himself would never be accused of possessing such an organ, he undoubtedly was blessed with another bodily feature that, for Marshall McLuhan, comes into its own with the invention of the telegraph. "The social hormone" is McLuhan's striking figure for registering the "organic character" of electrical communication: the telegraph "makes each of us present and accessible to every other person in the world."[8] As the author of more than ten thousand pieces of correspondence—including more than a hundred extant telegrams—James was undoubtedly a highly motivated and voluminous communicator.[9] Whether or not all this communication was in the cause of accessibility is another question altogether. But James does share with McLuhan a fascination with the telegraph as a technology for transmitting not just information but sensations; face-to-face with Captain Everard, the telegrapher is overwhelmed by how his body functions as a medium that replaces verbal messages with non-semantic analogs that, the less they say, the more desirable they become. "Her immediate vision of himself had the effect, while she counted his seventy words," James writes of the telegrapher, "of preventing intelligibility. *His* words were mere numbers, they told her nothing whatever; and after he had gone she was in possession of no name, of no address, of no meaning, of nothing but a vague, sweet sound and an immense impression" (843). At this high pitch of communicative passion, the telegrapher seems to indulge a moment of epistemological overreach ("she knew everything") that we as readers might resist but are fated to repeat (843). The story ends, and still its crucial words remain "mere numbers"—seven nine four nine six one—that let James's fiction avoid excessive "intelligibility," while at the same time, to borrow from McLuhan, achieve a "plastic form with a kind of nervous system of its own" (220). With the telegraph, McLuhan contends, "the entire world of the arts began to reach again for the iconic qualities of touch and sense interplay" (220). And James, we might say, is never more McLuhanesque—or modernist—than when he discovers that the messages whose effects we feel most deeply are sometimes those that literally communicate the least.

This chapter, then, is about the aesthetics of communication that operates in the late fiction of Henry James, with a particular focus on the telegrams and otherwise transmitted messages that occur with unexpected frequency, punctuating the course of *The Ambassadors* (1903) and, to a lesser degree, *The Golden Bowl* (1904). I will be concentrating on the dramas of "connexion"—the technical term, I want to call it, which James employs everywhere in this text to describe a type of relationship that is thick with equal measures of epistemological mystery and illicit sexuality, or more simply, the interesting type—that pattern his later plots in increasingly convoluted ways, beginning with *What Maisie Knew* (1897). As "communication" is itself a term suspended between abstractions of cognition and circumstances of technology, I turn to discourses that are capable of inflecting or complicating our sense of what fascinates James about a whole variety of mediated experience: from the give-and-take of language and dialogic gamesmanship that defines his "scenic" method to the massively articulate shows of thinking and reflection that are made to index consciousness; from the impossibly subtle idiom of the unspoken that his characters use as if a native tongue to the sharp and clipped yet somehow cunning telegrams that at once suggest the cryptic pleasures of the epigrammatic but just as surely signal what language is reduced to in those disenchanted realms of modern life—think of Mrs. Newsome's Woollett, or of Adam Verver's American City—that James wants always to keep at arm's length, if not a good deal further. An essential context for our understanding of James emerges, for example, from the popular cultural domain: a surprising number of love stories from the period trade on the narrative possibilities of instantaneous communication over distance, the same possibilities, I want to argue, that James exploits with sometimes excruciating convolution. James all but perfects a certain language of mediated experience in his later fiction, where experience itself is, by definition, circuitous and indirect. What matters more, I want to argue, is that even Henry James at times seems baffled by the subtlety of the grammar he devises in hopes of capturing the mediated textures of modern life and its rampant "connectibility."

The Novel of Circumlocution

Let me begin with a classic problem of James's compositional method—as he himself repeatedly describes and dramatizes it—that looms almost like a primal scene in his understanding of his own resistance to a specifically literary economy of information. When narrating the process by which many of his novels and longer short stories, or *nouvelles*, achieved their final forms, he often tells of how he overheard, or had related to him, some small anecdote, situation, or incident that later proves the "germ" for a work of fiction whose finished scale is out of all proportion to its original source. The New York Edition preface to *The Ambassadors* opens with one such account, as James insists that Strether's speech to Little Bilham in the second chapter of book 5 constitutes the "whole case" of the novel, inspired years before by a story told to James about William Dean Howells in Paris. "Nothing can exceed the closeness with which the whole fits again into its germ," James writes (*AM*, 34). Another aspect of this problematic compositional technique emerges in his correspondence, where he often worries that a particular "germ" refuses to conform to the length he has apportioned for its "whole." "As I wrote you the other day," James confesses to Horace Scudder in 1895, "I find in my old age, that I have too much manner & style, too great & invincible an instinct for completeness & of seeing things in all their relations so that *development*, however squeezed down, becomes inevitable—too much of all this to be able to turn round in the small corners I used to. I select very small ideas to help this—but even the very small ideas creep high up into the teens [of thousands of words]. This little subject ["The House Beautiful"]—of an intense simplicity—was tiny at the start; but in spite of ferocious compression—it has taken me a month—it has become what you see" (*LL*, 284). In this case, "The House Beautiful" had become a 25,000-word story with little hope of securing magazine publication. And James offers a version of this apology to editors throughout the course of his career—before, I should also point out, he takes up dictation and his narrative style mutates into a kind of writing that is determined by the prolixity of his speaking.[10]

Admiring James no longer requires a stylistic defense of his fiction's exceeding length and highly wrought "completeness." I am, however, interested in the language James employs in his defense against these accusations, or against pressures—from other writers' successes, from his own lackluster sales—that he experienced as their equivalents. I find it particularly striking that when James answers for his way of writing, or contrasts it to another author's more "direct" or more "immediate" style, he rarely elects to shift the valorizing categories to those that might better serve his own aesthetic. No doubt there is a measure of performative *noblesse* in his deferring to a principle of immediacy that he so obviously violates in his every sentence; and there is too a sense of resignation in his grudging acceptances that any fiction aspiring to a degree of popularity must communicate to the reader with greater clarity and consistency than his own. But as readily as he indulges these rhetorics, he insists that his writing, with all its rococo elements on full display, *is* immediate and direct. I want to consider more closely, then, the working model of communication that emerges from James's insistence that an ideal connection between text and reader is one in which "equivocation" and "redundancy"—to use two oddly evocative terms from Claude Shannon's mathematical theory of information—are simply inescapable.[11] I turn first to some curious advice James gives to keep one reader of his late fiction interested and attentive.

A few months after the publication of *The Ambassadors,* James writes to the Duchess of Sutherland urging her to engage the new novel at a deliberate, if not programmatic pace. Whether or not she followed his instructions to the letter, the appeal of the delicate procedure he begs of her is clear enough:

> Take, meanwhile pray, the *Ambassadors* very easily and gently: read five pages a day—be even as deliberate as that—but *don't break the thread.* The thread is really stretched quite scientifically tight. Keep along with it step by step—and then the full charm will come out. I *want* the charm, you see, to come out for you—so convinced am I that it's there![12]

James stresses that reading the novel at this steady gait will allow the duchess to match the time she spends with the text to the time the text itself represents, as though experience of his book will be intensified if it coincides with the temporality of the characters within.[13] The implications of such an unlikely mode of reading are particularly resonant with respect to *The Ambassadors,* which is constructed largely as a narrative of Lambert Strether's ineffectual delay of Chad's inevitable return to Woollett.[14] But it is the metaphor of connection ("*don't break the thread*"), and the emotive register in which James employs it ("I *want* the charm, you see, to come out for you"), that I want to pursue for now. The emphasis is James's own, and it strikes a familiar note of mindful care shot through with equal measures of affection and command. We might well imagine such orders being given by any number of James's characters, from the later novels especially, and hear the mix of brittleness and force that invites, yet also troubles, our attachment to Madame de Vionnet in *The Ambassadors,* to Kate Croy in *The Wings of the Dove,* or to Charlotte Stant in *The Golden Bowl.* Not one of whom, it is important to remember, gets what she wants when pitted against a character like Mrs. Newsome, Milly Theale, or Maggie Verver, who seem instead to use more elaborate means of making other people do what they are never really told. Thus while James is simultaneously domineering and imploring in his letter to the Duchess of Sutherland, the novels he is producing at this moment suggest that "mastery" (a loaded term for Jamesians) is rarely secured by means of blatant overture. Indeed, James's last three novels are fixated almost morbidly on the negative capabilities of communication—on the effects of reticence, of messages not delivered or somehow misunderstood—and so direct us, again and again, to fathom the consequences of exchanges between characters that do not happen.[15] We realize the strength of Milly's hold on Merton Densher when it is made clear that her final letter need not be read for both Densher and Kate to "know" its meaning; Maggie solidifies her triumph over Charlotte when, at a crucial moment of exposure, she so artfully accuses her of "nothing"; it is when Mrs. Newsome has stopped sending telegrams from Woollett (sending instead the Pococks) that Strether, "in the finer clearer medium of her silence," appreciates that her presence has taken on "a greater intensity," that "her vividness" has magnified into "almost an obsession."[16] It is as though throughout the novels of the major phase, communication and a range of behaviors that should stand for radical, even hostile alternatives to communication, are experienced as effectively identical, as little more than different ways of doing the work involved in connecting one person to another.

As with many of James's pronouncements on the novel, both formal and informal, his operating instructions for *The Ambassadors* show a relative disregard for fiction that sets out to communicate too straightforwardly. This is not to imply that he thinks that novels as a genre ought not to communicate, or that literature as such necessarily aspires to more meticulous and exalted uses of language. He does, however, at times suggest that both of these presumptions apply to *his* novels and to the type of literature they represent. In an 1890 letter to William Dean Howells, he lauds the "communicable rapture" that *A Hazard of New Fortunes* has aroused; the book, James writes to Howells, in praise both tautological and faint, is a "triumph of communication" because "you communicate so completely *what* you undertake to communicate."[17] An earlier letter finds James even less enthused by Howell's genius for observing and transmitting social fact: "I am surprised some times, at the thing you notice & seem to care about. One should move in a diviner air" (*LL*, 197). To Mrs. Humphrey Ward, James warns that in her latest novel (*Eleanor*), "your material suffers a little from the fact that the reader feels you approach your subject too *immediately*, show him its elements, the cards in your hand, too bang off from the first page" (*LL*, 317). James offers a humbler variation of the same critique to H. G. Wells, whose *Future in America* was published in 1906 just as James's own essays from his U.S. tour were being serialized. His ovation for Wells's "communicative passion" warms over rhetoric served to Howells some fifteen years before (*LL*, 441). And even though James takes himself to task in light of Wells's "vividness" and "force," his hyperbole is the rather awkward sequel to a stinging condemnation: James writes to Wells, "you tend always to simplify overmuch," before adding, "But what am I talking about, when just this ability & impulse to simplify—so vividly—is just what I all yearningly envy you?—I who was accursedly born to touch nothing save to complicate it" (*LL*, 441).

James incriminates himself with more conviction when he responds to Hugh Walpole's confession that parts of *A Small Boy and Others* just plain "defeat" him: "That is the pang & the proof that I am truly an uncommunicating communicator—a beastly bad thing to be" (*LL*, 523). But this pleading gesture is rendered arch by what comes next as James describes his own posture in the literary marketplace: "Here at least I said to myself is a thing at every inch of its way on the [level of] the meanest intelligence! [And yet, as it] would seem, I don't get flat *enough* down on my belly—there's a cherished ideal of platitude that, to make 'success,' I shall never be able to achieve" (*LL*, 523). For an acolyte like Walpole, James perhaps assumed, better by far that the Master be an "uncommunicating communicator" than to venture after the prostrations of—the scare quotes say it best—"'success.'"

Yet James does invoke, with respect to his late manner especially, an insistence on both economy and linearity as aesthetic principles worth honoring. Later in the same letter to Mrs. Ward, for example, he indulges in some hypothetical dialogue that captures perfectly how he argues on these topics: "I should have urged you: 'Make that consciousness full, rich, universally prehensile. . . . how, otherwise, do you get your unity of subject or keep up your reader's sense of it?' To which, if you say: How then do I get *Lucy's* consciousness, I impudently retort: 'By that magnificent and masterly *indirectness* which means the *only* dramatic straightness and intensity'" (*LL*, 317; emphasis in original). James first courts and then accentuates the paradox. The ungenerous might even translate this advice as something on the order of, "be more like James and less like Mrs. Humphrey Ward." But I would caution against such an easy claim of arrogance or ulterior motive. James's devotion to the indirect often operates at such a high pitch of assertion that it merits closer scrutiny, particularly as some of his most sophisticated accounts of narrative technique turn on the same vocabulary that we will later see in the fiction when he depicts, to shuffle his own terms slightly, the "intensity" of a telegraphic "indirectness."

The opening paragraphs of the New York Edition preface to *The Golden Bowl* rehearse the essence of James's practical advice for Ward with a considerable show of theoretical agility. "Among the many matters thrown into relief by a refreshed acquaintance with *The Golden Bowl*," he writes, "what perhaps stands out for me is the still marked inveteracy of a certain indirect and oblique view of my presented action; unless I make up my mind to call this mode of treatment, on the contrary, any superficial appearance notwithstanding, the very straightest and closest possible" (*GB*, xli). He argues that his practice of narrating draws not from his "own impersonal account of the affair in hand" but instead from a more mediated "account of somebody's impression of it," a "somebody" serving as "a convenient substitute or apologist for the creative power otherwise so veiled and disembodied" (*GB*, xli).[18] And though James goes on to say that, for *The Golden Bowl* at any rate, the text owes its main appeal to the fact that he chose *not* to deploy a surplus character to filter and reflect the narrative, it is his defense of the "indirect and oblique" that makes the stronger impression, all the more given that the preface ends with more talk of "communication," of "'connections'[that] are employable for finer purposes than mere gaping contrition" (*GB*, lxi). The first sentences of this preface certainly make a strong impression on Percy Lubbock: he seconds James, as if taking the Master's dictation, when he writes that "the simple story-teller begins by addressing himself openly to the reader, and then exchanges this method for another, and with each modification he reaches the reader from a further remove."[19] Such distance between author and reader promises a version of the uniquely mediated immediacy that James recommends to Ward. Thus Lubbock concludes, "The more circuitous procedure on the part of the author produces a straighter effect for the reader."

At the risk of anticipating too much of a later argument, I want to venture that the compulsive indirectness that James identifies as his method—and also his sense that this indirectness is in actuality direct, straight, and the guarantor of a phenomenal immediacy—represents more than a leap of critical fancy or mere vindication of his later stylistic turns. There is ample evidence of both of these rhetorical strategies throughout the prefaces, but I think neither adequately explains the historical significance of James's own "circuitous procedure" for making fiction. I am proposing that what James considers the major insight behind his favored "mode of treatment"—that is, the discovery that the most circuitous may be experienced as the most immediate—applies with equal salience to almost everything that happens to the characters he depicts in his three major novels from the first years of the twentieth century.

I want a certain emphasis to fall on "twentieth century": though it is not my aim to contrast James's early and late novels with complete thoroughness, I would suggest that the ostentatiously mediated textures of his later novels reflect a number of formal innovations that he actively pursues from the mid-1890s on, but also that these same innovations index ways in which he becomes more deeply absorbed, at this very moment, within the cultural effects of media technologies and the distinctly modern world of communications that they imply. Discussing James's "telegraphic realism," Menke argues that when the telegraph, as both a plot device and an emblem of modernity, is "stretched to the breaking point" in "In the Cage," we find it "may convey the messages of a telegraphic modernism" (215). Thus in an early novel like *The American* (1876–1877), when Christopher Newman admits that "in America, I conducted my correspondence altogether by telegrams," the emblematic status of the telegraph is clear enough, but it is still possible for James to imagine Paris as a sanctuary from the modernity that technology somewhat colorlessly symbolizes; "I have even bargained," Newman says, "that I am to receive no business letters."[20] And even as late as *The Tragic Muse* (1890), much the same symbolic scheme persists: it is with little gusto that Nick Dormer takes to the "many letters and telegrams" that are consistently associated in the text with Julia Dallow, Mr. Cateret, and the political domain in which they thrive, and "answering these communications" is clearly signaled as the opposite of the artistic isolation that Nick is after.[21] But by the later fictions, it is almost impossible to assume such conventional metaphorics, and we see that James does not just "stretch" the telegraph, as Menke would put it, but radically multiplies and distributes its presence so as to suggest that telegraphy has become, technically speaking, "ubiquitous."[22] *The Ambassadors* might be expected to conform to the imaginary geography of *The American*, and with Mrs. Newsome "no less intensely than circuitously present" by way of countless telegrams from Woollett, there is at least the invitation to register the difference between America and Europe as one determined by technology (*AM*, 44). We will see, however, that this is not the symbolic use to which James puts telegrams in his later novels. Nor does such extrapolating on "the international theme" go that far toward explaining all the figures of "connection" that owe their resonance to a language derived largely from the technicalities of communication.

With these various propositions in mind, I would like to give a sharp pull on the "thread" I have left dangling from James's directions to the Duchess of Sutherland. His New York Edition preface for *The Ambassadors* spends a good deal of time on the figure of Maria Gostrey and her function. Strether meets her in the first pages of the book, and she looms immediately as a romantic complication—not so much an overt rival to the mysterious Mrs. Newsome, who has dispatched her fiancé (Strether) to Paris to return her son to Woollett, but certainly a distraction that might slow the progress of his mission. We soon realize that Mrs. Newsome would be right to worry, for while Strether and Maria definitely do not pursue a romance, they do engage in elaborate and detailed conversations about every aspect of Strether's experiences. Yet their intimacy, as James explains in the novel's preface, is contrived almost entirely on our behalf as readers. Maria is "the most unmitigated and abandoned of *ficelles*," as James terms his character-observers who tend to operate at a verbose remove from the plot itself: "she is an enrolled, a direct, aid to lucidity" (*AM*, 47). The language evokes several colloquial senses of *ficelle* as a word suggesting the idea of "knowing" or "knowing the ropes"; and this latter expression reminds us that *ficelle* most literally refers to a small piece of string or thread. It is not on this echo alone that I find the preface so conspicuously prefigured in James's earlier letter concerning the "scientifically tight" appeal of *The Ambassadors*. He relies on his *ficelles* in other novels to produce narration by way of retrospective dialogue that effectively occludes the narrator himself (Fanny Assingham in *The Golden Bowl*, for instance, or the tellingly named Susan String*ham* in *The Wings of the Dove*). But what preoccupies James throughout his discussion of "quite the best, 'all round,'" of his novels, is an intricate dialectic between connection and disconnection that comes to provide both a thematic architecture for the text's plot and an aesthetic rationale for James's own hesitancy to communicate in his fictions. Such *ficelles* as Maria Gostrey permit a mediated variety of first-person address—first-person by proxy, so to speak, a technique that James believes essential "less to [his] subject than to [his] treatment of it" (*AM*, 47). "The interesting proof, in these connexions, being that one has but to take one's subject for the stuff of drama to interweave with enthusiasm as many Gostreys as need be" (*AM*, 47). Or put another way, once "one's hero" is effectively disconnected from the reader, there is no limit to the "connexions" that an author may invent, and no limit to the density of the circuitry—the scenes of conversation and communication, the surreptitious monologues, the covert moments of indirect address—that replaces the "looseness" and "fluidity" of first-person narrative with the "straightness and intensity," recalling the letter to Ward, of the Jamesian novel.

There are several scenes in *The Ambassadors* that allow us to realize the full significance of James's recourse to the telegraph as a means of materializing or reifying such aestheticized "connexions" within his fiction. A crucial moment occurs near the beginning of the novel; we have not yet learned Maria Gostrey's name, but we have discovered that she knows "Mr. Waymarsh of Milrose, Connecticut," the American lawyer from whom Strether has just received a message apologizing for a delay in his arrival. Thus Strether and the strange woman, without speaking a word about the matter, agree to spend a few hours together in the meantime:

> They moved along the hall together, and Strether's companion threw off that the hotel had the advantage of a garden. . . . He wanted to look at the town, and they would forthwith look together. It was almost as if she had been in possession and received him as a guest. Her acquaintance with the place presented her in manner as a hostess, and Strether had a rueful glance for the lady in the glass cage. It was as if this personage had seen herself instantly superseded. (*AM*, 58)

We know already that this is the "glass cage" of the hotel's telegraph office, and for a brief moment the novel looms almost as a sequel to "In the Cage." The second sentence of the novel informs us that a telegram, "reply paid," has preceded Strether to Chester (*AM*, 55). It is also quite suggestive, in light of what comes later, that the price of his reply has already been taken care of for him, that the economics of communication are already not in Strether's favor, long before we learn of his dependency on Mrs. Newsome and the money that she wires him. We will soon discover, after all, that Mrs. Newsome is the only benefactor of the high-minded periodical that Strether edits, making him as much her employee as any of the workers at the Woollett "manufacture" (96). Maria too has Strether at something of a disadvantage, and there is a hint of impropriety, a seductive charge and faint aura of the illicit, to the "strange inconsequence" of easy familiarity she inspires. Nor am I sure whether the various analogies she employs to "professionalize" her relationship to Strether—at first she is a "hostess," and subsequently she calls herself "a sort of superior 'courier-maid,'" and finally "a companion at large" (*AM*, 65)—dispels this aura or heightens it. When Maria confides that her lot in life is to "bear on her back the huge load of our national consciousness," it would seem difficult to take her statement as a euphemism for some ridiculously genteel form of prostitution, until, that is, she adds, "I don't do it, for instance—some people do, you know—for money" (*AM*, 66).

Yet the association of Maria and the telegraph girl is ultimately more provocative than conclusive. I take seriously the "as if" that James drops squarely at the end of Strether's fleeting perception that his new companion is somehow a sequel to the nameless information worker behind the glass. This is not to discount the importance of a crucial description of Maria as "the mistress of a hundred cases or categories, receptacles of the mind, subdivisions for convenience, in which, from a full experience, she pigeon-holed her fellow mortals with a hand as free as that of a compositor scattering type" (*AM*, 60); there are obvious similarities between the labors here figuratively located in a print shop and those undertaken at a hotel telegraph office or mail room, where "cases or categories" are also sorted, where people are assigned "receptacles" and "pigeonholed" so that their letters may be "scattered"—the context implies dispersal or distribution—according to some unlikely order. But in appearing to "supersede" the telegraph girl, Maria distinguishes herself from this functionary, and by extension, points the novel away from the petit bourgeois world of "In the Cage." The artfully contrived ambiguity in which James drenches Maria's class suggests instead a world where both the telegraph and the modern system of communication it represents have been deterritorialized, or better, distributed into the very texture of social life. We are being prepared for a narrative in which it will be difficult to discern anything allegorical about technology, a narrative in which the pleasures and anxieties of communication will be decidedly intricate and enigmatic, and precisely for this reason, more urgent and unnerving than anything we find in James's previous telegraphic fiction.

What this means on a larger scale is that the three novels of the major phase, for obvious reasons more encompassing and complicated than his *nouvelle* about a telegrapher, appear at first glance less motivated, less structured by problems of communication technology, when in fact there are countless instances, like this scene from *The Ambassadors*, that make sense only when we realize the extent to which James remains interested in thoroughly mediated experiences of connection—fantasies perhaps, but nevertheless compelling.

This is part of what makes James's novels so involving and uncanny in their depiction of modern life. And so exceptionally roundabout.

Falling in Love with Media

I have thus far been tracing a series of associations between James's insistence on the circuitous, at the level of narrative construction, and his interest in the telegraph as a central artifact of the modernity his narratives document. But it remains to be explained how and, more importantly, why two such radically different formal modes—the least concise of novels and the most abbreviated of verbal communications—become crucially "connected." In comparison to the hackneyed example of Ernest Hemingway, James obviously produced fiction that is demonstrably *not* telegraphic if we take this term to mean a kind of fiction that aspires to the minimally connotative, referential style we attribute to the medium. I would like to counter this common sense on two fronts. First, there is a great deal of popular fiction and iconography from the period that allows us to reconsider the status of telegraphic expression in the late nineteenth century, to describe more variously the cultural effects of this particular technology, and to account for a wider range of mediated experiences that were somehow constelled around the telegraph. Second, the fact that the most compelling of these popular materials are frantically, even ludicrously modern love stories, in which all the mechanics of the marriage plot are translated for a telegraphic world, suggests we might look less to James's linguistic surfaces and more to his semantics of romance, pleasure, and sexuality, in order best to gauge how his late novels communicate with the materialities of communication itself.

It was fundamentally James's inveterate indirectness that opened him to accusations of both depravity and decorum, especially when readers sensed that more carnal and voluptuous meanings loomed always on the other side of sentences so wrought and over-elegant. Jonathan Freedman, for example, has argued that James was entangled in debates about the "degeneracy" of British aestheticism throughout the 1880s and 1890s, and further, that his major novels were received, at least by some, as exemplary and therefore nefarious proof of this mode's most undesirable aspects.[23] The abrasive—though never tedious— Maxwell Geismar rehearses Wilde's sentiment at several points in *Henry James and the Jacobites*, a book known for its combination of strenuous close readings of James's writing and psychoanalytic invective against James's sexuality. Geismar condemns one passage from the *Notebooks* as displaying James's "true view" of the "physical passions," which is to say, "his curious process of refining them away, of converting the primary human drives into a sublimated sort of idealism, an ethereal sensibility."[24] "It is a world of 'liaisons' gone mad in the later Jamesian repressed and spinsterish world of sexual fantasies," Geismar rants elsewhere, "but these liaisons and secret affairs are 'experienced' only in talk, in gossip, in speculation. There is nothing direct, nothing physical ever described here, or experienced firsthand . . . just as there are no pleasures of the flesh, or of sexual love, no rewards, no satisfactions."[25] And while Geismar is old news to critics of James, one strain in his thinking is worth pursuing. Disembodiment—"nothing physical," "no pleasures of the flesh," "an ethereal sensibility"—is where James's too fancy style marries perfectly with his too timid sexuality. On this count, Geismar is preceded by several critics contemporary with James. A British reviewer of *The Wings of the Dove* calls its characters "abstractions of abstractions, shadows of shadows."[26] The American critic F. M. Colby undertakes a more extensive treatment of this Jamesian failing in two 1902 essays, titled respectively—and as if already at the service of our own critical lexicon—"The Queerness of Henry James" and "In Darkest James." The latter is a reluctantly approving notice for *The Wings of the Dove*, about which he admits that "by indefinable means, and in spite of the most wearisome prolixity . . . things you had supposed incommunicable certainly come your way."[27] But it is the former essay that makes a more subtle argument about the immateriality of James's prurience:

> In a literature so well policed as ours, the position of Henry James is anomalous. He is the only writer of the day whose moral notions do not seem to matter. His dissolute and complicated Muse may say just what she chooses. This may be because it would be so difficult to expose him. Never did so much vice go with such sheltering vagueness. Whatever else may be said of James, he is no tempter, and though his later novels deal only with unlawful passions, they make but chilly reading on the whole. It is a land where the vices have no bodies and the passions no blood, where nobody sins because nobody has anything to sin with. Why should we worry when a spook goes wrong? . . . To be a sinner, even in the books you need some carnal attributes—lungs, liver, tastes, at least a pair of legs.[28]

I think there is something essentially correct to what Colby says here— dated, yes, but still worth taking seriously. For Colby does not deny that there is "vice" in James, nor that a sense of something difficultly and obscurely erotic is an element of his fiction. It is rather that James is fascinated more with "vices" that are not well fitted to the conventional organs of transgression. "Why should we worry when a spook goes wrong?" What is the significance of sex without its "carnal attributes"? This last question could be phrased from a slightly different perspective: what precisely *is* sex without the viscera that Colby shies away from naming (he too is "policed," after all) when he eroticizes lungs and livers? Contemporary critics of technology, for example, now describe a whole array of computer-mediated entertainments and experiments that have quickened our sense of sexual possibility in the utter absence of body, flesh, and fluid.[29] But I also believe it likely that any answers patterned on these models, and on the discourse that surrounds them, would assume a fairly predictable shape. We should not project the disembodied pleasures of "darkest James" onto the technologies of our present without also acknowledging that there are eminently historical models for such representations of sexuality; as Claudia Springer reminds us, with regard to Denis de Rougemont, "the purest form of romance" in the Western tradition has long been predicated on "the idea of bodiless sexuality."[30] This is all to say simply that the pleasures of the telegraphic should not be overlooked if we are concerned with understanding an imaginary geography "where the vices have no bodies," a place where one can "sin" only with the organs of communication.

An illustration will help to clarify the argument I am making (fig. 1.1). It shows, in a central image surrounded by smaller, less detailed vignettes, the interior of a railway car, with two foregrounded figures who appear to be looking at each other, the girl on the right less obvious with her attentions, perhaps because she herself seems under the watch of two other figures, older and parental, in the seats behind her. This main scene depicts events narrated in the first few pages of "A Centennial-Telegraphic Romance," an anonymous story from *Lightning Flashes and Electric Dashes*.[31] Sydney Summerville, "a denizen of the Western Union main office," is taking the train to Philadelphia, where he plans to visit the Centennial Exhibition (101). While scanning the faces of his fellow passengers, he spots the "sweet, frank countenance" of the girl sitting opposite him. The story spares no hyperbole in describing the effect she has upon the young telegrapher: "To meet an utter stranger, and gaze in the unfamiliar eyes unthinkingly, and suddenly to find ones [*sic*] heart still and cold, while everything in the world underwent a grand, wondrous change, that is love at first sight—the sweetest, most divine and glorious of all love. It is worth life and worth death to love like that" (102).

A Centennial Telegraphic Romance.—Drawn by Frank Beard.
(See Paeg 31.)

FIGURE 1.1. "A Centennial-Telegraphic Romance." Frontispiece of *Lightning Flashes and Electric Dashes: A Volume of Choice Telegraphic Literature, Humor, Fun, Wit and Wisdom* (New York: Johnston, 1877).

The object of Summerville's new affections is traveling with her parents, and after they catch her exchanging long glances with a stranger ("Each looked at the other steadily, but with perfect modesty for perhaps ten seconds"), she blushes, frowns, and turns away. "But the frown speedily vanished and gave place to a sweet and much more becoming smile, which Summerville promptly and gallantly reciprocated. The lady seemed a little abashed at this, and in her embarrassment caught the little window fastener in her dainty fingers and listlessly thumbed upon it a moment. Presently she clicked, in tolerably fair Morse: 'I, I. That bright smile haunts me still'" (103). Of course Eva—her name, we later learn—does not expect her Morse transmission to be received; she is, in effect, thinking out loud in code. But Summerville improvises a sending key of his own and taps out a reply using his pencil on the car window. Their flirtation thus continues as Eva's mindful parents continue watching, no longer aware of any untoward looks and not hearing the much more involved flirtation that is unfolding amid all the noise and chatter. This is what is centrally pictured here: the surreptitious telegraphing of two smitten lovers, "strangers on a train," we might say, perfectly maintaining the public appearance of decorum—"nothing direct, nothing physical"—while rapidly and secretly committing acts of communication far outside the limits of propriety.

"A Centennial-Telegraphic Romance" incorporates several standard themes and plot devices that recur in mediated love stories of the period.[32] A morphology of these "wired" romances would take account of the following: (1) Trains pervade both the milieu and the figurative languages of these fictions; this reflects not only interdependence of communication and transportation networks in late-nineteenth-century America but also the central importance of the railway as an emblem of technological and social modernity, an emblem that these fictions often want supplanted in favor of the telegraph. (2) With almost the same intensity that these stories embrace the modernity of telecommunication, they revel in all that is most formulaic and conventional in the general discourse of love and romance; a lot of truly awful poetry, for example, punctuates "A Centennial-Telegraphic Romance," as if these texts are anxious to convince us that all the old, familiar sentiments will obtain under new conditions of media. (3) Following closely from this last element, these stories display a sometimes uncanny fascination with highly heterogeneous forms of textuality, incorporating not just poems and lyrics but also telegraphs, letters, Morse code, and popular song as materials for their verbal surfaces. (4) Plots, of course, are driven by confusions of identity that thrive when one is able to know only what may be transmitted telegraphically. Summerville first introduces himself to Eva with a false name to prevent entanglement in case her family is undesirable, and the vertigo of identity is only deepened when, having confessed his duplicity, Summerville, mistaking a telegram sent to Eva's cousin, who is also named Eva (!), believes himself abandoned for a rakish fellow operator. And more: a lover does not know what her beloved looks like and so is tricked into a relationship with someone inappropriately old or comically unattractive, or is led to believe, by some nefarious interloper, that someone else is actually the person with whom she has been communicating; one operator passes himself off as another, having "listened in" to a telegraphic courtship; people fall in love with operators of uncertain gender, age, and attractiveness. (5) Proximity does not preclude telegraphy; lovers engage in the most arcanely technical forms of communication even when present to one another. (6) Distance does not preclude sex, or at least, forms of communication that are freighted with a great deal of erotic suggestion and intimation; there is an urge to imagine figurative alternatives to consummation, some of which are almost ludicrously artless in their euphemistic referencing of the carnal and the physical.

We see evidence of this effort at both the top and the bottom of the "Centennial-Telegraphic Romance" image. The sketch of Cupid perched at a telegraph sounder is, I admit, a rather timid gesture toward an erotics of communication. More interesting—though, again, far from salacious—are the two hearts suspended from the wires that drape across the indeterminate space between the individual pictures of Summerville and Eva. The wires are purely decorative and iconic, given that both lovers appear to be engrossed with written mail instead of telegrams. Still, the hearts draw the viewer's attention to this space between, emphasizing the hard reality of their physical separation, making it literal and explicit at the very instant when it is rendered figurative and euphemistic. The emblematic hearts are obviously meant to signify, to serve as metaphors of "love"—being transmitted, bridging the paltry fact of distance, uniting what is apart—but at the same time, I think it possible to read these hearts as metonymic parts of bodies, as reminders of all that is not so easily telegraphed from place to place. They simultaneously make for a point of closure and interruption in a plainly sexualized circuit of romance; the wires break upon piercing each heart, which has the effect of underscoring their two-dimensionality and emptiness, especially when compared to the fully modeled figures in the railway car below. Are these hearts flat shapes or rounded volumes? Are they skewered and suspended *on* the wires, or are they somehow supposed to be imagined *inside* the wires, like the bulge inside a snake that has just swallowed a huge mass? Amid all the "semantic prattle," to use Barthes's phrase, about love and communication, all the redundancy of scenes where messages are being transmitted and received, these hearts are at once the symbolic key to whatever sense the image might make upon an initial viewing—along with the Cupid, they confirm, despite all that we do not know, that these scenes are from a love story—and yet they just as eloquently suggest ways in which this image, and the romance it represents, must necessarily remain inscrutable if it is to capture the mediated materiality of such a highly charged yet ultimately only telegraphic connection.

No matter how we read the hearts in the image, Barthes's *S/Z* remains remarkably appropriate for the occasion. The entire entry on "The Prattle of Meaning" is worth considering:

> For any fictional action . . . there exist three possible realms of *expression*. Either the meaning is stated, the action named but not detailed. Or, while the meaning is being set forth, the action is more than named, it is described. Or else the action is described, but its meaning is kept tacit: the action is merely connoted (in the strict sense of the word) from an implicit signified. The first two realms, in terms of which signification is *excessively* named, impose a dense plentitude of meaning or, if one prefers, a certain redundancy, a kind of semantic prattle typical of the archaic—or infantile—era of modern discourse, marked by the excessive fear of failing to communicate meaning (its basis); whence, in reaction, in our latest—or "new"—novels, the practice of the third system: to state the event without accompanying it with its signification.[33]

No less than ten acts of communication, in one sense or another, are figured in the illustration accompanying "A Centennial-Telegraphic Romance."[34] In the story itself, there are fifteen instances of quoted poetry; one of these quotations is itself situated within a letter that Summerville writes to Eva—there are three such epistolary transcriptions in the text, in addition to the entire opening "conversation," presented textually as dialogue though it is taking place in Morse code between Summerville and Eva on the train. The story, simply put, cannot stop communicating its own status as a story about the romance of communicating romantically—communications that often must augment, qualify, or clarify prior communications or miscommunications about a romance that consists solely of communications in the first place. This is not entirely a novel feature of "A Centennial-Telegraphic Romance," nor of the many stories like it. A highly self-conscious gamesmanship about the narrative possibilities of communication, and vice versa, is put on show in any number of epistolary fictions; it is not for nothing that Bernhard Siegert speaks of "literature as an epoch of the postal system."[35] But "A Centennial-Telegraphic Romance" takes its indebtedness to earlier literary models far too seriously, desperately wanting to prove that we are reading a story about love and not technology, and so it "prattles": "But love sometimes enters a life abruptly and unexpectedly. Love, as somebody has said, is a dear divine passion of the gods. It is the only thing in this world that makes the long interval between fourteen and seventy in any way acceptable. Life without love is an ugly, monotonous song; a low, wearisome, uneducated parrot's song that dolefully rings out in the dreary space, frightening the timorous traveler."[36] Thus the story describes the lovers' first meeting of glances; the accompanying illustration seems positively austere in deploying just two iconic hearts and a telegraphing *putto*.

Charles Barnard's cryptically entitled "— – — – — — –: An Electro-Mechanical Romance" also conforms neatly to the genre I described above. First published in *Scribner's* in May 1875—and then reprinted in several anthologies of telegraphic fiction and Barnard's own collection, *Knights of To-Day, or, Love and Science* (1881)—this story is superlative for its attention to the uncanny textuality of mediated love and for a plot involving what must be among the first acts of hacking in American literature. A telegraph operator is in love with an engineer, John, and since she can never be certain exactly when his express train will arrive, she teaches him her name in Morse ("K — – — A – — T — E –") so that he may sound it on his steam whistle whenever he approaches her isolated station. Thus it is several pages before we—meaning any readers unfamiliar with Morse, which I assume was and is the vast majority—are taught to read the story's title, and no sooner are we made technologically literate than language itself is rendered as pure sound when John's first call to his beloved is figured as a bar of music.[37] From name to code to noise in just a page. Their restricted network operates only so long, however, before another operator hears their signal and thus exposes their relationship, which is as much to say, its propriety, along with Kate's sexual respectability. Good girls do not have their names bellowed by the speeding "59" express. And so Kate seizes on the idea of a private line between John's engine and her office: "If we can manage to rig up another wire from her [the train] to our station we can make an open circuit, and as you pass . . . you can join it and—ring a bell in my office." They find half a mile of abandoned wire, Kate fashions a battery, and under cover of darkness, she instructs John in how best to lay the new line so that it takes advantage of, and is fully hidden by, the company's own poles and wires. It is this improvised and covert connection that warns Kate of an impending collision between the "59" and a train carrying the president of the railroad. She and John admit their illicit use of company materials to their employer: "Never did story create profounder sensation. The gentlemen shook hands with [John], and the President actually kissed her for the Company. A real Corporation kiss, loud and hearty." John is promoted on the spot to a position that pays enough for him to marry, and Kate is "fired" so that she may instead assume her new position as wife and mother, her expertise ("he was fairly dazzled by the brilliancy and audacity of her ideas") no longer needed for the domestic duties ahead.

"A real Corporation kiss" thus forecloses on both the pleasures of communicating on the sly and the ingenuity of a woman with superior technical know-how and imagination. The "private circuit" of two workers is quite literally "incorporated," with the effect of turning covert lovers into petit bourgeois man and wife. The codes of intimacy established, on a woman's terms, within the silences and spaces of modern life give way to the official proclamations of a patriarchal authority: "It is resolved . . . that the said operator be requested to resign." All this *is* the happy ending, and we have little reason to believe that such thorough punishment of possibility—ideology besting technology on every count—was intended to be read as anything but, in the story's words, the accomplishment of "a dream," "a paradise." The narrative shape of these fictions of technology almost never deviates from the standard course of romance. Perhaps this is to be expected: these are stories, for the most part, of lower-middle-class information workers longing only for unqualified middle-class status and its domestic comforts. The cultural price of imagining, with such fanfare, entirely new domains of mediated experience may well have been the affirmation of entirely retrograde social outcomes. Which means we must look for smaller moments in these works to remind us that not all the pleasures of communication lend themselves so readily to marriage plots.

When a "C" Loves an "N"

The plot of Ella Cheever Thayer's *Wired Love: A Romance of Dots and Dashes* (1880) turns on one of the most elaborately mediated courtships of its period—or any other, for that matter: Miss Nathalie ("Nattie") Rogers, an aspiring writer making ends meet as a telegrapher, strikes up a flirtatious "correspondence" with another operator, Clem Stanwood, who subsequently moves to the very town—and into the very boardinghouse—as Nattie; after misadventures typical to the genre—a crude, lower-class operator who has listened in attempts to pass himself off as Nattie's distant friend—Clem and Nattie decide to string a wire between their rooms so that their deepening relationship may proceed without the nosy meddling of their landlady, Miss Kling; after further misadventures typical to sentimental fiction more generally—Nattie mistakenly concludes that Clem has fallen in love with her friend Cynthia, an opera singer referred to, quite ominously, as "Cyn," while Clem mistakenly concludes that Nattie has fallen in love with his friend Quimby—our heroine and hero finally communicate to each other their true emotions; Clem proposes, Nattie accepts, and the novel ends much like any number of popular "romances" of the period, with the rites of marriage soon to promise domesticity and bourgeois status for the telegrapher and would-be author whose fiancé has been promoted to the ranks of management, a bright future with the company ahead.

Since *Wired Love was* published by the same firm that produced three anthologies of telegraphic literature, as well as several monthly periodicals covering all aspects of the industry, it is safe to say that the core of its intended audience was associated with nineteenth-century high technology in one form or another.[38] The novel's dedication is presented solely in Morse code, as are its final lines (fig. 1.2). Thus it would have taken anyone without a working knowledge of Morse some effort to read the novel through to its conclusion: "my little darling my wire." (I decoded the text using one of several Morse translators available online; there are delicious ironies in this, too numerous to mention.) I call attention to the text's last page not just because it is an oddity of book history but also because it typographically negates and disavows the movement from the mediated to the real that the novel has ostensibly been after for some 250 pages. When Cyn sees that Nattie and Clem are holding hands, that various miscommunications have been transcended and they now are "making love like ordinary mortals," she insists that "this will never do! We must end this romance of dots and dashes as it commenced, to make it truly 'Wired Love!'"[39] Clem proceeds to the telegraphic key that has been installed and "with his eyes looking straight into Nattie's," sounds a message "that [makes] her blush and seize his hand in shy and unnecessary alarm." But Nattie—concerned with decorum to the end—fears that another character might "read" the message as it arrives on the other set of telegraphic instruments next door. Thus Clem relents:

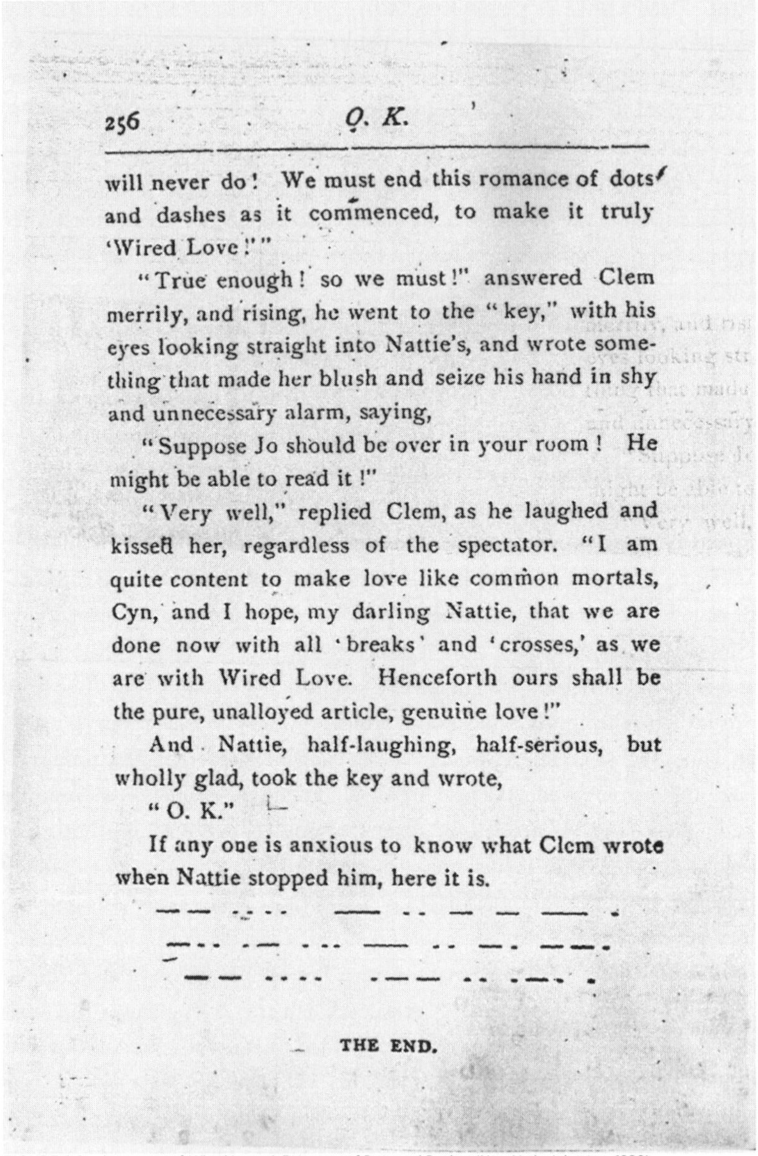

will never do! We must end this romance of dots'
and dashes as it commenced, to make it truly
'Wired Love!'"

"True enough! so we must!" answered Clem
merrily, and rising, he went to the "key," with his
eyes looking straight into Nattie's, and wrote something that made her blush and seize his hand in shy
and unnecessary alarm, saying,

"Suppose Jo should be over in your room! He
might be able to read it!"

"Very well," replied Clem, as he laughed and
kissed her, regardless of the spectator. "I am
quite content to make love like common mortals,
Cyn, and I hope, my darling Nattie, that we are
done now with all 'breaks' and 'crosses,' as we
are with Wired Love. Henceforth ours shall be
the pure, unalloyed article, genuine love!"

And Nattie, half-laughing, half-serious, but
wholly glad, took the key and wrote,

"O. K."

If any one is anxious to know what Clem wrote
when Nattie stopped him, here it is.

— — ·· ·· ·   — — ·· — — — — ·
— ·· ·— · ··   — ·· — · — · —·
—   · ·· ·   · — —   ·· ·—· · ·

THE END.

FIGURE 1.2. Last page of *Wired Love: A Romance of Dots and Dashes* (New York: Johnston, 1880).

"I am quite content to make love like common mortals, Cyn, and I hope, my darling Nattie, that we are done now with all 'breaks' and 'crosses,' as we are with Wired Love. Henceforth ours shall be the pure, unalloyed article, genuine love!" Nattie answers with a communication in Morse, "'O. K.'" and then we are left to read Clem's last transmission. That all this back-and-forth, this rampant communication—physical gestures of desire inspiring spoken declarations of affection, which are then translated into coded messages of devotion—utterly confuses "wired love" with the "unalloyed" is obvious. I think it also likely that Thayer brings this confusion on herself and wants her reader to revel in it, to enjoy the friction and delay of the encoded ending. Even a fluent operator of 1880, after all, could be expected to register the novelty of "reading" Morse as if it were a dialect of literary English. The title page of the novel announces that we are about to have "'The old, old story'—in a new, new way." Clem and Nattie might believe that medium and message are ontologically distinct, that "wired" love is not "genuine," but Thayer, it would seem, knows better. The end of her text short-circuits—the egregious pun is immanent in the logic of the narrative, in the visual layout of the final page—the "old" story of love and marriage and the "new" way in which it can now be consummated. The novel pronounces them man and "wire."

Accordingly, throughout the novel Nat and Clem are never so close as when they are communicating telegraphically or acting as if this were their only means of maintaining their connection. The spoken word and physical touch fail repeatedly to clarify the terms of their relationship; presence is much more problematic to their love than absence, and if proximity threatens always to attenuate their desire, distance provides both energy and inspiration. This is evident when Clem makes his first appearance as a character "in the flesh" at a dinner party that Nattie and Cyn have thrown together. Having been introduced only as another lodger's friend, Clem listens carefully as Nat describes the boorish and sexually aggressive operator who recently introduced himself as her "C." "Suddenly Nattie was disturbed by Mr. Stanwood drumming with a pencil on the marble top of the table," Thayer writes, and "with a slight start she listened more attentively to his seemingly idle drumming. Yes—whether knowingly, or by accident, he certainly was making dots and dashes, and what is more, was making N's!" In reply, she grabs some scissors, "the only adaptable instrument," and signs the question "Are you an operator?" Their Morse conversation continues beneath the din of party chatter, a secret and flirtatious exchange hidden, like some sonic equivalent of Poe's "purloined letter," in plain hearing. And instantly recognizing in the figure Nat has met as "C" an opera-tor from his former station, Clem is able to reveal his telegraphic identity in person: "Don't you 'C' the point? Can't you 'C' that you did not 'C' the 'C' you thought you did 'C' that day?" This sort of punning and play has marked their communication from the start and makes the code of the telegraph office into a ready language for drawing-room comedy. But it is Nattie's reaction that I find more striking than Clem's virtuoso banter: "Nattie's breath came fast, and her hand trembled so she could not hold the scissors. With a crash they dropped on the table, making one loud, long dash" (148–150). She is rendered "speechless" by Clem's confession—which means here a physical discomposure and failure of manual articulation. What results is an eruption of utter noise that causes others at the table to take notice, yet this noise is also a kind of cry that retains a phantom legibility. "One loud, long dash" would translate literally, in Morse, as "AAAAAAA." Her body speaks in code even when excited past the point of language.

A sexually explicit reading of Nattie's outburst may easily be imagined and is certainly available at this moment in the text. But of greater consequence is an earlier scene, from the first chapter of the novel, in fact, that treats the con-catenation of telegraphy and sexuality with even more euphemistic candor. As the novel opens, there is no Nattie and Clem—there is only "N" and "C," two abbreviations indulging in a little flirtation via telegraph, perhaps to no other end, in these initial paragraphs of the text, than to thwart the boredom of being but "the human portion of its machinery."[40] And Thayer is quite determined to press the gender uncertainty of the resulting come-hither communications. "I wonder if this smart operator is a lady or gentleman!" (10). Soon after this exclamation, Nattie is undone by a flurry of code sent by "this too expert indi-vidual of uncertain sex" (11); later "he—or she—" again bests Nattie with his or her fluency in Morse (19); Nattie again exclaims, "I do wonder if this 'C' is *he* or *she*!" (21); "C" answers, "Call me plain 'C'! Or picture, if you like, in place of your sounder, a blonde, fairy-like girl talking to you . . . " (23); and the chapter ends with Nattie still desperate "to know whether my new friend employs a tailor or a dressmaker!" (24). This is far too much homoerotic noise for a truly homoerotic fiction of 1880, and I doubt that many of Thayer's readers would have expected that a love affair in a "new, new way" meant a romance between two women. Such ham-handed innuendo—though pointedly provocative for some—could be assumed, for most, to reference a narrative possibility that will obviously not turn out. Still, the provocation is there, and it colors what I take to be the most exquisitely erotic moment in the entire novel. As "C"—be "C" he or she—is teasing "N" about her or his stumbles in Morse, Nattie must also contend with a customer in the office:

> And turning quickly around to scowl this persevering questioner into si-
> lence, Nattie's elbow hit and knocked over the inkstand, its contents pour-
> ing over her hands, dress, the desk and floor, and proving beyond a doubt,
> as it descended, the truth of its label—
> "Superior Black Ink!"
> And then, save for the clatter of the "sounder," there was silence.
> For a moment, Nattie gazed blankly at her besmeared hands and ruined
> dress.

$$(13-14)$$

Let me again insist that the ambiguous gender of the sender who has caused this telling, frenzied accident is something of a red herring. More important, to my thinking at least, is that such a classical and formulaic symbol of misbegot-ten female sexuality—a garment "ruined" and "besmeared"—is here enlisted as a figure of communication at its most visceral and carnal. Whether Nattie is the unconscious agent of this transgression on her purity (she herself knocks the inkstand over), or whether "C" has transgressed against her (she is telegraphed into submission), we cannot say. The concatenation of female sexuality and the materiality of a medium, however, could not be signaled more directly. As an instance of what Katherine Stubbs describes as the "all too visible, precariously hyper-embodied" status of female telegraph operators more generally in fiction of the period, this telling accident depends on a peculiar mix of mediums in order to communicate.[41] Like Nattie's later outcry at the dinner table, which is both noise and message simultaneously, the stain that marks her dress is ren-dered weirdly literal, as if the splattered ink leaves behind not a simple blot but the words spelled out by the letters "of its label." Of course this literalization is itself a ploy; she is not left with "Superior Black Ink" written on her body, but rather with a blot—semantically null, visual noise—that signifies far more than "the truth" behind its brand name.[42] Small wonder that the novel ends with Clem declaring Nattie his "little darling" and "wire" in Morse: they consum-mate their "romance" telegraphically upon their first mediated meeting. The verbiage does little more than make it all official, or "O. K.," to borrow the more economical locution that the novel uses for the title of its final chapter, where the marriage of Nattie and Clem signals, though perhaps does not deliver, a return to more conventional relations.

This circuitry of noise, technology, and sexual suggestion operates at too high a speed for the novel's rickety machinations of plot and melodrama: the inevitable narrative of marriage does not so much drive the mediated romance of Nattie and Clem as try its best to clean up the mess of unspecified pleasures left behind by "N" and "C" and whatever it is they do to one another from their respective stations. And this circuitry operates just as forcefully—which is to say indirectly—with no surrounding narrative to grant some measure of social codification to these fugitive pleasures of technology. Consider the following images (figures 1.3, 1.4, 1.5): the first shows the cover of a National Dictograph Company brochure from the early 1900s; the second consists of a sequence of illustrations from the brochure's pages that trace what has been spoken into the dictograph by the company's president; the third shows the same cover illustration of the president at his dictograph, but with the brochure open. From president to secretary—"It Has All Been Taken Down by the Stenographer," the final caption reads. "A Complete Record Is Available for the Man Who Forgets or Mislays His Memorandum"—we simply follow the red dot that is the "Master's Voice," from superintendent to foreman to electrical engineer to purchasing agent to some anonymous employee able to listen without a visitor overhearing, until the message at last arrives with the recording angel of the firm. Unlike Nattie in *Wired Love*, she remains impeccable in her composure and absorbed in her task. But she nevertheless provides this network of communication with its ultimate materiality—there is a red piece of colored paper glued onto the page of her picture in the brochure that is the dark dot that the viewer has been following all along. Thus when the cover is viewed without the pages properly aligned, we see instead a void, an empty circle cut into each page that looks exactly like what it is—nothing—without the garish prick of red that rather suggestively appears only when a woman is wired into the network. Our stenographer is "available" to any and all and no one in particular, to everybody "who forgets" or cannot place their "memorandum." Her prosthetic use-value is thus made clear. It is also important to point out that while several other dictographs (in fig. 1.4, the first three pictured starting at the upper left) have microphones like that of the president's, which makes them able both to send and to receive, the stenographer must face a protruding little box that obviously does nothing but talk at her (and not to her) all day long. There is, to put this

FIGURE 1.3. Cover of National Dictograph Company Brochure, circa 1900. University of California, Santa Barbara, Department of Special Collections, Manuscript #107.

all another way, a whole history of secretarial labor in this series of illustrations, and it certainly applies to this bit of office-supply ephemera.[43] But in a world where "wired love" is possible, we cannot be sure what other stories may be waiting for us when we think we are witnessing something as mundane and commonplace as communication.

The Superintendent Called Into the Conference [5]
Gives the Information Wanted Without Any Interruption to the Task in Hand

Then the Foreman, Who Estimates a Cost [7]
Supplies the Detail Wanted from Data Which is Before Him

The Electrical Engineer Also Called Into the Conference
There is No Opening or Closing of Doors, Giving of Directions to an Operator, Shouting or Helloing

At This Stage the Purchasing Agent is Consulted [11]

He is Heard as if the Other Members of the Staff Stood About Him

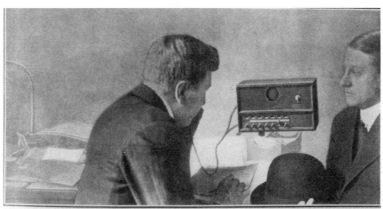

Visitor Cannot Hear Confidential Instructions from President [13]

Every Emergency Has Been Arranged For. This Shows What to Do When a Stranger Happens In

It Has All Been Taken Down by the Stenographer [15]

A Complete Record Is Available for the Man Who Forgets or Mislays His Memorandum

FIGURE 1.4. Sequence of internal images from National Dictograph Brochure, circa 1900. University of California, Santa Barbara, Department of Special Collections, Manuscript #107.

The President Confers with the Manager
Conversation Carried on as if They Were in the Same Room, Though Neither Leaves His Desk

FIGURE 1.5. Cover of National Dictograph Company Brochure (open). University of California, Santa Barbara, Department of Special Collections, Manuscript #107.

Mrs. Newsome's Cables

I have been describing telegraphic fictions that in no way merit the term "Jamesian." This is not to say that their appeal is merely topical, but rather that they offer, on the whole, little purchase for finely calibrated readings of their experiments in point of view, of their representations of "consciousness," of their elaboration at the level of the sentence, of their moral elegance and psychological eccentricity. These are not "dramas of discrimination," to borrow a phrase from James, but texts determined to articulate, with utter and convincing scrutability, a new phenomenology of communication. Shaped as much by the sheer "romance" of connection as by the material conditions of media technology, these fictions want to show—and maybe to shock a bit in the process—that distance and "immediacy" need not be experienced in opposition to one another. Proximity no more promises the physicality of a carnal embrace than separation stipulates that only words may be exchanged between resourceful young telegraphers in love. Niklas Luhmann best sums up the situation: "In all of this an innovative, typically Romantic paradoxy asserted itself: the phenomenon of vision, experience, and enjoyment *being enhanced by means of distantiation*."[44] He could just as well be speaking of James's later fictions and the difficult aesthetic that makes them early landmarks of literary modernism: "What perhaps stands out for me is the still marked inveteracy of a certain indirect and oblique view of my presented action; unless I make up my mind to call this mode of treatment, on the contrary, any superficial appearance notwithstanding, the very straightest and closest possible." There is nothing "scientifically tight," to borrow again from James, about the argument that is implicit in such a breakneck analogy. The rest of this chapter aims at explicating the analogy into a fuller and more historically concerned account of mediated experience in James's last three novels. These are long and various novels—I won't say that the account that follows is complete.

I first want to return to *The Ambassadors*, which features by far the greatest number of specific references to telegrams to be found in any of James's novels. It also inundates the whole world of telegraphic communication with the most conspicuously symbolic associations. And, in the figure of Mrs. Newsome—"no less intensely than circuitously present" when reduced to just a series of telegrams giving orders from Woollett—it presents a character who comes to embody a spectacularly unappealing form of American modernity as representing sheer disenchantment, rationality, and control. Nowhere are these aspects of her character more sublimely rendered than in the following passage from book 10, after Strether's odd disinclination to hurry Chad on his way has been communicated back to Mrs. Newsome. Strether's delay results in Mrs. Newsome dispatching her daughter, Sarah, and the rest of her family, the Pococks, to bring both Chad and Strether back to America; but at this point in the novel Strether seems much more determined to prolong his time in Paris than does Chad. The crucial description occurs just as Waymarsh, who Strether now realizes has been observing him and reporting back to Woollett all along, has informed him that Sarah Pocock is, after a short holiday, preparing to return home:

> He [Waymarsh] was brave in his way too, keeping nothing back, confessing all there was, and only leaving Strether to make certain connexions. "Is what Mrs. Newsome had cabled her daughter an injunction to break off short?"
>
> The grand manner indeed at this just raised its head a little. "I know nothing about Mrs. Newsome's cables."
>
> Their eyes met on it with some intensity—during the few seconds of which something happened quite out of proportion to the time. It happened that Strether, looking thus at his friend, didn't take his answer for truth—and that something more again occurred in consequence of *that*. Yes—Waymarsh just *did* know about Mrs. Newsome's cables: to what other

end than that had they dined together at Bignon's? Strether almost felt for the instant that it was to Mrs. Newsome herself the dinner had been given; and, for that matter, quite felt how she must have known about it, and, as he might think, protected and consecrated it. He had a quick blurred view of daily cables, questions, answers, signals: clear enough was his vision of the expense that, when so wound up, the lady at home was prepared to incur. Vivid not less was his memory of what, during his long observation of her, some of her attainments of that high pitch had cost her. Distinctly she was at the highest now, and Waymarsh, who imagined himself an independent performer, was really, forcing his fine old natural voice, an overstrained accompanist. The whole reference of his errand seemed to mark her for Strether as by this time consentingly familiar to him, and nothing yet had so despoiled her of a special shade of consideration. (411)

There is precious little "romance" to the telegraph here, and no "wired love" in the grim embrace of "Mrs. Newsome's cables." James imagines for us instead—even to the point of risking the gaudy pun on "cables"—the scene of communication as a theater of control, a gothic space where power is exercised from a vague remove, where "daily cables, questions, answers, signals" assemble into some conspiracy of data that will no doubt be used against us. The very phrase "remote control" is an early-twentieth-century invention; in fact, the *Oxford English Dictionary* dates its first recorded usage to 1903, the very year that *The Ambassadors* was published. What is perhaps most striking about this passage, however, is Strether's oddly sympathetic, even tender apprehension of the forces that are set on his undoing by returning him to Woollett, where he is, of course, expected to marry Mrs. Newsome. It is as though Mrs. Newsome exposes herself to Strether—he sees her "so wound up" and straining at "high pitch"—precisely when he comprehends how completely she has made Waymarsh into an instrument of surveillance and communication. Communication, it would seem, cannot *not* go both ways.

Strether's complicated pity for Mrs. Newsome—as if he is just slightly guilty about what he has driven her to do to him—is in keeping with the larger narrative shape of *The Ambassadors*, which will of course end with Strether on his way back to America, not to marry Mrs. Newsome but still resigned to life in what Ross Posnock aptly terms "the reformatory of Woollett."[45] In any event, James here at least partially retreats from an earlier moment in which Mrs. Newsome and Sarah Pocock are imagined in much less ambiguous terms.

I am thinking of a scene in book 8 that takes place soon after the arrival of the Pococks. Strether comments to Sarah's husband, Jim Pocock, that the second wave of "ambassadors" seems ominously peaceable—"You don't show your claws," says Strether, adding of Sarah in particular that "she isn't fierce. . . . I'm such a nervous idiot that I thought she might be." To which Jim answers, "They ain't fierce, either of 'em; they let you come quite close. They wear their fur the smooth side out—the warm side in. . . . They don't lash about and shake the cage." Then Jim extends the analogy still further: "And it's at feeding-time that they're quietest. But they always get there" (332–333). As Strether contemplates Jim's remarks and admits to their unflattering accuracy, he also realizes just what type of carnivore he has been antagonizing for the past three hundred pages by his refusal to execute his mission on behalf of Mrs. Newsome: "It was as if a queer truth in his companion's metaphor had rolled over him with a rush. She *had* been quiet at feeding-time; she had fed, and Sarah had fed with her, out of the big bowl of all his recent free communication, his vividness and pleasantness, his ingenuity and even his eloquence, while the current of her response had steadily run thin" (333). Again the reader encounters, as above for "Mrs. Newsome's cables," an aggressively material metaphor that seeks to render "communication" as something much more tangible and visceral than the mere exchange of messages on paper; and again, this effort to materialize "communication," to grasp at a phenomenology of media effects, could not possibly be more dissonant, in both tone and implication, than that which we saw earlier in the illustration from "A Centennial-Telegraphic Romance." James's telegraphic chains and chunks of flesh stand in drastic opposition to the hearts and Cupids decorating that previous iconography.

In a novel where the hero famously figures his accomplishment in altogether negative terms—"That, you see, is my only logic. Not, out of the whole affair, to have got anything for myself"—we might say that no longer being bound to Mrs. Newsome represents the sole result of Strether's actions. But before we can be certain that this is the inevitable outcome of the novel, there is a moment that suggests just the faintest outline of a possible narrative much different from the one that James is writing. The following passage describes what comes immediately after the scene in which Strether anxiously imagines the "transatlantic bridge" between the Woollett post office and the bank on Rue Scribe (a name well chosen for the circumstances), which is, I need hardly mention, another overt materialization of his emotional and economic tie to Mrs. Newsome. Unable to read his several letters from Mrs. Newsome in this space that has become so figuratively proximate to Woollett, he wanders throughout Paris for the better part of the morning before finding "his nook" in the Luxembourg Gardens and there examining his mail:

> Four of the letters were from Mrs. Newsome and none of them short; she had lost no time, had followed on his heels while he moved, so expressing herself that he now could measure the probable frequency with which he should hear. They would arrive, it would seem, her communications, at the rate of several a week; he should be able to count, it might even prove, on more than one by each mail. If he had begun yesterday with a small griev-ance he had therefore an opportunity to being to-day with its opposite. He read the letters successively and slowly, putting others back into his pocket but keeping these for a long time afterwards gathered in his lap. He held them there, lost in thought, as if to prolong the presence of what they gave him; or as if at the least to assure them their part in the constitution of some lucidity. His friend wrote admirably, and her tone was even more in her style than in her voice—he might almost, for the hour, have had to come this distance to get its full carrying quality; yet the plenitude of his con-sciousness of difference consorted perfectly with the deepened intensity of the connexion. (112)

There is much to note here, starting with the image of a chase ("had fol-lowed on his heels") which "recalls"—meaning it actually predicts—the pas-sage from the preface where James appreciates the "thrill" of his elaborate and rarefied methods by offering, as a lesser model, the racial melodrama of *Uncle Tom's Cabin*: "No dreadful old pursuit of the hidden slave with bloodhounds and the rag of association can ever, for 'excitement', I judge, have bettered it at its best."[46] We are also given to recognize, I think, a certain desperation in the sheer volume of "communications" that Mrs. Newsome has produced, and though it is possible to take this vulnerability as just a ruse for the ferocity it will become, I am struck by the particular tenderness with which Strether handles the ma-terials ("keeping these for a long time afterwards gathered in his lap"). James seems intent on establishing some basis for us to better appreciate the violence of Strether's reaction to later telegrams. Finally, there is the texture of his reverie itself, which is dominated by the phantasmic, mediated "presence" of his absent correspondent. The language mirrors the crucial articulation, again from the preface, of Mrs. Newsome's at once overwhelming and yet marginal status in the narrative ("no less intensely than circuitously present"). Thus there is an especially close relationship—indeed an implicit yet powerful analogy—between the experience of reading that James is describing in this passage and the experience of reading that he hopes that we are having. In other words, I see at work here an aesthetic logic more exacting than the conventional sense in which any character reading could be argued to provide us with a chance to feel ourselves projected into the text itself. What James dramatizes as Strether's experience of "deepened intensity" at a "distance" is nothing less than the phenomenology of indirect "communications" that he pursues across a range of writings on his own narrative techniques. The "connexion" between Strether and Mrs. Newsome, which seems most palpable when most spectacularly mediated ("her tone was even more in her style than in her voice"), idealizes an essential aspect of James's technique in his later novels.

No doubt this argument brings to mind the work of other critics who have scrutinized the deep complicity of James's fiction with various discourses that he presents as antithetical to both the style and the sensibility of that fiction. Thus Mark Seltzer tracks all the ways that James's art subscribes to the same protocols of managerial power that, in *The Ambassadors*, we find eventually pictured in Strether's image of Mrs. Newsome and her insidious "cables"; for Jennifer Wicke, it is the cultural grammar and ideology of modern advertising—Chad's intended specialty in Woollett—that patterns *The Ambassadors* despite the scorn James piles upon it.[47] And while it may be tempting to treat James's investment in languages of connection and communication as determined by, and corollary to, his traffic in these other discourses of modernity, I would be reluctant to accept such a flattening of James's messages to the mediums he might reference. Or put another way, the aesthetics of "connexion" between Strether and Mrs. Newsome change during the course of *The Ambassadors*, transforming from a mediated relationship emblematic of a "circuitousness" that James appears to hold in high esteem into something else entirely, into a relationship that James depicts in figures of such directness and surpassing "immediacy"—her controlling "cables," her "feeding" on his "communication"—that we are supposed to understand that there is no longer any real "connexion" between them. But it is not until his ties to Mrs. Newsome have demonstrably lost much of their "intensity" that Strether is able to comprehend their full pathology with any measure of insight or specificity. For James, a "connexion" that has an objective correlative really isn't one, which means that perhaps the most crucial scenes of communication we must contend with in *The Ambassadors* are precisely those that are most abstract and inexplicable, those most historically remote.

This is certainly how I would characterize the long scene that dominates book 11, where Strether unexpectedly encounters Chad and Madame de Vionnet and is made to see that their "virtuous attachment" is less "virtuous," or maybe more of an "attachment" than he had realized (187). For while several characters in the novel go to considerable lengths to inform Strether that Madame de Vionnet has been Chad's mistress all along, Strether has managed, against long odds, to keep himself uncertain about the full erotics of their tie. Given my larger interests, here is what I take to be the key passage in Strether's retrospective interpretation of the event that finally changes his mind:

> From the point of view of presence of mind it had been very wonderful indeed, wonderful for readiness, for beautiful assurance, for the way her decision was taken on the spot, without time to confer with Chad, without time for anything. Their only conference could have been the brief instants in the boat before they confessed to recognizing the spectator on the bank, for they hadn't been alone together a moment since and must have communicated all in silence. It was a part of the deep impression for Strether, and not the least of the deep interest, that they *could* so communicate—that Chad in particular could let her know he left it to her. (466)

It isn't going too far to say that no one has taken Strether at his word for more than forty years; what he identifies as "the deep impression" of the scene, we have invariably taken as screen or substitute, as some sort of circumlocution that speaks directly to what will not be signified when he realizes "that they *could* so communicate." Laurence Holland (in 1964) notes that this is important language because it testifies to the "shared communion" between Chad and Madame de Vionnet that is "at once the basis and the result of their intimacy"; but he also argues that Strether's illusions about this "intimacy" verge on the preposterous, given that it simply is not "credible that he would persist . . . in thinking that Chad's and Mme. de Vionnet's affair is an attachment without sexual consummation."[48] Kaja Silverman (in 1992) offers an explicitly Freudian amplification of Holland's sense of Strether's disproportionate response.

"What is enacted here is in effect a primal scene," she writes. "James's novels and short stories," she says, "return again and again to situations which, like Strether's visit to the French countryside, somehow reprise that fantasmatic moment where the child is first made aware of adult sexuality."[49] There is simply no such thing as a "deep impression" left behind by a spectacle of communication unless "communication" is taken immediately as a metaphor of sex, a ruse to let James talk around the presence of a more drastic and more carnal variety of connection. We thus revisit a familiar landscape of hesitation and repression, the timid heart of "darkest James," as F. M. Colby called it, "where the vices have no bodies and the passions no blood," the ultimate expression of Geismar's "ethereal sensibility": "There is nothing direct, nothing physical ever described here . . . no pleasures of the flesh, or of sexual love, no rewards, no satisfactions." I am not suggesting that either Holland—surely chief among the "Jacobites" who are targeted by Geismar—or Silverman subscribes to these particular misperceptions of sexuality in James. Just the same, they both admit that we grasp at signs of sexuality in Henry James only through the mediating misperceptions of his characters and narratives. A reader armed with a sufficient theoretical apparatus can disabuse James's verbal surfaces of their symptomatic fixations on "communication," of their polite contrivances to see always something else in the place where sex, as we all know, must certainly preside. The arguments I have been expounding in this chapter—about the aesthetics of James's indirectness, about the popular languages and iconographies of sexualized communication in the period—are finally aimed, I hope, at giving us a chance to understand the "pleasures" and "satisfactions" that *are* in James as something other than mistakes.[50]

"He had wanted to put himself in relation," James writes of Strether soon after his arrival in Paris, "and he would be hanged if he were *not* in relation" (122). On his way to Chad's apartment on the Boulevard Malesherbes, Strether has found himself "under the old arches of the Odéon" and indulges in some "[lingering] before the charming open-air array of literature classic and casual." What he experiences here as the rewards of being "in relation" nicely predict those pleasures that James will later attribute to "the idea of connectibility": "He found the effect of tone and tint, in the long charged tables and shelves, delicate and appetizing; the impression—substituting one kind of low-priced *consommation* for another—might have been that of one of the pleasant cafés that overlapped, under an awning, to the pavement" (122). On the one hand, the figurative logic of this moment could not be more conventional, with Strether simply borrowing from his immediate surroundings to characterize the appeal of these literary morsels, improvising the most available metaphor at his disposal. On the other hand, and in light of my particular concerns in this chapter, I would like to call attention to the way Strether "substitutes" a form of physical satisfaction for the "effect" of a specific medium, in this case, books. I would also be inclined to take seriously the carnal overtones that linger about the italicized "*consommation,*" which James leaves in the original French but which is transparent to its English analog and which heightens the illicit implications of the cheap thrills that Strether is after. James then mediates still more thoroughly this already "mediated" instant of "consummation": we are told that Strether only "edged along, grazing the table, with his hands firmly behind him. He wasn't there to dip, to consume—he was there to reconstruct. He wasn't there for his own profit—not, that is, the direct; he was there on some chance of feeling the brush of the wings of the stray spirit of youth" (122). Abstinence and self-denial are the major themes that James appears intent on sounding, and Strether rehearses these behaviors throughout the novel, culminating in the finely calibrated rejection of Maria Gostrey that leaves him with only his "wonderful impressions." "But nothing like *you,*" Strether answers when Maria points out that his "impressions" are still something; "it's you who would make me wrong!" (512). Yet it is precisely this moral economy—in which communications, no matter how elaborate and involved, cannot possibly count for consummation—which James exasperates and provokes at several critical junctures in *The Ambassadors*, in, I admit, a decidedly minor key, when toying with the equivalence of reading and eating, of Balzac and éclairs, but also in the language that surrounds the "intimacy" that Strether discovers between Chad and Madame de Vionnet when he sees them not talking to each other and yet being no less connected by their silent and encrypted network of imagined messages.

Thus we should consider carefully James's account of the Sunday afternoon that Strether spends at the home of the sculptor Gloriani, for it is here that Strether takes special delight in two very different moments of communication, first with Gloriani himself and then with Little Bilham, the struggling artist who is both Chad's friend and something of his "ambassador" to Strether while Chad waits to make his entrance early in the novel. The latter scene is more famous and unquestionably more verbose; indeed, Strether's extended discourse on the theme of fleeting time, intoned "slowly and sociably, with full pauses and straight dashes," constitutes, as we saw above, the "germ" of the whole novel as James remembers the drama of its composition (216). "It's not too late for *you*, on any side," Strether begins by saying, "and you don't strike me as in danger of missing the train" (215). Given the role that trains will later play, with Strether's "random" choice of line and destination allowing him to stumble on Chad and Madame de Vionnet, there is obviously some irony at work. We might also treat this passage as generally emblematic of all the talking Strether does through-out the narrative, to Maria Gostrey especially, which becomes implicated, by its very fluency and discursivity, in his attempt to extricate himself from the brutal dispatch and efficiency that come to dominate our understanding of how language itself must function back in Woollett. It is, however, Strether's earlier and far less noisy instance of communication with Gloriani on which I want to focus.

Arranged by Chad to be the site where Strether will first meet Madame de Vionnet, Gloriani's house and gardens are presented in adoring terms—adoring especially for the rich associations that emerge from the bare details of the scene. "The place was itself a great impression," writes James, "a small pavilion, clear-faced and sequestered, an effect of polished parquet, of fine white panel and spare sallow gilt, of decoration delicate and rare" (198). James describes not so much what Strether sees as what he thinks he sees; not "polished parquet" and "sallow gilt" for certain, but certainly their "effect." Such emphasis on sheer perception might bring to mind a host of truisms about the function of perspec-tive in James's fiction, about the basic operating procedures of consciousness as he imagines it at work, about the way he renders experience always at a certain stylized remove. The more that Strether indulges and attempts to comprehend "the admirable medium of the scene," the more his observations give way to abstractions, to "signs and tokens, a whole range of expression, all about him, too thick for prompt discrimination" (199). It is at this moment of information vertigo—James calls it an "assault of images"—that Strether fixes on the figure of Gloriani himself, "almost formidable," "a dazzling prodigy of type," "with a personal lustre almost violent" (199). This is telling and spectacular language, but hardly prepares us for what Strether finally makes of the encounter:

> He was to remember again repeatedly the medal-like Italian face, in which every line was an artist's own, in which time told only as tone and consecra-tion; and he was to recall in especial, as the penetrating radiance, as the

communication of the illustrious spirit itself, the manner in which, while they stood briefly, in welcome and response, face to face, he was held by the sculptor's eyes. He wasn't soon to forget them, was to think of them, all unconscious, unintending, preoccupied though they were, as the source of the deepest intellectual sounding to which he had ever been exposed. He was in fact quite to cherish his vision of it, to play with it in idle hours; only speaking of it to no one and quite aware he couldn't have spoken without appearing to talk nonsense. Was what it had told him or what it had asked him the greater of the mysteries? Was it the most special flare, unequalled, supreme, of the esthetic torch, lighting that wondrous world for ever, or was it above all the long straight shaft sunk by a personal acuteness that life had seasoned to steel? (200)

The central drama recounted by this remarkable passage is one of being "exposed"—which for James means at once that Strether believes he witnesses (is "exposed" to) the illuminating power of the "esthetic" and that Strether believes he is scrutinized by ("exposed" before) this same force; he is "sounded" by the spectacle of Gloriani's "radiance." Or maybe not: I say Strether "believes" because James's description of the sculptor as "all unconscious, unintending, [and] preoccupied" seems calculated to raise the possibility that this moment of "tone and consecration" is largely fantasy, the concoction of a starstruck American unfamiliar with the ways of Europe and its artists. It is this version of events that Strether credits when he realizes that so far as his sublime "vision" of Gloriani is concerned, "he couldn't have spoken without appearing to talk nonsense." The fact that another Gloriani, who passes briefly through James's *Roderick Hudson*, is an entirely different emblematic figure of the artist only adds to the undecidability that colors every aspect of this scene.[51] James leaves us with two questions, the second by far more involuted and elaborate, which depend utterly on another and more basic question that remains unspoken. What, if anything at all, has happened here? I have no definitive answer to this question and doubt very much there is one, but I think we draw nearer to a sense of what is most significant about this moment in *The Ambassadors* when we understand that this question is ultimately about "communication" and nothing more. Or less.

Thus while this early mention of "communication" seems innocuous enough, in light of the epistemological frenzy that will later descend upon the word when Strether encounters Chad and Madame de Vionnet, it is tempting to see in Strether's ravishment at Gloriani's merest glance and gesture an anticipation of the force with which the discovery of their connection will overwhelm him. Indeed, the "communication" that takes place between Strether and Gloriani is considerably more graphic and suggestive in its carnality. "The penetrating radiance," "the long straight shaft sunk by a personal acuteness"—this is language that seems assembled from conventions of erotic discourses, from an implicitly feminizing rhetoric of religious rapture and divine submission, to more explicitly homoerotic rhetoric, like that we might associate with Whitman's poetry of easy and immediate male intimacy, or with Pater's brand of sensual "aestheticism," or with accounts of sexual "decadence" that circulated with increasing visibility in the years after the Wilde scandal—which we know James followed closely.[52] I am not claiming that various languages of sexual implication are compatible, nor that James handles them in any systematic manner. All this erotic noise emerges not because "communication" stands for sex in some one-to-one equivalence predicated on displacement or sublimation but rather because "communication" in and of itself—between these men, in this place, at this time—somehow represents the most exhilarating and unnerving form of contact James can imagine. And because this is the case, because there is no direct link between communication and any concrete expression of sexuality, but rather this supremely circuitous sense that communication and a whole series of pleasures refer back to each other without priority or hierarchy, the languages of mediated experience I have been charting in James are inevitably resistant to being translated or rationalized into familiar categories of overt message and latent meaning. Indeed it is difficult to specify just who or what the central focus of Strether's affections is at almost any point in *The Ambassadors*. Here we see him reveling in "communication" with Gloriani; but as we saw much earlier, his relationship to Maria Gostrey is every bit as mediated and enticing; we later find James situating Strether in a "double connexion" with Maria and Mrs. Newsome (174); he is demonstrably charmed by the "fathomless medium" of Chad's amoral glamour; he momentarily wonders if even his "old relation" to "beautiful brilliant unconscious Mamie [the youngest Pocock]" is about to transform into something else entirely, and there are several occasions where it seems as if Jeanne de Vionnet is available in return for services rendered to her mother, Madame de Vionnet (378). Of course Strether elects to tie himself to no one in particular—which is perhaps the best possible tribute to his extreme capacity for the Jamesian pleasure and Jamesian virtue of "connectibility."

It would, however, be wrong of me to suggest that all of Strether's possible "connexions" seem equally appealing, or that his promiscuity of attachment and communication is formless and democratic. Whatever we think takes place between Strether and Gloriani, whether some inscrutable transmission of the "esthetic," some cryptic flash of homosexual rapport, or some fantasy involving both or neither, nowhere else in *The Ambassadors* does "communication" seem quite so dazzling and unconditional, so far removed from everyday instrumentalities of exchange and obligation, from the implicit social imperative to signify something—anything—that will give up its quantity of information if pressed enough. Elsewhere in the novel this is not the case. When Strether observes Chad and Madame de Vionnet in "communication," he catches them in an act of exceeding purpose and direction, an exchange that could not be less accurately described, recalling Gloriani's unique attraction, as "unconscious, unintending, preoccupied." And this should come as no surprise: despite all the elegance and aura of her ancien régime inheritances, despite the "dignity of distances and approaches" that marks her home in the Fauborg-St. Germaine, we might also remember that at first sight she "*differed* less," to Strether anyway, "differed, that is, scarcely at all—well, superficially speaking, from Mrs. Newsome or even from Mrs. Pocock" (211). Thus once back in Paris on the morning after their awkward threesome in the countryside, Strether receives "Madame de Vionnet's own communication" and, as we can imagine was true of Mrs. Newsome's "cables," this message too "consisted of the fewest words" (471). Woollett may well be a "reformatory" of rationalized production—though the only thing we know for sure that it produces, given Strether's famous refusal to name its signature commodity, is telegrams—but Paris is no less subject to "the common and constant pressure" of modern life. The pneumatic tubes that carry Madame de Vionnet's *petit bleu* to Strether imply a network architecture every bit as inescapable as that represented by America itself, and Strether seems finally no more enamored with Paris's "silver stream of impunity" than with Woollett's "discipline." Either the sordid publicity of the *Postes et Télégraphes* or an American empire of industry and advertising: that these are the only options left to Strether at the end of *The Ambassadors* tells us much about both the character and the limits of James's imagination. Something happened in Gloriani's garden. There will be no returning to know just what it might have meant.

The Intensity of Intimation

This account of *The Ambassadors* has led us to a point where the central contradiction about communication in Henry James now emerges in sharper focus. To put it simply: James romanticizes—and I use this word with quite specific valences in mind—the experience of communication while, at the same time, he indicts the telegraph itself on several counts. The novel does not seem to find much to its liking about the telegraph as a medium, and we finally see precious little pleasure associated with its poetics of rigor and compression, with its coercive instrumentality, and with the utter modernity, surely as apparent in Paris as in America, that this particular technology foretells. Mrs. Newsome's many cables represent a practice of communication that is no more appealing, in the end, than Madame de Vionnet's single *petit bleu*; Strether may be seduced by the entire apparatus of Chad's "transformation," but when Maria early on informs him that Bilham "has had every day his little telegram from Cannes" and that Chad too is playing the "game" by remote control, we are being prepared to realize just how thoroughly he has remained, or perhaps become, his mother's son (151). And if words like "communication" and "connexion" are to resonate at all historically in James, and not code only problems of psychology or phenomenology in his texts, we must account for how this language comprehends and exploits the telegraph in all its material and cultural particularity. How does James incorporate the telegram—short, direct, and shockingly imperative—into a world where communication is imagined as prodigious, convoluted, and decidedly circuitous? How does a telegram, if I may borrow from James's lament on his obscurity to Hugh Walpole, become an "uncommunicating" communication?

We may start answering these questions by noting a peculiar feature of James's late novels, which is so obvious that I hesitate to identify it as a formal strategy. I am thinking of the marked delay that occurs between the delivery of a telegram to a character and the revelation of its contents to the reader. Thus in *The Ambassadors*, Strether receives the crucial telegram from Woollett, "in the form of a scrap of blue paper," at the start of book 7's second chapter (286), and this communication remains just that—a mute artifact of modern life, pure medium without message—for the rest of the chapter. It is not until we turn the page to chapter 3 that this telegram speaks its information and we are able retroactively to make sense of the emotions and effects it has already produced. Clearly Strether is upset—he crumples the telegram in a small fit of violence, then drops it, picks it up, reads it again; these actions, exemplary of the writing-workshop dictum "show, don't tell," suffice to demonstrate the tenor of his agitation. And I would have little cause to fix on this altogether ordinary example of realist technique if not for James's employing this same narrative gambit, under marvelously more complicated circumstances, at an urgent moment of decision in *The Golden Bowl*. The scene in which I'm interested unfolds between Adam Verver and Charlotte Stant shortly after he has proposed; the Prince and Maggie have traveled to Italy, Maggie leaving Charlotte to entertain her father in her stead, and leaving her father to realize that Charlotte, as his wife, would "square" the network of relations in which the Ververs, at this early stage in the proceedings, believe they are involved. Little does Maggie know of Charlotte's prior relationship with the Prince, and thus little can she understand that she herself is motivating the circumstances that will soon allow her husband and her stepmother to pursue this relationship again. The reader, of course, knows all this and more besides, and so is able to appreciate the exquisite irony and fateful gamesmanship of Charlotte's agreeing to marry Adam only on Maggie's express approval. For this reason, chapter 13 begins, Adam "had written to his daughter" and "Maggie's reply to his news was a telegram from Rome" (168). This message, which Adam certainly thinks enough to satisfy Charlotte, simply reads: "'We start to-night to bring you all our love and joy and sympathy.' There they were, the words, and what more did she want?" (170). But from the superior vantage of her morally suspect point of view, Charlotte wants still more "words" from the Prince himself and signals her trepidation; Adam offers "secretly to wire him that you'd like, reply paid, a few words for yourself" (174). Charlotte's answer encompasses much of what is problematic about the novel's general economy of both information and marriage—"'Reply paid for him, you mean—or for me?'"; to which Adam's answer—"Oh, I'll pay, with pleasure, anything back for you—as many words as you like . . . not requiring either to see your message"—only adds to our sense that "pleasure" and "payment" are already too close by half (174). But with Charlotte and Adam still demurring back and forth, parsing about what is "*right*" when we know that *nothing* about this situation truly is, the following occurs:

> She had taken her boa and thrown it over her shoulders, and her eyes, while she still delayed, had turned from him, engaged by another interest, though the court was by this time, the hour of dispersal for luncheon, so forsaken that they would have had it, for free talk, should they have been moved

to loudness, quite to themselves. She was ready for their adjournment, but she was also aware of a pedestrian youth, in uniform, a visible emissary of the Postes et Télégraphes, who had approached, from the street, the small stronghold of the concierge and who presented there a missive taken from the little cartridge-box slung over his shoulder. The portress, meeting him on the threshold, met equally, across the court, Charlotte's marked attention to his visit, so that, within the minute, she had advanced to our friends with her cap-streamers flying and her smile of announcement as ample as her broad white apron. She raised aloft a telegraphic message and, as she delivered it, sociably discriminated. "Cette fois-ci pur madame!"—with which she as genially retreated, leaving Charlotte in possession. Charlotte, taking it, held it at first unopened. Her eyes had come back to her companion, who had immediately and triumphantly greeted it. "Ah there you are!"

She broke the envelope then in silence, and for a minute, as with the message he himself had put before her, studied its contents without a sign. He watched her without a question, and at last she looked up. "I'll give you," she simply said, "what you ask." (177)

There is then a moment of confusion as Adam thinks that Maggie has sent a second message. Charlotte tells him that this telegram is in fact from the Prince and offers to let Adam read it. "Not if it satisfies you," he answers. "I don't require it." He does ask whether the message is "funny." "No—I call it grave," is Charlotte's answer. And we know nothing more about this telegram until its contents are disclosed to us—several chapters and many, many pages later.[53]

This astonishing scene of communication no doubt owes much of its considerable effect to elements I would hardly characterize as subtle. For all that we're supposed to tremble at the difficulty of *The Golden Bowl*, this passage trades, with little shame or trepidation, on the theatricality of its irony and on the melodramatic flourish of a telegram that somehow does not let itself be read. James situates us squarely on the side of Charlotte here, and whether or not we sympathize or identify with her erotic brinkmanship, we are permitted the conspiratorial thrill of understanding, unlike Adam, that his marriage has been secured not only by means of telegram but by a telegram between two former lovers who are set now to become son-in-law and mother-in-law. In the popular techno-romances of prior decades, the course of "wired love," no matter how circuitous, was never so perverse and devious. But James also mediates our imagined access to this brazen, and at the same time clandestine, communication; we know more about the fatal telegram than Adam does, and this means everything, and yet we really don't know anything at all. No actual information has been given to the reader; no message has been delivered. We see only that this communication has made some tremendous difference and that its contents are apparently to remain a secret. This is a narrative device that wantonly invites all manner of anticipation about a future scene of scandal, shock, and exposure. I find myself reminded of the creaky histrionics that surround the discovery of Monsieur de Bellegarde's deathbed declaration in *The American*, and wonder if there wasn't at least an instant in which James, never able quite to shake the allure of melodrama, as Peter Brooks and William Veeder have made clear, was planning to have Adam, or maybe Maggie, come across a crumpled telegram, take it to a deathly quiet chamber, step into the glow of some solitary lamp or dwindling fire, and there "[force] a meaning from the tremulous signs."[54] ("Meaning" is forced instead from the shattered pieces of the golden bowl—an object as flamboyantly symbolic and "written" with associations as any artifact of media.)

But our interest in this scene finally does not depend on such speculations, however tempting they may be. Instead I want to emphasize the meticulous detail of James's description of the telegram's delivery, for it is this slow and curiously inefficient circuit of communication that best represents the media aesthetic of his later fiction. There is something languorous from the beginning about Charlotte's boa and the use she puts it to, as if it is the objective correlative of her intention to "delay" her answer to Adam's proposal. The uncanny emptiness and silence of the court—"so forsaken that they would have had it, for free talk, should they have been moved to loudness," or, I might add, if any "talk" in *The Golden Bowl* was ever "free"—give the impression of slow motion to the progress of the approaching messenger boy. Charlotte's concentration on his arrival and exchange with the portress seem of sufficient focus that the conventional indicator of passing time, "within the minute," seems more likely to be an accurate measure of the unfolding narrative action. And again, when Charlotte opens the telegram and "for a minute" looks at the paper in her hands, the specifying of an action's definite duration adds to the encompassing slowness of the larger scene. The portress provides a moment of animated and slightly comic counterpoint, yet we might also think of her as only retarding even more the eventual delivery of the message; both her gesture of "[raising] the telegraph aloft" and her officious announcement of its addressee would appear entirely superfluous given that she has already "met" Charlotte's "marked attention" and thus has little cause to make a spectacle of herself. I don't wish to imply that James completely isolates the telegraph from the associations we might expect: Adam and Charlotte are on the move, having traveled from Brighton to Fawns and now to Paris, and are already in thorough communication with Maggie and the Prince, who are on their way from Rome; so thorough, in fact, that the Prince's telegram arrives as if actually summoned out of thin air by Charlotte's stratagem of delay; the dizzying speed of modern life can go unmentioned here because it is the absolute precondition of the entire scene, the notorious "annihilation of time and space" need not be singled out because it has, as James might say, transformed the very medium of the everyday. That Maggie and the Prince—in Rome—are able to determine the outcome of a quiet conversation over lunch—in Paris—obviously holds a certain fascination for James, and precisely demonstrates what his wayward "communicative passion" might mean in terms of narrative practice. And it is easy enough to link this "indirectness" to various discourses of technology and communication that pattern what we have come to talk of as the "control revolution" of the later nineteenth and early twentieth centuries.[55] What sets James apart, I am suggesting, is his interest in the intimate effects of media, his sense that the same technologies that make it possible to extend language and consciousness over geographic distance also make it possible to distend and disfigure the idea of proximity itself, to imagine that "connexion"—whether conceived in social, psychological, sexual, or artistic terms—is best achieved, and most intensely registered, when as mediated and "circuitous" as possible. Thus even as the Prince's telegram serves to bring Rome and Paris into immediate apposition, it magnifies a modest hotel courtyard and the few feet across a luncheon table into spaces of staggering breadth and bewildering proportion.

And since I have argued that this telegram exemplifies a fundamental refusal in James's work to equate immediacy with intensity, it should come as no surprise that when we finally are allowed to read the Prince's message, the crucial words amount to no revelation whatsoever, but rather pay tribute to the allure of inscrutability. We learn the content of the message only to be told, her decisive action upon receiving it notwithstanding, that Charlotte still has no idea just what it means:

> That telegram, that acceptance of the prospect proposed to them—an acceptance quite other than perfunctory—she had never destroyed; though

reserved for no eyes but her own it was still carefully reserved. She kept it in a same place—from which, very privately, she sometimes took it out to read it over. *"A la guerre come à la guerre then"*—it had been couched in the French tongue. *"We must lead our lives as we see them; but I am charmed with your courage and almost surprised at my own."* The message had remained ambiguous; she had read it in more lights than one. (212)

"Quite other than perfunctory" is a wonderful way of phrasing almost everything that a telegram should not be. This is certainly not one of Mrs. Newsome's cables. Nor is it even slightly reminiscent of the romantic "prattle" that we saw everywhere in *Wired Love* or "K ——— A—— T — E -." James contrives a "message" of such ostentatious ambiguity that we cannot say for sure if it is written in French or English. Is it only the first idiomatic phrase that "had been couched in the French tongue," or has the rest of this document been unconsciously translated from some French original that existed solely in James's imagination, for the benefit of his audience? ("When I speak worse, you see," the Prince admits much earlier in the novel, "I speak French.") No amount of translation will clarify the guiding sentiment of this artfully opaque telegram; there is a striking ethical neutrality to its key terms ("charmed," "courage"), and this further mystifies whatever stand the message is or isn't taking on the question of Charlotte's mercenary daring and duplicity in marrying Adam Verver—which is as much to say, the Prince's own mercenary daring and duplicity in marrying Maggie. I am not suggesting that it was some great feat for James to craft a pair of sentences that can baffle us. My aim in citing this passage is rather to insist that James renders this particular message "ambiguous" in ways that profoundly contradict the cardinal virtues of its medium—the dazzling speed of telegraphic transmission, the sheer dispatch of information, the economy of language that has been compressed and coded to accomplish maximum efficiency. This telegram gives up its message slowly, if at all; it signifies little more than a miracle of equivocation, and does even that with exceptional redundancy and noise.

If we ask what larger meaning this minor formal victory of James's style over the medium of the telegraph has for the "indirectness" that patterns his literary project, especially in its major phase, the answer would seem to be that technology presented powerful new models for representing experiences of "connexion" that were already at the center of his familiar constellation of concerns.

Thus whereas *The Portrait of a Lady* is a novel in which passing references to the telegraph loom very small in its grand thematic architecture, one of its most important moments—when Isabel finally recognizes "the strange impression she had received . . . of her husband's being in more direct communication with Madame Merle than she suspected"—already looks ahead to later fictions in which these dramas will become absorbed in all the technicalities of modern media.[56] Perhaps as James lived longer away from friends and family in America, or as he gradually curtailed the manic sociability of his first years in Europe, or as several of his relationships with men, according to Wendy Graham, flowered into "passionate correspondence[s]," or as his own mode of writing evolved into the "circuitous" practice of dictation, it was to be expected that his fiction would become more responsive to the pleasures, costs, and compensations of media. Apart from these matters of biography, we might also see the tendency of his later works not just to reference various means of communication as realist window dressing but to incorporate a phenomenology of mediated experience as the very basis of their aesthetic structure, in light of the changed world he faced upon revisiting the "international theme" for his final novels. Like the popular telegraphic fictions he almost surely never read, James perhaps found it imperative to imagine the spaces of modernity "as a geography crisscrossed and demarcated by the constant circulation of messages, messengers and message delivery systems."[57] I take these last phrases from Tom Gunning's marvelous description of the world we see in Fritz Lang's films—hardly the first works one would turn to in search of insight into Henry James. But Mrs. Newsome is perhaps less different than we might think from criminal masters of manipulation like Dr. Mabuse (from *Dr. Mabuse the Gambler*) or the genius Haghi (from *Spies*). As we see in Lang, James comes increasingly to depict a world where space itself exists alongside a network of technologies—or better, alongside network technologies as such—that not only provide a parallel media-scape for human interactions but assume a more primary role as the place where such interactions are realized most dramatically. In this world of late James, even the impossibly "good" Milly Theale, from *The Wings of the Dove*, displays an almost fiendish talent for "communication."

When Merton Densher returns to London, waiting for word of Milly's death—"Mrs. Stringham," we learn from Kate, "is to telegraph"—he is "a haunted man" (458, 469). But instead of a telegram, Densher receives a letter from Milly, which he believes must have been written some time before her final spell of sickness. "The communication I speak of can't possibly belong," he says to Kate, "to these last days. The postmark, which is legible, does; but it isn't thinkable, for anything else, that she wrote" (487). They continue to discuss the unlikely letter, Kate wondering if Milly's writing on her deathbed does not "depend a little on what the communication is," and Densher answering, "A little perhaps—but not much. It's a communication" (487). An even thicker gothic aura assembles around this letter when Densher later realizes that "this thing has been timed" to arrive at Christmas Eve. Milly did much more than write as she died; she checked the delivery schedules from Venice to London, timed the speed of foreign mail, and seized on the only medium that would carry her last message at the properly slow pace—at the exquisitely slow pace—that would guarantee its overwhelming impact. She has been dead already for several days when Merton at last receives her letter, which Kate first assumes must be a telegram since, for a dying girl, speed should be a premium. But Milly is after another effect, and knows that she will achieve it only if her message makes its way to Merton through a more circuitous operation. One has few desirable options when pitted against such "magnificent and masterly indirectness," and so Kate throws this inescapable "communication," sealed and unread, into the fire.

Master, Dictator, Messenger Boy

Although there are many other James texts that show evidence of his deep interest in forms of media, and in what I have been calling the romance of communication, this moment in *The Wings of the Dove* most powerfully brings to mind a slightly different piece of writing—the famous "death-bed dictation" that James undertakes with the aid of Theodora Bosanquet shortly before his final coma. For obvious reasons, there is a pathos to this brief series of texts that is difficult to dispel. The image of the stricken Master, speaking as "Napoléone" on his wondrous "scheme" to redesign the Louvre—"It is, you will see, of a great scope, a majesty unsurpassed by any work of the kind yet undertaken in France"—confirms too many of our fantasies and assumptions about the outlandish grandeur and political unconscious of James's project in his fiction, especially in the later novels where his style becomes decidedly ostentatious.[58] It is this grand manner that Friedrich Kittler tries to capture by juxtaposing James directly with his deathbed persona: "From 1800–1815, Napoleon's noted ability to dictate seven letters simultaneously produced the modern general staff. His secretaries were generals and a marshal of France. From 1907–1917, a typewriter and its female operator produced the modern American novel."[59] This is Kittler at his most telegraphic, and there is much to disagree with: no literary historian would look for the invention of "the modern American novel" in James's output after 1907, nor is it quite fair to say that James "had become emperor" without noticing that he takes command of the Napoleonic decor, not the Napoleonic armies. Yet I respect Kittler's desire to situate James within a material history of communication technologies, for the modernity of James's texts is everywhere involved with networks of media, experiences of technology, and various "passions" for communication.

Whether James himself knew the pleasures of "wired love" is another matter. In letters to the young sculptor Hendrick Andersen, James inveterately imagines his written communications in physical terms, lending a remarkable sensuality to the way he figures the texture of their mediated relationship, especially after 1903.[60] "But please feel now, none the less, that I lay my hands on you and draw you close to me," James writes in one 1903 letter; "Every word of you is as soothing as a caress of your hand, and the sense of the whole as sweet to me as being able to lay my own upon *you*," he writes in 1904 (*HJL*, 269, 310). The tenor of this language seems strongly patterned after the "Calamus" poems from *Leaves of Grass*, and we know from Edith Wharton that James had almost altogether reversed himself, by 1904, on earlier criticisms of Whitman and would read his verse aloud with some degree of relish.[61] Perhaps this in part explains the slightly formulaic flavor of James's discourse as a lover at a distance, an observation I make not to question the intensity of James's ardor but to point out that—in communication, which is where I am most interested in his ardor anyway—he imagines the carnal equivalence of his connection to Andersen in a language both homoerotic and as conventional as any hearts sent via telegraph or little Cupids firing love arrows in Morse code. Thus James ends letters: "Goodnight, dearest Hendrick, I draw you close and hold you long," or "I embrace you, dearest Hendrick, ever so tenderly!" (406, 580). As Wendy Graham reminds us, Andersen was one of several men with whom James corresponded in a register of significant sexual connotation, and she claims that critics and biographers have consistently diminished "the erotic (that is, masturbatory) potential" of these letters.[62] Her parenthetical attempt to desublimate communication into the sex that it must surely screen and represent returns us to the scandalizing spectacle that Strether witnesses between Chad and Madame de Vionnet in *The Ambassadors*, and to the untoward stain Nattie suffers in *Wired Love*. Finally, though, it is my argument in this chapter that there are pleasures in the world of media that are particular and native to that world, pleasures that are not repressed or obligated into always more circuitous expressions but that persist and thrive on being mediated, losing nothing of their allure as they remain absorbed in all the technicalities of what is only and entirely communication.

It is along these lines that I understand James's "rage for connections," a temperament he describes in *The Middle Years*, some pages after the passage with which I began the chapter (*MY*, 578). Recalling his first encounter with George Eliot, he narrates a small domestic crisis involving a son of G. H. Lewes, suffering from "a violent attack of pain" and in need of medical attention. "It took me no long time," James writes, "to thrill with the sense, sublime in its unexpectedness, that we were perhaps, or indeed quite clearly, helping her to pass the time till Mr. Lewes's return—after which he would again post off for Mr. Paget the pre-eminent surgeon" (575–576). But as Lewes's arrival grows more noticeably delayed, the "*illustratively* great" Eliot herself seems anxious, and the moment between her and the young American turns "awkward." Then James has "the inspiration that at once terminated the strain of the scene and yet prolonged the sublime connection. Mightn't I then hurry off for Mr. Paget?—on whom, as fast as a cab could carry me, I would wait with the request that we would come at the first possible moment to the rescue" (577). These many years later, James writes, "I again feel myself borne very much as if suddenly acting as a messenger of the gods" (577). He admits that he was plainly starstruck, and specifically delighted to be of service to an author he so admired. His extreme reactions and emotions were, as he remembers them, "excessive": "It was by their excess that one knew them for such, as one for that matter only knew things in general worth knowing" (577). But James ultimately cannot name the source of his unmatched satisfaction at being used to pass along a simple summons, at performing the role of errand boy for a "master" in her moment of disturbance. In 1870 there are of course no telephones, and it gains little time to find the nearest telegraph office and send a wire across the city, which would then need to be delivered in person anyway. James is himself the only form of communication that is available. And so he learns that there are pleasures he cannot fathom in the alchemy of mediums and messages.

2
LOVE AND NOISE

Besides, when every body has his portrait published, true distinction lies in not having yours published at all. For if you are published along with Tom, Dick, and Harry, and wear a coat of their cut, how then are you distinct from Tom, Dick, and Harry?

HERMAN MELVILLE, *PIERRE*

In America everybody is, but some are more than others.

GERTRUDE STEIN, *EVERYBODY'S AUTOBIOGRAPHY*

When Gertrude Stein Checks In to Grand Hotel

The travesty of literary celebrity that Melville undertakes when the action of *Pierre* moves from the country to the city is as savage as it is, from young Mr. Glendinning's perspective, uncalled for. Disinherited, estranged from family and fiancée, impoverished, incestuously in love with either his mother or his sister, or both—becoming famous would seem to be the least of Pierre's problems. Then again, as he is molested from the start by the uncanny likeness of his father's image and the "ineffable correlativeness" it suggests, it is perhaps not out of character for Pierre to be worried, above all, about anything that might render him just a version of someone else.[1] For Pierre, to sit for a daguerreotype, to be "dayalized a dunce"—where once a "faithful portrait" marked the "immortalizing [of] a genius"—is to lose oneself within a democracy of mercenary and formulaic distinction; so we might say that for Melville, the mediating discourses and material emanations of fame work contrary to their own clamor, permitting not the apotheosis of the singular individual but rather the replication of a standardized type of celebrity, famous like most people are not, but also famous exactly like other famous people already are.[2] Melville thus assaults an American culture of celebrity in a highly precocious way, identifying at this early moment that what is most compelling about stardom has less to do with its scarcity and considerably more to do with its proliferation and promiscuity:

as Leo Braudy writes in his comprehensive history of fame in Western culture, "America pioneered in the implicit democratic and modern assumption that everyone could and should be looked at. This it seemed was one of the privileges for which the American Revolution was fought."[3] The overstatement here is only partly rhetorical. Stars do, after all, represent exemplary instances of the mediated life in America; they constitute a whole category of extravagantly mediated personhood, a whole species that is at home in the simulated, artificial worlds of publicity that have come to surround those technologies, film most of all, that have amplified fame and its effects out of all historical proportion. The logical extension of Melville's corrosive irony toward fame, a point that Braudy approaches more gingerly but just as surely, treats being a star as the same thing as being American, only more so: we are all looked at, we are all mediated, we are all spectacularly reproduced, and the lifestyles of the rich and famous are nothing more than variations on modern life in general, pitched at the level of allegory and dressed up to show a little, or sometimes a lot, of class.

No such concerns for Gertrude Stein, or so my other epigraph on American celebrity would have us think. Stardom here assumes an ontological status; it is a difference that makes a difference: a star is a star is a star is a star. She makes this remark in *Everybody's Autobiography*, the 1937 sequel to her astonishing best seller of 1932, *The Autobiography of Alice B. Toklas*, and these two texts will be my primary concern in this chapter, which is about the mediated life of celebrity in the 1930s and the particular iconography of fame found in Stein's popular writings. I am interested in what might be called the content of the form of Stein's fame. I will not be treating Stein's fame as a biographical footnote, nor as a catastrophe from which her writing failed to recover, nor as an extended performance of cultural subversion from within.[4] I would like instead to reconsider her stardom as an essential aspect of her literary production in the 1930s, a period in which Stein—all her otherness notwithstanding—finds herself strangely and belatedly embraced by American culture, perhaps in part because she describes the experience of celebrity in ways that constellate a distinctively modernist fascination with medium aesthetics within a broader sense of cultural response to a modernity distinguished by the pervasiveness of its media. That is to say, the life of fame she narrates, and which is pictured in the iconography that surrounds her, takes its particular shape within a world that depends on technologies of communication and representation whose influences are felt on a pervasive scale. "I of course did not think of it in terms of the cinema," Stein writes of her own modernity, "in fact I doubt whether at the time I had ever seen a cinema but, I cannot repeat this too often any one is of one's period and this our period was undoubtedly of the cinema and series production."[5] The joke being, of course, that Stein for once does not repeat herself, though evidence of a world doing things cinematically is abundant in the texts to which I will be turning shortly.

Stein's willingness to admit to cinema's influence—without ever having seen a movie—testifies with uncanny elegance to the profound importance of film for literary modernism as a whole, and for the unique "crossing and interplay of the life of media forms" that McLuhan observed in the languages of Eliot, Proust, and Joyce.[6] In this respect, Garrett Stewart is just the latest to argue that literary modernism must be understood, as Stein would say, in terms of the cinema. Writing of the non-semantic noise and "stray signification" that so many early-twentieth-century texts indulge and reproduce, Stewart proposes that "literary modernism begins, is always beginning, with such incursions of linguistic eccentricity in our habituation to lexical and syntactic code," and this patterns an entire network of "filiation" between "literary and filmic textuality."[7] Modernist writing, for Stewart, wants to face, and at the same time to contain, the materiality of words that may not always mean what authors say, nor even mean at all; and the "rough equivalent in film," he suggests, "is a surrender, induced by the text itself, to the optically unthought of the moving image" (266). Though voiced in the idiom of deconstruction, Stewart's modernism— predicated on the "surrender" to an unmeaning, technical constraint—is evocative of Clement Greenberg and the "instinctive accommodation to the medium" he celebrates in "Towards a Newer Laocoön" and elsewhere.[8] Phonemes and photographs constitute the "oscillating materiality" that show what modernism really is for Stewart, "beneath the shows of representation," and so we arrive again at a sense of modernism where the sensuous and visceral take precedent, and eventually win out against the text's intended content (266). "What thus glimmers into possibility," according to Stewart, "is a decisively new view of the convergence between the filmic apparatus and a whole stratum of literary writing tapped and maximized by modernism: namely, a technology not just of inscription or writing, but of 'style' itself" (286). Though not a figure that Stewart mentions, Stein would seem a perfect case of such "convergence." Hugh Kenner glances at this dimension of Stein's work in *The Pound Era*—in which he just barely glances at her anyway—when he describes her devotion to "a mystique of the word" that structures a literary enterprise "not related to a reader's understanding."[9] In Stein, "the words turn toward one another in a mathematic of mutual connection" that affirms "the aim and morality of style." If modernist writing, to return to Stewart, "vibrates with the undulant undoing of continuous signification"—the phrase already sounds like it was made for Stein—her texts aspire to this condition of play and excess with a forthright determination that is almost artless in its evasion of everyday semantics. Indeed, I can think of no better way to describe the vertigo of reading Stein than Stewart's summary judgment on what finally makes for modernism on the page: "Words don't make it through to you from a strictly communicating consciousness *that* way" (266).

And so Stein exemplifies the new mode of writing that Friedrich Kittler calls "the discourse network of 1900," which understands the medium of words as powerfully challenged by the ability of film and other "technological media" to record and store experience of every kind.[10] Stein's early experiments in automatic writing, which she pursued with Leon Solomon while both were students at Johns Hopkins, are one of several cases that Kittler uses to explain how film's capture of motion and human physicality, and the phonograph's capture of sound and human speech, result in the familiar modernist condition in which the "most radical extrapolation" of what writing can do is to "write writing" itself. "The ordinary, purposeful use of language—so-called communication with others—is excluded."[11] For many of Stein's best feminist critics, her turn away from the conventions of everyday grammar, syntax, and punctuation indicates her commitment to a language unwilling to suffer the rules of "Patriarchal Poetry," to invoke one very strenuous, though handily titled, example of her refusal to communicate.[12] Without attributing Stein's style to any politics, Peter Nicholls speaks effectively on behalf of a consensus that almost no one wants to contradict: "Stein's focus of attention travels consistently away from meaning to the texture of writing. Language begins to assume a new opacity" as it becomes less a medium of reference and more "a medium of consciousness."[13] Thus it seems only appropriate that when Stein is discussed explicitly with respect to film, she is situated alongside works of the cinematic avant-garde that similarly confound the limits and assumptions of classical Hollywood. For Susan McCabe, experimental films such as Man Ray's *Emak Bakia* can help illuminate Stein's "strategies of representation and embodiment," because their emphasis on "fragmented, repetitive bodies" and "decentered plots" parallels the "bodily disjunction" that Stein wants her reader to experience not as a thematic *in* her writing but *as* her writing. Stein aspires to reproduce techniques of cinematic modernism that are "otherwise unnoticeable in conventional narrative film."[14]

This chapter, however, argues that there is much that we can learn from thinking about Stein and Hollywood cinema in its most conventional and formulaic forms, and that her fascination with the medium of film takes on an unexpected shape in her popular writings of the 1930s—writings that demonstrate not only what happens when Stein tries to communicate with a wider audience but also the effects of such communication on her particular style of modernism. I am interested, in other words, in what Stein wants to communicate by self-consciously situating her popular writing—with its still palpable difficulty and opacity and aspiration to materiality and noise—in a world that she describes as cinematic for all the ways in which it permits Stein herself to register the effects of stardom and celebrity. If "the task of the modernist artist," as Stanley Cavell famously writes in 1969, when Greenberg's modernism still held sway, "is to find what it is his art finally depends upon," I want to suggest that Stein discovers that *hers* depends on Hollywood.[15]

I should also confess that the account of Stein that I will be developing itself depends on that flimsiest and most popular of narrative conventions, the coincidence. Stein's unlikely celebrity begins with the publication of *The Autobiography of Alice B. Toklas* in the summer of 1933, along with its concurrent monthly serialization in the *Atlantic*, which began in May of that same year. Written almost entirely in the fall of 1932, Stein's obscured autobiography and history of modernism is thus completed at the very moment when *Grand Hotel* (MGM, 1932) is commanding first place at box offices all over the nation that Stein had left, but never really left behind. Starring Greta Garbo, John Barrymore, Joan Crawford, Lionel Barrymore, and Wallace Beery—each among the most prominent and profitable stars of the period—*Grand Hotel* went on to earn more than $2.5 million (against just over $700,000 spent on production and distribution), as well as the Oscar for Best Picture of 1932. There is no evidence that Stein read Vicki Baum's best-selling novel from which the movie was adapted, nor is it at all likely that she saw *Grand Hotel* in Paris before starting work on her own narrative of cosmopolitan sociability amid the visual culture of modernism. It is this coincidence that I hope to make as historically meaningful as possible.

With this same film almost certainly in mind, Rem Koolhaas writes that "the 'Hotel' becomes Hollywood's favorite subject" in the 1930s because it functions not just as a space of visual possibility but also as a narrative readymade, "a cybernetic universe with its own laws generating random but fortuitous collisions between human beings who would never have met elsewhere."[16]

The cameo appearance—defined without elaboration in *The Dictionary of Film Terms* as "a screen role of short but memorable duration," often by an actor "who is usually a major film star or entertainment figure"—is the technology of characterization that responds most directly to this new fantasy of communicating interiors, thickly saturated yet eloquent with information, splendor, and human beings as visual surfaces in constant motion. For in addition to representing the perhaps prototypical film version of the "cybernetic universe" that Koolhaas describes, *Grand Hotel*, as I will soon argue, must also be accorded a special place in any history of the formal device at issue here, because what Irving Thalberg and the production team at MGM devised, for the first time, was a narrative film where even the biggest stars—because they were too many—made little more than cameo appearances. Yet *Grand Hotel* seems positively vacant by comparison if we consider the dazzling assembly of cameo appearances that practically choke the narrative of *The Autobiography of Alice B. Toklas*—in which four hundred different individuals are mentioned by name—and relent hardly at all in *Everybody's Autobiography*—in which another three hundred, that is, three hundred *more* names are deployed, referenced, and otherwise dropped as indirect but nevertheless telling evidence of just how well received, from Mary Pickford to Eleanor Roosevelt, Gertrude Stein was upon her return to America. Sheer numbers, though, tell only part of the story. I am finally interested in an elaborate iconography of modernity that locates the cameo appearance at an intersection of private lives and public spheres in American media culture, an imagined space that encompasses hotel and home alike, a world of cameo appearances that brings Gertrude Stein and Greta Garbo into an electrifying proximity too noisy and too mediated by far to be called contact in any traditional sense of the term. Though this was, unless biographers discover something to the contrary, as close as the two ever were.

The World of Cameo Appearances

In the 1990s especially, cameo appearances became so widespread as almost to command a genre of their own. "You Ought to Be in Pictures," announced a headline from the *New York Times*, "Everyone Else Is These Days."[17] And if not "everyone," then at least a tremendous parade of the marginally famous: Mort Zuckerman, Calvin Trillin, Ivana Trump, the late George Plimpton (the *Times*'s "king of cameos"), Erica Jong, and Ed Koch are among those mentioned in the story; off the top of my head, and I say this with a degree of embarrassment, I can think of cameo appearances by Brooke Shields, Mel Brooks, Carol Burnett,

George Segal, Don Rickles, Keith Hernandez, Jean Claude Van Damme, Yoko Ono, Billy Crystal, Robin Williams, Maureen Stapleton, Carroll O'Connor, Jerry Seinfeld, Beau Bridges, and Dick Gephardt—and these just on NBC sitcoms. Rosie O'Donnell, Joan Rivers, and Brooke Shields (again) on *Nip/Tuck*; Jennifer Aniston on *Dirt*; Britney Spears on *How I Met Your Mother*: seemingly every sweeps week and fight for higher ratings inaugurate an unceasing promotional hum of "special guest stars," suggesting that P. T. Barnum's "operational aesthetic" continues to function as the compulsory logic of "Must-See TV," for it is clear that a significant aspect of the attraction in such cases is all the apparatus at work in simply announcing the attraction itself.[18] This is not to say that the cameo appearance is nothing but a gimmick or a marketing ploy; it is, however, never *not* a gimmick, no matter its other semiotic ambitions. And so a film like Robert Altman's *The Player* (1992) or a series like *The Larry Sanders Show* or *Extras* depends on both a constant stream of cameo appearances and our pleasurable complicity with the very Hollywood star system that is being mocked; an aura of the "culture industry" at its most recursive and claustrophobic is always the point, and the cameo appearance seems the ideal formal device to signal an appropriately high self-consciousness without conscience. In this regard, Billy Wilder's *Sunset Boulevard* (1950)—with Gloria Swanson's captivatingly historicized performance as Norma Desmond, Eric von Stroheim's gothic turn as her butler, Cecil B. DeMille, Hedda Hopper, and all the "wax-works," including Buster Keaton and his one word of deliciously morbid, stone-faced dialogue—and Jean-Luc Godard's *Contempt* (1963)—featuring Fritz Lang as the director of the fictional version of Homer that is being filmed within the fiction of the film itself—must be accorded their ambiguous status as classically postmodern (with either term, or both, in scare quotes) examples of the skillful manipulation of cameo appearances. And it is no accident that both films are obsessed with the mortality of their medium, with the death of cinema at the hands of either television (Wilder) or Hollywood (Godard); the cameo appearances in each embody and allegorize fragments of a film history that is always about to be, or perhaps already has been, lost. As if stars in a world of cameo appearances don't die—they just get smaller parts.

Or put another way, the cameo appearance reproduces stardom in miniature, and I say this with more than just wordplay in mind.[19] In *The Savage Mind*'s famous discussion of *bricolage*, Lévi-Strauss observes that it is not simply the fact of representation, but rather the reduction in scale upon which almost all representation depends, that conditions our response to cultural artifacts and, more to the point, diversifies "our power over a homologue of the thing [represented]"— as smallness itself provides a "means" by which the object "can be grasped, assessed and apprehended at a glance."[20] This account of the miniature has a particular bearing on the cameo appearance. For as an eminently small phenomenon of celebrity, it trades on a mode of identification that remains somewhat removed from the totalizing engrossment in narrative that has long been the bottom line for classical Hollywood cinema. The cameo appearance might even be considered among the least of "attractions," to use Tom Gunning's famous term for any number of direct solicitations of the spectator that "rupture a self-enclosed fiction world"—but still, an attraction nonetheless.[21] The vast majority of cameo appearances effectively trivialize or "tame," as Gunning would say, the same moments of narrative limbo that they exploit; a walk-on by Marlo Thomas, Wayne Newton as "Wayne Newton"—these are not avant-garde gestures, any more than simply knowing the players in *The Player* without a scorecard is evidence of some superior distance from the film's domain.[22] The cameo appearance cannot help but be clever in every sense of the word; it is often precious or smug, but it also has the sly potential to allow us to borrow ownership of the means of pop cultural production, for it is finally *our* knowledge of the lesser-knowns and has-beens of film and TV history upon which the cameo appearance ultimately depends. Has there even been a cameo appearance if we do not recognize that guy from *Dexter* or what's-her-name, the one from that movie? The cameo appearance draws a charmed circle of self-congratulatory viewership, as if we too were part of this little family business that is the culture industry, where everybody knows everybody else in one giant network of relations that connects us not just to the star system but to the larger economy of entertainment and spectacle that it implies. Here, I suggest, is the most important aspect of the cameo appearance as stardom writ small: it offers, as Susan Stewart has observed of miniatures in general, "a diminutive, and thereby manipulable, version of experience, a version which is domesticated and protected from contamination."[23] A charm against the very system that proliferates it, the cameo appearance, like the dollhouse and other microscopic domains, creates "a tension or dialectic between the inside and the outside, between private and public property, between the space of the subject and the space of the social."[24]

At issue, then, is how we understand our strange yet familiar place in a world of celebrity that seems to enclose and isolate us simultaneously. The cameo appearance communicates, endlessly and without decision, between these two ways of describing just where we belong—outside or in?—in reference to the star system as a way of life, as a way of imagining the effects of a media culture that may well surround us all, but surrounds some more than others. The cameo appearance does not resolve, but rather puts on display the contradictory accounts of stardom with which this chapter began. It is a figure that refers to celebrity in both the dubious aggregate and the splendid particular, to celebrity as both a product of the assembly line and incandescent personality, spectacular and available for the rest of us to see, but probably never be. This is all much, much less than it was invented to accomplish.

◊

In December 1932 *Fortune* published a company profile of Metro-Goldwyn-Mayer, the largest and most successful enterprise in the world "devoted exclusively to the business and art of producing moving pictures."[25] What immediately follows this straightforward enough remark is a startling account, or perhaps I should say accounting, of all that adds up to compose the "business" side of the movie equation. From MGM's physical plant—"fifty-three acres valued at a trifling $2,000,000"—to its "twenty-two sound stages," "sixteen company limousines," "room for the practice of 117 professions," and "colored shoeshine boy outside the commissary [who] considers himself an actor because he frequently earns a day's pay in an African mob scene," no asset, it would seem, no matter how trifling or disagreeable, goes unrecorded; *Fortune* cites just over thirty-five figures on the story's first page alone, from the "50¢" oysters at the M-G-M dining hall to the "billion pairs of eyes" that watch M-G-M films. The company's sublime mathematics of scale are exhaustively detailed in a tone of dry sophistication, as if to remind the reader that big numbers are business as usual in the pages of *Fortune*, even if the movies are not; but at other moments, the outlandishness of the studio's bottom line appears to beggar both *Fortune's* sense of irony and its prose, as if to suggest that any complication of style or syntax would only interfere with the narrative adding machine:

> M-G-M's weekly payroll is roughly $250,000. On it are such celebrities as
> Marion Davies ($6,000), Norma Shearer, the three Barrymores, who get
> about $2,500 a week each, Clark Gable, Jean Harlow, Joan Crawford, Buster
> Keaton, Robert Montgomery, Marie Dressler (whose pictures take in more
> than any of the others'), Helen Hayes, Jimmy Durante, Conrad Nagel,

Ramon Novarro, Wallace Beery, small Jackie Cooper, who makes $1,000 a week, John Gilbert, and until very recently, Greta Garbo. Miss Garbo is likely soon to return from Sweden where she recently retired after amassing a fortune of $1,000,000. If she does return, she will doubtless have a chance to make another million. Actors' salaries are only a small part of M-G-M's outlay. The biggest and most expensive writing staff in Hollywood costs $40,000 a week. Directors cost $25,000. Executives cost slightly less. Budget for equipment is $100,000 a week. M-G-M makes about forty pictures in a year, every one a feature picture or a special picture. Average cost of Metro-Goldwyn-Mayer pictures runs slightly under $500,000. This is at least $150,000 more per picture than other companies spend. Thus Metro-Goldwyn-Mayer provides $20,000,000 worth of entertainment a year at cost of production, to see which something like a billion people of all races will pay more than $100,000,000 at the box office. *Motion Picture Almanac*, studying gross receipts, guesses at a yearly world total movie audience of 9,000,000,000. (51)

Some of these numbers no longer supply quite the same shock value now that a single film regularly costs more to produce than the year's global box office gross, and the scandalous salaries of the Barrymores and Norma Shearer, and even Marion Davies, are probably less than what Matthew McConaughey spends on his personal chef and trainer. But this is 1932, the worst year of the Great Depression in America and, of special importance, the worst year of the Great Depression in Hollywood. *Fortune* only hints at the story we could tell with the following figures: between 1930 and 1932, the domestic film audience erodes from 80 million to less than 55 million per week; the combined payrolls of the five major studios plummet from $156 million to less than $55 million, the "Polish immigrant who sometimes makes $500,000 a year" at MGM notwithstanding; these same five studios see their stock value decrease by almost 80 percent and their profits simply vanish, with net losses totaling $26 million by 1932 and only one major studio not in some sort of receivership. That studio, needless to say, is MGM, which will single-handedly generate an astonishing 75 percent of the industry's profits for the decade.[26]

Grand Hotel figures prominently in *Fortune*'s attempt to understand how MGM has done more than just survive the same economic crisis that has swamped its competitors. This being *Fortune*, due mention is made of the company's flexible debt structure and "conservatively amortized" inventory;

but this also being Hollywood, the explanation that is ultimately provided for MGM's prodigious bottom line is, strictly speaking, no explanation at all but rather a striking concession to the irrational alchemy of movie stardom, senseless and occult, and thus easy to deprecate even when it represents nothing less than the secret magic of the market itself. The "real clue" to M-G-M's preeminence, we learn near the article's close, is "the exuding of personality" by all those stars whose salaries are registered with such precision in the passage above, for "while there may be some dispute about M-G-M's acting, no one will deny that the M-G-M roster exudes more personality than any other in Hollywood" (122). All this "exuding" is performed by "a dozen of those hypnotic ladies who are asked to send their height, weight, bust dimensions and autograph to dreamy admirers all over the country," and though *Fortune* doesn't say what's asked of the men, we are still informed that MGM claims "a half-dozen male performers of equally mesmeric power" (122). In an example of the studio's promotional genius that *Fortune* reproduces, *Grand Hotel* appears as a virtual reification of MGM's commercial aesthetic on-screen. Setting a lobby poster for the film alongside a bombardment of come-ons to distributors—colloquial, ecstatic, cliché, and Yiddish, no less—the language reads like nothing so much as a premature Donald Barthelme pastiche of the very ad-speak it exemplifies (fig. 2.1).

Fortune later argues that films like *Grand Hotel* represent an altogether necessary modernization of the star system. "It is true that there are a diminishing number of pictures in the old movie tradition," the article notes of a "tradition" not yet twenty, with studios no longer churning out "pieces of utter whiffle for the display of some jerkwater matinee idol" (122). Instead, "what Mr. Thalberg substitutes for the 'star' system is a galactic arrangement whereby two or more 'stars' appear in one film . . . and so long as M-G-M keeps as much personality on tap as it has at present, so long can M-G-M hope to be well up in the Hollywood van" (122). The mixed metaphors here—from the cosmos to the bottling plant—might indicate just how unprecedented MGM's emphasis on the star system in "multiple" was at the time, though in retrospect the film seems a patent example of classical Hollywood. But Rudolph Arnheim, writing of *Grand Hotel* in his "Film Report" for 1933, after briefly rehearsing *Fortune*'s narrative of the film industry in crisis, uncorks a figurative reading of the movie that captures its strangeness with considerably more flavor: "*Grand Hotel* is a truly astonishing example of the culture of the American society film," he writes, adding that it offers evidence that Hollywood feels "forced, by the catastrophic

FIGURE 2.1. Advertisement for *Grand Hotel*, 1932.

failure of all proven attractions, to the desperate measure of collecting a whole bunch of stars in one single film, according to the principle that chocolate is good and herring is good, hence Garbo plus Beery must be really good!"[27]

The combination of Stein plus celebrity could have seemed no less strange at the time. And that Stein imagines a world of cameo appearances that matches the formal and thematic design of *Grand Hotel* almost exactly is the oddest of several "fortuitous collisions," recalling Koolhaas, between high modernism and

Hollywood that we will witness in this chapter. I am particularly interested in how the cameo appearance structures a kind of space in which people and technology are placed in communication. The cameo appearance is the most resplendent icon of Stein's experience of celebrity, which is itself an experience of the mediated life in America and abroad. "The thing is like this," Stein writes in *Everybody's Autobiography* as she attempts to reckon her new status as celebrity, "it is all a question of identity. It is all a question of the outside being outside and the inside being inside. As long as the outside does not put a value on you it remains outside but when it puts a value on you then it gets inside or rather if the outside puts a value on you then all your inside gets to be outside" (48). The star, in other words, is someone who has been turned inside out by the market and by media culture—which makes her just like the rest of us, especially in familiar accounts of the market and its effects on, or against, subjectivity.[28] Both Stein's writings in the wake of celebrity and *Grand Hotel* assume a self that is constituted in its very mediation, lost to all traditional notions of the private, and banished from the types of space historically constructed to house privacy in all its forms. Yet this mediated life of fame—visible, overheard, and thoroughly publicized—is not necessarily a life about which all is disclosed and in which nothing remains incommunicable to a world of others. It is a life of cameo appearances, where we experience everything in passing, in abbreviated gestures of familiarity and recognition that put precious little on display in showing us just what we want to see.

Celebrity from the Inside Out

"She always was, she always is," Stein writes of herself from the narrative remove of Toklas's impersonated voice, "tormented by the problem of the external and the internal" (112). *The Autobiography of Alice B. Toklas* registers this particular torment in a variety of ways, including, obviously enough, in the text's narration, performed as if "internal" to Alice B. Toklas when it in fact originates outside her in the person of Gertrude Stein. And though the language here is one of psychological disturbance, suggesting that Stein suffers the irreconcilable difficulties of inside and outside with the greatest sensitivity, the immediate frame of reference for this remark concerns aesthetic form more than emotional pain. While traveling in Spain, Stein's "style gradually changed," and where before her interests had been focused "only in the insides of people, their character and what went on inside them," she subsequently writes in response solely to "a desire to express the rhythm of the visible world" (111–112). To avoid all representations of interiority, to restrict language to details of sense and surface, is a "struggle" that Stein admits is ongoing, even as the surrounding narrative offers strong evidence that some sort of victory has been achieved. *The Autobiography of Alice B. Toklas* is an autobiography almost wholly void of psychological reflection, an autobiography that confesses to almost nothing that cannot be observed with the eye or ear.

This fact, however, hardly detracted from its popular success as a record of Stein and Toklas's life in the cosmopolitan city of Paris during "the heroic age of cubism." Looking back on *The Autobiography* from the vantage point of its sequel, Stein admits that Toklas thought that the book "was not sentimental enough" to be a best seller, though "later on when it was a best seller she said well after all it was sentimental enough" (47). We might take this remark as showing that Stein was well aware of the terms on which women's writing—and especially writing that achieved a measure of wide acclaim—tended to circulate; we might also wonder to what degree *The Autobiography*'s involvement with the language of domesticity, certainly a dialect of the sentimental, represented a canny strategy on Stein's part, an attempt, recalling Stewart's discussion of the miniature, to offer a "diminutive" or "manipulatable" account of modernism and modernity. Sara Blair suggests that Stein's work demonstrates that the private home provided "a dense site of distinctly modern" social experience in the years after World War I, and she argues persuasively that in such texts as "If You Had Three Husbands," we see that avant-garde literary production was often situated in a "changing form of domesticity."[29] That said, there is little sense that *The Autobiography* even counts as avant-garde. Bob Perelman describes Stein's best seller as deeply committed to the "domestication of modernist art and writing."[30] He means no great slight with this remark, but it is difficult to avoid the insinuation that *The Autobiography* represents a diminished achievement in light of other Stein texts, a view shared by many of her best critics.[31] Near the end of Toklas's story, just pages before the book's ruse of authorship is confirmed, we read the following attempt to isolate the narrative's retrograde domestic situation from its avant-garde aura: "She finds it difficult," Toklas muses, "to understand why we are not more modern. Gertrude Stein says that if you are way ahead with your head you are naturally old fashioned and regular in your daily life" (232). To come to this conclusion, however, one must first agree that a life lived amid a constant press of cameo appearances is, by any standard, "regular." And what we find inside the strangely domestic spaces of publicity at 27 Rue de Fleurus is a social world whose visible rhythm, paraphrasing Stein a bit, is both supremely frantic yet oddly without resonance. Stein imagines a space where interiority has given way to a version of what Blair terms "metropolitan sociality," and it is exactly this feature of Stein and Toklas's home that makes it the ideal environment for recognizing the modernity of Stein's writing.[32]

I want to begin with the fifth chapter of *The Autobiography of Alice B. Toklas,* "1907–1914," which records, and explicitly thematizes, the greatest proliferation of cameo appearances. "And so life in Paris began," we read, "and as all roads lead to Paris, all of us are now there, and I can begin to tell what happened when I was of it" (81). This gesture of inclusiveness toward all, of opening up a private space to any who might stop by, either physically or through the mediation of language itself, is a central trope of this, the text's longest chapter. Yet this promise that history will be simulated as if "you are there," as a newsreel might put it, is almost immediately revised and contained, its force lessened by Toklas's admission that the sheer proliferation of visitors to the Stein salon dampens the magnitude of their individual significance:

> The geniuses came and talked to Gertrude Stein and the wives sat with me. How they unroll, an endless vista through the years. I began with Fernande and then there were Madame Matisse and Marcelle Braque and Josette Gris and Eve Picasso and Bridget Gibb and Marjory Gibb and Hadley and Pauline Hemingway and Mrs. Sherwood Anderson and Mrs. Bravig Imbs and the Mrs. Ford Madox Ford and endless others, geniuses, near geniuses and might be geniuses, all having wives, and I have sat and talked with them all all the wives and later on, well later on too, I have sat and talked with all.
>
> (81–82)

While this series of interchangeable wives parades through 27 Rue de Fleurus, Toklas remains a constant around which a social comedy of broken marriages and mistresses swirls, the functional equivalent of Stein's spouse—for the purposes of domestic entertaining at the very least. The text is invitingly silent on the next step in a syllogistic logic that follows from the fact that Stein sits with "the geniuses" and Toklas with their wives. I will return to this silence, but for now I want to attend to the display of sociability that surrounds this telling moment of private life revealed for public view. Given that a dozen other "wives" are mentioned in the space of a sentence, what interests me about this passage is not so much the status of Toklas as the "wife of a genius," but the status of *any* self-representation under conditions demanding such rapid, superficial referencing.

At the risk of putting it too strongly, Stein dissociates interiority from privacy, from solitude, and most importantly, from meaningful perception in general. This is to say that *The Autobiography* pursues a range of representational strategies that try not to devolve into a conventional metaphorics opposing surface to depth, "external" to "internal." A surprisingly useful account of how such strategies might shape a poetics of self-display is offered by Bakhtin's description of Greek "rhetorical autobiography" from the essay "Forms of Time and Chronotope in the Novel," written sometime in the late 1930s, and certainly without any reference to Gertrude Stein. In this genre's particular "chronotope," as Bakhtin maps it, "there was not, nor could there be, anything intimate or private, secret or personal, anything relating solely to the individual himself, anything that was, in principal, solitary. Here the individual is open on all sides, he is all surface, there is in him nothing that exists 'for his sake alone.'"[33] This is not, for Bakhtin, a condition of clinical, existential isolation; on the contrary, the sense of a surrounding public is so intimate and enveloping that "this 'surface' on which a man existed and was laid bare, was not something alien and cold" (135). Instead, Bakhtin writes, "a man was utterly exteriorized but within a human element, in the human medium of his own people" (135). It is an ennobling, if not utopian, state of affairs for Bakhtin, gloriously prior to a life "drenched in muteness and visibility," before both "loneliness" itself and a loss of "the unity and wholeness that had been a product of [man's] public origin" (135). But for Stein, this "human medium" figures as an interminable series of cameo appearances—a public, so to speak, in two dimensions only. She represents life at 27 Rue de Fleurus so as to match Bakhtin's paradise of the public self in almost every regard save the most important—that is to say, the ultimate effect of all this living for public view. Stein and Toklas actually seem to imagine themselves as "exteriorized" for no good reason whatsoever. "It was an endless variety," Toklas says later in the chapter, "and everybody came and no one made any difference. There were friends who sat around the stove and talked and there were the endless strangers who came and went" (116). She describes a strange wasteland of publicity; and the terrain is more evocative of Eliot and his melancholic affectations than might be expected. The Stein salon functions like Bakhtin's chronotope of the classical public square, a void of privacy and interiority, but visible only in the form of fittingly modernist ruins. "Who else came. There were so many." "And no one made any difference."

Of the more than four hundred cameo appearances that preoccupy *The Autobiography of Alice B. Toklas*, a sizable percentage are found in the immediate vicinity of this remark, lending it an iconic status within the exhausting swells of social life at the Stein salon. Braudy describes the historical world of fame as one in which "names inundate us," and this is certainly true of Stein's world in Paris. In the ten pages surrounding Toklas's elegy for the less significant masses of friends and strangers at 27 Rue de Fleurus, the reader is treated to the following cacophony of proper names: Mildred Aldrich (who "adored cablegrams"), Henry McBride, Roger Fry, Clive Bell, Mrs. Clive Bell, and "many others" from the Bloomsbury circle, Wyndham Lewis, Augustus John, Lamb, and "throngs of englishmen," "Pritchard of the Museum of Fine Arts, Boston," "the Infanta Eulalia," Lady Cunard and her daughter Nancy, Jacques-Emile Blanche, Alphonse Kahn, Lady Ottoline Morrell "looking like the feminine version of Disraeli," "a roumanian princess" and her "cabman," William Cook and "a great many from Chicago," Raventos, Sabartes, "the futurists all of them led by Severini," Marinetti, Epstein "the sculptor," Dr. Claribel Cone, Etta Cone, Emily Chadbourne, Myra Edgerly, (Arnold) Genthe ("the well known photographer"), John Lane, Colonel and Mrs. Rogers, John Lane, Mabel Dodge, Edwin Dodge, Constance Fletcher, Jo and Yvonne Davidson, Florence Bradley, Mary Foote "and a number of others quite mad with fear," Siegfried Sassoon, Edith Sitwell, André Gide, Muriel Draper, Paul Draper, Haweis, Mina Loy, Harry and Bridget Gibb, Florence Bradley, Charles Demuth, Picabia "dark and lively," Marcel Duchamps "looking like a young norman crusader," Carl Van Vechten, Robert Jones, John Reed . . . And while the reproduction of such a list may seem excessive on my part, I should point out that even this taking of attendance leaves us far short of the total population Stein registers in these years, for not only are countless individuals abstracted within cryptic references to "everybody" and "others," but names continue to drop from the pages of *The Autobiography* at nearly the same relentless pace until the chapter ends with the eruption of war—the only event capable of checking this prodigious output of cameo appearances.

But this extravagant record of the "human medium" within which Stein and Toklas live is weirdly without a message. If we are told in advance that "no one made any difference," why provide us with this elaborate social registry in the first place, why subject us to this detailing of empty particulars? Thinking first in formal terms, there is a sort of musicality to all these proper nouns, a sensual experience of odd-sounding syllables and exotic pronunciations;

yet given Stein's antipathy toward the noun as a part of speech—"things once they are named the name does not go on doing anything to them and so why write in nouns"—it is unlikely that she would have been after these particular non-representational effects of language (*LA*, 210). Indeed, as Jennifer Ashton points out, Stein insists in many of her writings that names can do nothing but refer; "the liveliness of proper names," as Ashton puts it, is a "way of negating the very possibility" that reference will ever be lost.[34] For Stein, then, each of the four hundred proper names included in *The Autobiography* must denote a specific individual, even if the vast majority of these references have no connotative value for her reader. Thus the exhaustive accumulation of all these names, we might say, serves as an object lesson in what communications theory would describe as the difference between an utterance and information, which finally does not depend upon a logic of linguistic reference, as it does upon a felicitous match of code to context. And since information, to borrow from Gregory Bateson, is a difference that makes a difference, we should already know that none of the countless visitors who pass through *The Autobiography* can fully register in the end as individuals.

Rather, Stein seems intent on exploiting a phenomenon of social poetics, and what comes to matter about all these names is not their singularity as references to people but their accretion within space and time. Lecturing on "The Gradual Making of *The Making of Americans*," Stein observes that "it is something strictly American to conceive a space that is filled with moving, a space of time that is filled always filled with moving" (161). The cameo appearances of "1907–1914" indicate the workings of an American system of social production, a system that seeks to maximize the sheer numbers of social contact, to exaggerate out of all traditional proportion the ratio between public exposure and private remove, while at the same time minimizing the significance of any single event of personality. The figuring of the social as a dense network of comings and goings, without end or effect, recalls no one text so much as *The Great Gatsby*, where Nick Carraway tabulates "in the empty spaces of a [railway] time-table" the profligacy of names that circulate through an East Egg summer.[35] Fitzgerald's set piece articulates, perhaps as scathingly as one can, the relationship between a social life of extreme publicity and a deeper sense of space and time as produced by technology and its networks, whether material or metaphoric. Stein is not nearly so determined to render the technological mediation of her social space, though there is a possibility that Fitzgerald looms as an influence here.[36] To map Gatsby's glittering parties onto a rationalized grid of commuter transport requires a commitment to realist irony that Stein, for the most part, lacks. What results, however, is much the same: a disorienting democracy of attention is all but forced upon us, a vortex of characters in constant motion, some of whom are perhaps crucial, many of whom are clearly trivial, yet all of whom occupy the stage for the identical fleeting moment. Thus a strict representational economy is emphasized, an implacable distribution of mimetic resources that accords equal time to both the terminally obscure and the historically famous, the Infanta Eulaila on the one hand and John Reed on the other; in a world of cameo appearances it is incumbent upon the audience of readers to know the difference, to read *against* the reduction in scale and fashion their own highly personal surplus of meaning. Yet this distribution of attention is, by the same token, a flagrant travesty of narrative and historical logic; these cameo appearances leave little space for the protocols of standard autobiographical representation, for perceptible divisions between foreground and background, between major and minor characters, between Lady Cunard and Mina Loy. "Everybody brought somebody," Toklas notes, and while this is certainly hyperbole and readily explained by reference to Stein's fondness for both indeterminate pronouns and aggrandizing generalizations, this technically meaningless and oddly affecting sentence also represents, in the only way possible, the upper limit of social reference itself, a way of marking a superlative degree of intimate publicity beyond which there is nothing but more "endless strangers," more visits from more people looking at more pictures, more points of passing interest along an "endless vista through the years." There is an exhaustive redundancy to the feats of memory in *The Autobiography of Alice B. Toklas*, exhaustive not only of some readers' patience but of the notion of historical significance as well. "And everybody came and no one made any difference."

That is, almost no one. For despite the sheer speed at which this social scene moves past the reader, and despite the sheer number of names the narrative accumulates, it is still possible to trace different paths of reference through the thicket of cameo appearances. Toklas's passing remark that "everybody found the futurists very dull," as Marjorie Perloff has argued, refers not only to Stein's personal antipathy toward futurism and its violent, promotional ideology of the avant-garde but also to a larger network of her texts in which the language practices of Marinetti and others are subjected to political scrutiny and poetic play (or vice versa).[37] It is also possible to imagine a, strictly speaking, *historicist* attempt to locate Stein's dazzling swirl of social reference within what Stephen Greenblatt would call a "cultural poetics" that puts small denominations of "mimetic capital" into circulation.[38] That John Reed makes a brief and somewhat unpleasant appearance at 27 Rue de Fleurus momentarily places the aesthetic radicalism of modern culture in communication with the political radicalism with which Reed is famously associated, and such networks of intertextual meaning might well be pursued. And as theoretically "everybody" possesses some degree of historical resonance, from the Infanta Eulaila to the Princesse de Polignac, the intertexual horizons of *The Autobiography of Alice B. Toklas* are all but limitless, offering an infinitely extensive system of cultural reference and surface particularity, with each obscure dignitary or minor painter leading finally to some domain of signification outside the text itself. The cameo appearance thus represents a dream of potentially endless historicizing, a historicizing rendered trivial, marginal, and haphazard by the very form of utterance that instigates it. If you recognize the name Gertrude Atherton, you crack a portion of Stein's code, and if you do not, the text gives no indication whatsoever that you have missed something, no more than Stein seems concerned if the name Marcel Duchamps carries any more significance than Alphonse Kahn, each of which is subject to the same economy of the cameo appearance. A name is a name is a name is a name. The text all but aspires to a condition that David Shenk, writing at the height of dot-com culture in the late 1990s, called "data smog" in hopes of capturing the feel of living in an environment where information is too abundant for our own good.[39] Thus a familiar modernist aesthetics of difficulty—"opacity" as Nicholls might say, or for Stewart "continuous signification"—operates not because the text resists definitive interpretation but because it encourages endless annotation.

But as I said, there is at least one way to qualify the text's conceivably interminable historical "irreference," and that qualification is this: to say that every cameo appearance is formally the equal of any other is not to say that every cameo appearance is experienced equally by any reader. Different readers approach *The Autobiography* with different degrees of competence in the arcana of its period-specific acts of memory. For every reader who skims over "Lady Ottoline Morrell" without a thought—her name just noise on the page—there is another who knows a bit of her biography, and so has reason, however trivial, to link Stein and D. H. Lawrence, who had based a character in *Women in Love* on Morrell in 1920. All this name-dropping has the effect of producing different readers: some who find the text a richly nodal document of modernism's culture and some who find the text a useless show of social capital. The contingency of the cameo appearance lets it beg with equal authority to be taken for granted, missed entirely, or doggedly pursued; but in any case, the cameo appearances in Stein make a spectacle out of information. We might even say that Stein's name-dropping revels in the "theatricality" of information, a term I am borrowing from Michael Fried. This is to stress the potential "obtrusiveness" and "aggressiveness"—two especially disparaging aesthetics that Fried associates with 1960s minimalism—that are risked by any work of art whose effect depends on "the special complicity that that work of art extorts from the beholder."[40] Or put differently, to the degree that cameo appearances in Stein refer only to names that no reader, I think, is supposed to know in full—this is why the narrative is structured as a show of "inside" information from the early days of modernism—the text must also acknowledge that these names need not communicate at all, that they constitute a medium where "the materials do not represent, signify, or allude to anything; they are what they are and nothing more" (165). And it is against the presence of this noise, and the theater of sociality that constantly intrudes on Stein and Toklas at 27 Rue de Fleurus, that *The Autobiography* employs one of the final cameo appearances of "1907–1914" to confirm that while we have been watching names come and go, Stein has been absorbed in her writing all along.

The most important drama of recognition played out over the course of *The Autobiography of Alice B. Toklas* concerns none of the text's cameo appearances so much as it does Gertrude Stein herself. At the beginning of the narrative, Toklas is introduced as an uncanny appraiser of greatness, a person who has encountered genius "only three times . . . and each time a bell within me rang," well in advance, she informs us, of any "general recognition" by the public (5). That she and she alone recognized Stein's genius "on sight" is the initial rationale for the fiction of her narration, as we learn from such provisional titles for her faux autobiography as, "My Life With The Great," or "Wives of Geniuses I Have Sat With"—trotted out just before Stein's hand as author is finally revealed. This revelation, as critics of the text's first illustrated edition have noted, is quite literally literal; facing opposite to the final paragraphs of the text we find a photograph captioned, "First page of the manuscript of this book," a gesture that graphically returns us to the start of the text, now visible in its author's hand, and yet does so with some irony, for just how, in the end, are we supposed to identify this writing as belonging to Gertrude Stein (figure 2.2)? How is this "hand" any more conclusive as evidence of authorship than the fictive "voice" of the narrative itself? And why, for that matter, the first page of the manuscript?

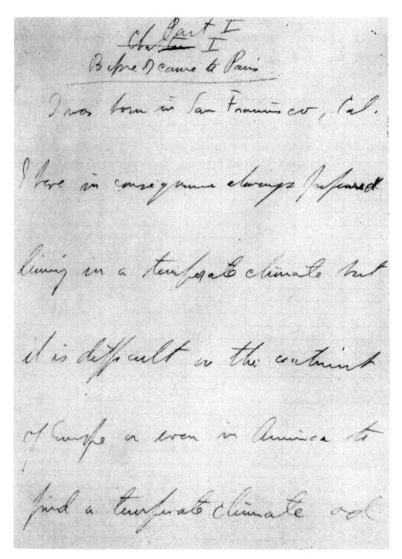

FIGURE 2.2. "First page of the manuscript of this book," from the first ed. of *The Autobiography of Alice B. Toklas* (New York: Harcourt, 1933).

This illustration turns Joseph Frank's famous aesthetic of "spatial form"—in which modernist literature aspires to "rival the spatial apprehension of the plastic arts in a moment of time"—into a kind of joke, a showy unveiling of the obvious that directs us back to the beginning of the book as if *now* we know to read it all differently.[41] It is also, of course, a joke about the meaningless materiality of the text, which is to say, that its deictic gesture—"first page of manuscript of this book"—does not denote "this book" at all, nor can it possibly confirm its author. The picture functions as what Katherine Hayles would term a "material metaphor," a figurative exploitation of the text's physical apparatus "that foregrounds the traffic between words" and books as technologies, mediums, or objects.[42] And in this respect, by including a picture of Stein's original manuscript, the text oddly enough recalls its own performance of displaced or distributed authority. "I always say," Stein writes, "that you cannot tell what a picture really is or what an object really is until you dust it every day and you cannot tell what a book is until you type it or proofread it. It then does something to you that only reading never can do" (106). Of course, Stein here writes about what Toklas does: experience the text as it communicates from one medium to another in a process that is perfect, strictly speaking, to the degree that it makes no difference. The typewriting of Stein's manuscripts gives Toklas a claim to textual intimacy with Stein that we as readers can never have, and that Stein, perhaps, cannot have herself. Kittler insists, echoing Jacques Lacan, that in the discourse network of 1900, where relays with and through technology have replaced communication between men and women, "there is no sexual relation between the sexes."[43] But Kittler also takes for granted that male authors and their female secretaries or, as they were objectified, their "typewriters," are the only players in this modern drama of mediation and textuality. The "genius" of *The Autobiography of Alice B. Toklas*, on the contrary, is to put these circuits of technology to work so that sexual relations within the sexes become, if not exactly possible, at least legible within the media environment that makes Gertrude Stein so famous.

That 27 Rue de Fleurus is the scene of Stein's writing is a fact of which we are continually reminded, beginning with the first edition's frontispiece illustration, a Man Ray photograph of Stein in silhouette at her desk, pen in hand, while Toklas occupies the background in a brightly lit doorway, her relationship to Stein's writing, as well as to the book before us, indeterminate—the title page of the first edition does not feature the name of an author (fig. 2.3).[44] These pictures, as James Breslin argues, make visible the displacement of authority that the narrative embodies in both its formal texture and its dominant thematics. The cameo appearance of Alvin Langdon Coburn, however, represents a moment of visibility, one that unexpectedly brings Stein into focus, not just as an author but, more importantly, as a star. "It was about nineteen twelve that Alvin Langdon Coburn turned up in Paris,"

FIGURE 2.3. Man Ray, "Photo of Gertrude Stein and Alice B. Toklas." Copyright © 2009 Man Ray Trust / Artists Rights Society (ARS), NY / ADAGP, Paris.

Toklas tells us near the end of "1907–1914," making this the chapter's penultimate cameo. She continues:

> He was a queer american who brought with him a queer english woman, his adopted mother. Alvin Langdon Coburn had just finished a series of photographs that he had done for Henry James. He had published a book of photographs of prominent men and he wished now to do a companion volume of prominent women. I imagine it was Roger Fry who had told him about Gertrude Stein. At any rate he was the first photographer to come and photograph her as a celebrity and she was nicely gratified. He did make some very good photographs of her and gave them to her and then he disappeared and though Gertrude Stein has often asked about him nobody seems ever to have heard of him since. (131–132)

This is one of the few cameo appearances that produces a specific narrative affect, a feeling that aspires to pathos but is perhaps more accurately described as the exhaustion of pathos, the weary realization that almost no one who has been mentioned in the preceding pages will ever be heard of again. To hark back to the critical vocabulary of Henry James, whose presence here quietly hints at a literary genealogy from the culmination of his career to the origin of Stein's, there is a certain tone to Coburn's visit, and this tone encompasses much of what the cameo appearance has to say about the emotional life of modernity: there are simply too many people to keep track of, too many events to register, too much history to write into the permanent record, even when that record is reduced in scale—thus extending the capacity of its memory—to a parade of cameo appearances.[45] This passage also makes clear that "celebrity" is one of the names designating this condition of extreme yet attenuated sociability, this blur of personality mediating between the intimate spaces of the home and a pubic sphere that lacks both limit and resonance, being both "endless" and making "no difference." But this is not at all what we see pictured in Coburn's photographs of Stein, images remembered as the first documents of her "celebrity," which represent a scene of writing almost entirely disconnected from the outside world. Thus even though Coburn's brief cameo is little more than "the appearance of a disappearance," to borrow a particularly resonant phrase from Alex Woloch's work on the function of minor characters, it makes a difference to Stein in that it christens the phenomenon of her celebrity and pays tribute to the materiality of the medium that distinguishes her literary status.[46]

In one Coburn photograph the page over which Stein works glows as a field of absolute whiteness matched visually to the extreme illumination of her forehead. The incandescence of the page recalls something of the ectoplasmic manifestations pictured in so much Victorian spiritualist photography, though in this case, there is no "other" erupting into our own world save that of Stein's own mental energies, the supreme consciousness that distinguishes the circuit between mind and page. Another of the Coburn pictures similarly fixates on the apparent dissolution of Stein's body into writing itself (fig. 2.4), as again Stein's rapt attention directs the viewer to the place in the image where it becomes impossible to determine just where the writer ends and the materials of writing begin. I should also add that writing is figured as anything but "automatic" in the Coburn series; in fact, the visual emphasis on Stein's powers of intention could hardly be stronger. But the profound modernity of Stein's writing is banished from the iconography of Coburn's pictures, where velvet robes, antique furniture, and an ostentatiously situated candle suggest that the technology of

FIGURE 2.4. Alvin Langdon Coburn, photograph of Gertrude Stein, circa 1914. Yale Collection of American Literature, Beinecke Rare Book and Manuscript Library, Yale University.

writing remains unaltered, despite the haunting presences of a modern visual culture that remains just slightly out of focus in the background, with its fuzzy mirror image of Gertrude Stein as already represented—Picasso's famous portrait dominates the deep center of the photograph—barely registering behind a foreground wholly dominated by Stein's absorption in the act of writing. Stein and her painted figure subtly mirror one another—the color of clothing is similarly dark, her face and forehead are likewise bright and focal, she is seated in both portraits, with her hands visible—but the author dwarfs her image. Indeed, Coburn's photograph almost renders Picasso's painting as the product of Stein's imagination; it floats above her head as if filling up a thought bubble. In this photograph, the act of writing radiates with a materiality that seems at once to "draw" on the visibility of modernist painting—the pun seems unavoidable since Stein could be seen as sketching here—even as the image quietly asserts the priority and specific inwardness of textuality.

So if this is what Stein looks like as a nascent "celebrity," neither fame nor recognition would seem to pose much of a distraction to the modern writer. Celebrity finally registers as no interference at all; the social noise at 27 Rue de Fleurus does not interrupt the ideal network of communication that relays the contents of the writer's mind to the page as if that page were as intimately connected to the body as the writer's own hand. The closed circuit of writing is impenetrable, and its technological apparatus is no apparatus at all but rather a perfect and seamless extension of the author and her identity. These photographs from 1914—fondly recalled by Stein in 1932 as the first images of her "celebrity"—depict a domestic scene of writing still isolated from the restless mobilizations of publicity, a space that remains "old fashioned and regular" despite the crowded assembly of endless cameo appearances and the pressures they apply to any stable notions of inside and outside.

Other accounts of the modern home at this same time imagine a radically different sort of domestic space: "In all its essentials," writes Norman Bel Geddes in *Horizons*, his 1932 fantasia of a streamlined lifeworld, "a house should be organized as a factory is. For it *is* a factory of a kind; and it is the most difficult kind of factory to run."[47] The writing factory at 27 Rue de Fleurus runs smoothly enough, according to *The Autobiography*, with Stein producing texts in great abundance while still managing to entertain a nostalgia for domesticity in the total absence of the solitude that is its defining condition. Some hint of this contradiction is visible even in 1914, for the old-fashioned candle is quite obviously not providing the brilliant illumination for the scene of writing the Coburn photograph depicts. The imaginary space of celebrity has a much different look—and sound—to Stein after she has actually achieved it, and this scene of writing gives way to a dizzying profusion of what we might call scenes of communication.

Ecstasies of Communication

There are limits to the modernity of Stein's Paris, and within the space of time narrated by *The Autobiography of Alice B. Toklas*, one such frontier is marked by the absence of the telephone.

As Gertrude Stein and I came into the café there seemed to be a great many people present and in the midst was a tall thin girl who with her long thin arms extended was swaying forward and back. I did not know what she was doing it was evidently not gymnastics, it was bewildering and looked very enticing. What is that, I whispered to Gertrude Stein. Oh that is Marie Laurencin, I am afraid she has been taking too many preliminary apéritifs. Is she the old lady that Fernande told me about who makes noises like animals and annoys Pablo. She annoys Pablo alright but she is a very young lady and she has had too much, said Gertrude Stein going in. Just then there was a violent noise at the door of the café and Fernande appeared very large, very excited and very angry. Félix Potin, said she, has not sent the dinner. Everybody seemed overcome at these awful tidings but I, in my american way said to Fernande, come quickly, let us telephone. In those days in Paris one did not telephone and never went to a provision store. But Fernande consented and off we went. Everywhere we went there was either no telephone or it was not working, finally we got one that worked but Félix Potin was closed or closing and it was deaf to our appeals. (97–98)

The basic units of narrative action in this passage are events of communication. The indecipherable bodily gestures of Marie Laurencin, the whispered exchange between Alice and Gertrude, the reports of animal verbalizations that annoy Picasso, and finally Fernande's striking entrance and grand distress over an eminently bourgeois catastrophe, which is as much to say no catastrophe at all. "One would like to ask," Freud writes in *Civilization and Its Discontents*, published just two years before, in 1930, "is there, then, no positive gain in pleasure, no unequivocal increase in my feeling of happiness, if I can, as often as I please, hear the voice of a child of mine who is living hundreds of miles away or if I can learn in the shortest possible time after a friend has reached his destination that he has come through the long and difficult voyage unharmed?"[48] To these zero-sum games of pleasure forced upon us by modern life, we might add Fernande's somewhat less dreadful dilemma: is there no positive gain in domestic comfort if the technology that spares me the labor of shopping cannot bring me my undelivered dinner? The "american way" to resolve this crisis, a solution about which Toklas seems somewhat ashamed, automatically involves an engagement with whatever means of technology are at hand, and even, if necessary, an actual trip to the grocery store, no matter how unaesthetic the hard facts of consumer life may be. Thus overlapping networks for the exchange of language and money are here designated as uniquely American priorities, the special province of the nation which, "having begun the creation of the twen-tieth century in the sixties of the nineteenth century is now the oldest country in the world" (73). This famous remark is readily confirmed, at least in terms of America's disposition toward the telephone, by an AT&T ad of 1935. "America leads in telephone service," it reads. "In relation to population there are six times as many telephones in this country as in Europe and the telephone is used nine times as much."[49]

The second chapter of *Everybody's Autobiography*, plainly titled "What Was the Effect Upon Me of The Autobiography," begins with a description of a new economy that conditions writing after Stein's surprising best seller. An indis-criminate theory of value that accorded every word the same dear status gives way to an inescapable "money value" that spectacularly commercializes some language while declaring other language worthless (40). Several critics and bi-ographers have pointed to a prolonged and, for Stein, entirely uncharacteristic period of writer's block as one result of her success.[50] But I am interested in another way that Stein's late celebrity and financial viability materialized them-selves in her daily life. Now able to sell even her earlier, unpublished works with some regularity, Stein acquires an agent, William Aspinwall Bradley, and takes dramatic steps to ensure that she and Toklas aren't quite so old-fashioned:

> So he was excited and I had to have a telephone put in first at twenty-seven rue de Fleurus and then here at Bilignin. I had always before that not had a telephone but now that I was going to be an author whose agent could place something I had of course to have a telephone. We are just now putting in an electric stove but that is because it is difficult if not impossible to get coal that will burn and besides the coal stove does not heat the oven and anyway France is getting so that French cooks do not like to cook on a coal stove. To be sure cooking with coal is like lighting with gas it is an intermediate stage which is a mistake. It would seem that cooking should be done with wood, charcoal or electricity and I guess they are right, just as lighting should be done by candles or electricity, coal and gas are a mistake, like railroad trains, it should be horses or automobiles or airplanes, coal, gas and railroads are a mistake and that has perhaps a great deal to do with politics and govern-ment and the nineteenth century and everything however to come back to my agent and to my success.
>
> It is funny about money. (45)

There is no accommodating the categorical modernity that this passage implies: the gradual progress of domestic technology in the background of *The Autobiography* is pointedly revisited here, not as a source of nostalgia but rather as a series of errors, an extended misrecognition of history's direction. Modernity, in short, is an all or nothing proposition; like the bumper sticker version of "America, Love It or Leave It"—horses or airplanes—but no straddling between then and now. "Everything" changes irrevocably with the modern, and though there is no way to know exactly what "everything" involves, I think it safe to say that "money" is at the root of it, and the telephone is among its most visible and audible signs. "And so Mr. Bradley telephoned every morning and they gradually decided about everything and slowly everything changed inside me," Stein writes just a paragraph later, "yes of course it did because suddenly it was all different, what I did had a value that made people ready to pay" (45–46). The telephone represents this larger network of communication that is identical to a larger network of exchange, making each transmission of mediated language a commercial transaction as well, an accumulation of economic determinants that "gradually" penetrates both home and self, rendering any vestiges of domestic individualism as backward as gaslight. Thus the telephone is a symbolic technology in several senses of the word, for it is not only a means of communication but also a metonymic figure for deeper historical and economic transformations. And though Stein appears to define with little difficulty just what the telephone is a symbol of, we should not ignore another aspect of the telephone in *Everybody's Autobiography*, an aspect featured prominently in *Grand Hotel* as well, in which phone calls are the very symbol of all that is modern because they symbolize nothing in particular, a telling background noise that consumes as much meaning as it transmits.

◊

One does not step inside the spatial and narrative world of *Grand Hotel* by walking through its massive revolving door and crossing its breathtaking lobby; one enters by way of the telephone. The ostentatious display of stardom in the film's opening credits, where each major actor, beginning with Garbo, of course, is treated to a premature curtain call, fades to black, and then fades in on what I want to call an establishing shot of the hotel's interior, but which really isn't, because the space it establishes is entirely *too* interior: the film's first images are of the hotel's switchboard, with the camera tracking over the heads of a series of nearly identical telephone operators, connecting and disconnecting a Babel of calls, a chattering polyphony of unspecified language, recognizable as English only in that the words "Grand Hotel" keep emerging audibly above the noise. And while we return to this space several times in the film's narrative, the switchboard remains totally "disconnected," architecturally speaking, from the interior of the Grand Hotel itself, within whose confines the entire narrative of the film takes place. We know only that these invisible channels of communication lead to narrative—a lot of narrative.

Fade to a man on the telephone. First Senf, the hotel porter played by Jean Hersholt, places a call to the hospital, begging to know if his wife has given birth yet, though he isn't permitted to leave his work even if she has. Then Otto Kringelein, the terminally ill petit bourgeoisie played to the hilt by Lionel Barrymore, calls home to let someone know he is staying at the "most expensive hotel in Berlin," where even this phone call costs "2 marks 90" every minute. Then Wallace Beery's archly German Herr General Director Preysing calls home to let them know he has safely arrived for his important meeting with a company from Manchester, a meeting upon which "everything depends." A woman named Suzette, the assistant to the famous ballerina Grusinskaya, calls the theater to warn them that "Madame will not dance tonight." Then Baron von Geigern, a jewel thief with the most impeccable class status of any of the film's characters, calls some anonymous criminal boss. "I need more money," he demands, "or I can't stay at this hotel much longer." We witness these calls from a position directly in front of each speaker, as if the movie screen was nothing more than the transparent wall of the telephone booth. The background remains largely out of focus, with just enough visual detail to let us know that there is motion and activity here, but not so much detail that our attention is drawn away from these intensely differentiated monologues—Hollywood character acting of the highest polish.

And then the sequence repeats itself. We return to each conversation a few seconds later, now in tight close-ups lasting only a few seconds, from which we cut away right in the middle of sentences, right in the middle of words. Thus Kringelein again: "I've taken all my savings and I'm going to enjoy spending it, all of it." Senf: "I can't, I'll lose my job. It's like being in jail." Preysing: "The deal with Manchester must go through." Suzette: "I'm afraid she will." And finally Kringelein: "Music all the time. Dancing. It's wonderful." These three minutes epitomize a narrative economy of montage, compressing almost all the information we need to make sense of the film's extensive plot: so much melodrama, so little time. The accelerating pace of the editing even invites a loose analogy between the general scarcity of money in the narrative and the special scarcity of screen time in the film, for the essence of *Grand Hotel* is that even its stars, because they are too many, make little more than cameo appearances, with Garbo around for only a scandalously brief twenty-some minutes.[51] The first line of dialogue in the film that is not spoken into a telephone is spoken directly to the viewer—or to nobody in particular—by Dr. Otternschlag, a scarred veteran of World War I played by Lewis Stone. His flat delivery and affected weariness exaggerate the resonance of the film's perverse moral—perverse, that is, because it evacuates meaning instead of condensing it: "Grand Hotel. People coming . . . going. Nothing ever happens." And the echo of Stein—or Stein's echo of Dr. Otternschlag, as the case may be—is unmistakable: "It was an endless variety, and everybody came and no one made any difference."

But something does happen that radically alters the film's visual logic, punctuating this opening scene of communication with a moment of spectacle that mutes, at least momentarily, Dr. Otternschlag's ironic commentary. The close-up of Lewis Stone fades, and we now see the crowded lobby of Grand Hotel from a vantage that is more or less at eye level, a true establishing shot in that the narrative space of the film is now immediately characterized: a world of gleaming surfaces, fancy dress clothes, a profusion of faces, constant movement. The "Blue Danube Waltz" begins, implying a social scene that operates with Viennese precision and splendid grace, though perhaps tending to the banal. The lobby of the Grand Hotel bears a resemblance in this sequence to that of the Hotel Atlantic in F. W. Murnau's 1924 film *Der Letze Mann*, at one time the most successful foreign film in U.S. history and almost certainly a point of reference here. Yet for all that these two films share at the level of locale and thematic emphasis, their particular visual techniques articulate radically different conceptions of space.[52] At the beginning of *Der Letze Mann*, we are already inside the hotel, descending toward the lobby in an elevator through whose grilled gate we see a scene of people in motion; the camera's point of view simulates the visual field of an unspecified yet embodied observer, a person with whom we walk out of the elevator and then across the lobby in a legendary and, for its time, technologically miraculous tracking shot.[53] And while the first shot of the full lobby in *Grand Hotel* depicts a similar interior design, its perspective could not be farther removed from the intimately subjective position in which Murnau situates us. *Grand Hotel* fades without warning to an overhead view of the lobby (fig. 2.5). This image gives some sense of the giddy perspective

FIGURE 2.5. Overhead shot of the lobby in *Grand Hotel* (MGM, 1932).

the viewer experiences, for while the sudden remove of our visual perspective from a crowded space, practically clogged with narrative, suggests a kind of surveillance and power over the microscopic scene below, this unexpected moment of visual abstraction—recalling a Busby Berkeley musical perhaps, and warped as if filmed in a convex mirror—also suggests a moment of harrowing weightlessness, as if all that was solid about social observation itself was about to melt into air.[54] Intricacies of character and plot are no longer visible from this celestial point of view, and though we soon return to "earth" and its noises, melodramas, and chattering dialogue, there is something about this brief respite from the narrative claustrophobia of the telephone booths that continues to haunt the opening sequence as it unfolds. This moment of pure visual display brings a whole architecture of modern life into focus. We see that there is an absolute dichotomy between the interior workings of the social machine and its reflection in the world of spectacle, between the switchboard's exposed bowels of tangled wires and faceless female labor and the shining spaces of circulation in the hotel's lobby. Like Gertrude Stein, to put it bluntly, *Grand Hotel* is tormented by the problem of the external and the internal, both in the melodramatics of its plot—a jewel thief hides behind the Baron's aristocratic veneer, a murderous villain lurks inside the stolid industrialist, without substance, and of course, inside the call girl and/or secretary played by Joan Crawford there beats a heart of gold—and also at the level of cinematic form. At no time in the film do we step outside the Grand Hotel itself; it is telling that the only glimpse we get of a space not contained within this interior is when we follow a hearse carrying the Baron's coffin out into the street; to check out of *Grand Hotel* is to move inevitably toward death.[55]

Nowhere after the opening sequence in *Grand Hotel* is so much accomplished with so much visual economy. The plot tangles forward, and characters meet and couple in almost every conceivable combination, as if the narrative was driven by some algorithm seeking to maximize each of its stars' screen time. Any description of the plot in detail is beggared by a rococo structure of interrelated events. The Baron meets Kringelein and then Flaemmchen (Joan Crawford) meets the Baron; then Kringelein meets Flaemmchen; then Preysing meets Flaemmchen, and later Kringelein and the Baron as well; once everyone has met everyone, the Baron makes his attempt to steal Grusinskaya's jewels but falls in love with her instead; Preysing makes his fraudulent business deal, and Flaemmchen becomes his sexual employee; Kringelein meanwhile tries desperately to seize what pleasures his dying body is capable of withstanding, a mission of petty hedonism that leads him first into conflict with his former boss, who happens to be Preysing, and then the Baron, who nobly refuses to steal from Kringelein despite his pressing need for money, and tries instead to rob Preysing, who kills him in the attempt. Thus Grusinskaya leaves for her next destination, unaware that her lover is dead; Preysing leaves for home

financially ruined and under arrest; Kringelein leaves with Flaemmchen, planning to spend on her whatever time and money he has left; Senf the porter
learns that his wife has given birth safely; Dr. Otternschlag, with the film's last
line of dialogue, returns us to where we started in the first place: "Grand Hotel.
People coming . . . going. Nothing ever happens." The film ends with nothing
of the visual flourish that distinguishes its opening. In fact, after those first few
minutes described above, it settles into a relatively workaday mode of narrative
cinema, perpetually crowded and quickly paced, but never again approaching
the speed of its opening montage of telephone calls, and never again indulging
in a moment of pure visuality that matches the strangeness of the spectacular
overhead shot that occurs soon after.

In many ways, the opening sequence of *Grand Hotel* serves as the perfect
illustration for the "amazing hotel-world" that is the Waldorf-Astoria in 1905,
when Henry James visits it in *The American Scene*. As soon as he enters the
lobby, James writes, the thickly mediated space of the hotel's interior "quickly
closes round him," and the observer is "transported to conditions of extraordi-
nary complexity and brilliancy. The air swarms, to intensity, with the *characteristic*, the characteristic condensed and accumulated as he rarely elsewhere has
had the luck to find it."[56] This well-known section of *The American Scene* has
been read from a variety of critical perspectives, and to these I would add my
own observation that what James seems to stumble into here is the world of
cameo appearances, where a traditional poetics of character has given way to
one based on speed and scale.[57] "That effect of violence in the whole communication," James argues, "results from the inordinate mass, the quantity of presence, as it were, of the testimony heaped together for emphasis of the wondrous
moral" (78). The "moral" that he derives from his visit to the grand hotel is, not
surprisingly, sharper than that of Dr. Otternschlag, for James at least tries to isolate a cultural logic within the bewildering confusion of the Waldorf-Astoria's
lobby, concluding that the "general truth" of this space lies in the "practically
imperturbable" relation between "form and medium": "here was a conception
of publicity *as* the vital medium organized with the authority with which the
American genius for organization, put on its mettle, alone could organize it"
(81). The conditions of supreme publicity that James describes at the Waldorf-
Astoria result only in part from the brute facts of population and motion, and
depend as much, if not more, on the complex arrangement of aesthetic display
and economic imperative that becomes, so to speak, the very air one breathes.[58]
These are not, however, conditions conducive to narrative; there is no "story"

to tell about the "hotel-word," there is only a special effect and dream-vision to be described, "a gorgeous golden blur, a paradise peopled with unmistakable American shapes" (81). Perhaps it is this "paradise" we see from our fleeting vantage point suspended above the Grand Hotel's lobby, a lobby whose floor, as Donald Albrecht notes, bears a striking resemblance to a chessboard, an image that would no doubt appeal to Henry James as well, who witnesses in the hotel lobby "the sharpest dazzle of the eyes as precisely the play of the genius for organization."[59]

More surprising by far is that *Grand Hotel* serves as the perfect illustration for Gertrude Stein's *Everybody's Autobiography*, a text that features several scenes of communication that reproduce the film's opening sequence with uncanny fidelity. We left Stein having just had telephones installed at both 27 Rue de Fleurus and her summer home at Bilignin. But the telephone is ringing in *Everybody's Autobiography* long before Stein narrates the how and why of its relatively belated installation in her domestic world. The text begins with a short introduction that promises all the pleasures of a sequel—"Alice B. Toklas did hers and now anybody will do theirs"—yet the paragraphs that follow appear determined to provide as little continuity as possible from *The Autobiography of Alice B. Toklas*. We learn right off that Alice Toklas objected to the "B"; that Stein has been thinking a lot about Dashiell Hammett; that someone named Miss Hennessy carries a wooden umbrella. And while it is possible to pursue a phantom narrative logic to these distractions—Toklas's discomfort with how Stein named her might index larger questions of her "voice" in *The Autobiography*; Hammett's presence at the beginning suggests a connection between this book and the detective fiction that Stein was both reading and, in a highly experimental mode, writing—I am more interested in how this introduction seeks to represent a state of distraction as such, that is to say, a state of distraction that Stein equates with her newly earned status as star. "It is very nice being a celebrity," Stein writes, "a real celebrity who can decide who they want to meet and say so and they come or do not come as you want them" (2). Stein wants "celebrity" to name an experience of sovereign social power, a new order of agency in the public world. The actual workings of this power, however, involve a network of telephone calls and social contingencies that matches anything we see and, as importantly, hear in *Grand Hotel*:

So Alice Toklas rang up Mrs. Ehrman and said we wanted to meet Dashiell Hammett.

She said yes what is his name. Dashiell Hammett said Miss Toklas. And how do you spell it. Alice Toklas spelt it. Yes and where does he live. Ah that said Alice Toklas we do not know, we asked in New York and Knopf editor said he could not give his address. Ah yes said Mrs. Ehrman now what is he. Dashiell Hammett you know The Thin Man said Alice Toklas. Oh yes said Mrs. Ehrman yes and they both hung up.

We went to dinner that evening and there was Dashiell Hammett and we had an interesting talk about autobiography, but first how did he get there I mean at Mrs. Ehrman's for dinner. Between them they told it.

Mrs. Ehrman called up an office he had at Hollywood and asked for his address, she was told he was in San Francisco, then she called up the producer of The Thin Man he said Hammett was in New York. So said Mrs. Ehrman to herself he must be in Hollywood. So she called up the man who wanted to produce The Thin Man and had failed to get it and he had Hammett's address. Mrs. Ehrman telegraphed to Hammett saying would he come that evening to dine with her to meet Gertrude Stein. It was April Fool's Day and he did nothing and then he looked up Ehrman and it was a furrier and no Mrs. Ehrman and then he asked everybody and heard that it was all true and telegraphed and said if he might bring who was to be his hostess he could come and Mrs. Ehrman said of course come and they came. His hostess but all that will come when the dinner happens later.

(2–3)

There is a confusing tedium to this story's iteration of phone calls and telegrams, and it is obviously this tedium upon which its comedic ambition is based, as this anecdote amuses only insofar as it demonstrates to excess its own lack of narrative interest. Yet we might also notice a preciousness to the story's pursuit of redundancy, for while it details an acceleration of social media I'm sure we believe we already know too well, I think Stein treasures each event of communication required to bring Hammett to the dinner table. The flat syntax and hurried rush of noun and verb suggest there is nothing really to hold the reader's attention, and it is almost maddening to work through the particulars of exactly the kind of story we might expect to have condensed into some far less cumbersome form. But what's perversely interesting about this story is the illogic that looms behind its tedium: why does Mrs. Ehrman know to call Hollywood once she is told that Hammett is in New York? and what exactly does that last sentence mean? what tense are we left in? what temporality is being narrated? This story is, after all, comedic in the grand sense as well: "The theme of the comic is the integration of society," Northrop Frye reminds us, but just what sort of society is integrated by this extravagance of phone calls breeding ever more phone calls, and increasingly unmanageable amounts of mediated language adding up to ever decreasing amounts of meaning?[60]

A high society is certainly one answer. We do not, after all, look to the world of celebrity for economic representations of poverty and lack. And in historical terms especially, this comedy of communication is marked with signs of class and cosmopolitan privilege that had not yet lost their novelty in 1930s America. The number of telephones actually declined slightly in the first years of the Depression, this according to *Communication Agencies and Social Life*, a 1933 report produced by the President's Research Committee on Social Trends, which also documents for the "average" American an interval of roughly one and a half days (four for long distance) between phone calls, and more than six months between telegrams.[61] Stein thus accounts for several months of communication in just a few minutes, and though I do not want to make too much of this sociological contrast, I think it safe to say that *Everybody's Autobiography* relishes its own peculiar class decadence. "Every class has its charm and that can do no harm as long as class has its charm," Stein writes later in the text; neither the sound of nursery rhyme nor the metaphysical caveat that follows, "and anybody is occupied with their own being," salvages such a statement, whose inconsiderate politics are mitigated only by their glibness (173).

When Stein returns to America in 1934–35, at a time when Depression-era iconography routinely equated impoverishment with technological antiquity, her complete fascination with a world where telegrams are dispatched without a second thought and the telephone rings constantly places her, as we shall see, in closer communication with Hollywood cinema than with any other cultural discourse of the period. The telephone was an essential emblem of class status and modernity, as Donald Albright has observed, whether on the desk of Jon Fredersen in Fritz Lang's *Metropolis* (1927) or on that of Larry Day, the absurdly wealthy stockbroker played by Douglas Fairbanks, Sr., in Edmund Goulding's previous film, *Reaching for the Moon* (1931)—his desk has sixteen phones on it, more than the entire lobby of Grand Hotel (fig. 2.6); and there are moments in the film when he "needs" each and every one, making deals with London and the Bourse, buying low and selling high, a manic vision of the economy that had been, until recently, doing big business. While it was certainly possible by the 1930s to treat the telephone as just another appliance in

FIGURE 2.6. Desk of Larry Day in *Reaching for the Moon* (MGM, 1931).

the standard American home, or as scenery around the office, it was also possible to make the telephone seem like a superlative necessity for those who make deals and live high—or must have dinner with Dashiell Hammett on a day's notice.[62]

Or, we might pursue another line of argument. That such scenes reference an iconography of class is still to insist on *reference* itself as a possibility under these conditions of rampant communication. As the camera cuts from phone booth to phone booth in *Grand Hotel*'s lobby, as Stein details the obscure signifying chain that finally brings her and Dashiell Hammett into actual contact, are we not witness to systems of media that serve no end so much as their own immense elaboration? Baudrillard makes what has become a common enough postmodern observation when he writes, "There is no longer any transcendence or depth, but only the immanent surface of operations unfolding, the smooth and functional surface of communication."[63] This seems to diagnose what we see in *Grand Hotel* and *Everybody's Autobiography*, because for all the noise of telephone calls and cameo appearances, there is also something relentlessly "functional" about these excesses of mediation itself, and even as we find ourselves increasingly unable to translate all these media events into a narrative or structure of reference, we also marvel at their uncanny fertility, the way each call breeds another call, each telegram breeds another telegram, and yet somehow the circuits of social life still manage to get closed, and thus Hammett shows up for dinner without ever knowing who invited him or why. What matters most, after all, about the telephone calls at the beginning of *Grand Hotel* is not who the characters are talking to on the other end of the line, but rather how their individual conversations talk to one another, establishing purely discursive relationships between these characters in advance of their later interactions in the real world. The film's two hours play out a game whose rules are established five minutes into the narrative, with all its subsequent combinations of star and plot already accounted for.[64]

In this regard, the scenes of communication I am describing look much like that depicted in an unlikely illustration of Baudrillard's point: Norman Rockwell's 1948 painting *The Gossips* (fig. 2.7). For all of Rockwell's obvious skill at representing physiognomy and affect, the fact remains that what this painting is about cannot be represented at all. The circuit of communication is perfectly and justly closed; "what goes around comes around" is no doubt this painting's homiletic teaching. Just *what* goes around, however, is irrelevant to the image. Rockwell's America has no shortage of juicy improprieties—perhaps a little drinking problem, some out-of-wedlock flirting at the ice cream social—and any of them might be captured in this image of transmission. That this image takes the form of a series of cameo portraits, disembodied profiles assembled in a montage of communicative action, suggests yet another aspect of its relevance to my discussion here. It is as if the very speed of the imaginary message demands that Rockwell start drawing the next figure before finishing the previous one, just as the pace of *Grand Hotel*'s editing finally overtakes the film's dialogue. And like the opening sequences of both *Grand Hotel* and *Everybody's Autobiography*, Rockwell's *Gossips* captures a network of total publicity that is both intimate and empty, a circuit that finally closes around nothing at all. More radically than Goulding or Stein, Rockwell presents us with an image of pure communication—pure, that is, because it is completely uncompromised by reference and takes place nowhere in the real world. Familiar as we all are with countless Rockwell images of small-town America, it is easy to imagine the shady streets, barbershops, coffee shops, and quaint kitchens where all these exchanges are happening, but it is precisely the absence of these spaces that makes this image so compelling. "The simulation of distance . . . between the two poles of the communication process is,"

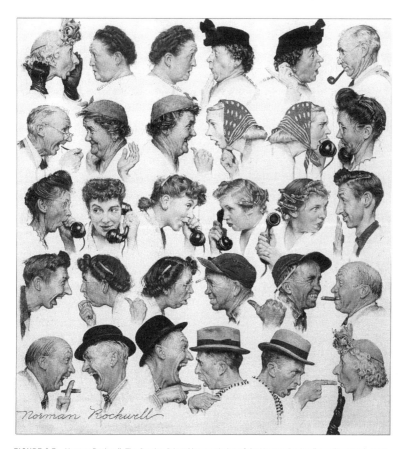

FIGURE 2.7. Norman Rockwell, *The Gossips*. Printed by permission of the Norman Rockwell Family Agency. Copyright © 1948 The Norman Rockwell Family Entities.

Baudrillard writes, "just a tactical hallucination. . . . 'Reality' has been analyzed into simple elements and recomposed into scenarios of regulated opposition" (142). Nothing could be "simpler" than a Norman Rockwell painting, especially one that depicts what is, after all, only the children's game of "telephone" at work in the world of adults. Yet this painting crystallizes one of the most radical conclusions we might draw from the scenes of communication that open both *Grand Hotel* and *Everybody's Autobiography*: that "communication" itself no longer exists to bear our representational burdens so much as we exist for its perpetuation—at whatever cost, and on terms we need not understand.

The Static of Sex

Stein concludes the introduction to *Everybody's Autobiography* by relating another anecdote of her newfound celebrity, though this second story aims at teaching a much different lesson about American fame and its consequences. Also different is the particular technology of fame at the heart of the matter. Stein's dinner with Hammett is the product of what we would now call "networking," a late-modern verb that was still almost exclusively a noun in the 1930s.[65] The introduction closes, however, with Stein offering one of literature's first accounts of the photo opportunity, a practice of celebrity that indexes fame's iconic dimensions just as surely as the noise of telephoning captures something of fame's extreme discursivity. What Stein makes clear at the beginning of *Everybody's Autobiography* is that being a celebrity demands a great deal of communication—both verbal and visual.

While in New York during the first weeks of her U.S. visit, Stein and Toklas are asked to a tea at which "a short little woman with a large head" is present, and also a woman to whom Stein pays little attention until someone informs her that she is Mary Pickford, "America's Sweetheart." "We were asked to meet each other, Mary Pickford and I," Stein writes, ". . . and then, I do not quite know how it happened, she said suppose we should be photographed together. Wonderful idea I said" (5). But as the story continues, Stein begins to understand that celebrity involves a subtle calibration of competing interests and desires for publicity. There is an economy of fame, a logic of supply and demand that keeps some stars apart even as it brings others together. Mary Pickford's cameo appearance becomes crucial for *Everybody's Autobiography* because it hints at this underlying economy, and also suggests that not "everybody" might want to have their picture taken with Gertrude Stein:

> It is funny about meeting and not meeting not that it makes any difference if you don't you don't if you do you do. Nathalie Barney was just telling me that her mother often asked her to come in and meet Whistler. Even if you do not care about his pictures he will amuse you, she said, but Nathalie Barney was always busy writing a letter whenever her mother happened to ask her and so she never met him. Mary Pickford said it would be easy to get the Journal photographer to come over, yes I will telephone said some one rushing off, yes I said it would be wonderful we might be taken shaking hands. You are not going to do it, said Belle Greene excitedly behind me,

of course I am going to I said, nothing would please me better of course we are said I turning to Mary Pickford, Mary Pickford said perhaps I will not be able to stay and she began to back away, Oh yes you must I said I will not be long now, no no she said I think I had better not and she melted away. I knew you would not do it, said Belle Greene behind me. And then I asked every one because I was interested just what it was that went on inside Mary Pickford. It was her idea and then when I was enthusiastic she melted away. They all said that what she thought was if I were enthusiastic it meant that I thought it would do me more good than it would do her and so she melted away or others said perhaps after all it would not be good for her audience that we should be photographed together, anyway I was very much interested to know just what they know about what is good publicity and what is not. (5–6)

There is of course no way to know just what's happening "inside" Mary Pickford as she decides against a photograph with Gertrude Stein. The collective wisdom of those at the scene articulates a sort of second law of thermodynamics for the rich and famous, making any net gain for Stein necessarily a net loss from whatever publicity Pickford might garner. We might also pursue another explanation, one that takes special notice of Nathalie Barney's mention here and questions whether something about the sexuality of Stein's modernity contributes to Pickford's concerns that the association "would not be good for her audience." Barney, after all, was a significantly more notorious lesbian than Stein, having been memorialized in a 1914 book entitled *Letters to an Amazon* and having long presided over a Parisian salon that easily rivaled the artistic and literary glamour of 27 Rue de Fleurus. That Barney's lone cameo appearance in *Everybody's Autobiography* occurs in such close proximity to Pickford's vague discomfort is hardly conclusive, but it is certainly curious, which is how Stein's sexuality seems to figure for many while she is on tour in the United States. The indirect communication—or better, direct miscommunication—of her homosexuality is very much the point of a headline like "Gertrude Stein, Not a Freak, Limits Her Audiences to Five Hundred," an announcement made by the *New York Herald Tribune* on October 29, 1934, about a sold-out lecture. As Terry Castle notes, "freak" was one of several words used from the eighteenth century forward to disclose lesbian identity without saying it out loud, and while references to Stein's linguistic eccentricity often trafficked in a vocabulary of the weird ("the babblings of the insane," according to one article in the *New York Times*), the play of sexual innuendo strikes me as highly intentional here, especially in relation to other press coverage from the period.[66] "'Yes, I Am Married,' Says Gertrude Stein," according to a *New York Herald Tribune* story on May 13, 1935. Perhaps playing off Stein's own teasing approach toward Toklas's de facto married status in *The Autobiography*—*Wives of Geniuses I Have Sat With* reads one alternate title weighed at the end of the narrative—Stein's immediate qualification, "I mean I am married to America, it is so beautiful," only accentuates the sexual indeterminacy that surrounds the relationship between Stein and Toklas in the public imagination of the period. "Has Gertrude Stein a Secret?" asks B. F. Skinner in the pages of the *Atlantic* in 1934. The ostensible subject of his investigation into what he calls her "true second personality" is not her sexual identity but rather her early exposure to automatic writing while a psychology student at Harvard. Gertrude Stein most definitely has a secret: that she authored, along with Leon M. Solomon, a scientific paper titled "Normal Motor Automatism." This is hardly the stuff of which pornography is made, and there is little titillation to be had from exposing Stein as—what else?—a former medical student; but on another level, what matters more is that something about Stein encouraged this flirtation with her homosexuality even as it remained ostentatiously undisclosed by the abundant references to her "mannish" attire and her affection for her secretary and "traveling companion," whom Stein sometimes calls "Pussy," according to one newspaper article.[67] Has Gertrude Stein a secret? The answer is of course "yes" and by the way, it's not about sex.

The question in which I am interested, however, does not concern our knowledge about Stein's sexuality—what did Mary Pickford know and when did she know it?—so much as it concerns the means by which knowing sex is transposed into a question concerning communication itself. I could pursue this line of argument on largely theoretical grounds, revisiting "the epistemology of the closet" and the "open secret" of homosexuality in modern culture, or Castle's departure from each.[68] But what continues to surprise me is that I don't have to: the communication of sexuality and desire is in fact an explicit concern of both *Everybody's Autobiography* and *Grand Hotel*, and both texts are determined to make the noises of sex as loudly as possible while demurring from any representations of sex as such, a strategy of oddly carnal reticence that depends, somewhat perversely, on telephones on the one hand and dogs on the other. This is not to say that either telephones or dogs function as mere indexes of lesbian sexuality; the circuits of suggestion and intimation that link dogs, telephones, and sex are rather far from direct, and it is the excessive verbosity of such a mimetic circuitry that seems finally to make it so appealing to all involved.

Consider the following sequence of events concerning Stein's servant, an "Indo-Chinaman" named Trac. By this point in *Everybody's Autobiography* Stein has made a kind of Orientalism into a repeated motif, around which various attitudes toward race and identity coalesce, though this is a matter that warrants a full discussion at some later time.[69] I want to focus instead on the way Stein suspends the sex of Trac's object of desire within a flurry of media and communication (in its older sense as well, signifying physical transit and not just the exchange of information):

> Trac did not go out in the evening, that is to say he did not like to go out in the evening because if he did it might be frightening and he began to talk about everything. . . . And then he began to talk about having a comrade with him. Yes we said. But will he come, well no said Trac he will not not when I tell him how it is about not going out, yes but when there are two of you you can go out we said well anyway said Trac it is very distracting and I do not work well when I am distracted, yes we said but you said you would, yes he said well I will write to my comrade again.
>
> Three days after he announced the comrade was coming. That is fine we said to tell him to telegraph the train by which he is leaving and we will go and call for him we said. Yes said Trac here is the letter. Yes we said but this is written by a Frenchwoman she is writing for him, no said Trac that is the comrade, what said we, yes said Trac that is the comrade, what said we, yes said Trac that is the comrade. Oh no we said not at all, and I said, if I want a Frenchwoman I will choose her, not for me said Trac, no I said no you have to telegraph her off I said, it is too late said Trac she has her ticket, well telegraph it off we said, I have no address says Trac besides she has started. Well I said come on we will meet her and Trac and I went to meet her. We met her. She was the largest fattest Bretonne I have ever seen and dear me. Well there we were. (164–165)

To say that this is all "very distracting" is, I think, to speak directly to what matters most here. Earlier in *Everybody's Autobiography* Stein writes, "A distraction is to avoid the consciousness of the passage of time" (61), but clearly what is avoided in this passage is the gender of Trac's "comrade," and among the letters, telegrams, and arriving trains, it is difficult to know just who wants a French-woman and who, if anyone, will pick her out. The reader, like Stein herself, expects Trac to be bringing a man home: the heterosexual option here is the altogether perverse one. But Stein's characteristic parataxis allows for, and perhaps actively demands, a great deal of misinterpretation, as ever more information is relayed by syntactic inversions and the same pronouns are repeated without regard for their antecedents. While some sense of the normal order of things—in terms of sex, if not exactly ethnicity—returns when all this communication comes to an end, we are still left with the impression that the speed at which modern life is lived can breed a certain promiscuity, a sexual energy that cannot be fully con-tained because it is always in communication, somewhere in the wires and all the mediated language that they carry back and forth. The mediated character of modernity, simply put, makes for strange bedfellows—never mind sexuality.[70]

I want to make an explicit comparison between this moment in *Everybody's Autobiography* and one of the most memorable sequences in *Grand Hotel*, again not because any direct influence is likely, but rather because the sheer coinci-dence of certain devices, technically speaking, illuminates something crucial about the mediated life that both texts describe. I am thinking of a sequence near the end of the film that brings several plot lines to a dark culmination by connecting them to one another by means of the telephone. Garbo's last scene in *Grand Hotel* (save a few seconds that show her final departure from the ho-tel) takes place immediately after Preysing has killed Baron von Geigern, hav-ing caught the genteel thief in the act of stealing from his suite. This scene is morbidly concerned with the telephone as well: Preysing beats von Geigern to death with a telephone, and the reaction to the crime is registered immedi-ately by the hotel's switchboard operator, herself a witness to the crime over the open phone line. When the film then cuts to Grusinskaya's suite for Garbo's last scene, the telephone remains an overdetermined presence in the narrative. The essence of the scene is that Grusinskaya is completely ignorant of her lover's death by telephone, and this point is made clear with truly melodramatic re-dundancy. Garbo first notes, "The music has stopped." She pauses, then adds, "How quiet it is tonight! It was never so quiet in the Grand Hotel." Still deter-mined to communicate its irony, the film next has Garbo turn to a large bou-quet and observe, "Those flowers . . . make me think of funerals." It is now that she picks up the phone and asks to be connected with Baron von Geigern. The next shot cuts to a dimly lit interior, a ringing phone, and the Baron's dachs-hund alone on the bed, craning its neck toward the phone, which will, alas,

FIGURE 2.8. Greta Garbo on the telephone, *Grand Hotel* (MGM, 1932).

never be answered. We cut back to Garbo as she responds to the voice of the operator (though we do not hear it ourselves): "Well, keep ringing. He must be asleep." What is striking about Garbo's monologue from this moment until its conclusion is that it is not, technically speaking, the soliloquy it sets out to be. Garbo hums. She pleads to the telephone, "Come and fetch me, *mon cheri*, I'm longing for you. I haven't been asleep." She takes the phone from her face and cradles it like a baby, like her lover's head, like an object that has been invested by cathexis with a wild surplus of longing and desire (fig. 2.8). "I kept thinking that you, that you might come to me," she says. All this lover's discourse pours out to the lover who can no longer hear it, which is not at all to say that no one is listening. For Garbo's next line is another answer to the silent interruption of the operator: "But he must answer. Ring . . . ring . . . ring! Oh *cheri*, why don't you answer the phone please?" And after another short pause, Garbo again instructs the operator, "Yes, yes, yes. Ring, ring." Twice then, we are reminded that Garbo's monologue is also dialogue, surreptitious and overheard by the operator, whose vantage is both quietly instrumental and deeply voyeuristic, and in this latter regard, whoever she is, she listens in much the same way we do in the audience—not just hearing Garbo as she makes love through—and to—the telephone, but *overhearing* her.

The caption beneath this image of Garbo on the phone, taken from an "official" 1980 MGM biography, reads more suggestively than anything I would dare invent to describe this scene's implications for *Everybody's Autobiography*: "She related to objects so magically that leading men were often not missed. In *Grand Hotel*, Garbo's best love scene was played to a telephone."[71] It would be surprising to find any reactions from the actual time of the film's release that were so forthright with their innuendo, but this should not cause us to discount the possibility that at least some in the audience took note that Garbo was, however vicariously, making love to a woman on-screen for one of the few times in her career. That this erotic exchange also depends entirely upon the technology that keeps this other woman off-screen is the aspect of this sequence I want most to emphasize: the telephone represents a whole matrix of sexual possibility that any contact in the flesh must necessarily terminate, and so in a very strange way, the hint of something lesbian here is perhaps less troublesome than what is offered by the joke that gets this hint across, namely the possibility that no one person might be as desirable as the elaborate network of devices and discourse that takes his—or her or their or our—place. "I want to be alone," Garbo's signature declaration of erotic inaccessibility, takes on a different meaning altogether in the age of the telephone, when isolation itself becomes a state of intense arousal and promiscuous connectedness.[72] What informs a great many narratives of mediated desire—whether concerning the telephone, or as we have seen, the telegraph—is the stubborn indeterminacy of that "you" who is wanted on the other end of the line. There is an exquisite degree of communicational malfunction at work in both the low comedy of Trac's surprising romance and the high melodrama of Madame Grusinskaya's misdirected wooing; one might even say that "perverted" is just the right word for how these messages are interrupted, rendered somehow wayward, left unanswered, and ultimately relayed to "wrong numbers." At the same time, to speak as Ellis Hanson does of "the telephone and its queerness" is to imagine a sexualization of technology that is considerably too precise for either *Grand Hotel* or *Everybody's Autobiography*, at least so far as the story of Trac's long-distance, and then troublesomely present, "comrade" is concerned. Sex of any kind—between men, women, or men and women—would close the circuit, threatening the very field of sexual possibility that remains open so long as sex itself remains an impossibility. The price of the medium, to return to McLuhan, is the massage—the embodied, the sensual, the physically material.

FIGURE 2.9. Francis Barraud, *His Master's Voice*, 1899.

Yet something of the carnal does inhere in these frantically mediated sexual encounters, and I think it might best be pinned down by recalling for a moment the performance of the only other actor to appear on-screen during this sequence of *Grand Hotel*, and that's the Baron's dog, Adolphus. Simply put, there is a direct connection between the carnal and the canine at this point in the film, and this emblematic relationship emerges with even greater force in *Everybody's Autobiography*. For the dog's symbolic function throughout *Grand Hotel*, as a conventional sign of the Baron's deep goodness despite his compromising choice of profession, also indexes, albeit fleetingly, one of the most pervasive icons of the period. Why a dog here? And why a dog in *Grand Hotel*, where any and all relations are subject to the deadly interference of speed, money, and technology? Perhaps there is a more than distant relation between Adolphus and Nipper, the famous "Victor Dog" of Francis Barraud's 1899 painting, which subsequently became the trademark image of the Gramophone Company and later the exclusive property of RCA (fig. 2.9). As Michael Taussig has argued, this image seeks to codify and memorialize a notion of "fidelity" in several senses of the term, both as a characteristic of the phonograph and its "mimetic superpower" and as a moral sentiment, an encompassing "loyalty" that will persist no matter how confounded by new technologies of the virtual and the simulated.[73] The sentimentality of this picture, alternatively known by the title

"His Master's Voice," is more than matched by its modernity; for even as Nipper provides a deeply comforting image of technology's new subject, the phonograph at which he puzzles is the occasion for a series of questions that the image itself does not answer, not the least of which concerns the fate of the master whose "voice" the picture names but of course cannot make visible. Whether a record of the dead, or of the merely absent, the voice of the phonograph speaks from a position of great loss: the original Nipper belonged to the artist's dead brother. It is in this regard especially that Adolphus shares a curious and melancholic kinship with the "Victor Dog." Nipper answers to a machine as if it were its master; Adolphus turns to the phone as if it were the Baron; and on the other end of the line, Garbo seduces the phone as if it were her lover. All three look to the "magic" of technology to compensate for the man they miss, which is not the same thing at all as the man they *need*. Whatever consummation—of heterosexual desire, of marriage plot—this dachshund's cameo appearance marks as impossible, Adolphus also signals a new series of erotic possibilities, of connections that Grusinskaya might not have chosen for herself but that, as Garbo's performance makes memorably clear (one must simply hear her plead with the telephone, "Ring . . . Ring . . . Ring!"), are exploited with considerable emotive hyperbole. A bizarre love triangle indeed emerges between Garbo, a telephone, and a dachshund: human, machine, and animal in a single, inoperable circuit of sexualized communication, each imparting a fetishized functionality upon the next point in the relay—Adolphus in place of narrative and sexual closure, the telephone in place of the absent male lover, the operator's voice in place of the audience, and the whole complicated network of desire and displacement beggaring by comparison any "love scene" between Garbo and Barrymore that a different ending would allow. There is, to put the matter simply, a lot more desire to go around when all it *can* do is go around.

A constant refrain throughout Stein's writings of the later 1930s, in both *Everybody's Autobiography* and *The Geographical History of America* (1936), is the crisis of identity she registers with every repetition of the sentence "I am because my little dog knows me."[74] The accumulated force of this oddly sentimental, ontological declaration as it resonates through Stein's writing suggests another unexpected coincidence with *Grand Hotel*. And accumulate it does: "I am I because my little dog knows me" begins the play "The Question of Identity" in *The Geographical History of America* (99); later in the play, the relationship is complicated—"I am I because my little dog knows me, even if the little dog is a big one"—but the basic terms that relate identity remain unchanged;

and near the end of *The Geographical History*, Stein borrows the language of a children's song, as if to stress the dramatic simplicity of her dilemma: "The person and the dog are there and the dog is there and the person is there," Stein writes, "and where oh where is their identity" (234). The very popularity she enjoys after the publication of *The Autobiography* is widely considered to have initiated Stein's identity troubles, and while recent critics, such as Charles Bernstein, have looked elsewhere, to "Stein's triple distance from the ascendant culture (gender, sexual orientation, ethnicity)," in search of ways to understand "I am because my little dog knows me," *Everybody's Autobiography* offers strong evidence that this sentence and its many variations address more particular problems of fame, publicity, and a new economy of writing.[75]

Recall that Stein's first act of popular, and thus financial, success is to purchase a coat and two collars for Basket (a white poodle named for a similar dog in James's *The Princess Casamassima*) (41). Stein's first moment of anxiety about success is similarly triangulated by reference to her poodle; thus just a few pages later, she writes, "It is funny about money. And it is funny about identity. You are because your little dog knows you, but when your public knows you and does want to pay for you and when your public knows you and does not want to pay for you, you are not the same you" (46). There is an instant of hesitation when the hint of chiasmus suspends her identity, along with "you" her reader, amid dog and public, money and no money. This grammatical travesty of cause-and-effect logic—who exactly is it that pays for "I" the reader? what public knows "me" in the privacy I share only with the book itself?—is pursued with even more gusto later. "I had always been I because I had words that had to be written inside me," Stein insists, "and now any word I had inside could be spoken it did not need to be written. I am I because my little dog knows me. But was I I when I had no written word inside me" (66). The spoken—a category that Stein extends to include the newspaper—is language without resistance, "and so writing naturally needs more refusing" (48). But was Stein Stein without writing, with reporters hanging on her every spoken word? Such grammar provides an excess of "refusing," performing the writerly resistance to too easy representation that Stein worries over in the aftermath of her fame. What such a performance does not provide, however, is an answer to the very question it poses, for this kind of language, as Bernstein rightly concludes, is more concerned with "holding off naming to see what otherwise emerges" than with making some stable determination of what "identity" is and what dogs have to do with it.[76] The dog in all these formulations is a figure of indeterminate yet absolutely essential feedback, placing one effect of identity—"I am"—in communication with a cause that causes nothing, even as it displaces questions of identity onto questions of relation—"because my little dog knows me." It is not so much *what* the little dog knows—who can know, after all?—but *that* it knows, that allows Stein to change the rules of the game. "But we we in America are not displaced by a dog," Stein writes in *The Geographical History*, "no no not at all not at all displaced by a dog" (100). But "displaced by a dog" is exactly what Stein is in America, her hesitating disavowals notwithstanding, and it is this way of being displaced that gives Stein a language capable of simultaneously deferring from, and referring to, the phenomenon of celebrity, as an experience of language, of class, of publicity, and eminently one of mediation. Like Adolphus in *Grand Hotel*, Stein's "little dog" also has some bearing on knowledge of a more intimate sort.

"Everything changes," Stein notes soon after the telephone is installed at 27 Rue de Fleurus and the summer house in Bilingnin. "I had never had any life with dogs and now I had more life with dogs than with any one" (49). This is, on the one hand, a simple statement of biographical fact: having purchased Basket in 1929, Francis Picabia gives Toklas and Stein a chihuahua, which they name Pépé (a perhaps impolitic nod to its imagined ethnicity). But on the other hand, Stein and Toklas's "life with dogs" is a sly suggestion of the domestic itself, a way of acknowledging "community property" and putting on display an erotic relationship that was otherwise unrepresentable. I confess that I am taking some license here, and perhaps reading too much into the accompanying details of Stein and Toklas's daily existence. Yet isn't there a difference between an image like the Man Ray photograph that serves as the frontispiece to the first edition of *The Autobiography* (fig. 2.3) and this Cecil Beaton photograph from 1938 (fig. 2.10)? and isn't it the dog that makes this difference especially telling? Around 1934 we see a marked shift toward pictures of Stein, Toklas, and their dog(s); a 1994 visual biography of Stein features half a dozen such images, none of which date from the period between 1929 and 1934, even though Basket was an available prop during those years as well.[77] As oblique family portraits, images like these evidence, at the very least, a willingness to play with an iconography of domestic intimacy that seems not to have been so appealing just a few years earlier. As suggestively as any buzz of innuendo surrounding Stein and Toklas in U.S. press coverage of their lives and travels, a "life with dogs" discloses their mediated partnership and shared affection; that these are not particularly brazen aspects of homosexuality in no way delimits their sly refashioning of

FIGURE 2.10. Cecil Beaton, "Gertrude Stein and Alice B. Toklas," 1936. Courtesy of the Cecil Beaton Studio Archive at Sotheby's.

the utterly normative—a "life with dogs"—as the potentially curious. As critics have been pointing out, Stein did pursue a variety of strategies for the representation of sexuality throughout her career, most notably in texts such as the early novel (later published as) *Q.E.D.* or in poems such as "Lifting Belly." What we see in images like this Beaton photograph, and read in Stein's constant references to the dog's life, testifies to a much different representational strategy that falls just short of reference to a space of privacy that may, or just as well may not, hold sexuality as its defining secret. In this regard, the sense of a formal interiority that one gets from Beaton's photograph is revealing in exactly the degree to which it is the opposite of risqué. Framed on its left edge by one opened door, with Stein standing before another in the right middle ground and Toklas sitting in the far depths of the image past still one more threshold, the photograph establishes both a thematics of entrance into closed interiors and an overwhelming formal insistence on classical perspective, enforcing a strict geometry toward the vanishing point of Toklas herself, strikingly illuminated and captured with great depth of field. Stein offers more resistance to our inward scrutiny than does Basket, who seems not so much a Cerberus in lamb's wool, on guard against deeper penetration, but rather on par with Toklas, matched in their shared diminution in respect to Gertrude Stein. What might Stein's gesture of discipline be preventing? Is Basket about to leap up with affection, obscuring Toklas from view entirely and thus ruining the picture? Or is he instead being kept in place, ensuring that the whole "family" is arranged just so for the camera? This captured moment of drama between Stein and Basket, whatever its irrecoverable meaning, also has the effect of keeping us, as viewers, in our place: we enter the recesses of the image solely on Stein's own authority, though to what end that authority is directed only her little dog knows. Toklas is demurely situated in anticipation of some "wives of genius" to sit with, while Stein commands not only the family dog but also the viewer's access to the private confines of the home. Yet even this rather conservative reading of the image (of somewhat limited biographical accuracy, too) unleashes, as I ruefully might put it, the possibility of a domesticity entirely between women, and an equivalent of marriage in which the "man of the house" is a strictly performative role, a fiction of gender that anybody, or better still, "everybody," can effect.

Given the utter impossibility of any physical intimacy between Stein and Toklas as they are represented in this picture—indeed, Toklas is so thoroughly distanced here that at first glance she could be mistaken for a child—I am tempted to argue that the price to be paid for any imagining of same-sex domesticity is the comprehensive repression of the sexual. That Basket is so sternly kept down suggests that there is little chance of opening the door and catching sight of some unexpected show of compromising, carnal animality. But I would not want to go so far as to accuse this image of telling what Catharine R. Stimpson calls the "lesbian lie," the politically fraught untruth "that no lesbians lie abed here," which Stimpson insists must be read *through* before any sense can be made of Stein's more popular writings of the 1930s.[78] The semiotic function of dogs in and around *Everybody's Autobiography* is no more or less sexually misleading than a remarkable bit of euphemism we find at the end of *The Thin Man* (1934), the very film, coincidentally enough, that is being made from Dashiell Hammett's best-selling detective fiction when he makes his crucial cameo appearance in Stein's narrative of her American tour. For not only does the film version of *The Thin Man* employ the telephone throughout as the only visible sign of the eponymous figure at the center of all the mystery, intrigue, martinis, and *entendre*; it also concludes with a scene of considerable interest in light of Stein's life of publicity as a "life with dogs." Nick and Nora Charles, played by William Powell and Myrna Loy, retire to their sleeping compartment aboard the cross-country train on which they're bound for California. Nora instructs Nick to put their terrier, Asta, in bed with her; Nick has different arrangements in mind, and with a caddish "Oh yeah?" throws Asta on the top bunk, where he paces back and forth for a few frames before he lies down and covers his eyes with his paws in a gesture of effectively pornographic propriety. (Cut to a shot of the speeding train as the music swells for the closing credits: "California, Here I Come.") In the aftermath of the Hollywood Production Code, sex of any kind was subject to new protocols for on-screen representation, and even the hint of a wholly normative coupling between man and wife thus demanded a circuitous symbology, decorous and yet transparently suggestive of exactly the sex that so insistently was not being shown.

It is guesswork on my part to wonder if *The Thin Man* actually informed *Everybody's Autobiography*, though Stein does carry on a running discussion of detective fiction and Dashiell Hammett throughout the book, and she had just completed *Blood on the Dining Room Floor*, her own peculiar contribution to the genre. That said, the connection is worth pursuing a bit further. Because there is clearly no "heterosexual lie" upon which *The Thin Man* depends; the dog does not represent the obliteration of sex so much as its translation into a more arcane symbolic language, one more mediated but hardly bent on the epistemological denial of what's going on in the bunk below. Asta chastely covers his eyes precisely because he knows, which is as much for the text to admit that we know too as we watch from our considerably less intimate vantage point. What Basket knows is a problem of considerably greater elusiveness, and I am not suggesting that Stein's repeated references to dogs in and around *Everybody's Autobiography* indicate a simple structure of displacement undone with a single interpretive gesture. "I am because my little dog knows me" neither announces out loud nor secretes away the truth of Stein's sexual identity, but rather communicates that identity in much the same way that the telephone communicates her social identity as a celebrity or her economic identity as a best-selling author: with a great deal of interference.

There is just one instant of raw, unmediated connection in *Everybody's Autobiography*, and Stein's representation of this encounter says much about the strange publicity of sex in a culture that is saturated with media. Stein describes an incident between two dogs that seems to beg the question of just what must be repressed in the making of a public "Gertrude Stein," but as this question shades almost imperceptibly into one about technologies of representation, it becomes clear that a "life with dogs" is no alternative to the mediated life of fame and celebrity. The unknowable interiorities that are signified by all these little dogs are always in communication with the outside world. As early as 1913, in *A Long Gay Book* (published in 1933), Stein had claimed that "a life which is private is not what there is."[79] But even if private life *isn't*, perhaps the exposure of one's privacy may still be limited to nothing more than the occasional and fleeting cameo appearance, such as that which punctuates the passage below. To prevent the thread of the narrative from becoming lost—a situation practically guaranteed by Stein's narration—let me say up front that the story involves Stein and Toklas trying to get to Chicago in time to see an opera. "If things do not take long," Stein begins aphoristically, "it makes life too short." She continues in the next paragraph:

> They telephoned there is plenty of time if you come by airplane. Of course we could not do that we telephoned back, why not, they said, because we never have we said, we will pay for your trip the two of you forward and back they said, we want to see the opera we said but we are afraid. Carl Van Vechten was there while all this was going on, what is it, we explained, oh nonsense he said of course you will fly, we telephoned back we will pay for the three of you. All right we said and we had to do it. Everybody is afraid but some are more afraid then others. Everything can scare me but most of the things that are frightening are things that I can do without and really mostly useless unless they happen to come unexpectedly do not frighten me. . . . I told all this to Carl and he said I am coming and so we did not think about it again. We went on doing what we were doing and then one day we were to meet Carl and fly and we did very high. It was nice. I know of nothing more pleasing more soothing more beguiling than the slow hum of the mounting. I had never even seen an airplane near before not near

enough to know how one got in and there we were in. That is one of the
nice things about never going to the movies there are so many surprises. Of
course you remember something, two little terriers that belong to Georges
Maratier began fighting their servant had been visiting her uncle who is our
concierge and the two of them a wire-haired and a black Scottie both fe-
males they should not but they do were holding each other in a terrifying
embrace. The girl came and called me, people always think that I can do
something, anyway as I went out I always go out when I am called I remembered I had never been near a dog fight before I remembered in the books
you pour water on them so I called for cold water in a basin and poured it
on them and it separated them. The white one was terribly bitten. Reading
does not destroy surprise it is all a surprise that it happens as they say it will
happen. But about the airplane . . . we liked it and whenever we could we did
it. They are now beginning to suppress the noise and that is a pity, it will be
too bad if they can have a conversation, it will be a pity. (195–196)

Here we witness a still more perverse coupling of dogs and telephones. This
highly impacted sequence of narrative, which begins with a now familiar scene
of communication, is all but overwhelmed by whatever it is that takes place
between those two female dogs, "holding each other in a terrifying embrace":
"they should not but they do." To remark, blandly and without affect, that "of
course you remember something," and then to illustrate the axiom by remembering *this* of all things, suggests the manifestation of a sexual unconscious that
has been all but banished from the surface of the text itself, as if only by means
of this seemingly random act of memory can Stein let us know what all the
text's "little dogs" have known from the beginning; that even the young girl on
the scene assumes Stein's familiarity with such erotic violence further adds to
the sense of overdetermination, to the sense that here is something startling
and revelatory about Stein and sex—much has been made, after all, from moments in Henry James and others that are altogether less "bestial" and pornographic than this.[80] Yet there is also a deliberateness to the choreography of this
passage's shock effects that brings to mind a different mediating context for the
significance of this sexualized outburst, which strikes me as having more to
do with the throwaway reference to cinema than might be guessed. For Stein's
passing comment about never "going to the movies" and the "nice things" that
result does manage to imply a sort of reverse phenomenology of surprise as a
basic provision of film experience. What Stein in effect describes is a particular

susceptibility to being astonished that survives only so long as the movies are avoided, or phrased another way, a mental conditioning provided for by film that accommodates us to modern life, circumscribing our psychic exposure to a new concentration of traumas, spectacles, and violent stimuli.

The "two little terriers" whose frenzy of bodily contact Stein so inexplicably remembers are, I admit, about the last things that would seem to "correspond to profound changes" in the modern subject's sensory field; but there they are, making a tremendous spectacle of themselves, and right in the middle of a passage where such notable icons of the modern as airplanes and telephones barely register in comparison.[81] The exchange of telephone calls about the trip to Chicago, for instance, marks the twelfth or thirteenth appearance of this very set piece, with each recapitulation further quieting the noisy strangeness of the new communicative environment of celebrity that Stein enters at the beginning of the text. The possibilities of electrical media are treated here as simple conventions for the representation of reported dialogue, as if "we telephoned" carried the exact semantic weight of "we said." And of course it shouldn't: the whole point of the passage is that time and space have, in fact, been annihilated according to program, that *now* "there is plenty of time" in America, because communication by telephone and airplane indicate a new temporality that might not make sense, but doesn't appear too disturbing for all the disjuncture it involves. The bland, all-purpose adjective "nice" defines the three-word sentence that encapsulates Stein's first experience of flight. This suggests an amenable modernity, at least until the movies are mentioned and the narrative abandons its own "slow hum" for a violent memory.

Stein has almost nothing kind to say about the movies in her account of the very tour on which she repeatedly proclaimed their historical significance. Thus, in "Portraits and Repetition," one of her public talks from 1934–35, Stein says that "funnily enough the cinema has offered a solution" to the demands of a modernist portraiture by combining seriality and singularity in the same technology of representation; but in *Everybody's Autobiography*, the cinema figures more as problem than "solution," and the trouble involves what Stein describes as a new kind of publicity to everyday life in the cinematic America she observes. Writing of "the wooden houses of America," Stein notes that "less and less there are curtain and shutters on the windows ... and that worried me"; she then goes on to draw a much larger conclusion about how open windows make good neighbors in America, whether you want them or not, since "as everybody is a public something and anybody can know anything about any one and can know any one then why shut the shutters and the curtains and keep any one from seeing, they all know what they are going to see so why look" (189). Stein's logic here seems to assume a social network of universal surveillance, with the power to look so democratically distributed that nobody, as Stein might say, needs to exercise it because "everybody" else, in their transparent homes, has already made sure that there will be nothing to see. Yet Stein also evokes something of the relational identity she formulates around the little dog who knows her, except in this case, the other one who knows who makes us what we are implies a self of maximum publicity, not indeterminate privacy. And when Stein returns to the subject of domestic space in America just a few pages later, she argues that this social visibility is a patently cinematic condition: "In America they want to make everything something anybody can see by looking. That is very interesting, that is the reason there are no fences in between no walls to hide anything no curtains to cover anything and the cinema that can make anything be anything anybody can see by looking" (202). And when confronted with her own spectacular image on-screen, Stein retreats with just the slightest hint of an anti-modernism that we rather might expect of Henry James or Henry Adams: "I saw myself almost as large and moving around and talking I did not like it particularly the talking, it gave me a very funny feeling and I did not like that funny feeling. I suppose if I had seen it often it would have been like anything you can get used to anything if it happens often but that time I certainly did not like it and so when the Warners asked us to come and lunch we did not go" (288–299).

Stein's discomfort here with what she was simultaneously declaring to be the representative medium of her period indicates an inconsistency in her position, a blind spot, quite literally, where the cinematic modernity that she imagines is finally reckoned against her having almost no firsthand experience of the movies. We might well expect this moment to ratify the fantasy of celebrity that Stein indulged in *Photograph*, a 1920 play that also considers the question of a mechanically reproduced self, but at a moment of relative obscurity in Stein's career. "For a photograph we need a wall," the text begins, "Star gazing. / Photographs are small. They reproduce well. / I enlarge better."[82] But perhaps by the time of *Everybody's Autobiography*, Stein has learned that publicity is governed by a different genius, and so she tells Charlie Chaplin, of all people, that "having a small audience not a big one" is what has produced, perversely enough, her amazing popularity in America (292). Thus the very magnitude of cinematic exposure threatens to violate this principle of the market, potentially delivering to Stein an audience so sizable that it could leave her without "publicity" altogether.

Or, what finally gives Stein a "funny feeling" about the movies might be the threat of exposure of a wholly different kind. For there is still that inexplicable cut in the narrative from the shock effects of film to the little terriers of Georges Maratier; the conceit of a syntactic connection between the two ("of course you remember something . . .) resolves nothing, and though the dialectical image of "the movies" juxtaposed with the erotic is certainly suggestive, I hesitate to call it decodable, much less transparent—like the houses of America—in making visible a sexuality that Stein wants to keep inside but that film itself somehow forces out. The representations of mediated sexuality in Stein's texts of the 1930s defy such gothic alternatives, such logics of *either* repression *or* unconscious revelation. "I am because my little dog knows me" implies nothing so much as a zone of privacy within the language of identity, a way of showing who you are without saying what you are. Language, simply put, is the technology that allows Stein and Toklas to make little more than cameo appearances in the very texts in which they star. Bennett Cerf, Stein's chief promoter at Random House, didn't know how much he was saying when he called her "the publicity hound of the world."

Gertrude Stein Superstar

The cultural circuitry that this chapter has described can be closed, at least for the time being, thanks to a last series of coincidences that occasion a cameo appearance by Garbo herself in the larger drama of celebrity that surrounds Gertrude Stein for the rest of her career, and continues to affect her reputation right down to the present day. Writing to Carl Van Vechten in the winter of 1940, with the German occupation of Paris a little more than three months away, Stein confesses that she would like to make another trip to America, though not for just any reason, and certainly not to escape the threat of war. What looms between Stein and America is the prospect of a second lecture tour, both an absolute necessity if she and Toklas are to pay their own way and also the less desirable by far when weighed against Stein's "dream that Hollywood might do the Autobiography of Alice Toklas [*sic*]":

> I would like to go over but to lecture three or four times a week for a number of weeks does not really seem to me as if I would like it, of course we cannot go over without making money and there it is, . . . they could make a very good film out of [*The Autobiography*] and then they would pay us

large moneys to go out and sit and consult and that would be all new and I would like that.[83]

The dream of "large moneys" for small labors in Hollywood is hardly Stein's invention. It is, however, a fantasy that rarely plays out in the mythology of the movie business, sometimes carrying a lucky actor to stardom, but often involving the author who risks Hollywood—in *What Makes Sammy Run?* (1941) and *The Last Tycoon* (1941), in *Sunset Boulevard* (1950) and *In a Lonely Place* (1950), in *The Player* and *Barton Fink* (1991)—in rather more harrowing and even fatal plots; "the death of the author" is a worn-out conceit in Hollywood, just another slightly stale "high concept" long before it takes the academy (ours, as opposed to the one that gives out Oscars) by storm. But this has nothing to do with what worries Van Vechten when he answers Stein a few weeks later. His enthusiasm, as it was regarding almost anything Stein proposed, was flamboyantly whole-hearted. "I talked to Bennett [Cerf] about the motion picture possibilities of *The Autobiography*," he writes, "which are ENORMOUS, but motion picture people are peculiar. You can't approach *them*. They must approach *you*. I think the time to take this up is when you are lecturing in Hollywood" (670). Thus Van Vechten assumes the rhetoric of both adoring fan and Hollywood insider, relating the rules of the game and the "peculiar" anthropology of the deal, what Stein should and shouldn't expect along the way to seeing a film version of *The Autobiography of Alice B. Toklas* become a reality. "Of course you would have to appear in the picture," Van Vechten adds, as if offering just another piece of knowing advice. "Even Greta Garbo and Lillian Gish couldn't be you and Alice" (670).

In a tremendous reversal of her prior uneasiness over seeing herself on-screen, Stein replies with a measured endorsement of the general plan, writing back to Van Vechten in April 1940 that several lecture-bureau agents "seem to think that Alice B. might be done in Hollywood," and moreover, that she is willing to go him one better in casting a film version of *The Autobiography* that consists solely of cameo appearances, not just by Stein and Toklas but by everybody, all the "endless strangers" and passing social presences. "Perhaps we all could go out and act in it," Stein ventures, "all that are spoken of in the book I think it would be fun" (671). She unfortunately says nothing in particular about Van Vechten's hyperbole that even Garbo would be insufficient in the role of "Gertrude Stein," which might not have sounded like hyperbole at all given Stein's profound sense of her own significance, captured best in her instruction to the reader of *The Geographical History* to "Think of the Bible and Homer think of Shakespeare and think of me" (109). Nor can we know from her reply whether Stein perceived—or for that matter, whether Van Vechten intended—a deeper play of allusion in referencing Garbo, the star of *Queen Christina* (1933), among the most famous de facto lesbian films of all time, and the subject of sexual gossip and Hollywood innuendo of which, I've no doubt, the magnificently well-connected Van Vechten was aware. But such historical intrigue takes place *inside* a moment of communication that is knowable to us only along the gleaming surface of its language. Garbo's cameo appearance in the Stein–Van Vechten letters seems to me a perfect example of its kind: because of the speed at which it moves and the dimension it does not have, we are left with both more and less information than we are due, as everything would make sense without a passing reference to Greta Garbo, yet once this reference it made, we can't help but feel like there could be more to it, more explanation, more context, more "referent" to the reference itself, which is exactly what the cameo appearance is designed to avoid in the first place, for it is finally a sign that stays a sign no matter how many networks of signification we may assemble around it. All we can be sure of, in other words, is that Garbo is treated as an icon, and not as an icon *for* anything, save perhaps the condition of being an icon. Still, the reference seems anything but empty, and so we keep looking at the opaque interior, at the blankness inside the figure's outlines, and we keep thinking there is something we might have missed, something momentary, in passing, fading into the background.

In April 1940, though, all such concerns were soon to be rendered, in a word, academic. "Well anyway spring does come," Stein writes after expressing her hopes for "Alice B." in Hollywood, "and things do happen" (671). "Things" did: Paris was occupied in June; and Stein and Toklas remained in Bilignin for the duration of the war, where they were left more or less unmolested by both the Nazis and the Vichy regime, owing perhaps to the very extent of Stein's fame and her connections to the United States, or, less appealingly, to her friendship with Bernard Faÿ, later convicted of collaboration and for more, it is safe to assume, than the influence he peddled with the Germans to save Stein's art collection.[84] So while it is easy enough to condemn as escapist this whole discussion of the film version that wasn't of *The Autobiography of Alice B. Toklas*, we might also remember that any avenue of potential escape was, on the contrary, an eminently practical concern, and that beneath all this fantasy and flattery about Stein trumping Garbo and an all-star cast of hundreds reproducing the salad days of modernism, Hollywood might represent not just Stein's "dream" of stardom and of money without labor, but of safety as well, of a security in being visible and exposed on film and in America, conditions she dreaded in 1935 but that we can hardly fault her for finding more enticing by comparison a few years later. When the war was over, Stein did in fact find herself once more before the movie cameras, the featured interview in a U.S. Army newsreel entitled *A G.I. Sees Paris*, proving that she surpassed Garbo on at least one front, that of endurance—to put it bluntly—in the courting of publicity. Thus a historical turn of events that would have seemed truly astonishing to anyone in America in 1940, and more improbable than any dream of Hollywood loosed in the correspondence of Gertrude Stein: that Stein would be making another film appearance some five years after the most famous star in the world had, without warning, forever vanished from the screen. I hesitate to suggest for even a moment that Stein managed to outshine Garbo, especially since there was such a profound incandescence to Garbo's resistance to fame in the last fifty years of her life. Technically speaking, however—and this is, of course, a phrase I take seriously—Stein did manage to outlast Garbo in the eye of public

FIGURE 2.11. U.S. Army press photograph from the filming of *A GI Sees Paris*, 1945. Courtesy of the Bancroft Library, University of California, Berkeley.

visibility, and that should count for something. A final image should bring this rather vague sense of significance I am evoking into sharper resolution.

We see Gertrude Stein seated in her home, and the nation's camera is rolling (fig. 2.11). Alice B. Toklas is nowhere to be seen, nor is there much evidence of the idiosyncratic, "mannish" wardrobe that was noted so compulsively by the press a decade before. Even the decor of the apartment, when compared to that pictured in the Coburn photographs of 1913, or those of Beaton in the late 1930s, seems almost tacitly to have mutated into a new kind of space, to have domesticated itself into a "grandmother's house," complete with flower baskets, candy dishes, and bric-a-brac atop all available surfaces. In short, almost every detail of the photograph conspires to convince us that we are witness to a scene of capitulation that was expected all along: the avant-garde, after all, is born to acquiesce in most classical accounts of its history; it fights the good fight for as long as it can, but every story then ends the same way, necessarily and programmatically, with a drama of co-optation that shows just how grave, now that it's gone, this last threat to the order of things has been. But the series of cameo appearances I've described in these pages, should, I hope, upset any feelings of nostalgia we might have for a radical poetics of identity that was lost when Stein "went Hollywood," and prevent just as surely any feelings of reflexive condemnation we might have about a "culture industry" that produces only ideology and unpleasure. What Gertrude Stein's last star turn shows is that being thoroughly mediated—by the nation, by capitalism, by technology, by language—is not always the same thing as being exploited, turned inside out, left empty of that which made you you, as Stein herself might put it. Or we can at least hope, so long as there is that little dog in the picture, staring right back through the camera that everybody else has agreed to ignore, as if knowing what no one else knows, and what no one else could say even if they did, not the Army, not Gertrude Stein, and certainly not me.

Part Two
Records

3
SOUNDTRACKS: MODERNISM, FIDELITY, RACE

Besides the pleasure I derived from actually listening to the rolls, a very distinct part
of my enjoyment, when I operated my phonograph consisted in watching the visible
changes that the regulating system underwent when the mechanism was started or
stopped . . . this succession of metamorphoses, was for me as great an entertainment—or
nearly as great—as to listen to the sounds that the sound box extracted from the black,
more or less scratchy wax of the rolls.

MICHEL LEIRIS, *SCRATCHES*

"Say It with Music"

The title of Irving Berlin's 1921 hit, written for the first of his *Music Box Revues*,
invokes a modernist aesthetic we all know well, though perhaps set to other music. The echoes of Provençal troubadours accompany Ezra Pound's pronouncements on behalf of the sensibility he wants twentieth-century poets to recover
by attending to rhythm and "melopoeia," or by following his Imagist imperative "to compose in the sequence of the musical phrase."[1] No map of Eliot's *The
Waste Land* is complete until allusions to both Wagner and "that Shakespeherian Rag" have been duly scrutinized for how they synthesize the demotic
and classical as leitmotif, thus discovering, in the *Gesamstkunstwerk*, one model
of fragments successfully shored against their ruins. When Langston Hughes in
The Weary Blues (1926) or Sterling Brown in *Southern Road* (1932) captures the
forms and textures of black music in his writing, his sources may well be vernacular, but the results are no less Eliotic in their reverence for the "amalgam of
systems of divers sources" from which modernism can be made.[2] James Weldon
Johnson introduces his book of verse-sermons, *God's Trombones* (1927), by emphasizing that he too has tried to "make it new" by scrupulously avoiding the
hackneyed linguistic forms associated with local color and Paul Laurence Dun-
bar: "The Negro poet in the United States, for poetry which he wishes to give
a distinctively racial tone and color, needs now an instrument of greater range

than dialect; that is, if he is to do more than sound the small notes of sentimentality."[3] If we look to European modernism and the avant-garde, this tendency toward musical analogy seems only more pervasive: from Dada experiments with a poetry of noises to the dazzling city "symphonies" of avant-garde film in the 1920s, we hear the old refrain, even if we don't know where we first heard it, or occasionally can't remember who wrote the words: *"All art constantly aspires towards the condition of music."*[4]

The media aesthetic that Walter Pater offers in this famous sentence from *The Renaissance* (1873) provides Clement Greenberg with an important line of argument in "Towards a Newer Laocoön," his 1940 essay on the "superiority of abstract art," which is, in its own way, as much a standard of the period as any Berlin show tune.[5] One of the essay's two footnotes pays tribute to Pater's "ideas about music," upon which Greenberg could be said to improvise his far more programmatic—if not prejudicial—account of medium-specificity as the necessary consequence of modernism's renewed appreciation for materiality. This is an argument whose refrain takes many forms later in the twentieth century, in response to Jackson Pollock or to debates surrounding each new style of the moment from minimalism to video and post-photography. But its essential character is best experienced in the original, where Greenberg's foreshortened history leaves ample space for his impossibly sure pronouncements:

> Only when the avant-garde's interest in music led it to consider music as a *method* of art rather than as a kind of effect did the avant-garde find what it was looking for. It was when it was discovered that the advantage of music lay chiefly in the fact that it was an "abstract" art, an art of "pure form." It was such because it was incapable, objectively, of communicating anything else than a sensation, and because this sensation could not be conceived in any other terms than those of the sense through which it entered consciousness. . . . The emphasis, therefore, was to be on the physical, the sensorial. "Literature's" corrupting influence is only felt when the senses are neglected. The latest confusion of the arts was the result of a mistaken conception of music as the only immediately sensuous art. But the other arts can also be sensuous, if only they will look to music, not to ape its effects, but to borrow its principles as a "pure" art, as an art which is abstract because it is almost nothing else except sensuous. (31)

Greenberg's insistence on the lack of semantic meaning within "pure" musical expression pushes toward a caricature of late-nineteenth-century aestheticism. It is not simply the case that music might teach the other arts that their mediums were, in fact, their messages, but that music promises to disabuse them of the notion that they should have messages at all.[6] "Literature" earns its scare quotes because it most clearly represents the idea—and also the practices and institutions that enforced this notion in Greenberg's version of the nineteenth century—that art had sacrificed sensation and materiality in the hopeless and historically mistaken project of "communicating" anything save the pleasures most appropriate to its own technologies. Saying it with music is the last, best way of saying nothing. And saying nothing leaves us with a modernism wholly present and immediately experienced because it communicates the sensuality of its medium in the form of messages we can never finally read.

Of course, the status of music, as both communicative action and "sensuous" form, is not nearly so high-minded in the hands of Irving Berlin. His lyrics make it plain that to "say it with music" is more carnal and conventionally provocative than any scenario we might contrive from Greenberg's sense of how works of art and human bodies come together. "Music is a language lovers understand," Berlin writes, "Melody and romance wander hand in hand / Cupid never fails assisted by a band / So if you have something sweet to tell her / Say it with music / Beautiful music." At the risk of over-reading Tin Pan Alley poetry, the work done here by "with" (say it *with* music) is by no means transparent: when Berlin suggests in the refrain that "Somehow they'd rather be kissed / To the strains of Chopin and Liszt," he not only plays a little with what we might call, using Greenberg's cherished terms, the purely abstract appeal of serious music, but also pictures a scene where music enables and accompanies an erotic gesture that is a sufficient signal on its own. Even without music, a kiss is a kiss is a kiss. But not so for the "tender message" that Berlin's love-struck speaker has "deep down in [his] heart," where it remains as the song gives voice to his failure to communicate "just exactly what I want to tell you." What makes this song felicitous as a substitution for, and performance of, the message it does not disclose—saying "it" with music *instead* of words—is the kiss it may effect, which, as the chorus goes, is just as likely to occur by listening to Liszt or Chopin and waiting for the susceptibility that their wordless virtuosity ensures.

None of these nice distinctions make a difference for Theodor Adorno. "All too willingly, the hits give their contingency a sexual meaning which is by no means an unconscious one," he writes in "On Jazz" (1936), and given his sense of what jazz was, his hostility applies much better to Berlin than to Louis Armstrong or Duke Elllington.[7] Popular music traffics in a sexuality that is all too obviously the answer to every would-be lyrical invention or formal gesture that contributes to the scandal of its sensual appeal. "The more absurd the nonsense, the more immediate its *sex appeal*," Adorno writes, putting *sex appeal* in deliberate English, all the better to disgust. "The pace of the gait itself," or so Adorno insists when speaking of the tempo at which jazz makes dancers move, "has an immediate reference to coitus; the rhythm of the gait is similar to the rhythm of sexual intercourse" (486). The posturings are so severe that mere citation seems sufficient to indict Adorno on the familiar charges of a hypertrophied elitism. And still he manages to find an even more visceral and revealing scenario to relish for what it darkly says about the music that he hates. Describing how "the new dances have demystified the erotic magic of the old ones," Adorno writes of "some so-called *dance academies*, where *taxi girls* are available with whom one can perform dance steps which occasionally lead to male orgasm" (486). The italics again mean English, which for Adorno, says it all.

As T. J. Clark observes, one danger of the fixation on mediums in modernism is that it risks short-circuiting when the "straightforward desublimatory force" of the desire for materiality (sensation, affect, physical response) gets interpreted as the entirety of its program. Modernism, for Clark, can tread perilously close to the fantasy that audience and artwork might meet as "bodies imagining each other," and the resulting mediated empathy—or perhaps better, empathy *with* media—is just "intercourse lightly disguised."[8] The problem for many early figures interested in the medium-specific qualities of popular music and, after the invention of the phonograph, new technologies that allowed for its revolutionary materiality on record and in the home, is that the fantasy that Clark describes might no longer be "disguised" at all. As Gilbert Seldes puts it with perfect mock anxiety in *The Seven Lively Arts* (1924), "The popular song is so varied, so full of interest, that for a moment at least one can pretend that it isn't vulgar, detestable, the ruin of musical taste, and a symptom of degeneracy."[9] Less easy with the implications of new musical technologies (and thus all the more effective at communicating their appeal), Constant Lambert describes a modern world of "music in decline" with even more libidinal peevishness than Adorno. "We live in an age of tonal debauch," writes Lambert, "where the blunting of the finer edge of pleasure leads only to a more hysterical and frenetic attempt to recapture it. It is obvious that second-rate mechanical music is the most suitable fare for those to whom musical experience is no more than a mere aural tickling, just as the prostitute provides the most suitable outlet for those to whom sexual experience is no more than the periodic removal of a recurring itch. The loud speaker is the street walker of music."[10]

I do not mean to take Lambert at his hysterical word on the sexuality of recorded sound. But as in Adorno, the excessiveness of the protest hints that the "mechanical romanticism," as Lambert puts it, that surrounds the phonograph and other musical technologies might prompt fantasies of mediated "debauch." Consider one advertisement for "The Edison Phonograph," from the early 1900s, which features a pair of adoring listeners utterly composed before the newest "form of musical entertainment" (fig. 3.1). The canisters spread out on the table—a musical bouquet to match the pink roses, which the man no doubt has brought as well—assuredly contain the "love songs" that lead the list of genres, including "dances," "funny songs," and "ballads," that the phonograph allows its owner to bring home. Neither man nor woman, though, appears excited to any degree approaching the sort of gratifications upon which Adorno fixates; the man shows the slightest measure of animation with his open mouth, but given that their bodies touch, if at all, somewhere just above the elbow, I think it safe to say that none of the conventional proprieties are endangered. Indeed, what seems most odd about the image is just how little interest each has in the other, despite all the romance in the air; the man and woman are entirely absorbed by the phonograph itself. It is the machine that has managed "to attract . . . and then to arrest . . . and finally to enthrall the beholder, that is . . . to call to someone, to bring him to a halt in front of itself, and hold him there as if spellbound and unable to move."[11] This is Michael Fried on the psychology of attention that emerges in eighteenth-century French painting, which Fried makes central to a genealogy of modernism within which many of Greenberg's cherished figures comfortably reside. The resonance helps to remind us of the important place that scenes of listening, and of listening to music in particular, hold within Fried's model of absorption; nor is this the only discourse of response that rehearses the uniquely seductive appeal of music as a tenet of comparative aesthetics.[12] Adorno captures the essence of these aesthetics and their exchange value in the age of mechanical reproduction when he observes that "music, with all the attributes of the ethereal and the sublime which are generously accorded it, serves in America today as an advertisement for commodities which one must acquire in order to be able to hear music."[13] "To the Edison Phonograph," the ad copy opens, "can be applied the old saying: 'A pleasure shared is a pleasured

FIGURE 3.1. Advertisement for the Edison phonograph, circa 1910. Collection of the author.

doubled.'" This couple is absorbed in stereo. Their feelings for the phonograph at once double, and double *for*, their feelings for each other. Yet it also seems that this much desire cannot be communicated without at least a hint that amid all this erotic mediation somebody might be a two-timer whose love is not his own to give. The striking visibility of the man's wedding ring—it is hard to miss as we follow the horn of the phonograph to the center of the image—makes me want to find its match on the woman whom he is courting with all the flowers and records. Since she is not wearing one, how are we to know if this phonograph is playing a tune that puts us in the parlor with Berlin or in the gutter with Adorno?

◊

If such intimations of mediated passion in all its forms—for bodies and machines—disclose part of what Seldes has in mind when diagnosing, with some approval, the "degeneracy" that popular music represents, another moment celebrating Irving Berlin in *The Seven Lively Arts* signals a different network of associations. Describing the sensibility and style that "has torn to rags the sentimentality of the song which preceded it," Seldes identifies two crucial figures making the music that has America "tearing a passion" in the twentieth century:

> A neat, unobtrusive little man with bright eyes and an unerring capacity for understanding, appropriating, and creating strange rhythms is in the foreground, attended by negro slaves; behind him stands a rather majestic figure, pink and smooth, surrounded by devils with muted brass and saxophones. (69)

The latter figure, Seldes tells us, is the white jazz musician Paul Whiteman, the former is Berlin, and the black figures behind the man behind the music invoke a familiar dynamic of "love and theft," to borrow from Eric Lott, in the history of how white entertainers and composers have depicted their sympathetic expropriations of black culture. These black figures, for Seldes's readers in the 1920s, would likely have summoned the specter of the "hot coon" whom rival songwriters accused Berlin of keeping at his disposal, ready whenever he needed a new hit. "You know, Irvy," says composer Henry Waterson to Berlin in one of several renditions of this mythology, "there's a story circulating on Broadway—that the reason you can turn out so much gold ragtime is because you got your own coloured piccaninny tucked away in a closet!"[14]

The tale of Berlin's "hot coon in the closet" began to circulate from the moment "Alexander's Ragtime Band" became a breakthrough hit in 1912. Scott Joplin long held that the tune was his own, and family members later recalled that Joplin cried whenever he heard it. Joplin also revised at least one song from his opera *Treemonisha* because he felt that Berlin had plagiarized from melodies he could have heard performed in the months before the show premiered.[15] "Because our whole present music is derived from the negro," as Seldes freely admits, there is no distinction between the vagaries of inspiration and outright acts of taking when contemplating the origins of ragtime.[16] The accusations surrounding Berlin only rendered metaphorical what was literally the case: that American popular music, at the turn of the century and after, depended in ever more elaborate ways on material associated with, or produced by, African Americans.

The pervasive influence of black music on U.S. modernism has been amply, even exhaustively, documented. This chapter proceeds from a different sense of how we might understand the relationship between musical form and racial content in the medium-specific fantasies that constituted the period's fixation on the sensuality and expressive physicality of music. But rather than treating race as subject matter that we recover only when the self-involving logics of modernist formalism are rejected, I want to show that the matter of race was part of what this formalism hoped to capture from the start. Or put differently, race was already so inscribed in the language surrounding new technologies that communicated the immediacy of music like never before, that it was difficult for the musical aesthetic of modernism to register its appeal without recourse to a whole network of racial meanings and iconographies that projected fantasies of blackness onto the medium of recorded sound—making U.S. modernism itself into a kind of feedback loop between race and technology. And while we might expect a culture of recorded sound that flourished with the popularity of black music to invoke, if only indirectly, the histories of slavery, segregation, and racial experience, we might not think to find such matters central to various modernist works concerned with music as a medium whose allure depends entirely on its saying nothing. The modernism I describe below is best able to idealize the medium of music by way of working through its other, elaborate devotion to race figured as a medium: as a physical, material limit to expression that becomes aestheticized as a vehicle for communication. This means that race, as I explore its fascination here, emerges less as the sign of what remains natural and authentic within the circuitous mechanics of recorded sound, and more as the material result of modernism's own commitment to the pleasures of both technology and technique.

Why should the sound of music made by machines provide us with occasions to perceive an uncanny mediating blackness? Adorno would say that anyone who believes that race can be communicated by music is hearing things, and thus he holds that the "relationship between jazz and black people" is utterly superficial: "the skin of the black man functions as much as a coloristic effect as does the silver of the saxophone" (477). This is language calculated to attack and shock; not for nothing is Adorno writing here under his pseudonym,

"Hektor Rotweiler." Yet even as he tries to nullify whatever racial meanings black music might be assumed to reproduce, Adorno remains fascinated by the "form of the phonograph record" itself and preoccupied by the "black pane of composite mass," which ultimately does not appeal like other artworks but looms instead like "black seals on the missives that are rushing towards us from all sides in the traffic with technology."[17] As surely as the couple in the Edison ad, Adorno is oddly enraptured with the materiality of recorded sound and cannot turn away. It is hard to say if he discovers here, in the physical reality of the medium, some echo of the "blackness" he finds nowhere in the message when he listens to black music. But for others, such technically fantasmatic connections are the stuff that modernism is made of.

The Racial Apparatus

Nowhere does the phonograph more powerfully make material an aesthetic of racial experience than in the prologue to Ralph Ellison's *Invisible Man* (1952). "Perhaps I like Louis Armstrong," the nameless narrator writes, "because he's made poetry out of being invisible."[18] In the incandescence of his spectacularly illuminated "hole" in Harlem, with its 1,369 lights "wired" everywhere across the ceiling, the Invisible Man listens to jazz on his "one radio-phonograph" while dreaming that he might someday produce a sonic splendor equal to the total wattage he has thus far managed to seize in his "battle with Monopolated Light & Power" (7). "There is a certain acoustical deadness in my hole, and when I have music I want to *feel* its vibration, not only with my ear but with my whole body. I'd like to hear five recordings of Louis Armstrong playing and singing 'What Did I Do to Be so Black and Blue'—all at the same time" (8). So much machinery for making music seems an appropriate ambition given that the Invisible Man can see himself "in the great American tradition of tinkers. That makes me kin," he says, "to Ford, Edison, and Franklin. Call me, since I have a theory and a concept, a 'thinker-tinker'" (7).

Since the Invisible Man's scene of maximum technology recalls, with terrific irony, such famous sites of American engineering know-how as Edison's complex of workshops in Menlo Park, it is only fitting that his "theory" of technology also echoes nineteenth-century attempts to understand the implications of the phonograph. "If this invention had taken place in the Middle Ages," the Count du Moncel writes in 1879, "it would certainly have been applied to ghostly apparitions, and it would have been invaluable to miracle-mongers."[19] But Ellison's prologue, even as it resurrects this imagery of recorded sound, also anticipates the ways in which a later generation of critics, and especially film theorists, will come to conceptualize the importance of invisible voices—"a voice whose source one cannot see," to borrow from Mladen Dolar—not just to film history but to the experience of modernity itself.[20] This phenomenon and its consequences are explored most fully by Michel Chion, who adopts the term "acousmatic" (from *music concréte* inventor Pierre Schaffer) to designate "a mode of listening that is commonplace today, systematized in the use of radio, telephones, and phonograph records," all of which allow us to hear, in the "here and now," something that isn't really there.[21] "Why all these powers in a voice?" Chion's answer makes clear his indebtedness to both Freud and Lacan: "Maybe because this *voice without a place* that belongs to the acousmêtre takes us back to an archaic, original stage: of the first months of life or even before birth, during which the voice was everything and it was everywhere" (27).

Or maybe not; Chion's notion of the acousmatic strikes me as useful enough without a psychoanalytical account of its origins. All the more, in respect to Ellison, given the story Chion recounts from Diderot's *Encyclopédie* about the ancient Pythagorean sect whose members dubbed themselves "acousmatics" because they were resigned to listen to their master only from behind a curtain, choosing to deprive themselves of seeing what they wanted most intensely to hear (19). Applying both to the Invisible Man's relationship to Armstrong— and, of course, to our relationship to the Invisible Man—the uncanniness of the acousmatic, which Ellison indulges *avant la lettrê*, provides for a curious but crucial form of freedom, another way for the Invisible Man to "slip into the breaks" where "time stands still" (8). If the acousmatic, as Dolar writes, "always displays something of an effect emancipated from its cause," this may well be the only emancipation that the Invisible Man can achieve so long as he must operate on the "lower frequencies."

Ellison, however, had access to other channels and published one of his first pieces after *Invisible Man* in *High Fidelity,* the famous magazine for audiophiles. The essay "Living with Music" (1955) describes a different acousmatic drama, though the setting is oddly reminiscent. "In those days," Ellison writes of his "tiny ground-floor-rear apartment," the choice was "either live with music or die with noise. And we chose rather desperately to live. In the process our apartment—what with its booby-trappings of audio equipment, wires, discs and tapes—came to resemble the Collyer mansion."[22] Making reference to the Harlem home where Homer Collyer starved to death after his brother and caretaker Langley was killed by a falling pile of debris (the brothers were compulsive hoarders), the allusion is appropriate to the fifties' craze for stereophonic sound. With articles in *House Beautiful* observing that "hi-fi addiction, like any other kind, can be carried over to excess," and even *High Fidelity* suggesting that the "audiomaniac" might need psychiatric care, it is no surprise that Ellison strikes a mildly anxious tone and argues self-defense.[23] On the other side of one thin wall "was a restaurant with a juke box the size of the Roxy"; another wall just barely muffled "a night-employed swing music enthusiast who took his lullaby music so loud that every morning at nine Basie's brasses started blasting my typewriter off its stand" (4). The "chaos of noise" to which Ellison is exposed includes a host of "preaching drunks," a cacophony of traffic, dogs and cats, and, one floor up, an aspiring singer who provides the essay with its central tension. For while Ellison is battling the "writer's block" that all this noise induces, he also sympathizes with the artist just upstairs; he knows "something of what the singer faced" from his own memories of jazz musicians in Oklahoma City, and from his days as a youthful trumpet player more than capable of "[tormenting] the ears of all not blessedly deaf with imitations of the latest solos of Hot Lips Page, the leaping right hand of Earl 'Fatha' Hines, or the rowdy poetic flights of Louis Armstrong" (8). Because the aims of this unseen voice so closely parallel those of Ellison himself—"could I," he asks, "an aspiring artist, complain against the hard work and devotion to craft of another aspiring artist?"—he is reluctant to impose silence on her by the usual means. (The swing aficionado next door, however, makes him "desperate enough to cool down the hot blast of his phonograph by calling the cops" [6].) Ellison decides to fight "noise with noise," pushing the upper limits of his Philco and realizing an unexpected peace of mind in the very opposite of quiet, in the music of Kathleen Ferrier, "that loveliest of singers" played at the greatest volume that he can muster (10). So he buys some more Ferrier records and upgrades his equipment:

> Between the hi-fi record and the ear, I learned, there was a new electronic world. In that realization our apartment was well on its way toward becoming an audio booby trap. . . . I heard David Sarser's and Mel Sprinkle's Musician's Amplifier, took a look at its schematic and, recalling a boyhood acquaintance with such matters, decided I could build one. I did—several times—before it was measured within specifications. And still our system

was lacking. Fortunately my wife shared my passion for music, so we went on to buy, piece by piece, a fine speaker system, a first-rate AM-FM tuner, a transcription turntable and a speaker cabinet. I built half a dozen or more preamplifiers and record compensators before finding a commercial one that satisfied my ear, and finally we acquired an arm, a magnetic cartridge, and—glory of the house—a tape recorder. All this plunge into electronics, mind you, had as its simple end the enjoyment of recorded music as it was intended to be heard. I was obsessed with the idea of reproducing sound with such fidelity that even when using music as a defense behind which I could write, it would reach the unconscious levels of mind with the least distortion. (10–11)

With this much technology to deal with—"and still our system was lacking"—it is a miracle he ever finished *Invisible Man*. For "a defense behind which [he] could write," he obviously has more hi-fi than he needs. Ellison has more hi-fi than he can hear.

What is remarkable about Ellison's account of his adventures in high fidelity is the degree to which his investments in technology, in every sense, keep shifting between a fetish for its material forms and a fantasy of its ideal invisibility. Ellison desires an aesthetic of "fidelity" that assumes a prior, absent scene of sound that only technology, by way of the most ornate circuits of mediation, can reproduce. There is a curiously double logic, then, to the insistence on listening to "recorded music as it was intended to be heard": by definition, such music is performed in order to be reproduced, and even the genre of the "live" recording is engineered to guarantee a sound that no one at the performance may ever hear, which means that experiencing recorded music as "intended" means precisely experiencing it *as* recorded. Jonathan Sterne puts it elegantly in his discussion of how the "conflicted aesthetic of recorded sound," as fashioned by audio professionals and the music industry over the course of the twentieth century, demanded that "technology as a vanishing mediator continually be set in conflict with the reality that sound-reproduction technologies had their own sonic character."[24] Of course Ellison's "mediator" does anything but vanish, to play off the Fredric Jameson that Sterne himself is referencing; the apparatus not only consumes the whole apartment ("it was worth your life to move about without first taking careful bearings") but also represents an object answering to some obsession Ellison comically, excessively enacts but, like any proper fetish, cannot entirely explain. Indeed, all this technology is wired to reach "the unconscious levels of mind"—Ellison's own "lower frequencies"—where the dream of "fidelity" has given way to a sensory overload, which in turn has faded into a weird, regressive reverie that, if a "necessary defense" for writing, seems to identify artistic inspiration with the experience of total mediation.

Or as T. S. Eliot famously contends, the writer has "not a 'personality' to express, but a particular medium, which is only a medium and not a personality, in which impressions and experiences combine in unexpected ways" (42). So too does Eliot's insistence on "technical excellence" seem slyly literalized in Ellison's extreme involvement with wires and records, transistors and tape; and in a fitting, Eliotic twist, the high technology of the new medium is there to afford a deeper, more appreciative regard for the "dead poets and artists" who came before. For Ellison, this allows for a provocatively—though not entirely unexpected—emphasis on a democratic sense of culture as a phenomenon of contact and juxtaposition. His commitment to aesthetic universalism might also, and more directly, function as an extension of W. E. B. Du Bois in *The Sounds of Black Folk* rather than an Eliotic echo; which is to say that Ellison knows his "native culture," but also knows that he must "love it unchauvanistically."[25] In this noisy world where Ellison is "living with music," this love finds its medium in a curious form of broadcasting, because the "tradition" that Ellison wants the "individual talent" upstairs to absorb has considerable static to overcome.

The aspiring artist one floor up brings out the best in Ellison's hi-fi by bringing out the worst in him. He confesses that "instead of soothing, music seemed to release the beast in me" (11). In a "war of decibels," his "music system" and all the wattage it can muster battles against however many pounds of pressure that his neighbor and "her diaphragm" can produce (12). But the conflict involves far more than volume:

If, let us say, she were singing "Depuis le Jour" from *Louise*, I'd put on a tape of Bidu Sayão performing the same aria, and let the rafters ring. If it was some song by Mahler, I'd match her spitefully with Marian Anderson or Kathleen Ferrier; if she offended with something from *Der Rosenkavalier*, I'd attack her flank with Lotte Lehman. If she brought me up from my desk with art songs by Ravel or Rachmaninoff, I'd defend myself with Maggie Teyte or Jennie Tourel. If she polished a spiritual to a meaningless artiness I'd play Bessie Smith to remind her of the earth out of which we came. Once in a while I'd forget completely that I was supposed to be a gentleman and blast her with Strauss's *Zarathustra*, Bartók's *Concerto for Orchestra*, Ellington's "Flaming Sword," the fame crescendo from *The Pines of Rome*, or Satchmo scatting "I'll be Glad When You're Dead" (you rascal you!). Oh, I was living with music with a sweet vengeance. (12)

This is, first off, an astonishing show of cultural capital, mixing jazz and classical music, relative obscurities and middle-brow sensations, and delivering it in what amounts to an "aria" of information—the virtuosity of Ellison's detailism is there, at least in part, to amplify the politics of race that he never mentions. So while I do not disagree with Alexander Weheliye when he notes that Ellison turns his apartment building into a "collective space to be shared" by way of all this musical exchange, especially since Ellison and the singer end their conflict with a peaceable, "live-and-let-live" reduction of volume on both sides, I cannot help wondering how race figures in this compromise.[26] Ellison, after all, never says whether his singing neighbor is African American; maybe he intends for readers to assume that she is black, given the neighborhood soundscape of "preaching drunks," Count Basie, and the blues. Yet when Ellison chastises his upstairs neighbor for "American slave songs sung as if *bel canto*" (6) or for "[polishing] a spiritual to a meaningless artiness," I think it more than possible to hear her—or rather, to hear Ellison hearing her—as white, or at the very least, as not black enough for the material. Their acousmatic relationship is at once color-blind and racially involved. Thus in responding to the singer's "artiness" with Bessie Smith, Ellison wants to "remind her of the earth out of which we came," but so much depends on who "we" are here: are "we" two African Americans struggling to find a happy medium among aesthetic options that resonate across the arbitrary racial lines of segregated U.S. culture, yet also anxious about "polishing" our black identities to a "meaningless" luster and another "coloristic effect" of the kind Adorno sees through? Or are "we" black and white neighbors, socially isolated, but able to hear our way to a satisfying compromise once the singer has learned to mark "the phrasing of great singers," which in the case of slave songs would mean reproducing black music "as it was intended to be heard," because Ellison himself was so "obsessed" by all its technicalities (13).

However one wishes to understand the communication that takes place between Ellison and his neighbor, it is clear that race pervades this scene of musical assault and pedagogy, protection and programming. Realizing the full scope of Ellison's desire to use recorded sound as a medium that makes race intricately material, even if it might not make its meaning clear, also helps us catch the note of melancholy with which Ellison ends the story of his first, beloved hi-fi. "We have long since moved from that apartment and that most interesting neighborhood," he writes, reminding us that the famous author of *Invisible Man* can afford a better, quieter part of town, "and now the floors and walls of our present apartment are adequately thick, and there is even a closet large enough to house the audio system; the only wire visible is that leading from the closet to the corner speaker system" (13). He can still hear the sounds of "past experience" in his memories of "phonographs shouting the blues in back alleys," or "washerwomen singing slave songs as they stirred sooty tubs in sunny yards," but like all memories that have found their proper place, the machinery that makes possible their storage and retrieval has largely disappeared. (Memories, we might recall from Freud, are only the "materialized portion of my mnemic apparatus, the rest of which I carry about with me invisible."[27]) Ellison's homemade hi-fi no longer occupies an outsized portion of a small urban apartment; his surroundings have gentrified to a degree that requires him to channel his obsession with technology into the single wire leading to the closet where his former "passion for music" has its home, the secret tangle of wires and circuitry safely sublimated out of view. He is less the "tinker" and more the mid-twentieth-century incarnation of the bourgeoisie for whom, returning to Adorno, the materiality of technology, in the flesh, is yet another object of repression. "The fate of the gramophone marks this development in a striking manner," Adorno argues, since "in their brassiness, they initially projected the mechanical being of the machines onto the surface." But then, he mordantly observes, "in better social circles . . . they were quickly muffled into colored masses or wood chalices."[28] It is as if the very mechanism that provided Ellison with such a thoroughly pleasurable "defense" against the noises and distractions of the city now represents a seduction he will no longer advertise but of course cannot bring himself to sacrifice—and so he renders it nearly invisible, leaving only a little wire to remind him of the apparatus he has put away.

This sense of longing for an object whose function is to mediate some *other* sense of longing seems to parallel— if not, more accurately, to predict—the variety of affect that will come to fascinate a generation of film theorists, Christian Metz and Jean-Louis Baudry chief among them, for whom the subject's identification with the cinematic "apparatus" structures a whole psychology of media spectatorship and perception. To align Ellison with this brand of criticism is less to read "Living with Music" as evidencing a familiar Freudian logic of lack and substitution—he fiddles with his stereo because he must deny any more visceral encounter with his upstairs neighbor—and more, to remember that the desire for mediated experience often takes on far less orthodox forms. Which is in part to suggest that Ellison's investment in his audio apparatus constitutes the kind of media fetish that Metz would recognize and diagnose accordingly as "the point of departure for specialized practices" and as a desire that is "all the more 'technical' the more perverse it is."[29] "Living with Music," then, is about a curious nostalgia for a medium that, because it makes mediated experience itself the object of desire, seems to lose the more it gains since it is finally the interference and indirection of communication—the "chaos of noise," as Ellison puts it—that is most jeopardized by any medium that might actually deliver high fidelity.

"It is not possible," Jürgen Habermas contends, "to want to communicate *and* to express oneself unintelligibly or misleadingly."[30] For this to be true of Ellison, we must conclude that even when he confesses himself a "beast" intent on phonographically acting out against his neighbor, he remains intent on establishing the validity of his appeal for understanding, and so hopes to have her recognize his need for a quieter scene of writing. But Ellison seems to prove instead that it is possible to want communication while at the same time wanting to express oneself as circuitously as possible, thus treating the message you may have in mind to elaborate forms of mediation and distortion, none of which render it unintelligible, but all of which nonetheless make its felicitous transmission into an affair entirely of the "lower frequencies" where opportunities for confusion are profound.

The Humanola

Here is a scene from the childhood of George Gershwin, as pictured in Sigmund Spaeth's *At Home with Music* (1946), a book of lessons in taste and tradition aimed at the "new audience for good music" which, Spaeth assures us, "is being developed largely through radio and phonograph records" (fig. 3.2).[31] If these technologies distinguish "the soundscape of modernity," to borrow from Emily Thompson, that by the late 1940s could be largely taken for granted, this illustration returns us to its ground zero: a young boy stands in rapt contemplation before an automatic piano, his head cocked thoughtfully to the side, his hands crossed behind his back to accentuate the precocious, intellectual

FIGURE 3.2. George Gershwin as a child from Sigmund Spaeth's *At Home with Music* (Garden City, New York: Doubleday & Company, Inc., 1946).

character of his deep absorption in both the music and the workings of the machine itself. There is nothing childish about the repose of his response—indeed, the emphasis appears squarely placed on the concerted lack of any visible reaction to the music he is hearing. The young composer is the picture of composure, and this awful pun seems almost the point, for as Isaac Goldberg, Gershwin's first and most adoring biographer, writes, "He had been a 'hard' kid. At six . . . he was almost as blasé and worldly wise as he is today."[32] Perhaps what we see here is evidence that Gershwin, at an early age, had already acquired the sort of "stimulus shield" that Walter Benjamin so famously imagines as necessary armature for a twentieth-century urbanite; or perhaps Gershwin, born far too early to enjoy the hi-fi that Ellison uses to screen out the city from his site of artistic imagination, simply had to develop other coping mechanisms to translate all this noise into the music he would later fashion. Goldberg catalogs the racket that Gershwin later treats as raw material: "The clatter of rollers over asphalt," "the din of the elevated overhead," "the madness of the traffic below," "the cracked tones of the hurdy-gurdy," "the blatant bally-hoo of the honky-tonk," "the blare of the automatic orchestra as the merry-go-round traced its dizzy circles through Coney Island's penny paradises," "the plaintive wail of the street singer across the obbligato [*sic*] of a scraping fiddle." This litany strives for a poetry of its own, with more than an accidental emphasis on alliteration, and more quasi-onomatopoeic patter than mere description warrants, but the sound of music Goldberg wants to evoke is finally Gershwin's own: "There were the earliest rhythms that sound not only from his first hits but from his most ambitious orchestral compositions. . . . It is young New York, young America, seeking a voice for its holiday spirit, its crude exaltations" (53–54).

From Gershwin's own memories of his enchantment by the pianola, which Goldberg quotes in his biography, we know that this is not necessarily a scene where race and music are involved. "One of my first definite memories," he recalls for Goldberg, "goes back to the age of six. I stood outside a penny arcade listening to an automatic piano leaping through Rubinstein's *Melody in F*. The peculiar jumps in the music held me rooted. To this very day I can't hear the tune without picturing myself outside that arcade on One Hundred and Twenty-fifth Street, standing there barefoot and in overalls, drinking it all in avidly" (54). The illustration from *At Home with Music*, then, is a free translation of this crucial childhood memory. Gershwin is placed inside the arcade, not at the window, which has the effect of shifting the emphasis from the sound of Rubinstein's composition to the vision of the automatic piano "leaping" through the song itself. This is, I admit, a minor liberty on the part of Spaeth's illustrator, but it makes it possible to imagine a far stranger scene of identification and inspiration. It is as if the sheer act of picturing this primal scene of Gershwin's self-formation recovers something that his own accounts must circumscribe or disavow: what first awakens his musical desire is not just the "peculiar jumps" of Rubinstein but the brilliant workings of technology. We see here another variation on one of Eliot's crucial lessons about the relationship between tradition and the individual talent— namely, that making art, in every sense, is an expression of "impersonality."

I seize on this privileged term from Eliot knowing that he never intended for it to suggest such an unabashed preoccupation with technique. Poetry is famously defined as "an escape from personality," but Eliot adds immediately that "only those who have personality and emotions know what it means to want to escape from these things" (43). To extend his praise for Dante and Shakespeare to the pianola is to literalize "impersonality" almost beyond recognition; that said, when Eliot suggests that it is in "depersonalization that art may be said to approach the condition of science," the modernity of affect he desires is clearly meant to resonate with the condition of modernity as such (40). For that matter, the famously despairing moment when a technology for reproducing music makes an appearance in *The Waste Land*—"When lovely woman stoops to folly and / Paces about her room again, alone, / She smoothes her hair with automatic hand, / And puts a record on the gramophone"—can be seen to index the very methodology of a text that works by making "different voices" present. ("Eliot's poem itself," observes Juan Suárez, "is based on zapping through a prerecorded literary archive which seems to be kept on the air at different frequencies."[33])

There are many ways, then, in which the aesthetic of modernist impersonality seems not just the precursor to, but the very image of, contemporary articulations of the post-human.[34] The bygone pianola—already long an object of nostalgia when *At Home with Music* appeared in 1946—was an engineering marvel that depended on the same punch-card technology as the Jacquard loom, an early-nineteenth-century invention widely cited as one of the first fully programmable machines, and the ancestor to the "difference engine" of Charles Babbage, the Hollerith Tabulator, and the "universal machine" of Alan Turing—even if an arcade in Harlem might seem an unlikely place for an impressionable young modernist to encounter an avant-garde example of "the materiality of informatics," as Katherine Hayles would say. The marvel of the player piano, moreover, was its ability to produce an amazingly detailed and precise inscription of a musical performance; the pianola had no "personality," but by the 1920s the best models produced by the Ampico Corporation possessed elaborate recording mechanisms that used spark chronographs to "write" on sheets of papers with electricity. As the pianist closed the circuits that were wired to the keyboard on a master instrument, sparks captured not only every note but also the exact velocity of the hammer as it struck, the force of the pedal, the duration of every note.[35] What Gershwin experiences, then, is both a recording of Rubinstein's *Melody in F* and its uncanny embodiment. The pianola does not "play" recorded sounds so much as use a coded sequence of information to reanimate a lifeless form with the "personality" of an artist who remains powerfully distant from the scene where his smallest gestures and passing turns of phrase cannot help but fascinate the discriminating subject amid the masses seeking only entertainment. This portrait of the musician as a young man shows us a perfect modernist already functioning at the height of its inhuman powers.

◊

"On 28th Street the song business developed to gargantuan proportions." This is how David Ewen, writing in *The Story of George Gershwin* (1943), describes

the emergence of Tin Pan Alley at the start of the twentieth century.[36] Named
for the legendary racket made by all the composers, music publishers, and theatrical producers concentrated within several city blocks, the neighborhood
that Ewen pictures for us appears anything but chaotic. Gershwin's first years
as a professional songwriter unfold against a background marked by the overwhelming scale and rationality of the music business, with the future legend as
lost as Melville's Bartleby, just another information worker going through the
obscure motions of what the system asks of him:

> [Tin Pan Alley] became a huge machine, disgorging songs out of its busy
> mouth. And it was an efficient machine. Tin-Pan Alley separated songs into
> a number of categories: the humorous vaudeville ditty, the ballad, the love
> song, the ragtime melody, later the "blues" songs, still later the "mammy"
> songs. Each department boasted its special composers and each its corps
> of expert musical stenographers to assist these composers in putting down
> their ideas on paper.
>
> It was a highly selective and delicate mechanism that created song fash-
> ions and then produced songs to meet the fashions. (41)

The modern musical assembly line works not to the "fascinating rhythm" of
later George and Ira Gershwin fame but rather to the singularly "inflexible
rhythm" of Horkheimer and Adorno, which they inevitably discover in every
style and genre that the culture industry produces. Employed as a studio pianist performing new songs for potential publishers, Gershwin, Ewen adds a
few pages later, "was expected to do his work automatically, to be a machine
inside a machine. Even at its best, playing the piano from morning till dusk,
six days a week, was sickening drudgery" (47). Goldberg calls this period in
Gershwin's life a time of virtual imprisonment in "Plugger's Purgatory," where
the constant selling of songs went on interminably (69). With neither irony nor
the slightest nod toward the hyperbole he risks, Goldberg expects his readers
to sympathize completely with his sense that Gershwin was, in point of fact, a
"Keyboard Slave."

It is perhaps hard for us to take this in the spirit of its original under-deter-
mination. We have learned from Jeffrey Melnick and Michael Rogin, among
others, to proceed with some caution whenever a sense of Jewish identity
gets mediated by way of an analogy to African American identity through the

metaphorics of slavery.[37] Figuring Gershwin as a "Keyboard Slave" may represent, however haphazardly, an example of what Rogin terms "Jewish blackface," and such performances of race were so compelling as identifications precisely because they were so unconvincing as imitations. According to this logic, calling Gershwin a "slave" no more makes him black than calling him a "machine" makes him, albeit anachronistically, a cyborg. What these gestures want to communicate is not just a logic of identity but a whole mode of production, or at least a sense of how a particular network of cultural and economic practices comes to shape our relations to the object world of media technologies, and vice versa.

Or, put differently, the readiness to represent Gershwin either as a jazz-playing "keyboard slave" or as a living, breathing "automatic piano" speaks to the tremendous over-determination, in U.S. culture of the late nineteenth and early twentieth centuries especially, that structures the analogy between blacks and machines long after slavery itself has become a memory. As Bill Brown argues, we still confront the "ongoing record of the ontological effects of slavery" across a wide range of discourses that trouble—and are troubled by—the "increasingly artificial" character of "modernity's distinction between human subjects and inanimate objects."[38] "Slavery provides a particular historical form," writes Stephen Best, for working through the ways in which "persons are treated as things, and things as persons."[39] Best describes how, in the decades after the Civil War, both popular culture and the law traded on a language of personification to extend the precedents of slavery so as to guarantee that black culture and intellectual expression were continuously marked by the pernicious "thingness" that whites projected onto African Americans. Joel Dinerstein tracks a closely related network of analogies between blacks and machines from the vantage point of modernism's complicated embrace of jazz in the 1920s and 1930s. Thus Le Corbusier believes that "the Negroes of the USA have breathed into jazz the song, the rhythm, and the sound of machines."[40] And Gershwin implicitly agrees when he recalls that the first intimations of *Rhapsody in Blue* came to him "on the train, with its steely rhythms, its rattle-ty bang," in which he hears "a sort of kaleidoscope of American—of our vast melting pot, of our national pep, of our blues."[41] Just whose blues does Gershwin want to reproduce? Race pervades the machine aesthetic of modern culture, mediating, for white artists most of all, the sometimes precarious desire to embody and reflect technology's "impersonality" without becoming just another body plugged in to its objectifying rationality. Race is what happens when you become the medium of someone else's instrumentality.

Gershwin had his first hit in 1919 with "Swanee," but only after Al Jolson heard its "hidden possibilities" and decided to feature the song in his latest blackface spectacle. The astonishing success of "Swanee" may have delivered Gershwin from his bondage in Tin Pan Alley, but his celebrity did not reach its highest pitch until the February 12, 1924, debut of *Rhapsody in Blue*. With its premiere performance on Lincoln's birthday, the piece was widely and preposterously compared to one of the fallen president's most famous compositions: "For was not the *Rhapsody in Blue*," asks Gershwin biographer David Ewen in the 1940s, "the Emancipation Proclamation for a Negroid music expression?" (96). The appropriately named Paul Whiteman, whose orchestra played Gershwin's score that night, also remembered the concert as an "Emancipation Proclamation, in which slavery to European formalism was signed away."[42] There is little to say about such stupendous fantasies of racial feeling, and the politics they entail, that has not been said by Rogin. This may be blackface only at the level of rhetoric, but still it manages to communicate "heightened authenticity and American acceptance for the (Jewish) individual, subordination for the anonymous (black) mass" (118). Yet neither Rogin's account nor those of others have much interest in Aeolian Hall, where the famous concert took place. As one of New York's most important concert halls in the 1920s, the choice of venue is remembered, when remarked upon at all, for signaling the desire for status on the part of Gershwin and Whiteman, and for helping to confer the legitimacy of the "classics" to jazz-inflected modernism in America. A gift to the city from the Aeolian Corporation, the space, just like the company itself, took its name from the mythic instrument that made music without any form of human intervention. In Coleridge's famous poem about this curiosity of ancient technology, the Aeolian harp—its strings caused to vibrate by the winds they capture—is said to sound like "a soft floating witchery of sound / As twilight Elfins makes."[43] But the Aeolian Corporation did not make its millions selling harps plucked by "gentle-gales from Fairy-land." It was the leading U.S. manufacturer of player pianos.

◊

An earlier model of "automatic piano" entertains Jim Burden, the narrator of Willa Cather's *My Ántonia* (1918), on a cold night in Black Hawk, Nebraska, where even in March "the scene of human life was spread out shrunken and pinched, frozen down to the bare stalk."[44] For Burden, sent away from Virginia to live with grandparents in the Midwest, the unexpected appearance of "Blind d'Arnault, the Negro pianist" (116) not only punctuates the "dreary monotony" of a bleak Nebraska winter but also inspires him to all but sing his own version of "Swanee," with a sentimentality every bit as saturated by plantation mythology as any Tin Pan Alley tribute to "Dixie":

> [D'Arnault] was a heavy, bulky mulatto, on short legs, and he came tapping the floor in front of him with his gold-headed cane. His yellow face was lifted in the light, with a show of white teeth, all grinning, and his shrunken, papery eyelids lay motionless over his blind eyes.
>
> "Good evening, gentlemen. No ladies here? Good evening, gentlemen. We going to have a little music? Some you gentlemen going to play for me this evening?" It was the soft, amiable, Negro voice, like those I remembered from early childhood, with the note of docile subservience in it. He had the Negro head, too; almost no head at all; nothing behind the ears but folds of neck under close-clipped wool. He would have been repulsive if his face had not been so kind and happy. It was the happiest face I had seen since I left Virginia. (118)

This startling description dehumanizes d'Arnault for his "repulsive" physicality ("almost no head at all," "nothing behind the ears"), while at the same time making his body express emotions that are most intimately Burden's own, as he is no doubt making his "happiest face" since leaving Virginia. Serving as the objective correlative for what the narrator himself is feeling is just the first of many mediating feats that d'Arnault will perform.

The novel thus proceeds to stress two connected yet not entirely compatible aspects of d'Arnault's virtuosity. On the one hand, Burden refers to the mindless physicality of d'Arnault's piano playing—and since he has figuratively decapitated the already blind musician in the passage that introduces him to the novel, it should come as no surprise that Burden posits a radically embodied, tactile relationship between the musician and the instrument itself. "Through the dark he found his way to the Thing," writes Cather, narrating the story, which Burden oddly seems to know by heart, of Blind d'Arnault's first encounter with the piano. The meeting of these two bodies produces a moment of contact at once infantile and erotic, a mix that is not that theoretically difficult to imagine but that nevertheless makes for a surprisingly sexy moment in a rather chilly novel.

"He touched it softly, and it answered softly, kindly," Burden tells us, and then "he shivered and stood still. Then he began to feel it all over, ran his fingertips along the slippery sides, embraced the carved legs, tried to get some conception of its shape and size, of the space it occupied in the primeval night. It was cold and hard, and like nothing else in his black universe" (120). We might hardly notice the racializing pun on d'Arnault's blindness—"his black universe"— given the almost pornographic intensity with which Burden reconstructs the way these two black bodies meet and touch. To the degree that d'Arnault's perceptive apparatus evokes a "primeval" mode of communicating with the world—the piano does, after all, *answer* his caress—it confirms the fundamental viscerality, borrowing from Brian Massumi, that "immediately registers excitations gathered by the five 'exteroceptive' senses even before they are fully processed by the brain."[45] The racializing pun, however, keeps this object lesson in "the autonomy of affect" beholden to a more pedestrian, indeed lascivious, fantasy of blackness. What Massumi would identify as "subsensate excitation" Burden attributes to a "sense of rhythm that was stronger than [d'Arnault's] other physical senses," which means that when he does start playing, he provides the familiar sight of "a Negro enjoying himself as only a Negro can" (121).

On the other hand, the novel also tries to understand d'Arnault's unthinking attachment to the piano as an expression of pure mechanics. We read, for example, that before d'Arnault began to play, "he approached this highly artificial instrument through a mere instinct, and coupled himself to it, as if he knew it was to piece him out and make a whole creature of him" (120). Even as the "artificial" nature of the piano stands in contrast to the basic animality of d'Arnault's "instinct," there are signs of a much deeper connection between them, an affinity that recalls what Mark Seltzer has called "the body-machine complex," which takes its most radical form by imagining the "radical and intimate *coupling* of bodies and machines."[46] The emphasis on *coupling* is Seltzer's own, but it calls attention to Cather's use of the same word to characterize d'Arnault's attachment to the instrument that quite bizarrely makes him "whole." How exactly would adding a piano to a blind man "piece him out" in such a way as to complete him? The logic is aggressively prosthetic, even as the language seems only to further deconstruct d'Arnault, as if the very process by which he acquires an "artificial" organ of expression reifies his inhumanity as nothing, in the end, but an assemblage of odd parts and broken faculties. Burden at one point during the performance in Black Hawk sees d'Arnault "[swaying] in time to the music, and when he was not playing, his body kept up the motion,

METZLER'S

"Humanola"

RETAIL
PRICE:

£25

Net Cash,

*together with
offer of £2
worth of
Music Rolls
to every
Purchaser*

FREE.

Its Popular
Price
extends its
Selling
Radius
far beyond
that of
any other
Piano
Player.

*Terms and Particulars
on application to:* **METZLER & CO. (Ltd.),** ⌈*And of all Local
Dealers*

40-43, GREAT MARLBOROUGH STREET, REGENT STREET, LONDON, W.

FIGURE 3.3. Advertisement for Metzler's 'Humanola,' circa 1900.

like an empty mill grinding on" (118). Here, d'Arnault appears as machine-like as any of the countless musical automata produced throughout the eighteenth and nineteenth centuries, or perhaps as the "Humanola" (fig. 3.3), one of several devices that were designed to play standard pianos using a series of "fingers" aligned to strike the keyboard. In an image advertising a different version of such a machine (fig. 3.4)—here called the "Needham Paragon"—we see this peculiar form of musical prosthesis in action. The woman "playing" the Paragon as it plays the piano controls only for tempo and volume; the hammers that strike the piano keys are programmed according to whatever roll is put inside. Like d'Arnault, the woman in this picture represents a void of musical awareness or intention. But she knows how to touch a machine and make it make music for her, which is, as we shall see, a power over "things" like Blind d'Arnault that white people are determined to exploit.

Of course, when Cather's narrator marvels at d'Arnault's "absolute pitch" and "remarkable memory," it is easy enough to consider him the virtual equivalent of a phonograph as well. In this regard, it is apt that when he first attempts

The Needham Paragon

A Song Without Words

NEEDHAM PIANO & ORGAN CO.
96 Fifth Avenue, New York

FIGURE 3.4. Advertisement for the Needham Paragon, circa 1910.

to play his mistress's piano—when he is still a child and, more importantly, still a slave, as Burden recalls his long, strange career—he starts with an uncanny act of reproduction. "He began to finger out passages from things Miss Nellie [his master's daughter] had been playing," explains Burden, "passages that were already his, that lay under the bone of his pinched, conical little skull, definite as animal desires" (120–121). So great are d'Arnault's mimetic abilities that what he later hears seems to have miraculously been inside him all along—he comes loaded with all the software, so to speak, that he will ever need—even though this means he is not displaying superior "memory" so much as superior programming. "He could repeat, after a fashion, any composition that was played for him," Burden informs us. "He wore his teachers out. He could never learn like other people, never acquired any finish. He was always a Negro prodigy who played barbarously and wonderfully" (121). Race again gets abruptly enlisted to mediate between the "animal" and the "mechanical"—either way, inhuman—understandings of d'Arnault's spectacular musical capacities, which ultimately devolve onto the circuitry of his identity, "always a Negro prodigy" who was "a Negro enjoying himself as only a Negro can." Blind d'Arnault, no matter what else he may be, is a wonder of the technology of blackness.

Cather modeled her portrayal of d'Arnault on the popular nineteenth-century performer "Blind Tom," who was born Thomas Wiggins in 1849, but known better as Thomas Bethune after the name of the white family who owned him and his parents until the end of the Civil War. In 1894, while still a college student, Cather contributed an unsigned review of Blind Tom's concert in Lincoln to the *Nebraska State Journal*. But while the review anticipates much of Jim Burden's response to Blind d'Arnault in *My Ántonia*, it does not treat Tom's performance as an occasion for racial nostalgia so much as an experiment in techno-cultural speculation. "He is a human phonograph," writes Cather of Blind Tom, "a sort of animated memory, with sound producing powers."[47] At the concert Cather attended, for instance, a "Professor Lichtenstein of the Western Normal" tried to best Tom's duplicating powers with a quick rendition of Louis Gottschalk's "Tremolo," and though Cather judged the resulting attempt by Wiggins something of a disappointment, she admitted that he "did much better than one would expect."[48] Throughout the long course of Tom's career, as Stephen Best has pointed out, his performances inspired "a patent frustration in attempts to cut the border between the aesthetic and the mechanical."[49] Blind Tom made countless audiences marvel at his "surfeit of mimetic power," which Michael Taussig, whose phrase I am borrowing here, suggests that white observers have long associated with racial difference. This projection of racial meaning works, as Taussig puts it, "to reinstall the mimetic faculty as mystery in the art of technological reproduction, reinvigorating the primitivism implicit in technology's wildest dreams."[50]

In the first decades of the twentieth century, Americans did not need to revisit some fetish world of the anthropological imagination to see what such

FIGURE 3.5. Advertisement for the Victor Talking Machine Co., circa 1912. University of California, Santa Barbara, Department of Special Collections.

a techno-primitivism meant in racial terms. Consider an advertisement for the Victor Talking Machine Company, which dates from sometime after 1911 (fig. 3.5). I call attention to this date because a particular innovation in phonograph design is here put on display—the first Victrola models with internal amplifying horns, the familiar brass trumpet now aimed down and placed behind cabinet doors. As a marketing strategy, this allowed the phonograph to be sold as both fine furniture and high technology, and it distinguished such machines as this Victrola XVIII, with its price set at $300, from the run of down-market Edisons and Victors that continued, well into the 1920s, to offer up their inner workings to the listener. Thus it is not immediately clear just what this image shows, and without the accompanying copy—*"Their inevitable choice—the VICTROLA"*—we would have little reason to suspect a record player sitting at the right edge of the picture, conveniently illuminated by the spotlight of a floor lamp. There is, however, no mistaking that this is a mis-en-scène besotted with a symbology of class: an older, distinguished set of parents and their daughter, dressed for dinner, a lovely Oriental screen and curtains marking off the space of *their* listening and leisure from the dining room where the black maid deals with dishes on the table. The family and their home are strenuously not luxurious; the sense of scale here is close and intimate, and the screen as much as announces the perfectly bourgeois attempt to exaggerate the distances within domestic space; the mother would probably ring a little bell to get the maid's attention from what couldn't be a distance of more than fifteen feet. A phonograph whose mechanics have been gracefully sublimated behind elegant curves and smooth veneers thus makes the ideal addition to a home where the experience of music has been respectfully repressed and disembodied, another dirty business, like cooking, cleaning, or clearing away the dishes, with which a comfortable white family need no longer bother.

Phonograph and black woman are thus locked in a two-way network of analogies: both perform physical labors, whether making music or washing dishes, that white people would prefer to avoid; as providers of domestic service, both represent markers of status and class in which they themselves take no interest; and as machines, neither need ever be worried about or given a voice in deciding if they are going to operate as directed. I might also point out that the image all but demands this particular reading: the space between screen and curtains, in which the maid stands revealed, rhymes perfectly with the just slightly open doors of the Victrola, as if *who* we see at the table should quiet any urge we might have to see *what* is inside the record player. The unsettling modernity of hearing music without instruments or musicians is translated into terms drawn from a more traditional form of household technology: the archaic rituals of chattel slavery are retrofitted for new times and social conditions. "The highly developed taste in art," reads the copy in a 1911 advertisement from the Victor Talking Machine Company, "is satisfied with nothing less than the best which the wide world has to offer. Logically and inevitably such a taste demands the instrument which Caruso has selected as his mouth-piece; which Farrar has selected; which John McCormack and Galli-Curci and Alma Gluck—and a host of other leaders—have selected to be their 'other self.'" But while this would suggest that the Victrola quite simply replaces musicians with music, their bodies with the sounds their bodies have made, I do not think this imagined circuit between Caruso and consumer is so easy to close—because it also appears that the Victrola has selected, as its "other self," a black woman whom we are invited to watch while others listen to the music that the phonograph puts at their service.

The Autobiography of an Ex-Phonograph

When James Weldon Johnson's *The Autobiography of an Ex-Coloured Man* (1912) invokes the specter of various thefts and transgressions by white songwriters in the early days of ragtime, he is not describing ancient history so much as trying to break the news. First published anonymously in the same year as Berlin's "Alexander's Ragtime Band," Johnson's book features a narrator who wants to impress upon his readers that much of the credit being given to the originators of the new sensation is misdirected; white men such as Berlin have earned their money, adulation, and acclaim just for transcribing what they have heard black musicians play.[51] Their reproductions are indeed mechanical and represent the opposite of originality, the work of men who are little more than what Bruno Latour might call "writing-down-machines."[52] Ragtime, the ex-colored man insists, was invented by "Negro piano-players who knew no more of the theory of music than they did of the theory of the universe, but were guided by natural musical instinct and talent. . . . These players often improvised crude and, at times, vulgar words to fit the melodies. This was the beginning of the rag-time song. Several of these improvisations were taken down by white men, the words slightly altered, and published under the names of the arrangers. They sprang into immediate popularity and earned small fortunes, of which the Negro originators got only a few dollars."[53] Writing some twenty years after Johnson, Huges Panassié argues that "the phonograph is most precious to jazz" because "the record is the only medium there is for preservation of tonal improvisations which, without records, would be lost forever."[54] But the ex-colored man knows otherwise: there already were technologies, perhaps not so sophisticated but equally pervasive, that functioned to inscribe, in more material forms, the fleeting and immediate pleasures of black music. They were called white people.

In the media ecology of *The Autobiography of an Ex-Coloured Man*, writing is effectively a racial attribute of whiteness. If there were no "ex-coloured man" there would be no need for him to write his "autobiography," for it is not the contents of his experiences that inspire their reproduction as a text but rather the idea that "in writing the following pages" he is "playing with fire" and courting a "diabolical desire" to confess the great secret that he has "passed" into the white world. He announces that his revelation will turn the "little tragedies" of his life into a "practical joke on society," but in the end, the note he strikes is more plainly melancholy in its regret that he has "chosen the lesser part" and sold his "birthright for a mess of pottage" (3, 211). As Cristina Ruotolo rightly argues, "From his 'ex-colored' and alienated position at the end of the novel, he can only gesture as a silent writer toward a realm of African American sound that, safe from the commodifying, imitating, and fetishizing ears of white America, has been returned to an imagined, if now inaudible authenticity."[55] According to this elegant formulation, Johnson's narrator wants us to believe that he has killed his "colored" self to preserve a far more valuable black aesthetic from being mediated right out of existence. The death wish that de Man discovers at the heart of autobiography—a genre in which, as de Man famously contends, "death is a displaced name for a linguistic predicament"—doubly patterns the logic of whiteness in Johnson's text, which asks us to mourn the black person that the narrator once was, while it leaves the narrator himself anonymous and nameless, a pure void of personhood.[56] But when Johnson's narrator elects to become "ex-coloured," the novel gives us no account of what he actually has lost. Maybe because he has nothing to lose. Walter Benn Michaels has an easy mark in *The Autobiography of an Ex-Coloured Man*, which features a narrator who looks back on his own life with such regret, at least in part, because he cannot survive the vicious logic immanent to the most literal understanding of race: as Michaels puts it, "Either race is the sort of thing that makes rejecting your racial identity just a kind of passing, or passing becomes impossible and there is no such thing as racial identity."[57] And so the ex-colored man has nothing in the end but a fiction of racial being he cannot let die, and his "fast yellowing manuscripts, the only tangible remnants of a vanished dream" (211).

We cannot appreciate the full meaning of this final gesture—which materializes the racial death of the ex-colored man in the technology of writing—without tracing how the novel and its narrator, from the start, align the aesthetic power of blackness with the sensuous, spontaneous immediacy of music. Recall the novel's plot: born in Georgia, the narrator moves to Connecticut with his mother while still a young boy, and there he enjoys a largely idyllic childhood before learning one day at school that he is black, just like his classmate "Shiny," whose dark skin and appearance he had formerly mocked; from this point forward, he identifies himself as black, even as he fixates on the "ivory whiteness" of his skin and "the softness and glossiness" of his dark hair, which makes his face "appear whiter than it really [is]" (17). After his mother dies, he decides to attend Atlanta University, but after his meager savings are stolen, he finds work in a Jacksonville cigar factory before making his way to New York, where he becomes a professional gambler, and finally a musician in the employ of a white patron who takes the now "coloured" man to Europe; here, his aesthetic ambitions awakened by European classics, he decides to return to the United States and collect black music throughout the South in hopes of assembling a symphony from his folk materials. But when he witnesses a terrifying lynching, he experiences an unbearable "shame at being identified with a people that could with impunity be treated worse than animals" (191). Now as an "ex-coloured man," he returns to New York, determined neither to "disclaim the black race nor claim the white race" (190); succumbing to what he calls "the money fever," he earns a small fortune and marries a white woman who dies giving birth to the second of their children (194).

This summary does little justice to the centrality of the ex-colored man's musical experiences within the shape of the narrative as a whole. Among his earliest memories he recalls how he first learned music by listening to "some old Southern songs" his mother liked to play (8). Unlike the other hymns that she "picked out"—which I take to mean that she read from a score—the narrator insists that "in these songs she was freer, because she played them by ear" (7– 8). We as readers are almost certainly supposed to know that these "Southern songs" are in fact black spirituals, and there are other details in the ex-colored man's account of his musical education that communicate more than a hint of the racial identity that he himself does not yet realize he has. Consider, for example, how he describes the particular attraction that the piano holds: "Whenever she started toward the instrument," he writes of his mother, "I used to follow her with all the interest and irrepressible joy that a pampered pet dog shows when a package is opened in which he knew there is a sweet bit for him" (8). In light of the ex-colored man's eventual disavowal of race because he cannot bear "being identified" with a people "treated worse than animals," his likening of himself to a dog already sketches the trajectory of his self-hatred. This language also recalls aspects of Blind Tom's similarly inhuman attraction to both music and the technology of the piano. Whether or not Johnson wants us to hear these echoes is hard to say, but in his own autobiography, *Along This Way* (1933), he mentions Blind Tom as one of the "well known" figures about whom he reads in James M. Trotter's *Music and Some Highly Musical People* (1881), a compendium of black musical biographies featuring a striking account of Thomas Green Bethune.[58] Such circumstantial evidence aside, the emphasis that Johnson places on reproduction and improvisation—on feats of memory and sheer performance—patterns the ex-colored man's musical abilities on those we saw attributed to Blind Tom. And so not only does the narrator "follow" his mother to the piano in a show of animalized fidelity, but soon he can "play by ear all of the hymns and songs" his mother knows; he does learn to read music, but "preferred not to be hampered by the notes," and his first formal teacher "had no small difficulty at first in pinning [him] down to notes" (8–9). "I used to stand by her side," the ex-colored man recalls of his mother when she played, "and often interrupt and annoy her by chiming in with some harmonies which I found on either the high keys of the treble or the low keys of the bass" (8). There is perhaps nothing out of the ordinary in this interaction between mother, child, and piano save the precocious talent that the ex-colored man displays, but all this looms differently when Johnson indulges in some leaden symbolizing by having his narrator confess to a "particular fondness for the black keys" (8). The piano, in effect, communicates the sense of racial identity that the ex-colored man has no reason to believe that he should have.

The ex-colored man's career takes a decisive turn when he encounters a figure who represents a powerful variation on the musical aesthetic that shapes his own childhood. To the degree to which these primal scenes of inspiration suggest a coherent set of preferences—for playing by ear over reading, for improvising over following the notes, for affect and impulse over rote performances of any kind—he does not find them completely realized until he ends up in New York, where he not coincidentally finds them completely racialized:

> I realized that in a large back room into which the main room opened, there was a young fellow singing a song, accompanied on the piano by a short, thickset, dark man. After each verse he did some dance steps, which brought forth great applause and a shower of small coins at his feet. After the singer had responded to a rousing encore, the stout man at the piano began to run his fingers up and down the keyboard. This he did in a manner which indicated that he was master of a good deal of technique. Then he began to play; and such playing! I stopped talking to listen. It was music of a kind I had never heard before. It was music that demanded physical response, patting of the feet, drumming of the fingers, or nodding of the head in time with the beat. The barbaric harmonies, the audacious resolutions, often consisting of an abrupt jump from one key to another, the intricate rhythms in which the accents fell in the most unexpected places, but in which the beat was never lost, produced a most curious effect. And, too, the player—the dexterity of his left hand in making rapid octave runs and jumps was little short of marvelous; and with his right hand he frequently swept half the keyboard with clean-cut chromatics which he fitted in so nicely as never to fail to arouse in his listeners a sort of pleasant surprise at the accomplishment of the feat.
>
> This was rag-time music, then a novelty in New York, and just growing to be a rage, which has not yet subsided. (98–99)

There are two performers here, and the ex-colored man is little interested in the one who sings and dances, perhaps because the "coins" thrown by the crowd make all too clear the latent influence of minstrelsy—a black musician may well possess "a good deal of technique," but stereotypes still pay. The more significant attraction is the music, which the narrator describes according to a logic that moves from amazement ("such playing!") to expert appreciation with surprising speed. Does the ex-colored man surrender to the "physical response" that ragtime demands? Are those his feet and fingers marking time? His head "nodding" to the beat? I ask because his detachment from "the barbaric harmonies, the audacious resolutions"—a detachment performed by naming them as such—while testifying to his talent and trained ear, also allows him to make a record of the performance that parallels the exploitative transcriptions "taken down by white men." The passages detailing these crimes of reproduction in fact follow on the scene above, and they render the ex-colored man's first response to ragtime as an odd but also—in light of his own conflicted sense of racial designation—entirely appropriate mix of black and white. He hears as if with perfect double consciousness that this music should at once communicate to him with a sensuous immediacy that, like his mother's spirituals and "Southern songs," signifies the blackness that he shares with the pianist; but at the same time, no matter how "abrupt" or "intricate" or "unexpected" they may be, he takes down every key change, octave jump, and chromatic run with a formal precision that distinguishes whites' appropriations of a style that does not belong to them "by natural musical instinct."

In 1912, when Johnson anonymously published *The Autobiography of an Ex-Coloured Man*, such appropriations would have pointed in the direction of Irving Berlin; in 1927, when Carl Van Vechten convinced Johnson to republish the text in his own name and identify it as a novel, the reader would have had Gershwin, Whiteman, Jolson, the members of the Original Dixieland Jazz Band, and countless others at whom to level the ex-colored man's indictment. But at the moment Johnson's narrator is describing—"the beginning of the rag-time song"—the likeliest figure to associate with the originary theft of "improvised" black performances then codified as white compositions was Ben Harney, whose *Ragtime Instructor* first appeared in 1897 and consisted solely of transcriptions that Harney claimed to be his own.[59] Musicologists and historians debate the originality of the songs that Harney popularized, with Tom Fletcher, in 1954, characterizing him as "the first Caucasian to translate ragtime to the piano," and Ian Whitcomb in 1987 referring to the "red-haired youth from Kentucky" who "had picked up his tricks from the Other America."[60] Or maybe he is Other too: Edward Berlin cites a 1913 newspaper purporting to reveal that Harney was a black man passing for white, which would make his transcriptions racially authentic by the standards of the ex-colored man at least, even if he only wrote them down as other Others played them.[61] Most recent sources dispute the possibility that Harney was African American, but in the context of Johnson's novel, even the slightest gesture of racial suspicion helps to underscore how the very notion of an "instructor" in the sounds of blackness—allowing anybody access to "tricks from the Other America"—already reproduces the formalities of passing, if not the fact. "Harney was not content to exploit the new craze of ragtime," writes the same Isaac Goldberg who celebrated Gershwin for "Swanee," in *From Ragtime to Swingtime: The Story of the House of Witmark* (1939); "he had the instinct of the codifier. He wanted to trap the theory behind the fact, and to set it down as a method that others could learn."[62]

◊

Ben Harney's performances, as remembered by Isaac Goldberg and Isidore Witmark, "included the 'ragging' of such popular classics as Mendelssohn's *Spring Song*, Rubinstein's *Melody in F*, and the *Intermezzo* from Mascagni's 'Cavalleria Rusticana,' which he would first play in their orthodox form. The effect was startling" (155). The ex-colored man's performances, as remembered by the anonymous narrator who was once the "best" ragtime pianist in New York, marshaled all his "knowledge of classic music" and "achieved some novelties which pleased and even astonished my listeners" (115). "It was I," the ex-colored man writes, "who first made rag-time transcriptions of familiar classic selections. I used to play Mendelssohn's 'Wedding March' in a manner that never failed to arouse enthusiasm among the patrons of the 'Club.' Very few nights passed during which I was not asked to play it. It was no secret that the great increase in slumming visitors was due to my playing" (115). Not content to claim his rightful place—though not, of course, his name—as the originator of the ragtime vogue for variations on the classics, Johnson's narrator seems also to want credit for anticipating the phenomenon that becomes the Harlem Renaissance.

His celebrity at the "Club" attracts the special attention of one white "slummer" who becomes the ex-colored man's patron, as well as serving as a "friend who was the means by which [he] escaped from this lower world" (115). Described as a "clean-cut, slender, but athletic-looking man," whose every movement bore the "unmistakable stamp of culture," this nameless millionaire is a figure redolent of an affected dissatisfaction and melancholy from the start, "languidly puffing cigarettes" as he sits alone, dispensing five-dollar tips to the ex-colored man with clockwork regularity for a month before propositioning him about "an engagement" (116). The performance begins with the ex-colored man playing classical music, "according to a suggestion from the host" (117). But for the "decidedly blasé" guests at the dinner, this sort of music is "only an accompaniment to the chatter," and after the first selection, the ex-colored man is largely ignored—until he receives his signal from the host to "[strike] up one of [his] liveliest rag-time pieces," which certainly prompts a version of the "physical response" that the ex-colored man experienced, but here the effect is far more extreme (117–118). It is not simply that now he has the full attention of an audience who has exhausted "every resource . . . that might possibly furnish a new sensation or awaken a fresh emotion"; his virtuoso playing, when he performs his "rag-time transcription of Mendelssohn's 'Wedding March,'" commands their bodies too, and soon "the whole company involuntarily and unconsciously did an impromptu cake-walk" (119–120).

This makes for a curiously self-regarding scene of imitation and performance: a black musician, who only looks white, plays a ragtime "transcription" of white music that seizes on white bodies and causes them "involuntarily and unconsciously" to dance like black people. The frenzy with which all racial identities at issue here get thoroughly confused—do the guests know the ex-colored man is black? might their cakewalk only mirror the act of simulated blackness they think that they are witnessing? how "unconsciously" does this transcribed "Wedding March" mean to echo the miscegenations, both literal and figurative, that inform this scene?—seems precisely to be the point of the evening's entertainment. The spectacle of such contagious inauthenticity brings to mind the reason LeRoi Jones treats ragtime so dismissively: "Northern Negro pre-jazz music," he writes in *Blues People* (1963), "was almost like the picture within a picture, and so on, on the cereal package."[63] Ragtime, simply put, is black music that has been processed and denatured, an easily consumed commodity synthesized, at every stage, from artificial ingredients. Jones has scorn to spare for this "kind of bouncy, essentially vapid appropriation of the popularized imitations of Negro imitations of white minstrel music"; the resulting mix of musical aesthetics evokes a modern world in which all signs of racial integrity have faded into "the hopelessly interwoven fabric of American life where blacks and whites pass so quickly as to become only grays!"[64] Of course "passing" here does not suggest the romance of racial ambiguity that it might for Ellison in "Living with Music," or even Johnson in *The Autobiography of an*

Ex-Coloured Man. Jones's pun instead implies the melancholy attitude he assumes toward any African American aesthetic that renders itself so available for reproduction that it no longer communicates even the slightest hint that it was, at least originally, the expression of a living, organic blackness.

Thus the image on the cover of sheet music for the "Castle Innovation Tango" (fig. 3.6) would, from Jones's vantage point, show much the same thing

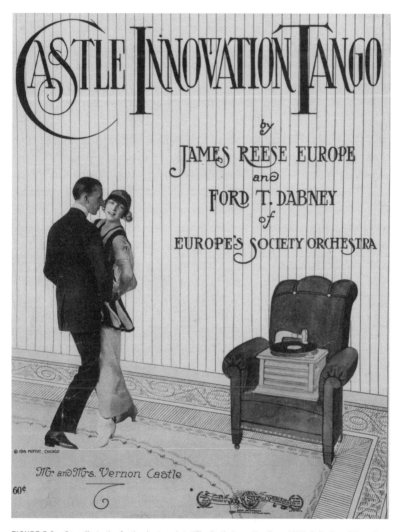

FIGURE 3.6. Cover illustration for the sheet music to "The Castle Innovation Tango," 1914. Collection of the author.

as the scene that the ex-colored man has just described. Here we see Vernon and Irene Castle dancing along to music coming from a small phonograph perched on an armchair. The Castles were two of the most successful American performers of the 1910s, the most prominent icons of the period's craze for social dancing, and the tight, though not exactly carnal embrace in which they are pictured would have been familiar to their many fans. Though they are perhaps best remembered for making the fox-trot into something of a national sensation, their singular "innovation" was a modern style of couples dancing that married speed to a potentially quite provocative insistence on close physicality—which is exactly how they are pictured in this illustration showing their bodies so tightly clasped to one another that Vernon's other leg has mysteriously vanished between those of his wife. Black musicians composed many of the tunes to which the Castles danced, and their association with James Reese Europe was especially important, for it was his Society Orchestra—a smaller version of his 150-member Clef Club Orchestra that played the first show of popular music at Carnegie Hall in 1912—that traveled with the Castles on several national tours, and also provided music for a majority of their New York stage performances. "It was we who made colored orchestras the vogue of Fifth Avenue," Irene Castle writes in a 1958 autobiography. "We booked Jim Europe's orchestra, the most famous of the colored bands. Jim Europe was a skilled musician and one of the first to take jazz out of the saloons and make it respectable."[65] One consequence of such "respectability" is easily extrapolated from this image of black music that has been utterly domesticated: the phonograph makes it possible for white people to tango in ragtime, dance a maxie, or "do an impromptu cake-walk" if they are in the mood, all without requiring the services of, or inviting any contact with, a black musician in the flesh. The logic of this substitution is so obvious—the music we cannot hear rhymes with the bodies we cannot see, and both mediate the signs of race that animate the scene—that it is easy to look past the fact that there should not, technically speaking, be a phonograph in the picture in the first place. Why put a phonograph on the cover of piano music? If we learn to play the "Castle Innovation Tango" for ourselves, why do we want a phonograph at all?

Let me begin answering these questions by posing yet another: why is the phonograph sitting down? On acoustic grounds alone, an easy chair is an odd place to put a record player, but this is not my point. I am fascinated instead by the way this image lends an almost human presence to the phonograph, as if this were *its* living room, as if the Castles were dancing for *its* entertainment.

The effect I am describing partly comes from the mix of media from which the picture has been fashioned: the photographic Castles do not seem entirely at home here; the plane of the picture is too flat to accommodate their scale, and their realism is rendered weightless and uncanny when set against the sketched-in walls and hand-drawn carpeting; even the chair, which is somewhat modeled as an object in three dimensions, is more cartoonish than photographic. If the phonograph is here by mistake—an instance of visual catachresis, since what it should be is the piano on which this music may be played—so too are the Castles, who have both stepped into a space where media technologies reside more comfortably than human beings. Which is to say that if this phonograph is strangely anthropomorphized by being given the seat of honor for a command performance by the celebrated Vernon and Irene Castle, then it also figures an aesthetic that is more powerfully realized and embodied when its author is altogether mediated. When someone buys a copy of the "Castle Innovation Tango"—a white consumer, if this cover is taken at face value—and sits down at the piano, that person will become the instrument of James Reese Europe and Ford Dabney, two black musicians who, like Johnson's ex-colored man, possess the ability to make white people move at their command, perhaps not always "involuntarily and unconsciously" but still by means of an elaborate system of racial fantasy and remote control. The Castles can plainly dance without their all-black orchestra, but they need some object to materialize the racialized aesthetic that their bodies at once express and sublimate in their curious performance for the phonograph itself. The same circuitous arrangement that translates ragtime into something more "respectable" all but inscribes the presence of race wherever there is a technology for making music.

It is this network of displacements and associations that informs the ex-colored man's experience of being used by his white patron as a virtual pianola. After the success of his first private performance, his new "millionaire friend," as the ex-colored man comes to call him, offers an exclusive "contract" guaranteeing "lots of work," but also with the following "stipulation": "that I should not play any engagements such as I had just filled for him, except by his instructions" (120). But the terms of this contract, freely entered, to be sure, seem to invite comparison to the slavery's protocols of ownership and objectification. It is not just that the millionaire treats the ex-colored man as a commodity— "occasionally he 'loaned' me to some of his friends"—but also that the character of their relationship suggests both the possessiveness and the implicit show of psychic need associated with the bonds between a master and his slave.[66] "He would sometimes sit for three or four hours hearing my play," the ex-colored man writes of his strange and wealthy patron, "his eyes almost closed, making scarcely a motion except to light a fresh cigarette, and never commenting one way or another on the music" (121). This absorption without affect stands in decided contrast to the giddy exuberance of the "impromptu cake-walk" that the ex-colored man inspired before; his music has a far different effect upon the millionaire, whose compulsion to consume is coded as decadent and narcotic, an addiction which demands that the ex-colored man outdo what any phonograph or player piano of the period could achieve—hour upon hour of continuous operation, perfectly reproducing song after song after song without requiring any human agency or attention. "The man's powers of endurance in listening often [exceeded] mine in performing," the ex-colored man admits, "yet I am not sure that he was always listening. At times I became so oppressed with fatigue and sleepiness that it took almost superhuman effort to keep my fingers going; in fact, I believe I sometimes did so while dozing" (121). What seems "superhuman" here is the ability of the ex-colored man to play automatically past the point where he surrenders consciousness, and there are gothic overtones to the only explanation that he can offer to account for why he permits himself to be used so absolutely: "During such moments this man sitting there so mysteriously silent, almost hid in a cloud of heavy scented smoke, filled me with a sort of unearthly terror. He seemed to be some grim, mute, but relentless tyrant, possessing over me a supernatural power which he used to drive me on mercilessly to exhaustion" (121). For all its resonance with a language of mediated experience that would not be out of place in Du Maurier's *Trilby* (1894)—with Johnson imagining the ex-colored man in the hold of a Svengali who renders him the instrument of corrupting musical desires—the bond between Johnson's narrator and his patron develops into a "familiar and warm relationship" (121). "I am sure," or so the ex-colored man wants to believe, that his "friend" the millionaire "had a decided personal liking for me" (121). But we can only know for certain just how affectionately the ex-colored man comes to feel toward this "relentless tyrant," who sometimes "loans" him out for friends to have at their disposal: "I looked upon him at that time as about all a man could wish to be" (121).

◊

A fine romance and a strict division of labor: the ex-colored man works tirelessly at the piano while the white millionaire listens insatiably, and each seems to get something that he needs from the relationship. Johnson's narrator is "paid so . . . liberally" that he can afford to overlook the ways he has been possessed, and his patron is distracted from "the thing which seemed to sum up all in life that he dreaded—time" (121, 143). We later learn, in fact, that the millionaire's attachment to the narrator is as much therapeutic as homoerotic, and he eventually commits suicide sometime after losing his "superhuman" musical accompaniment. "As I remember him now," the ex-colored man writes of an ex-white man whose actual oblivion conveniently prefigures the self-inflicted racial death that structures the narration, "I can see that time was what he was always endeavoring to escape, to bridge over, to blot out; and it is not strange that some years later he did escape it for ever, by leaping into eternity" (143). Their double suicides—both literal and otherwise—are best understood as pathological enactments of the alienation that draws them to each other in the first place. Between the two of them we witness a scale-model version of the "new organizational network for the economy of music" that Jacques Attali attributes to "the advent of recording"; "in this network," Attali continues, "each spectator has a solitary relation with a material object; the consumption of music is individualized, a simulacrum of ritual sacrifice, a blind spectacle."[67] Neither the white millionaire, as musical consumer, nor the ex-colored man, as music-making "object," manages to get out of this relationship alive.

On this evidence we might conclude that the "strong bond of affection" between the ex-colored man and the ex-white millionaire is rather desperately revealed, after both have killed those aspects of themselves they least could bear, to have been doomed from the beginning. Even at its highest pitch, their intimacy remains an affair of substitutions and deferrals:

> This man of the world, who grew weary of everything and was always searching for something new, appeared never to grow tired of my music; he seemed to take it as a drug. He fell into a habit which caused me no little annoyance; sometimes he would come in during the early hours of the morning and, finding me in bed asleep, would wake me up and ask me to play something. This, so far as I can remember, was my only hardship during my whole stay with him. (131)

Here the appeal of the ex-colored man as the perfect medium for making music suggests as well a desire for proximity and contact that communicates, for Cheryl Clarke and several other readers of the novel, a "covert" acknowledgment that the same period which witnesses the rise of ragtime witnesses too the growing prominence of Harlem as one of New York's most important centers of gay culture. As Clarke would have it, the fact that a moment such as this appears determined to misrepresent the millionaire's desire to have sex as, on the contrary, his desire to have his piano played, is itself the proof that Johnson's narrative of passing is also about "illicit sexuality (including homosexuality)."[68] I do not disagree. But I would insist that even if the millionaire only gets into bed with the ex-colored man to hear some ragtime, there is something sufficiently erotic about their relationship—precisely because it shows a white passion for black music and its mediums—that speaks to a variety of equally compelling pleasures that are possible when we surrender to our deepest feelings for technology.

Jan Matulka's 1929 painting *Arrangement with Phonograph* strikes me as a perfect illustration of this point (fig. 3.7). Matulka's expressive strategies rely haphazardly on any number of modernist aesthetics that are beyond the scope of Johnson's novel: a fauvist saturation of color, an appropriately flat geometry evocative of cubism, a touch of surrealism in the moody nighttime sky, and of course a selection of objects that perhaps confess too easily their influences, from the African mask that claims the left side of the canvas for the "primitive" to the banjo, at center, which could be taken as the counterpart to so many guitars in Picasso's still-lifes. These are analogs, not attributions; the banjo, to cite one departure, has a cartoonish curve that owes relatively little to cubism in its strictest incarnations, and the mask, to cite another, traffics in a more explicit mode of racial caricature. That said, this mask of blackness also features, as its distinctly visible "other" side, a white profile with blond hair. And at the very least, this whiteness troubling the "arrangement" of racial signifiers—including the banjo, an instrument with its roots in West Africa, which here has been given an unsubtle phallus for its neck as if to confirm the sexual potency of black culture—might make us wonder about the record playing on the phonograph. Is it a low-down, dirty blues or some whitewashed approximation? The black mask seems to emerge from the recesses of the white mind; the black mind seems to produce a crown of white skin and blond hair. Whose racial fantasy is being dreamed upon this moonlit night? And what music puts us in the mood?

The circuitry connecting race and recorded sound in Matulka's *Arrangement with Phonograph* presents us with a modernist predicament of mediation: everything that this image says with music has a flip side that undoes the logic of

FIGURE 3.7.   Jan Matulka, *Arrangement with Phonograph*, 1930. Smithsonian American Art Museum.

identity that it asserts. Music does not so much communicate a sense of racial meaning as provide a form and apparatus onto which both the ex-colored man and the white millionaire can project their love of the technologies that they need so desperately to express their otherwise damaged and divided selves. I would argue, moreover, that the ex-colored man continues to indulge such compensatory, mediated pleasures right up to the bitter end of his life's story. Having "passed" into white New York society, and with a small fortune earned in real estate speculation, the ex-colored man meets a white woman at a "musi-cal" and is immediately captivated by everything about her, from her voice to what can only be described as her overwhelming whiteness. "She was as white as a lily, and she was dressed in white. Indeed, she seemed to me the most daz-zling white thing I had ever seen," the ex-colored man confesses, before then attempting to convince us that "it was not her delicate beauty which attracted" him so much as her voice, "which made one wonder how tones of such pas-sionate colour could come from so fragile a body" (198). By this point in the novel, however, it is hard to read this loving appreciation without also wonder-ing how the narrator now understands the sounds of "colour" that once came from his own white body; his passion makes him anxious to admit that he has "Negro blood" inside his veins, even as his feelings "melted away [his] cynicism and whitened [his] sullied soul and gave [him] back the wholesome dreams of [his] boyhood" (200–201). Not wanting to marry her "under false colours," he decides to spill his secret: "Then I told her, in what words I do not know, the truth. I felt her hand grow cold, and when I looked up, she was gazing at me with a wild, fixed stare as though I was some object she had never seen" (204).

But even when language fails him, and his "incoherent words of love" seem only to confirm that in the eyes of his potential wife he is finally just a thing that no white woman could truly love, the ex-colored man still has recourse to the medium in which he has never failed to charm. Of course this means saying it with music: at a properly respectable "card party," far removed from both the blaring "Club" and the blasé decadence of the millionaire, he sees the woman of his impossibly white dreams—who "seemed even a trifle paler"—and joins her at the piano as she starts to play, "very softly, as to herself," the opening bars of Chopin's Nocturne No. 13 (207–208). "I felt that the psychic moment of my life had come," he writes, and when she calls him by the "Christian name" his readers never know, he realizes that their romance has overcome his race, and he hears her say, "I love you, I love you, I love you" (209). As if her act of repetition calls for an echoing gesture from the ex-colored man, he answers her by "[taking] her place at the piano and [playing] the Nocturne in a manner that silenced the chatter of the company both in and out of the room" (209). As an episode in the social history of the piano, nothing could be more conventionally bourgeois than this making of matches to a soundtrack of the classics; the piano, according to Arthur Loesser, "can be seen as a feature in the physiognomy of a certain way of life, the way of moneyed middle-class people" of the kind the ex-colored man becomes, a people who "wanted an instrument that could play any tone loud or soft from bodily impulse at the whim of an instant, that could reflect the free, incalculable play of 'feeling' within their hearts."[69] Thus this moment is described by one critic as a performance where the ex-colored man "ultimately dissolves . . . resistance to miscegenation by, in effect, dissolving his blackness" in the perfect reproduction of a piece of music catering to the "middle-class white society" to which he is resigned to join.[70] Yet I would argue that this moment also reverberates with the sounds of race—of "passionate colour" in every sense—that were so irresistible in the strains of the ex-colored man's ragtime transcription of the "Wedding March." His fiancée, just like the millionaire before, is privy to the secret that the white man at the piano really isn't who or what he seems, and that his playing, for all its fidelity and expressive power, also communicates a troubling instability of identity, a series of mediations between black and white, machine and human being, or put more literally, between piano player and player piano.[71] This may well be when the ex-colored man sells his "birthright for a mess of pottage." But in this "psychic moment," when demonstrating to his fiancée just how effortlessly he reproduces music for her pleasure, the ex-colored man also reminds her, for better or for worse, what it technically is that she is marrying.

J. Scott Fitzgerald, Wired for Sound

"With the advent of the new media," Mladen Dolar observes of the phonographic era that is modernity, "the acousmatic property of the voice became universal, and hence trivial . . . all we see is some technical appliance from which voices emanate, and in a quid pro quo the gadget takes the place of the invisible source itself. The invisible absent source is substituted by the gadget which disguises it and starts to act as its unproblematic stand-in" (63). This pervasive mediation of voice and sound is certainly the historical condition from which Ellison and Johnson both attend. But I would also hope that nothing about the ways in which these works imagine the poetics of this substitution— which puts media technology in the place of some body, individual, or identity that makes music—appears even for a moment "unproblematic" with respect to race. Any apparatus that becomes a medium for racial communication in America is almost automatically, or so it would seem, transformed into a fetish, invested with excess meaning, and apprehended as an object fascinating not only for the messages it can deliver but also for the noises it cannot suppress. It would be a mistake, I think, to presume that these media effects and fantasies are somehow secondary or ephemeral—distractions at the level of content, that return us to a self-deluding ideology of form, a logic of modernism circumscribed, as Fredric Jameson argues, "in terms of technique and of technical developments within the medium itself."[72] To the degree that aspiring to the "condition of music" marks a particularly compelling version of this medium aesthetic, I have tried to keep at least partial faith with its own protocols and operations while at the same time pursuing connections to a larger world of media technologies to suggest a different archaeology for modernism's past and a different trajectory for its future. So while I have looked to other explanations for why these modernist representations of recorded sound take the shape they do—the widespread influence of primitivism, the rampant commodification of racial authenticity, the afterlife of slavery as a cultural phenomenon, the emblematic status of the machine—I would also like to insist that some of the most compelling constellations of race and technology are best understood as products of an extreme commitment to experiencing the materiality of a medium.

The fiction of F. Scott Fitzgerald provides the perfect test for such an argument. I say this not just because his prose so often strains toward precisely those sound effects—alliteration, assonance, periodicity—that count as "musicality" in the everyday language of literary evaluation, nor even because these recurring stylistic features help sustain the sense of "lyricism" that is the signature of every aspect of his writing, from its tone and local textures to its ideology and thematic emphases. One could, I think, almost pick a paragraph at random to prove the case, but I would like to proceed from an example that is far more motivated. This is how the protagonist of *The Beautiful and the Damned* (1922), Anthony Patch—a "distinct and dynamic personality" whose abiding irony cannot prevent his final crack-up—recalls his mother, who died when he was five:

> His memories of the Boston Society Contralto were nebulous and musical. She was a lady who sang, sang, sang, in the music-room of their house on Washington Square—sometimes with guests scattered all about her, the men with their arms folded, balanced breathlessly on the edges of sofas, the women with their hands in their laps, occasionally making little whispers to the men and always clapping very briskly and uttering cooing cries after each song—and often she sang to Anthony alone, in Italian or French or in a strange and terrible dialect which she imagined to be the speech of the Southern negro.[73]

As with seemingly every hero in Fitzgerald, there is the lost object and the romance of the aesthetic that can never quite manage to restore it. The long, paratactic sentence that describes his mother's singing provides a syntax for this melancholy, extending its grammatical construction to encompass more absence with every comma splice, mourning for her death even as the ornate use of the historical present obscures the event itself within a self-regarding contemporaneity, which is entirely associated with, if not predicated on, the experience of art. Whatever timelessness there is to treasure here depends on music. And the various repetitions ("sang, sang, sang"), alliterations ("balanced breathlessly," "clapping . . . and cooing cries," "Anthony alone"), and moments of assonance ("music-room," "hands in their laps," "speech of the Southern ne-gro") attempt to communicate a psychology of character by way of an indulgent formalism that, for all its attention to what Greenberg would call the "immedi-ately sensuous" aspects of its medium, all but telegraphs each and every thing it wants to say.

It is just as telling that a version of black music—distorted, off-key, and so inauthentic that it doesn't fool a five-year-old—appears in the background of the scene, for as critics such as Michaels, Michael North, and Mitchell Breitwi-eser have pointed out, while few of Fitzgerald's fictions are concerned primarily with race, there is no escaping the signs of its mediating influence in many of his major works, and in *The Great Gatsby* (1925) most of all. Breitwieser un-derstands the extravagant production number that Gatsby stages for his guests as emblematic of the novel's divided attitude toward race; on the one hand, jazz is obviously synonymous with Fitzgerald's epoch, representing modernity as such with all its "energy and velocity," and hints at "an erotic vitality early lost in an effete society (but still effective among African Americans)"; on the other hand, the lengths to which Fitzgerald goes to specify that the characters in *The Great Gatsby* are hearing not jazz but rather its degraded approximation, reveal that the modern world is warped not only by white fantasies of black exclusion but also by the "imperfect repression of qualitative racial difference [that] ensures that the cultural coding of race will necessarily entail the her-meneutic code." This means, according to Breitwieser, that such repression is always incomplete, and therefore perceptible in the narrative contortions that continuously invoke the very racial signs they would otherwise displace.[74] Or, as North puts it, the "black body represents a material reality that cannot be aestheticized by any medium, no matter how modernized."[75]

Black bodies and black music, then, bring the noise to white America that makes it "into this land of jazz," where, in the words of *The Beautiful and the Damned*, Fitzgerald's characters "[fall] immediately into a state of almost au-dible confusion" (640). But by the end of the novel, Anthony Patch is more than just confused. After waiting for most of the narrative to inherit his grandfa-ther's fortune, only to have a contested will deprive him of any money, he lapses into insanity just as a verdict in his favor is returned. His nervous breakdown, however, is the opposite of a surprise to any reader "listening" carefully to a bit of music Anthony hears a coat-check girl singing just a few pages before: "*Out in—the shimmee sanitarium / The jazz-mad nuts reside. / Out in—the shimmee sanitarium / I left my blushing bride*" (784). Anthony's grandfather disinherits him because of a debauched scene he stumbles into when he surprises Anthony with a visit; and his arrival comes as a complete surprise because no one in the house, where the "melancholy cadences" of drunken song mingle with "'Poor Butter-fly (tink-atink), by the blossoms wait-ing' on the phonograph," can hear the telephone when he calls to say he is almost there (656). On both of these occasions, the virtual soundtrack not only tells us more than everything we need to know—a "Poor Butterfly" waiting for his money, he will go "Jazz Mad" before he gets it—it reveals a commitment to communicate so obvious that the effect is less one of tone or lyric mood than, again, one of Barthes's "semantic prattle."

Fitzgerald cites a range of music that draws more narrowly from popular styles and genres, which means that he tends to avoid the sharp juxtapositions of high and low (Wagner and that "Shakespeherian Rag") that famously define, for example, Eliot's allusive technique in "The Waste Land." Which is not to say that Fitzgerald always gives his readers music that is easy to decode, especially given that a sense of exceeding presentness and ephemerality is itself part of the message his fiction often seems most intent upon delivering. The archive of popular music in Fitzgerald that Ruth Prigozy very helpfully reconstructs—numbering more than seventy specific titles—now reads much like the antiquarian arcana of Eliot or Pound. Indeed, I am far better informed by virtue of my chosen field and its acculturating traditions about the significance and implications of, say, the "Dirge" from John Webster's *White Devil* than I am about the nuances of "Three O'clock in the Morning" from *The Greenwich Village Follies of 1921*, or "Three Acts of Music" from *No, No, Nanette*, each referenced in *Tender Is the Night*. That the materials of modern popular culture are uniquely subject to such instantaneous archaism speaks to the bulk in which such works are produced and to the speed with which they are consumed, and both of these phenomena conspire to make for something of what Benjamin has in mind when he writes about "all the difficulties posed by an attempt to render an account of the immediate past."[76] But if Fitzgerald's use of what amounts to literary background music—whether performed by characters themselves, on record, or overheard—suggests a practice of citation parallel to the collage aesthetics of high modernism proper, it also evokes cinematic modes of musical accompaniment, especially in respect to the exhibition protocols of silent film. Much of the music Fitzgerald cites and incorporates has little intertextual relevance at all; it is quite simply there, as Prigozy notes, "to create a particular mood" (56). Like the "cue sheets" produced by music publishers and other companies in the "photoplay music" industry—and here I am relying on Rick Altman's recent work on sound in silent film—what often matters for Fitzgerald is less the reader's knowing where a particular song or lyric is from and more the ability of the music, no matter how unfamiliar, to index an affective tone or generic register of emotion.[77] Given Fitzgerald's fascination with film, not to mention his later years in Hollywood, this should come as no surprise; he had the inclination from the start, and eventually the experience, to reproduce a version of film music in narrative form.

Yet Fitzgerald's pervasive indexing of music, to the exact degree that it simulates a cinematic style of accompaniment from the silent era and anticipates the emergence of full scores and soundtracks in the sound era that follows, also aims to reproduce an experience that the "almost audible" medium of writing cannot possibly achieve. This is not a matter I wish to treat with too much drama or theoretical exaggeration: the point of Fitzgerald's recurring references to musical performance and recorded sound is not to manufacture pathos over writing's inability, as a technology, to make noise; and I say this knowing full well that much of his aesthetic attitudinizing reflects a patently Romantic sensibility, one no doubt traceable to such iconic allegories of art's portentous silence as Keats's "Ode on a Grecian Urn." Moreover, I admit that many of the moments I have been citing could be said to display a certain anxiousness about the "confusion," contingency, and immediacy of sound, which is precisely what the insistence on writing's arbitrary rationality, especially as understood by Derrida, wants to chasten.[78] I am interested in scenes where music functions as little more—but just as crucially, as nothing less—than white noise, aspiring to invisibility and pure ambience, but still somehow determined to communicate a sense of racial meaning in the most circuitous way we can imagine.

Consider, for example, Fitzgerald's early short story "The Offshore Pirate," which first appeared in 1920 and was later collected in *Flappers and Philosophers* (1920). It is a love story whose plot unfolds entirely against a soundtrack of black music, which is not there to remind us, recalling Breitwieser, that race must be constantly repressed, so much as artificially reproduced because it just happens to provide the perfect medium for white people to express their feelings for one another. The story opens with the wealthy, spoiled Ardita Farnham, who is determined to scandalize her uncle, whom she is visiting in Florida. "A yellow-haired girl reclined in a wicker settee reading *The Revolt of the Angels*, by Anatole France," she is loudly refusing to go ashore—she is on her uncle's yacht, anchored off Palm Beach—and keep a date that has been arranged for her with

Toby Moreland, the son of a family friend "from the circles in which [she has] presumably grown up."[79] But Ardita, sucking on a lemon and involved with a Russian described by her uncle as "a confirmed libertine," wants only to stay at sea; she cares nothing for the publicity that the story of her affair is causing, and she even goads her uncle by daring him to "have it filmed": "Wicked clubman making eyes at virtuous flapper. Virtuous flapper conclusively vamped by his lurid past" (73). So she stays on board as evening comes, when she hears the sound of men singing "in close harmony and in perfect rhythm to an accompanying sound of oars cleaving the blue waters" as they approach the yacht: "seven men, six of them rowing and one standing up in the stern keeping time to their song with an orchestra leader's baton" (74). The lyrics of the song itself are largely nonsensical—"*Oyster and rocks, / Sawdust and socks, / Who could make clocks / Out of cellos?*"—but there is no mistaking that it is supposed to sound like ragtime given that the white leader, who of course conducts, and the "negroes," who man the oars, are eventually announced as "Cutis Carlyle and his Six Black Buddies" (74, 94). What neither we nor Ardita learns until the end of the story, though, is that this interracial group of ragtime pirates is a fiction; "Curtis Carlyle" *is* Toby Moreland, and his "Six Black Buddies" are, as Toby's uncle says after arriving on the scene, "six strange niggers" hired as props to outfit Moreland's turn as exactly the sort of suspicious character for whom Ardita would fall. And fall she does: as the "negroes' voices" drift in with one last song, Ardita tells Moreland that she wants him to lie to her "just as sweetly" as he knows how for the rest of their lives together (96).

It is hard to overstate the degree to which the romance that unfolds between Ardita and Moreland, aka "Carlyle," is mediated by race, which is to a similarly profound degree mediated by music. Curtis Carlyle, or so Ardita is led to believe, was born to a poor white family in Tennessee—so poor, in fact, "that his people were the only white family in their street" (79). He spent his childhood with "a dozen pickaninnies streaming in his trail," and this early proximity to black life, this "association," Carlyle calls it, "diverted a rather unusual musical gift into a strange channel" (79). After the ex-colored man, however, the idea that a nominally white boy would provide a "channel" for black music does not seem odd at all: when Carlyle remembers—which is to say, when Moreland invents out of whole cloth—"a colored woman named Belle Pope Calhoun who played the piano" and describes how he "used to sit beside her . . . and try to get in an alto with one of those kazoos that boys hum through," we are returned to a primal scene of mediation that prepares a young boy to later earn his living reproducing black music with genuine fluency and feeling for its racialized aesthetic (79). When the "ragtime craze" swept the nation, Carlyle formed the "Six Black Buddies" with five boys he grew up with and a "wharf nigger" from New York and set out on the vaudeville circuit; soon after, "he was on Broadway, with offers of engagement on all sides, and more money than he had ever dreamed of" (79). But his success brings him no satisfaction, though he puts it to Ardita in a considerably more telling phrase when he laments that he was tired "playing the role of the eternal monkey, a sort of sublimated chorus man" (80). Thus his new career as pirate, thief, and kidnapper marks some desperate attempt to reclaim the whiteness that has never been securely his. Yet the essence of his appeal to Ardita, as Moreland must be seen as knowing from the start, rests entirely in his miscegenated status as "poh white," which is to be born a medium—a "strange channel"—for the blackness that accompanies him no matter where he goes (79).

Both Fitzgerald and Moreland treat these black musicians as narrative accessories for a jazz-age aesthetic that seems no less effective for being artificial. The allure of jazz, even when it sounds as "haunting and plaintive as a death-dance from the Congo's heart," is irresistibly modern, and in light of my concerns, modernist as well: it allows people to "channel" any fantasy of race that might help them get what they desire. According to this logic, the materiality of the medium is something to indulge and then dispose; Moreland and Ardita won't always have—or need—six black men making music in the background to communicate the love that they now have for one another.

◊

Oddly enough, it proves much harder to sustain a romance that begins with nothing but a phonograph. I take this as one of the admittedly most obscure conclusions we can draw from the marriage of Dick and Nicole Diver in *Tender Is the Night* (1934), which tracks the course of their relationship from psychiatrist and patient in Switzerland, to husband and wife on the French Riviera, and finally to its bitter end, when Nicole leaves Dick for Tommy Barban and Dick returns to the United States, where he fades into obscurity somewhere in upstate New York.[80] The last novel Fitzgerald lived to finish, *Tender Is the Night* turns quite explicitly on psychoanalytic technicalities: we learn in "Book 2" that Nicole's initial infatuation with Dick represents "a transference of the most fortuitous kind," and it is possible to understand the dynamic that eventually destroys the Divers' marriage as an extension of this therapeutic process (120). Or so Fitzgerald's rather clinical reading of their crack-up would have us believe.

In keeping with this logic, Nicole's affair with Tommy is not only healthier because he is not, and never was, her doctor, but also because her desire for his more brutal, aggressive masculinity—he is, after all, a mercenary whose "business is to kill people" (35)—shows the full extent of her recovery from the schizophrenia for which she is being treated. "She knew that for her the greatest sin now and in the future was to delude herself," the narrator writes of Nicole's mental state as she considers leaving Dick for Tommy. "It had been a long lesson but she had learned it. Either you think—or else others have to think for you and take power from you, pervert and discipline your natural tastes, civilize and sterilize you" (289–290). This is a fittingly American variation on what it means to be cured in psychoanalytic terms; self-knowledge is just an intermediary along the way to believing that one has the "power" to do whatever one would like, which should above all else feel "natural." Tommy makes the ideal object for Nicole's desires so long as their primitivist inclinations are the measure of their health. With "his handsome face . . . so dark as to have lost the pleasantness of deep tan, without attaining the blue beauty of Negroes," everything about Tommy Barban, from the echo of "barbarian" in his name, to his coloring, which leaves him just short of black, speaks to a figure who has not been "civilized" in the slightest (269).

Blackness mediates almost every aspect of Nicole's character: she has a daughter, with Dick, named Topsy; her older sister, reflecting on her "free and easy manner," is "sensibly habituated to thinking of her as a 'gone coon'" (157); as a young girl, she was the victim of incest by her father, Devereux Warren, the patriarch of a wealthy family who, though from Chicago, has a name that would not be out of place in Faulkner; and this crime seems to have left a stain, as the color of her skin is repeatedly remarked as "ruddy, orange brown," or "brown," in contrast to the young actress Rosemary Hoyt's "raw whiteness," which Dick and others try to preserve on the beach and elsewhere (6, 14, 5). The difference nicely registers the fact that Rosemary, who will pursue her infatuation with Dick for the first part of the book, is fresh meat for the jaded socialites who take her up because they have seen her in the movies. (She has just wrapped production on a film called *Daddy's Girl*, a title that further encrypts incest into the novel's atmospherics.) "We wanted to warn you about getting burned the first day," Rosemary is told, "because *your* skin is important" (7). This is advice about the dangers of exposure—of getting burned—that a budding star would know to take to heart; as Richard Dyer reminds us, "the codes of glamour lighting in Hollywood" were developed to accentuate the "glow and radiance" of such early icons as Lillian Gish and Mary Pickford.[81] It is far too late, however, for Nicole to be so white. When we first see her in the south of France in 1925, already "darkened," her appearance only reproduces signs of race that Dick experiences in a far more visceral form when Nicole takes him and a record player on a picnic in 1917.

To say that Dick and Nicole's love affair, especially in its first stages, is highly mediated seems a staggering understatement. The language of psychoanalysis and its therapeutic structures of relation intervene on their initial meeting, which Nicole's first psychiatrist, Dr. Gregorovius, deliberately contrives to produce the "transference" necessary for Nicole's treatment; then Dick receives "about fifty letters from her written over a period of eight months," a frenzy of communication that renders this "transference" powerfully material to the narrative itself, which tracks the course of her recovery by way of an elaborate epistolary set piece (121). We are treated to excerpts from Nicole's one-sided correspondence that are supposed to show "a marked pathological turn" giving way to a "richly maturing nature" (121). More readily apparent, at least in light of my particular interest in Fitzgerald, is the novel's attention to the visual layout of these letters, which are reproduced with their "original," by which I mean utterly fictitious, page breaks still intact and marked by the parenthetical 2's:

If you come here again with that attitude base and criminal and not even faintly what I had been taught to associate with the role of gentleman then heaven help you. However, you seem quieter than the others,

(2)

all soft like a big cat. I have only gotten to like boys who are rather like sissies. Are you a sissy? There were some somewhere. (121)

Or again:

I think one thing today and another tomorrow. That is really all that's the matter with me, except a crazy defiance and a lack of proportion. I would gladly welcome any alienist you might suggest. Here they lie in their bathtubs and sing Play in Your Own Backyard as if I had my

(2)

backyard to play in or any hope which I can find by looking either backward or forward. They tried it again in the candy store again and I almost hit the man with the weight, but they held me.

I am not going to write you any more. I am too unstable. (124)

In a novel where the aspiration to high modernism marks, in the figure of the careerist hack writer McKisco anyway, a cynical program to ape "Antheil and Joyce," or sell cheap variations "on the idea of Ulysses," there is perhaps reason to wonder whether such lavish attention to the materiality of communication is Fitzgerald's own belated gesture toward a more technically difficult aesthetic (10). Yet I would prefer to see these odd displays of typographic noise, which say quite literally nothing about the messages they interrupt, as preparing us to realize, along with Dick, that Nicole is most seductive when her charms are altogether specific to her medium.

The next time Dick sees Nicole in the flesh, music is on her mind: "I have some phonograph records my sister sent me from America," she tells him, and adds that she knows "a place to put the phonograph where no one else can hear" (135). She tries to gauge whether her new favorite songs—such obscurities from the hit parade of 1917 as "Hindustan," "I'm Glad I Can Make You Cry," "Wait Till the Cows Come Home," and "Good-by Alexander"—compare to what Dick has heard in Paris (135). Still instructed by Dr. Gregorovius to encourage her flirtations for therapeutic reasons, Dick agrees to a moonlight walk, and after stopping briefly to retrieve the phonograph that Nicole has carefully placed along the way to their chosen destination, the evening's entertainment can begin. This long scene displays every feature of the modernist preoccupation with race and recorded sound that I have been describing here:

> They were in America now, even Franz with his conception of Dick as an irresistible Lothario would never have guessed that they had gone so far away. They were so sorry dear; they went down to meet each other in a taxi, honey; they had preferences in smiles and met in Hindustan, and shortly afterward they must have quarreled, for nobody knew and nobody seemed to care—yet finally one of them had gone and left the other crying, only to feel blue, to feel sad.
>
> The thin tunes, holding lost times and future hopes in liaison, twisted upon the Valais night. In the lulls of the phonograph a cricket held the scene

together with a single note. By and by Nicole stopped playing the machine and sang to him.

"Lay a silver dollar
    On the ground
And watch it roll
    Because it's round—" (135–136)

The evocative first clause does most of the heavy-lifting in the first paragraph, which devolves into a pastiche of lyrics assembled from the records in Nicole's collection—a collection that must include a copy of "The Darktown Strutters' Ball," one of the first jazz hits, and the source for the fragment about the "taxi, honey."[82] (The all-white "Original Dixieland Jazz Band" released a version of this very song in 1917, and it is widely considered the first jazz record.) The resulting nonsense is just hard enough to parse that Fitzgerald salvages the "thin" tunes, and even slighter, secondhand escapism, to suggest the power of the charms to which Dick will soon succumb. And there is reason to suspect that part of what Dick finds so appealing—so familiar, so like America—is the sound of black music as only a white body can reproduce it:

On the pure parting of her lips no breath hovered. Dick stood up suddenly.
    "What's the matter, you don't like it?"
    "Of course I do."
    "Our cook at home taught it to me:
        'A woman never know
            What a good man she's got
        Till after she turns him down . . .'
    "You like it?"
    She smiled at him, making sure that the smile gathered up everything inside her and directed it toward him, making a profound promise of herself for so little, for the beat of a response, the assurance of a complimentary vibration in him. Minute by minute the sweetness drained down into her out of the willow trees, out of the dark world. (136)

The crucial lyric is likely Fitzgerald's own, and my evidence for its racial inflection is purely circumstantial. In light of the relays between race and other technologies of musical expression that this chapter has explored, I am inclined to believe that the Warrens' cook, like the maid in the Victrola ad, was black. It also seems plausible to think that Nicole, responding to what she may take as Dick's disapproval of her singing, must produce this explanation to account for just why an otherwise normal American girl— unmarked by any sexual catastrophe now that she is cured—would know a song like *that*. She is not channeling another pop confection along the lines of "Hindustan," nor even "The Darktown Strutters' Ball"; it sounds instead as if the family cook has taught Nicole the blues, and for Fitzgerald's readers in the 1930s, or so I would assume, the echoes of Bessie Smith or Ma Rainey would be pronounced, though this technically makes Nicole's performance an anachronism.

For Luhmann, a modern "semantics of love" is predicated on the idea "that there can be such a thing as experiencing a meaning which cannot be communicated, because the assertion of difference between utterance and information destroys itself in relation to the meaning in question."[83] The Western discourse of romantic love, as it developed in the eighteenth and early nineteenth centuries, had to conceive a language that described a world of feeling "that transcended all means of expression"; yet this same language also had to provide a stable social medium for a new psychology and politics of intimacy that imagined marriage as a relationship of mutual transparency and affective symmetry (128). Two people who answer singly as "Dicole" have such a marriage in spades. We see here the moment of perfect communication that makes this marriage possible: "everything inside" Nicole is "directed" at Dick, whose flustered, clumsy, painfully transparent silence could not possibly be more legible and obvious within the "semantics" that Luhmann describes. No "complimentary vibration" is required to telegraph his desire. Thus Nicole, responding to Dick's non-response, "stood up too, and stumbling over the phonograph, was momentarily against him, leaning into the hollow of his rounded shoulder" (136). The record player all but propels them to this first embrace, which makes not only for an intensely mediated carnal moment but also for an experience of racial meaning that cannot be communicated. No matter how seductively Nicole tries to give Dick "everything inside her," he still seems more enchanted by the mysterious "sweetness" for which she is just a medium, which flows into her out of America, out of the "thin tunes" on the phonograph, out of the family cook back home, "out of the willow trees, out of the dark world."

The romantic moment that Dick and Nicole share with one another and a phonograph is one of many in the novel where Fitzgerald's references to music, sound, or other, more contrived acoustical events provide an index to the status of their relationship. Early in book 1, for example, we witness an exchange between Dick and Nicole that features his entirely gratuitous reliance on a megaphone to let her know that he has decided they should throw a dinner party. "He had many light mechanical devices," Fitzgerald notes, but on this occasion anyway, their use is less a matter of necessity than of compulsion: "The ease with which her reply reached him seemed to belittle his megaphone," but still Dick "stubbornly" insists on amplifying his own voice for no particular reason (27). The image of a husband so anxious to be heard reveals a marriage for which communication, we can safely say, is something of an issue—and certainly a well-schooled Freudian such as Dick would wonder why it was so easy for Nicole to "belittle" his male apparatus. When the narrative recounts the first years of their relationship in book 2, however, another ostentatious sound effect allows us to realize, in retrospect, that Dick was not simply anxious that Nicole might be turning a deaf ear to his control and care, but also perhaps trying to recapture the uncanny intimacy of their prior connection. I am thinking of a conversation they have in a hotel salon—"a room of fabled acoustics"—where they are able to hear each other across a crowded room from forty yards away (150). Not only can they speak "naturally" at a distance and yet achieve an effect of startling intimacy, but the private character of their communication can be treasured amid the noise of public life and social scrutiny (150). "*You realize the people in the center of the floor can't hear what I say, but you can*," Nicole says to Dick, since voices carry in this peculiar fashion only for speakers stationed at the far corners of the room. Or as Nicole's sister, Baby Warren, explains the trick by way of a revealing analogy, "A waiter told us about it . . . Corner to corner—it's like wireless" (151). Thus Nicole again proves her mastery when it comes to exploiting the medium at her disposal, whether phonographic or architectural. On the other hand, Dick's taste for "light mechanical devices" notwithstanding, he displays no comparable expertise; indeed, many of his experiences with technology leave him comically unmanned, and phone calls seem to cause him especially acute distress.

Near the end of *Tender Is the Night*, the phone rings and Dick comes to the rescue of Mary North, a former member of the Divers' circle, and a friend, both described as "ladies of connection" (302). The call inspires the following reflection on the moral of his story:

He would have to go and fix this thing that he didn't care a damn about, because it had early become a habit to be loved, perhaps from the moment when he had realized that he was the last hope of a decaying clan. On an almost parallel occasion, back in Dohmler's clinic on the Zürichsee [in reference to Nicole], realizing this power, he had made his choice, chosen Ophelia, chosen the sweet poison and drunk it. Wanting above all to be brave and kind, he had wanted, even more than that, to be loved. So it had been. So it would ever be, he saw, simultaneously with the slow archaic tinkle from the phone box as he rang off. (302)

This moment makes explicit that a kind of circuitry connecting phonographs and telephones looms in the background of Dick's own understanding of the logic that has determined his career. He has been, from the moment Nicole turned on her record player in 1917, at the mercy of whatever medium a woman might elect to use; and the slightly garbled allusion to *Hamlet*, a play in which "poison" most famously (in the murder of Hamlet's father) enters the body through the ear, further renders Dick, at least in his own self-serving imagination, a victim of all that he has heard. So much now seems "almost parallel" to something else that we can perhaps forgive Dick his confusion. The ringing of the telephone "simultaneously" produces an effect of synaesthesia and anachronism, with its "archaic tinkle" calling forth a vision of past experience that lasts only an instant before Dick must answer to its urgency. But amid this flurry of allusions and conflations, none is more revealing than the convergence, within this last analysis of Dick's character, of two traits familiar to any reader of *The Great Gatsby*: the desperate romanticism of Gatsby himself ("he had wanted . . . to be loved") and the reactionary posturing ("he was the last hope of a decaying clan") of Tom Buchanan, who worries that "the white race . . . will be utterly submerged" by the "rise of the colored empires," with Gatsby's mysteriously mongrelized identity as a harbinger of things to come.[84] Though Buchanan may succeed in fending off Gatsby's challenge to his family and marriage, in *Tender Is the Night*, the "clan" that Dick would champion is finally routed, and the victory belongs not just to Tommy Barban but also to the powerfully mediated form of modernity that Nicole herself embodies.

I take this as the outcome of the noisy three-way exchange between Dick, Nicole, and Tommy that follows on Dick's last, heroic turn in answer to Mary's phone call. The scene begins with Dick and Nicole, as is their custom, getting their respective "haircuts and shampoos" in adjoining rooms at the hotel salon—as if Fitzgerald needed to remind us just how little challenge Dick, at this point in his pathetic alcoholic decline, can offer to the battle-hardened mercenary who has seduced his wife (307). Nicole sees Tommy enter the men's side of the salon and anticipates "some sort of showdown" between Tommy and Dick, the substance of which we first overhear in "fragments" since Fitzgerald focalizes the narration from her vantage in another room. In a novel so attuned to acts and rituals of communication, we know of course, as does Nicole, to read through their clipped civilities—"Hello, I want to see you. . . . serious. . . . serious. . . . perfectly agreeable."—and understand their sharp insistence (307). Tommy's message is clear enough to Dick, or so it seems, for he immediately takes Nicole, still in the midst of getting her hair cut, to a nearby café where Tommy is waiting to see them both. A waiter sits the three of them down, and as they order drinks, Dick asks for his scotch and soda to be made with an almost impossibly suggestive brand of whiskey:

> "The Blackenwite [*sic*] with siphon," said Dick.
> "Il n'y a plus de Blackenwite. Nous n'avons que le Johnny Walkair."
> "Ca va."
>> "She's—not—wired for sound
>> but on the quiet
>> you ought to try it——"
> "Your wife does not love you," said Tommy suddenly. "She loves me."
> The two men regarded each other with a curious impotence of expression. There can be little communication between men in that position, for their relation is indirect, and consists of how much each of them has possessed or will possess of the woman in question, so that their emotions pass through her divided self as through a bad telephone connection. (308).

"Blackenwite" was how French waiters referred to a once popular whiskey sold under the English name "Black and White."[85] Of course Dick will settle for Johnny Walker, but his first impulse is toward a term that effectively displaces the plain fact of Nicole's cuckoldry onto a fantasy of miscegenation, with Tommy's vague ethnicity now registering as fully "black," as it combines with Nicole's "white," to loom as just the sort of threat that Dick would want to vanquish on behalf of his "decaying clan." Dick's choice of whiskey even allows

Fitzgerald to echo a similar scene from *The Great Gatsby* in a brilliantly convoluted fashion: in chapter 7, when Tom Buchanan confronts Gatsby about his attentions to Daisy, he sees them as part and parcel of a modern decadence toward "family life and family institutions" that will soon "throw everything overboard and have intermarriage between *black and white*" (emphasis added; 130). Dick reproduces the materiality of Buchanan's signifiers with no apparent understanding of their sense. Fitzgerald turns him into a kind of human phonograph, who mechanically and unconsciously gives voice to words that mean far more than he can know, and this strikes me as an incredibly original way for Fitzgerald to repeat himself. Tommy also sounds like something of a broken record in respect to Gatsby—"'Your wife doesn't love you,' said Gatsby. 'She's never loved you. She loves me.'"—but here is where the parallels stop. Dick hardly mounts a defense after Nicole admits that she has "gotten very fond of Tommy," and though she wants Dick "to take the initiative" and fight, he seems "content to sit with his face half-shaved matching her hair half-washed" (310). This is Gatsby's tragedy half-baked, played the second time as farce.

But this is not the only way Fitzgerald quotes himself in this amazing scene: the lyric that provides the crucial background music for this exchange is also his composition, which is especially appropriate given that a song using a language of high technology to imagine a woman's sexual availability cannot help but recall Nicole's uncanny reproduction, with the aid of a phonograph and her family's cook, of "America" in book 2, a performance culminating in the bit of blues Fitzgerald writes expressly for her. We are now better able to grasp what is important about these simulations of intertextuality that Fitzgerald indulges. They first of all draw him still closer to a twentieth-century world of popular music that, as we saw for James Weldon Johnson and others, was everywhere shaped around performances of racial identity that were, in turn, reflections of and improvisations on a wider network of material practices dependent on such acousmatic technologies as the phonograph and the player piano. This means that we might think of Fitzgerald not only as a particularly acute listener when it comes to the influence of music as a medium of modern culture, but also as a curious sort of practitioner in his own right; if Johnson starts out as a lyricist who turns from Tin Pan Alley to literature by way of a fictional autobiography of a musician, Fitzgerald devises fictional Tin Pan Alley lyrics to pattern his own literary texts by way of an aesthetics of imaginary reference and information. In *Tender Is the Night*, this fabulation-in-song further means that Fitzgerald is the true source of any racially suggestive noise that we hear coming from Nicole; that is, her blackness is exceedingly fictional, for not only is the Warren family cook quite obviously a character in a novel, but the music that Fitzgerald attributes to her, which I think many readers would assume is the citation of a "real" song Fitzgerald would have known, is just another work of fiction. These are moments of allusiveness that exemplify less the modernist immersion in popular materials that we associate with Joyce and Eliot than the anticipations of a postmodern gamesmanship that we associate with Pynchon or Nabokov. All of which is to return to the problem of Nicole's blackness in *Tender Is the Night*—the performances and innuendos that make her whiteness register as a kind of whiteface—and to marvel at the circuitousness of the racial logic that Fitzgerald forces us to confront. Even as Dick tries to take his stand against the dark "barbarian" who is pillaging his "clan," the narrative itself reminds us that such fictions of racial being and identity are fundamentally outmoded. In the foreground, we see a rehearsal of Tom Buchanan's nativism in conflict with Gatsby's mongrelized modernity; but in the background, we hear enough to realize that everything is already "blackenwite." The trouble with Nicole is not that she allows too "little communication" between black and white (Tommy and Dick), as though she were "a bad telephone connection." On the contrary, the problem is that Nicole has been "wired for sound" from the beginning: she is a perfect medium of racial communication, capable of recording the slightest traces, residues, and performances of black identity and then reproducing them with breathtaking fidelity. The mediums that communicate the sounds of blackness—technologies including phonographs, player pianos, and white people—speak to a phenomenon of racial experience in which precisely those relations that are altogether "indirect," like those finally channeled through Nicole, are also the most resonant and involved.

◊

This last scene of Dick and Nicole's marriage is given over to a multitude of voices: Dick and Tommy in both French and English, the waiter, Nicole, and "an insistent American" pushing copies of the *Herald* and the *New York Times* (309). Thus, like so many scenes in Fitzgerald, it reads as if it were constructed, at least in part, for its theatrical or cinematic possibilities. Fitzgerald made his second trip to Hollywood in 1931, just before starting work in earnest on the manuscript that would become *Tender Is the Night*, and the commercial failure of the novel helped speed him back there later in the 1930s. But even before

Fitzgerald had firsthand experience in laboring on screenplays, there are extended passages of closet drama in *The Beautiful and the Damned*, and countless moments in *The Great Gatsby* where Nick Carraway's first-person narration restricts itself to little more than speech tags, stage directions, and notes about decor. Because my concern has been with the phonograph in *Tender Is the Night*, I have looked past what is, for almost all the novel's readers, the pervasiveness of its fascination with cinema as both visual medium and harbinger of modernity. Michael North and others have written insightfully on these matters, and such attention to Fitzgerald and film has begun to expand our sense of his fiction's situation within a media ecology.[86] To that end, it seems worth noting that Fitzgerald dissolves the marriage of "Dicole" in a scene featuring two types of acousmatic voice, one of which suggests the strong influence of cinema. We "hear" this as the diegetic music that punctuates the turn from Dick's chitchat with the waiter to Tommy's overt assault. The other disembodied voice belongs, of course, to the narrator himself, whose elaborate figuration of Nicole as "a bad telephone connection" offers Dick an instant to compose himself, which he uses, pathetically, but fittingly enough, to change his drink order ("Donnez moi du gin et du siphon"). Both of these voices use a language of technology to sexualize Nicole, and both speak with a degree of irony that Dick is in no position to appreciate:

> "She's—not—wired for sound
> but on the quiet
> you ought to try it——"

We have seen before what happens when Nicole is "wired for sound," and even when she is not—meaning, literally, that no microphone is amplifying and transmitting the sounds of her infidelity in the flesh—Tommy is free to "try it." The syncopating dash, in other words, lets us weigh each syntactic option in the lyric, so that we can read "not" out of the sentence and recall Nicole and her phonograph in book 2, even as Dick is made to realize that another erotic circuit has been closed just out of earshot. Fitzgerald's simile comparing Nicole to a telephone is also acutely double-voiced: what Dick is rather bluntly being told, after all, is that Tommy has passed much more than his "emotions" through Nicole's "divided self," which is to say that the reason she is now a bad "connection" is because she operates a party line. "Nicole found a note saying that Dick had taken the small car and gone up into Provence for a few days by himself. Even as she read it the phone rang—it was Tommy Barban from Monte Carlo, saying that he had received her letter and was driving over. She felt her lips' warmth in the receiver as she welcomed his coming" (290). This scene of communication immediately precedes the chapter in which Nicole and Tommy consummate their affair; in this context, the erotics coded within the image of her lips warming and Tommy "coming" could not be more explicit. Phone sex has made Dick into a cuckold several pages before the carnal act itself is demurely referenced by an ellipsis: "she forgot about Tommy himself and sank deeper and deeper into the minutes and the moment.... When he got up to open a shutter and find out what caused the increasing clamor below their window, his figure was darker and stronger than Dick's" (294). And lest we overlook just what this "darker" man portends, the "noise" disturbing their post-coital reverie comes from a group of Americans singing out a bastardized rendition of "Dixie."

At these moments, Fitzgerald says with music what could not be expressed any more directly about the character of Nicole's sexuality. All the intimations of blackness and racial mixing, I would argue, enter the novel in such highly mediated forms—as background music, acousmatic voices, sound effects, performances of technology—because Fitzgerald wants us to recognize that Nicole's racialization is a patent artifice, a screening fiction cobbled out of second-order signifiers for which the novel finally has no referents. This is, to borrow and revise from North, an aestheticization of race that Fitzgerald can accomplish in the medium of the novel insofar as he can aestheticize, in the first place, all the other, different mediums of modern life that now register and communicate a sense of race. Blackness may well come into *Tender Is the Night*, as North insists, in "weirdly inappropriate ways" (139). But technically speaking, none of the devices—narrative and otherwise—that literally communicate the presence of race for Fitzgerald seem odd or unfamiliar in their contexts; telephones, phonographs, and popular music are actually the opposite of strange within the pervasive modernity recorded in his fiction. Indeed, I hear the incessant noises of blackness in *Tender Is the Night* as signs of Fitzgerald's understanding that for Americans such as Dick Diver even the most outlandish and artificial stories involving race may still be easier to hear than those about the "inappropriate ways" of white people. Thus incest remains unspeakable while the sounds of miscegenation fill the air. Rosemary Hoyt, after all, is the star of a movie called *Daddy's Girl*, and the title tells us, in the first pages of the book, everything we need to know—more than most of the characters in the novel *can* know, long before we learn the truth about Nicole's illness and its cause. But film is largely silent in the novel, and so it must literally communicate in code or shorthand, as Fitzgerald goes to almost impossible lengths in order to remind us.

Because the scene of Tommy and Dick's "little communication" about, and through, Nicole is set on a particular afternoon in July 1929 when the Tour de France arrives in Cannes ("Boys sprinted past on bicycles, automobiles jammed with elaborate betasselled sportsmen slid up the street" [307]), Matthew Bruccoli and Judith Baughm are able to reconstruct a rather precise chronology for the plot of *Tender Is the Night*.[87] Thanks to their efforts we know that the scene in which Nicole learns that her father is in Lausanne takes place in the summer of 1928, when Dick is consulting on the case of the young Chilean homosexual at the very hospital where Nicole's father, suffering from the effects of alcoholism, has come to die. Nicole never sees her father again; he checks out of the sanitarium and disappears just before Nicole's train makes it to Lausanne, and so the chapter ends with Dick and Nicole sitting together in a hotel near the station, where they stop to get a drink and hear a record: "Some one had brought a phonograph into the bar and they sat listening to The Wedding of the Painted Doll" (252). Bruccoli and Baughm inform us that Fitzgerald here refers to a "popular song of 1929," with lyrics by Arthur Freed and music by Nacio Herb Brown.[88] A helpful gloss for one of the more obscure references in the novel, but not for understanding what it means for Dick and Nicole to be listening to this song in the summer of 1928, the year *before* Freed and Brown wrote it for MGM's *The Broadway Melody*, the studio's first all-talking feature film, which premiered in 1929.

The original sheet music for the song makes clear that it was "introduced" in this MGM production, which was released in February 1929 and became a major box office hit that helped drive the studio's conversion to sound filmmaking on a massive scale. Of course Fitzgerald, with so much music filling up the sonic backgrounds of his fictions, can be forgiven for a minor confusion about one particular song's date. We may choose to ignore—as most readers of *Tender Is the Night* no doubt have—the fact that he has Dick and Nicole listen to a record that could not possibly have existed. There is no communication without noise, after all, and at worst this anachronism introduces a bit of static to the novel's attempt to convey the mediating texture of its historical moment. That said, it is

FIGURE 3.8. Cover illustration for the sheet music to "The Wedding of the Painted Doll," 1929. Collection of the author.

hard to look at the cover illustration for "The Wedding of the Painted Doll" and wonder whether the slip here is acutely overdetermined (fig. 3.8). The image of two children dressed up as bride and groom means to evoke the song's novelty lyrics about a wedding between toys—Red Riding Hood, Buster Brown, and the Jumping Jack have "jumped into town" to "look at the little cutie, look at the little beauty, look at the little doll, it's her wedding day"—but everything about this mix of fantasy and childish sexuality appears cruelly ironic as part of the soundtrack for Dick and Nicole's failing marriage, and just cruel as an echo of Nicole and her father's incestuous relationship.[89] Fitzgerald's slip can thus be made Freudian without much effort; his citation of a song that cannot possibly be heard becomes another way for the text to register the primal scene of sexual trauma that it incessantly defers.

Let me suggest another reason why Fitzgerald needs to have us "hear" what no one could have heard in 1928. A world away from what is happening to Dick and Nicole in *Tender Is the Night*, Hollywood is undergoing the transition from silent film to sound. The character of Rosemary Hoyt puts these two worlds into communication, as several critics have observed. On his first trip to Hollywood, in 1927, Fitzgerald met Irving Thalberg and later used him as the template for the character of Monroe Stahr in *The Love of the Last Tycoon* (1941). Though not as famous an expression of Thalberg's style (and MGM's prestige) as *Grand Hotel, The Broadway Melody*, and especially its production number for "The Wedding of the Painted Doll," enjoys a curious place within film history. After seeing the first version of the number, Thalberg ordered retakes—as he often did—but since MGM was filming its first "all-singing, all-talking" movie, this provided the opportunity for a crucial technical innovation. Convincing Thalberg that the recorded soundtrack of the song made during the original filming was already very good, a sound engineer proceeded to have a new version of the number shot with the performers dancing to the synced playback of their first performance.[90] The clear advantages of this practice for making musicals—the potential for more elaborate choreography and increased camera movement—soon helped make it standard throughout Hollywood. Having singers lip-sync their performances to already recorded vocals also became standard practice, making it possible for actors who sang poorly, or not at all, to star in musicals. The use of this technique recalls, however, another common practice of the early sound era: the remaking of silent films as talkies by having them "retrofitted," to borrow a term from Donald Crafton, with music, sound effects, and post-dubbed dialogue.[91] Here it is irresistible not to mention that Freed and Brown write a song in 1925, "Singin' in the Rain," that later gives its name to Freed's masterpiece as a producer at MGM, where his unit was responsible for many of the studio's most famous musicals. *Singin' in the Rain* (1952) is a film preoccupied with the traumas and possibilities that follow on the arrival of sound in Hollywood. At the end, Don Lockwood (Gene Kelly) and Cosmo

Brown (Donald O'Connor) pull back the curtain to reveal that the beautiful voice belonging, on-screen at least, to Lina Lamont (Jean Hagen) belongs instead to Kathy Selden (Debbie Reynolds), who has had to dub over not just Lina's singing in the fictional silent-drama-turned-sound-musical, *The Dancing Cavalier*, but all her dialogue as well, since Lina's nasal tone and grating accent defeat the studio's most strenuous efforts at voice instruction. In the late 1920s, silent films turned into sound films in this elaborate, artificial fashion were often called "goat glands" in honor of the period rage for impotence treatments involving liquid extracts made from animal testicles, which were then ingested, or surgically "grafted" into the patient's scrotum—Yeats and Freud were among the better-known recipients of this procedure, the Steinach operation.[92]

All this, then, to suggest that Fitzgerald's premature citation of "The Wedding of the Painted Doll" introduces an almost impossibly encrypted network of relays between technologies of artificial sound and artificial sexuality. I should say, for the record, that it is hard to imagine a reader in 1934 for whom Fitzgerald's own musical contribution to *Tender Is the Night* would not seem almost as appreciably obscure. That is, no one has ever "heard" the song that Fitzgerald writes to accompany and inform the end of Dick and Nicole's marriage. This piece of music is just as historically impossible—and as impossible, in its way, for us to read—as the phonograph that plays "The Wedding of the Painted Doll" the year before it is released. The lyric sounds so plausibly like so many of the actual lyrics that Fitzgerald quotes throughout the novel and his fiction overall, that it is easy, in fact, to imagine a reader or two in 1934 who would have sworn they knew that tune, and perhaps tried to hum the chorus in hopes of bringing back the memory of a piece of music that no one ever had been—or ever will be—able to hear. Don't you know that song? "She's—not— wired for sound . . . " How does it go again? Thus for Fitzgerald to "say it with music" is, against all odds and expectations to the contrary, to say it in his own words: the effect of reference he is after suggests that writing is now situated in a world of other media, and that we must read as if their noises, inscribed upon the silent page, form a fantasmatic soundtrack that communicates more than what the novel otherwise could tell us. But the message Fitzgerald chooses to deliver in this particularly convoluted fashion is finally anxious about such mixed aesthetics and their strange and potent virtuality. For while the Steinach operation was a glorified vasectomy, and the various elixirs made from monkey testicles were used solely to increase male virility, it is as if Nicole has been sexually augmented and transformed by a kind of "goat gland" procedure in the equally peculiar Hollywood sense of the phrase. Recording studios, radio stations, and sound stages, after all, were the only places in 1934, aside from *Tender Is the Night*, where the words "wired for sound" had any meaning. They remind us that Nicole's voice has never been her own. She is "wired for sound" when she mouths the music from the records on her phonograph, and when she reproduces songs the family cook has taught her. From the beginning of the novel, she has been a weird vessel for the communication of a racialized aesthetic that does not belong to her, that is audible only through Dick's increasingly anxious perceptions of a modern world entirely too noisy and confused, and in the end, too "blackenwite" for his liking. But we would do well to remember that Fitzgerald gives us ample cause to realize that we should not believe everything we hear in *Tender Is the Night*—much less everything we don't.

Race Records

This chapter has explored a culture of recorded sound that, even as it exemplifies a modernist concern with the aesthetics of media, has shown little regard for what in Greenberg's terminology we might call the "purity" of a more medium-specific understanding of the differences between phonographs and pianolas, between the audiophile technology of Ellison's hi-fi and the cinematic sensibility that makes Fitzgerald's *Tender Is the Night* so completely "wired for sound." My concern has been instead with a more pervasive and consistent network of meanings, iconographies, and implications that associate rather freely amid various media, and with the modernity they register. The racialized aesthetic that I have here recovered is, to borrow from our contemporary idiom of technology, powerfully "cross-platform" in its ability to operate in literature and film, art and advertising, and in figures otherwise remote from one another, as Gershwin, Ellison, Cather, James Weldon Johnson, and Jan Matulka. In work after work, technologies of recorded sound invoke race as the very essence of their instrumentality and appeal, their acousmatic fascination. Nowhere is this more apparent than in *Tender Is the Night*, where Fitzgerald suggests that Nicole's troubling and provocative sexuality is not just inseparable from but finally equivalent to the mediated sounds of race that she simultaneously channels and embodies. She communicates—and communicates between—the "more immediate and more powerful sensations" of music and a desire for the effects of race, and in this respect she echoes the uncanny performances of identity that make Johnson's "ex-coloured man" into a virtual "humanola." The more intimate these figures become with the materiality of their given mediums, the more "blackenwite" they seem. "There has been, is, and will be," Greenberg admits, "such a thing as confusion of the arts." What Greenberg describes, with perceptible remorse, as the impossibility of painting or writing to sustain music's "almost complete absorption in the very physical quality of its medium" means that some return to the semantics of communication is inevitable for any artist working in essentially impure forms corrupted by their proximity to mere "literature."[93] This account of U.S. modernism's elaborate circuitry of racial noise and media aesthetics has shown that there is no fetish for the technicalities of a medium that is not connected to the histories that determine the possibilities of its message.

Richard Wright's "Long Black Song" from his 1938 collection of stories, *Uncle Tom's Children*, provides a last and graphic variation on this lesson. Set in the rural South sometime after World War I, the story concerns a young wife and mother, Sarah, whose former lover has died in combat and whose current husband, Silas, seems an insufficient substitute for all that she has lost. "There had been cooking and sewing and sweeping and the deep dream of sleeping grey skies in winter. Always it had been like that and she had been happy. But no more. The happiness of those days and nights, of those green cornfields and grey skies had started to go from her when Tom had gone to war. His leaving had left an empty black hole in her heart, a black hole that Silas had come in and filled. But not quite. Silas had not quite filled that hole."[94] There is nothing subtle about the language Wright employs to suggest that Sarah's melancholy doubles for a form of sexual desire; the figurative "hole" at the center of her character migrates easily enough from her "heart," to where we might otherwise assume that Silas does his best to fulfill her body's needs now that Tom is gone. If Sarah's inner life, as we might expect for Wright, can be made crudely legible with just a few sentences, it takes considerably longer to understand the world of noise and sound in which we find her at the start of "Long Black Song." The story appropriately begins with the lyrics of a lullaby that Sarah sings to try to keep her baby quiet, but its crying grows "louder and louder" until she takes down an old clock for it to play with (104). The child first attacks the clock with bare hands—"Bink! Bink! Bink!" is Wright's attempt at onomatopoeia—but Sarah, fearing for her child's safety, gives her a stick with which to continue the assault (104). "She heard each blow landing squarely on the top of the clock," and Wright signals the change in timbre by switching to "Bang! Bang! Bang!" as the noise repeats throughout the opening pages of the story (104–107). And then more noise: a "dull throb like she had heard that day Silas had called her outdoors to look at the airplane" turns out be a car approaching on the dirt road from town; Sarah thinks at first that Silas may have gotten a ride back from his trip to buy supplies, but when it stops she sees instead a white man "with a huge black package under his arm" (107). He is selling a combination graphophone and clock for fifty dollars, which Sarah insists they cannot afford and do not need. "We git erlong widout time," she tells the salesman; but he presses forward with his pitch, in part because he sees the broken clock that Sarah's baby is demolishing, and in part because he has been told that Silas is in town, and from the way she sees him "looking at her breasts," we know that he might want to make more than just a sale (108). But even as Sarah notices his interest, she perceives it as more infantile than lascivious ("Hes jus lika lil boy"); and the salesman in turn sees Sarah as strangely childish in what appears to him her striking isolation from modernity itself ("I don't see how in the world anybody can live without time") and her reliance on the sun's rising and setting to mark the passing days (108). Wright outlines the allegory of this encounter between white (technology) and black (nature) with no more subtlety than he conceives of Sarah's sexualized psychology. What happens next in "Long Black Song" does not so much elaborate on these aspects of the story as execute them with bitter, programmatic clarity.

So the salesman unpacks "the big black box" and pulls out "a square brown graphophone" (108). This simple descriptive language is oddly racialized by Sarah's fascination with the graphophone, which mixes a desire for its sheer materiality with an improbable projection of maternal feeling; she is immediately dazzled by the gold accoutrements and glowing finish of the wood, but only because the luster of the graphophone "reminded her of the light she saw sometimes in the baby's eyes. Slowly she slid a finger over a beveled edge; she wanted to take the box into her arms and kiss it" (109). Why does she want to turn this icon of white modernity into a black baby? Sarah's infantilizing of the graphophone seems part and parcel of her earlier effort to disavow the salesman's sexual attention to her body, and these denials of eroticized communication between black and white only anticipate the spectacle that Wright will make from Sarah's absence of volition when she eventually succumbs to the salesman's advances. Of course she outwardly resists, repeatedly saying, "Naw, naw" and thinking to herself, "hes a *white* man! A *white* man! Naw! Naw!" (112). But Wright also lets this scene unfold precisely as a misogynistic fantasy of interracial rape, or rather, its impossibility: black women such as Sarah may say "no" to white men, but her body sends a different message when we read that "her loins ached," that "she felt her body sliding," that "a liquid metal covered her and she rode on the curve of white bright days and dark black nights and the surge of the long gladness of summer" (112–113).

The problem with this language is its close proximity to a kind of literate pornography that it simultaneously reproduces and obscures. I am more interested, however, in the way that Wright prepares us for this rush of carnal violence with a scene of purely mediated experience that anticipates its every turn. The graphophone, for Wright, is finally not a toy. And whatever innocence Sarah tries to feign is immediately dispelled when the music starts to play:

She smiled. The white man was just like a little boy. Jus like a chile. She saw him grinding the handle of the box. There was a sharp, scratching noise; then she moved nervously, her body caught by the ringing coils of music.

> *When the trumpet of the Lord shall sound . . .*
> She rose on circling waves of white bright days and dark black nights.
> *. . . and time shall be no more . . .*
> Higher and higher she mounted.
> *And the morning breaks . . .*
> Earth fell far behind, forgotten.
> *. . . eternal, bright, and fair . . .*
> Echo after echo sounded.
> *. . . When the saved of the earth shall gather . . .*
> Her blood surged like the long gladness of summer.
> *. . . over the other shore . . .*
> Her blood ebbed like the deep dream of sleep in winter.
> *And when the roll is called up yonder . . .*
> She gave up, holding her breath.
> *I'll be there . . .* (109)

The perspective shifts radically after the sentence in dialect allows Sarah to repeat her earlier refrain. With the "noise" of the graphophone, the narrative assumes a different voice; metaphors spill down the page in a very deliberate display of literary technique, right down to the alternating lines from a hymn, "When the Roll Is Called Up Yonder," that effect a patently modernist juxtaposition of high and low, sacred and profane. The voice that we have come to recognize as Sarah's own—to this point, the story's third-person narration has been focalized through both her perspective and her language—is supplanted by these two new voices that are at once more lyrical, more distant, and more artificial. The effect is beautiful and pernicious: the vivid ecstasy not only confirms the presence of the erotic tension that Sarah has so far tried to disavow, but it does so in a language that will return when the salesman physically presses himself upon her. Thus this eroticized aesthetic experience produces a sequence of figurative and physical markers that will return, on just the next page, to aestheticize a sexual encounter that can be read at worst as rape, and at best as some desperate blur of anguish and predation. Sarah's blood again will "surge," and she will hold her breath; "white bright days and dark black nights" will again give way to "the long gladness of summer." "Echo after echo" will connect the mediated pleasure of recorded sound to whatever it was that the graphophone salesman did to her after the music stopped.

Wright marshals the whole of his formidable skills to ensure that we can never know what happened. But when Silas comes back and discovers the salesman's straw hat in the bedroom, he is neither sympathetic nor beset with questions of interpretation. He seizes on the graphophone as the material evidence of Sarah's infidelity, and destroys it with a show of rage against the "white ape"—a bitter play on common slurs associating black men with sexually aggressive beasts—before chasing Sarah from the house with threats of violence (118). From the vantage of the outlying field to which she has fled, Sarah witnesses the revenge that Silas wreaks upon the salesman when he arrives the next morning, with another white man, to close the deal, or at least retrieve the graphophone. Silas whips him brutally, and then shoots him as he tries to run back to his car; but Silas fails to kill the other man, who escapes to town and there assembles the group of men—perhaps a lynch mob, perhaps the law—whom Silas fights until he himself is trapped inside the house, which catches fire in a hail of bullets, burning him alive while Sarah "[waits] to hear his call" (127). But he dies "without a murmur," and the grim silence of his last stand against the overwhelming force of white authority speaks well enough to the politics and symbolism Wright wants to get across (127). Wright depicts these episodes of male conflict as mute tableaux that we see through Sarah's eyes: "They faced each other, the white man standing up and Silas sitting down; like two toy men they faced each other. She saw Silas point the whip to the smashed graphophone" (122). Which is not to say that Wright dispenses with all narrative sound effects in the absence of the technology that occasions their appearance while also structuring their form. "Dimly she saw in her mind a picture of men killing and being killed," the story catches Sarah thinking. "White men killed the black and black men killed the white. White man killed the black because they could, and the black men killed the white men to keep from being killed" (120). It is surely no accident that this circuit of attack and retribution plays in Sarah's consciousness like a broken record.

When Wright published "Long Black Song" in 1938, this familiar figure of technological malfunction, which survives for now despite its obsolescence in a digital culture of bits and information, would have felt right at home. I say this despite the fact that my use of it on this occasion is technically incorrect: graphophones, like the machine that brought so much mediated pleasure to the couple in the Edison ad with which this chapter started, did not play records in the form of discs; rather they used cylinders made primarily of wax. Edison's stubborn commitment to this particular medium can be traced back to his earliest experiments with the phonograph, and though later innovations such as the "Blue Amberol" cylinders of the early 1910s boasted superior sound quality and increased durability, by 1913 the disc recordings pioneered by Berliner for use on his gramophone had become standard in the industry. The Edison Company began selling its own "Disc Phonographs," but continued to lose out to Columbia, Victor, and other manufacturers; all production stopped in 1929 and the history of the graphophone came to an end. Since "Long Black Song" is set at some unspecified moment soon after World War I, Wright's revival of— and strenuous attention to—the graphophone is not quite anachronistic, but it does seem an odd detail to emphasize in a ferociously political story that in no way seems to imagine itself capturing a moment in American race relations whose time has passed. To have his fiction turn on an outmoded technology was one way for Wright to register the uneven development of the black South; his characters, after all, are "Uncle Tom's Children," and we should not expect such subjects of history to have the latest instruments.

But this is not, I think, the only reason Wright puts a graphophone at the center of the network of race and sex and media that he pitilessly designs in "Long Black Song." Like so many of the other texts and images this chapter has explored, in this story Wright is interested in what Jonathan Sterne describes more generally as "the eros of communication," which structures our attachment to technologies of recorded sound, and which often takes the form, as we have seen, of "love and longing for the machine" itself.[95] Wright also reproduces almost every aspect of the modernist fascination with the sensuous immediacy of music, and with the delirious, enabling possibilities for racial vicariousness and contact that it materializes. For all of this, Wright could just as well have used a phonograph. The crucial function that the graphophone alone allowed was the ability to make records as well as play them. Edison sold blank cylinders that could be used for home recording; the amplifying horn served also as a kind of microphone to collect and concentrate a source of sound; the needle that tracked the grooves of the record doubled as a stylus that inscribed. Thus Silas (stylus) finally treats the body of the graphophone salesman as if it were a graphophone in the flesh: "he simply stood over the dead white man and talked out of his life, out of a deep and final sense that now it was all over and nothing could make any difference" (125). And at one point in the excruciating monologue that follows, Silas speaks what I take to be the central motivation for this "long black song" he puts on record: "Ahm gonna be hard like they is! So hep Gawd, Ahm gonna be *hard!* When they come fer me Ahm gonna *be here!*" (125). In the fire and bloodshed that end the story, we realize how hard Silas becomes. But since he dies in ostentatious silence, it is only when he talks into the body of the white man that Silas can be "heard" ("*hard*"), that we can "hear" ("*here*") his words as they are taken down in dialect and italicized on the page as if to guarantee these double meanings. Only a graphophone, or its human equivalent, will do. This is medium specificity with a vengeance.

4
THE NEW PERMANENT RECORD

As a rule, information is something to preserve, garbage is something to be destroyed.
However, both can be looked on as a kind of waste product, a physical burden, and for
contemporary society both are among the most pressing problems of the day.
An ancient Sufi saying states that a heavy load of broken pottery and a heavy load of
books are the same for the donkey.

BILL VIOLA, *"THE PORCUPINE AND THE CAR"*

On Creating a Disposable Past

History often stinks—which is perhaps why, just a year after opening, the National Archives installed a special "vault for the fumigation of records," pictured here in a 1935 photograph from the *Second Annual Report of the Archivist of the United States* (fig. 4.1).[1] We see two men loading a cart of old documents, some bound in leather, others loose or tied with ribbon, into the smooth metal maw of the treatment chamber, which stretches who knows how far past the left edge of the photograph; maybe we are supposed to estimate the vault's size from the fact that there are only two trucks visible—a full load, as it were. A sense of the compartment's interior dimensions—roughly ten feet deep, five feet across, and six feet high—is confirmed by an accompanying description in the archivist's *Report*: "This chamber, which weighs over 6 tons and has a capacity of 300 cubic feet of records at one fumigation, is the largest vacuum vault used for the treatment of books and documents in the world" (41). A superlative machine. No doubt made in America. Four circular gauges and what is possibly a barometer dominate the black octagonal panel mounted on the vault's exterior. Here, workers monitor the vacuum produced by the massive turbine mounted on top of the chamber, as well as the concentrations of ethylene oxide and carbon dioxide within. These gases, which the *Report* assures us are "non-flammable and non-toxic to man," prevent the damaging spread of the

FIGURE 4.1. Anonymous photograph from the *Second Annual Report of the Archivist of the United States, For the Fiscal Year Ending June 30, 1936*, Washington, D.C.: United States Government Printing Office, 1936.

molds and mildews that are pandemic among the materials to be housed in the National Archives: "Although a preliminary survey of Government records in the District of Columbia by the National Bureau of Standards and the Department of Agriculture indicated that only approximately 10 percent of the archives coming to the National Archives would need fumigation, experience has shown that all materials in boxes and many documents in other types of containers should be fumigated as soon as received. This procedure is being followed" (41).

The past imperfect sounds the proper note of bureaucratic impersonality, although, on this matter at least, rhetorical vagueness is also the most honest approach. From the Division of Accessions, we learn that a total of 2,192,144 cubic feet of materials have thus far been designated for the archives, and this does not yet include what preliminary surveys of the Departments of War, Treasury, Commerce, and Navy will designate for storage once completed. At 300 cubic feet of documents per fumigation—and more than 2 million cubic feet of materials with more on the way—we see in the image a "procedure" that will be "being followed" for some time. Nothing here discloses just how thoroughly on the wrong side of an economy of scale these two men are, but the sheer bulk that must be borne by the task of memory that the archives undertakes does seem to prompt a moment of historical melancholy, even dread, just a few years later at the beginning of another *Annual Report*: "As the wheels of Government go round," a bureaucrat poetically writes, "they grind out a ceaseless stream of records, which, like the salt ground from the magic mill in the fairy tale, has become so great in volume that it threatens to engulf everything in its path."[2] There are plenty more truckloads of history where these two came from.

I begin with this photograph, despite its narrow audience of government functionaries, because it recalls some of the more charged and pervasive iconographies of 1930s America, and harbors an unlikely allegory about the relationship between modernity and history, one that looks to technology as a means to preserve and ultimately transmit a material past that appears at best an inconvenience and at worst a threat—to both itself and us. We might first describe this photograph as showing "men at work" amid "modern machines." I take both these phrases from Lewis Hine's *Men at Work* (1932), which prefaces its images of aerial construction on the Empire State Building and skilled labor on assembly lines with the proposition that "the more you see of modern machines, the more may you, too, respect the men who make them and manipulate them."[3] I am not suggesting that a similar sense of social mission motivates the archives photo—a close look at the finely creased pants of the man lower on the ramp indicates a suit-and-tie employee in a smock, not the class of worker who interested Hine. But whoever took this photograph was likely familiar with a range of Depression-era scenes of labor, especially those aimed at offering more ameliorative images of modern work—the style of image favored by the U.S. government's "official" documentary aesthetic as it turned away from the more overt politics of Dorothea Lange, Ben Shahn, and others.[4] Though not a picture of a modernizing project on the order of the Hoover Dam, the photograph pays tribute to the power of "consensus about shared national goals" that Terry Smith describes as central to the effort on the part of many New Deal agencies to show government making "effective" progress in the face of ongoing strain and crisis.[5]

By the same token, I am not suggesting that the archives photo was taken simply because the fumigation vault exemplifies a perfect icon of machine-age styling and design, and so participates in another equally pervasive mode of visual culture in the 1930s. With its smooth and regular geometries, metallic textures, and biomorphic turbine—which could, with a little more streamlining, merit comparison with the "20th Century Limited"—the vault is a ready-made precisionist icon, expressing the functionalist aesthetic that designers such as Raymond Loewy and Norman Bel Geddes helped to promote and popularize (fig. 4.2). The immaculate enameling on the vault's side panels could be from a

FIGURE 4.2. "The Twentieth-Century Limited." Advertisement for New York Central System Railroad, circa 1937.

new Frigidaire. Indeed, almost every visual element of this massive and unromantic piece of engineering confirms some aspect of the constellation of stylistic preferences, squarely in the Bauhaus lineage, that Philip Johnson celebrated in the Museum of Modern Art's famous "Machine Art" exhibition in 1934. "The beauty of machine art depends often upon rhythmical as well as upon geometrical elements—upon repetition as well as upon shape."[6] How better to appreciate the sleek steel ribs that provide for the vault's structural support? "Machine art, devoid as it should be of surface ornament, must depend upon the sensuous beauty" of enamel, aluminum, or steel.[7] How better to describe the essence of the vault's stark appeal? It would seem, in short, that the picture is the work of a photographer who understood something of the aesthetics and attractions that went along with—that in the 1930s depended on—the spectacular utility of the machine we see here.

I need not be so circumspect about the allegory I see this photo putting into service. This is a picture of modernity, not just because it shows such an imposing piece of technology, but because it envisions an emblematic fiction in which the old and new meet in a moment of stylized proximity and contact. The story goes something like this: the past is a mess, unwieldy in its cluttering and at times overwhelming presence in a world where it seems less and less to belong; modernity is a name we give to the experience of knowing that the past no longer speaks to us directly; and so we box it, tag it, and put it away, all in order to lend it a new kind of status—as history, as archive—which relies on a series of operations that at once translate the past into a dialect of the modern and help us make sense of whatever language it may once have used to communicate. I've just mixed my metaphors here, setting out to describe history as a stubborn kind of materiality, only to arrive at history as an expressive idiom; and this slip from things and objects to mediums and messages is itself one of the symptomatic conditions of U.S. modernism with which this chapter will contend.

If the archives photo asks that we consider history as an exercise in treating waste, it also asks that we think about waste management as a problem that turns on the materiality of information. In the 1950s these truckloads of paperwork would likely be on their way to getting microfilmed and thrown away, and today they would get scanned and digitized—before recycling, or so we hope. To the degree to which we believe that either of these alternatives would accomplish what this photograph depicts—the preservation of historical materials—we effectively ratify a contemporary view that, to borrow from

Katherine Hayles, "[puts] materiality on one side of a divide and information on the other side."[8] According to this logic, which Hayles approaches skeptically, it follows to think of information, despite all our computers, hard drives, fiber-optic cables, and server farms, "as a kind of immaterial fluid that circulates effortlessly around the globe while still retaining the solidity of a concept." The archives photo shows no evidence of such an attitude toward information, and little sign of the intention to dispose of the material on display, which retains far more "solidity" than a concept does. What makes this anonymous image so strikingly modernist in its constellation of history and technology is not just the fact that in the 1930s this laborious process of fumigation was cutting-edge archival practice; it is also that it renders the materiality of the vault itself as compelling as all the documents it has been built to save. Or said differently, this photograph shows us that it is impossible to think about preserving history as content without first going to work on history as form, and that it requires a considerable investment in technology to conceive of such an undertaking in the first place. It takes, in other words, so much technology to get at our materials that we are always at risk of being swallowed by the mechanics of our efforts. I admit that the fumigation vault does not at first glance resemble the other technologies whose fetishized appeal this book has tracked. And only in what was, by the 1930s, an archaic sense of the term could this image be said to depict a scene of "communication" (the transport of the documents, for example, up the "communicating" ramp into the chamber). Yet if we are willing to grant—as Stanley Cavell proposes, drawing on Clement Greenberg—that a medium, in the last analysis, is "something through which or by means of which something specific gets done," this fumigation vault may well represent a modernist aesthetic in more than just its streamlining. Its function helps to define the difference that its mediation makes: through the vault, we remain attached to the materials of history and feel the past more viscerally by means of the technology that affects it.

The implications of the archives photo allow us to consider both the problems and the possibilities of a mediated history—which is exactly what, by the 1930s, a great deal of America's history looked like. The photo wants to promise that the past will be rescued by the technologies of modern life, and that nothing of its texture will be lost in the translation. But to embrace this image of historical mediation is to understand that we increasingly rely on technology itself as "something through which" we access or retrieve a past whose materiality has been not just refreshed but sorted, organized, and managed. My hope in this chapter is to find ways to appreciate some of the technologies that the period invented to manage its own accumulation of material. There are "no ideas but in things," as William Carlos Williams first declares in 1929, but sometimes there are more things than we can process.[9] This is one reason why history is not so easily modernized, and if the archives photo does not make this fully clear, we will examine in the following pages a range of figures and projects from the 1930s that do—including Williams, Lewis Mumford, George Oppen, Charles Sheeler, *Let Us Now Praise Famous Men*, and *The Index of American Design*. I want to revisit the modernist aesthetic that promised to remember and record the past like never before and to understand better how the mediated history it makes could lead to something of a crisis. Are there ideas in everything? And if there are, how do we know which things to keep and which to throw away? It risks anachronism to borrow from computer science and suggest that U.S. modernism was shaped by its devotion to various "object-oriented" databases that flourished in the period and accumulated history as an endless series of items ("a ceaseless stream of records"), which were themselves imagined as artifacts of information that must communicate if they are to matter. As Lev Manovich insists, the "genre" of database—defined most simply as "a structured collection of data"—is a cultural form that modernism in part anticipates, so it is only fitting that we can see so many figures of the 1930s experimenting with their own object orientation, so to speak, as an aesthetic that could bring them closer not just to the materials of the past but to the technologies that informed them.

The priority and allure of material objects—and old objects especially (relics, artifacts)—is one of the most familiar themes in writing of the 1930s, and it is once again a central preoccupation of critics returning to modernism's culture. Bill Brown has recently argued that "the modernist's fetishized thing—excised from the world of consumer culture, isolated, refocused, doted upon, however momentarily—is meant to be saved from the fate of the mass-produced object."[10] We might consider Susan Stewart's suggestive work on the poetics of the miniature and the souvenir as a precursor to Brown, insofar as she stresses the ways in which we embrace and treasure the materiality of such objects to the exact degree that they confront the everyday assumption of exchange and functionality.[11] My own debts and allegiances to such work will emerge as we proceed, but this chapter is also determined to explore a less familiar network of materialist discourses that attributes the allure of objects less to their intrinsic qualities as things and more to their capacities as mediums. I am concerned with what might be called the mediated life of history itself in American culture, and the texts that are my interest in this chapter ask a series of questions about media technology and the archival past that are curiously and, sometimes, perilously suspended between moments of exhilaration when history looks ready to be saved by modernism's informational aesthetic and desperation when this aesthetic looks to threaten even what it most strenuously wants to remember. This is a threat I might bring into sharper focus by confessing that although I know better, I still sometimes look at the archives photograph and see two men loading history into a monstrous oven—pristine, grisly, efficient.

◊

Perhaps my sympathies are misplaced: there is a good chance, after all, that somewhere in the National Archives the documents we see in this picture remain to this day, in one form or another, while the vault is almost certainly landfill or long ago melted down for scrap. Almost nothing ages worse than high technology.

And for that matter, the math I alluded to above is not on the side of the vault: one trip almost done, only 10,000 more to go before 1935's accessions will be taken care of, though at any pace slower than 30 trips per day, this first stage of the archives' preservation program will drag on well into 1936, by which point another 5,649,415 linear feet of records ("found in 5,659 separate rooms") will arrive, most of them mildewed and demanding fumigation.[12] The amount of materials we see—48 boxes worth, maybe 3 feet of records in each—makes for a paltry synecdoche of the whole that remains. The "fairy tale" indulged a few years later in the opening sentences of the National Archives' *Seventh Annual Report* gives us a much more accurate picture of the situation than all the exact figures and sober projections: "a ceaseless stream of records . . . so great in volume that it threatens to engulf everything in its path." This image bears a dark lesson about the abundance of modernity's historical production, and strikingly corresponds to one of the most famous moments in Benjamin's "Theses on the Philosophy of History." Perhaps all beleaguered archivists think alike: if the "angel of history" bears witness to "one single catastrophe which keeps piling wreckage upon wreckage and hurls it in front of his feet," he also experiences "progress" as a version of the desperate accumulation of material that plagues the author of the National Archives' *Annual Report*.[13]

Still, the archives photo assumes a confident investment in technology that remains a signature of U.S. culture in the Machine Age, as Smith and others have observed. In its streamlined functionalism, as I suggested, the vault is virtually a schematic for the aesthetics of precisionism—a term used to characterize a loosely affiliated group of writers, painters, and photographers in the period, including Charles Demuth, Morton Schamberg, and Charles Sheeler, to whose work I will later turn. Precisionism has been described as less a movement than a shared preoccupation with what at first appears an eccentric set of materials: early cubism, Duchamp, American arts and crafts, photography, and, most crucially, industrial technology and design.[14] What patterned these preferences was an emphasis on control, detachment, intellection, and restraint; precisionism concentrates a strain within American modernism that Hugh Kenner tellingly attributes to "people who spend much time operating machinery" and thus "find it easier on the whole to shape their emotions to the abstract or the inanimate."[15] Alfred Barr, who later became the first director of the Museum of Modern Art, is credited for first naming Sheeler and others in his circle "precisionists" in 1927, but the term had already been employed to describe a modernist aesthetic by Marianne Moore in her 1923 poem "Bowls." She may have not spent much time operating machinery, but the second half of Kenner's formulation certainly applies:

> by this survival of ancient punctilio
> in the manner of Chinese lacquer-carving,
> layer after layer exposed by certainty of touch and unhurried incision
> so that only so much color shall be revealed as is necessary to the picture,
> I learn that we are precisionists,
> not citizens of Pompeii arrested in action
> as a cross-section of one's correspondence would seem to imply.[16]

The poem invokes a familiar structure of Romantic lyric—the projection of ideas onto things, as in Keats's "Ode on a Grecian Urn"—but only to reject this model of subjectivity as inapplicable and outmoded. Our "correspondence" with each other might be too emotional and overwrought; and we should write with more reserve and less animation, since, not being "citizens of Pompeii," it is not as if our world is ending. But our relations with the material might be getting better, and Moore's speaker has learned to appreciate a cooler aesthetic that relies on the "unhurried" dedication to technique. Nothing of the speaker is "exposed" in her intimate attention to the materials at hand, which comes into focus not as the product of her sympathies and attachments ("correspondence" happens elsewhere) but as her temperate, composed reaction to what she sees. Lisa Steinman speculates that "Bowls" may have been inspired by a photograph by Paul Strand, but even in the absence of such a direct connection, we can see in Moore's poem a play of image-making technologies: the flash that "arrests" the victims of Vesuvius "in action"; the precise "incision" that reveals color.[17] "It does not make sense to speak of Precisionism without considering photography," writes Ellen Handy; for while few precisionists sought overtly photo-realistic effects, there is an inclination toward the "modern, technical, objective, hard-edged" sensibility popularly associated with the straight photography of Strand and later Walker Evans.[18]

This particular precisionist affinity returns us to the iconography of the archives photo and its highly "technical" response to the management of historical materials. If Strand and Evans departed from the pictorialism of Alfred Stieglitz by rejecting stylistic affectations (filters, tinting) that obscured the mechanical "objectivity" of the photographic image, we might say that the fumigation vault aspires to an equally transparent relationship to the material it processes. But I would also like to trace the period's fascination with a mechanics of visual perception and depiction that, for all its streamlining, reveals a more mediated experience of a materiality that resists rendering its objects cleanly and efficiently. Precisionism's model of objectivity as an aesthetic end—a model informed by, and idolized in, photography itself—so depends on the powers of technology that it is often difficult to look past all the operations that are necessary to produce a work of art that can render its own means effectively invisible. In this respect, another of Moore's poems, "An Egyptian Pulled Glass Bottle in the Shape of a Fish," reads like an allegory about photographic ways of seeing that are anything but immediate:

> Here we have thirst
> And patience, from the first,
> And art, as in a wave held up for us to see
> In its essential perpendicularity;
> Not brittle but

Intense—the spectrum, that
Spectacular and nimble animal the fish,
Whose scales turn aside the sun's sword by their polish. (*MM*, 173)

Moore's bottle offers an amazingly compact lesson in "thirst" and "patience": this is a poem describing a bottle that looks like a fish, and which therefore can hold the liquid that the fish needs in order to live, but would have to turn itself inside out to have. Or put differently, the "shape" of the bottle itself calls attention to the desire for a particular medium—the fish's "thirst" for, or to be in, water—that the bottle, as a work of art, can easily objectify but can never, no matter how patiently we wait, make available. If we see the bottle as a fish, its "essential perpendicularity" is confirmed: as a container, it is necessarily at cross-purposes with its subject—a fish forever out of water. At the same time, it is not art's purpose, as Moore makes clear, to satisfy such naive and immediate "thirsts" for literal representation; the bottle is not a fish, but only "in" its shape. And since "wave" can just as well refer to light, the fish's utter isolation from its natural medium only confirms that to see anything at all, we must be thoroughly immersed in a medium of our own. Indeed, Moore's paratactic grammar challenges us to realize that "the spectrum" itself constitutes our vision of "that / Spectacular and nimble animal the fish"; the appositional construction of the sentence suggests a syntactical correlative for visual experience, since we don't so much see objects but rather the light that they refract and "turn aside." This is practically a parable of Barthes's sense of photography as an "emanation of the referent" that depends on the "radiations" of light that touch us when we see; technically, this is a condition for normal optical perception as such, but art here rewards our "patience" by making the "brittle" truth that we see nothing in and of itself into a game of scrutiny, displacement, and transformation. Moore provides us with an especially "intense" reminder to look more kindly on our mediums, because no matter how much we may think they isolate and interfere, it is far worse to think how we would feel if they were taken from us.

What attracted a precisionist aesthetic almost irresistibly to photography was its ability to satisfy the "wish to view the world" that Cavell identifies as a particular "automatism" of the medium itself.[19] This is to say that photography answers not simply to a desire for better views of the world (for more accurate or convincing representations), but to a desire "for the condition of viewing as such" that "takes the responsibility for it out of our hands." Photography, for

Cavell, "automatically" produces the same experience of detachment within the workings of a medium that Moore would have us learn from looking at a fish-shaped bottle. Writing in 1937 on the occasion of the first comprehensive retrospective of photographic images at the Museum of Modern Art, Beaumont Newhall took a less poetic approach to the impersonality of photography, which he called "basically a way of fixing the camera image by the action of light upon a substance sensitive to it."[20] In stressing this material fact of the technology, Newhall sounds a theme that later critics of photography will transform into its specific medium aesthetic, from Susan Sontag ("to photograph is to appropriate the thing photographed") to Barthes ("the photograph is literally an emanation of the referent") and, most recently, to Patrick Maynard (photography "is simply the physical marking of surfaces through the agency of light and similar radiations").[21]

For many modernists, the appeal of such an aesthetic was patterned on the assumption of photography's superior and unavoidable immediacy, on the idea of a technology that could do nothing but communicate the image of anything that was there when the shutter opened—producing, in Barthes's words, "a material vestige of its subject."[22] As Michael North has demonstrated, modernism was especially devoted to the promise—hard-wired, so to speak, into the very idea of the camera as a thing that sees—of registering the world by way of a "more indexical sign, a kind of trace previously produced only by nature."[23] And if we take our cues from Williams's own spare lyrics about red wheelbarrows ("So much depends upon . . .") or plums in the icebox, we might rightly conclude that photography inspired a modernism that aimed for objectivity even at the risk of seeming, well, cold. But for all of precisionism's rhetoric of impersonality and sheer technique, it also invited artists and writers to perform a surprisingly affected tone toward objects and traded on an almost moral sense of dedication to the materials at hand. In 1938 Constance Rourke's highest praise for Charles Sheeler pays tribute to his work's rigorous attention to physical detail "that may without too much exaggeration be called dedication to the object."[24] There are many moments when a modernist respect for objects and their forms becomes instead a more visceral desire to possess and reproduce a feeling of materiality that belongs not so much to objects as to the mediums we use to show how much we care for them. Thus Louis Zukofsky gives us an image that seems to show that for a poet to demonstrate his commitment to greater and greater "objectification" is for him to indulge the fantasy that he can cradle his own writing in its arms: because "there exists, tho it may not be harbored as solidity in the crook of an elbow, writing (audibility in two-dimensional print) which is an object or affects the mind as such."[25]

We might well wonder what the unknown author of the fairy tale that starts the National Archives' *Report* for 1941 would have made of all this "respect for the object" and devotion to "writing" that rests tangibly "in the crook of an elbow." In the archives, after all, both the object status of texts and the physical pressure of writing's variously material incarnations take on a different reckoning; a modernist fetish for the materiality of the text is programmed into the system, but also rendered slightly foolish, when it becomes necessary to take stock of discourse by the linear foot and by the ton. It is this way of experiencing history—as aggressively, even uselessly material—that is captured with a certain gnostic flair by a story with which Bill Viola begins his essay "The Porcupine and the Car": A friend gives Viola a huge quantity of used audiotapes "retrieved from the garbage at his office," which would seem the perfect gift, or so Viola initially thinks, for the multimedia artist who has everything. "Thrilled at the prospect of unlimited free recording time," Viola writes, "I got an idea to set up a tape recorder right in the center of activity in my house, the kitchen, and to try and record everything that went on."[26] And so he records for a full week whatever happens to happen (idle chatter, or cooking a meal), making sure that the tape is running if there is any noise at all for the microphone to pick up. But Viola's rapture with the total documentary of his everyday soundscape vanishes almost instantly when he must face the first batch of what results: "when I had accumulated well over 24 hours of tape, I suddenly realized a distressing thought. I would need 24 hours, exactly the time it took to record, to play all this stuff back. Furthermore, if I kept this up, say, for a year, I would have to stop after six months to begin playing back, and if I got really ambitious and made it my life's work, I would have to stop my life when it was only half over to sit down and listen to all the material for the rest of my life, plus a little additional time for rewinding all the cassettes" (59). The problem is not so much one of fidelity—there is no doubting the accuracy of the record produced by the apparatus he employs—as of economy; what modern technologies of representation make possible are extensions of memory that are so complete, so massive in their accuracy and so easy to accumulate that the work of making a viable history becomes the work of forgetting. For every load of papers on its way to the vault, how many more should simply be left to the fungus? "The total quantity of records received during the fiscal year 1941 exceeded by 35 percent the quantity of records received in any previous fiscal year" (*Seventh Annual*

Report, 18). If not for the outbreak of war, why expect fiscal year 1942 to prove any different?

It is a commonplace in accounts of modern life in America that there is finally never enough history left behind; that the sheer pace of technological change, the inexorable capitalist fixation on the new, the inurement to rootlessness that comes naturally to a sprawling nation of immigrants—all these conspire to bring about an attitude toward history that is neglectful at the core. Van Wyck Brooks's call for a "usable past" stands among the most famous indictments of modern America's insufficient respect for history itself, and several of the texts I will consider in this chapter echo both the rhetoric and the substance of his accusation; and yet we will also see that what makes the American past seem somehow unusable to a great many in the 1930s is precisely the fact that there is too much of it.[27] The idea of a national memory—patterned on and mediated by all the technologies that modernity can muster—presents a formidable challenge because these very technologies, even as they crowd out archaic fragments and traditions that remain, also allow us to make records of the past in astonishing magnitude. When history becomes a problem not of loss but of excess and even abundance, then the material status of the mediums that bear it, no matter how efficient they might be, is impossible to manage. At such a moment, the appeal of getting rid of mediums is tangible, and the desire to burn away the archive's physicality—so as to better keep the content of its massively decaying forms—is not just understandable but irresistible. Thus a contemporary "ideology of immateriality," to borrow from Hayles, distinguishes digital culture—where information is a prized abstraction that must be free to communicate across platforms—from the analog world of modernism, where specific mediums tried to keep their messages to themselves.[28] But U.S. modernism stages a version of this conflict within its own practices of historical representation in the 1930s, as the attraction to materiality must face the consequences of the accumulations it can inspire, and then fight the urge to just throw everything away and make it new. I am after a better understanding of how technology makes history—a "procedure," returning to the language used by the National Archives, still "being followed" to this day.

Archival Aesthetics

"How are media the subjects of history when doing history depends on so many tacit conditions of mediation?"[29] I borrow this provocative question from Lisa Gitelman because it applies with particular resonance to works from the 1930s that reflect on the centenary of photography, when the medium itself became an object of history. Soon after organizing his groundbreaking exhibition of photography at the Museum of Modern Art, Beaumont Newhall published what became the first complete history of photography from its origins to the present. The following year, Robert Taft published his exhaustive social history, *Photography and the American Scene* (1938); Benjamin had already published his essay "A Short History of Photography" in 1931, which was itself a review of two new books that had just revisited the early decades of photographic practice in Europe. And as we will shortly see, this sense of a once new medium turning old is a concern for many others in the period.

But I also take the spirit of Gitelman's provocation to apply more broadly to the mix of media archaeology and "medium-specific analysis" that this book has pursued from the start.[30] That is to say, my own interest in revisiting the histories that emerge around a modernist aesthetics of the medium has been powerfully informed by my sense of the degree to which contemporary media culture has defined itself against this language of modernism, even as it pursues a similar network of aspirations toward more sensuous and visceral experiences of communication. Benjamin pays tribute to the effects of such presentist historiography by way of an elaborate simile that appears a few pages before his vision of "the angel of history": "As flowers turn toward the sun, by dint of a secret heliotropism the past strives to turn toward that sun which is rising in the sky of history."[31] Taking the photograph in the National Archives as a historiographic model, on the other hand, suggests far less natural procedures for producing a past that, however recalcitrant, will always in the end surrender to the priorities of the present. In this respect, Derrida provides a surprisingly direct account of how such histories are made, although I doubt that anything so prosaic as fumigation figures within the logic of historical "technique in general" that he describes in *Archive Fever*: "the technical structure of the *archiving* archive also determines the structure of the *archivable* content even in its very coming into existence and in its relationship to the future."[32] For Derrida, no form of technology for making history can have a transparent relationship to the materials it encounters in the archive. This is not just because the "technical structure" of the present conditions how we understand the past, but rather because "content" is always—and already was—an emergent property of form. To my ear at least, the unintended echo of McLuhan is remarkable. History proves another case where the medium is the message.

Derrida's insistence on the radical presentism of the archive—indeed, its technological determination of the past—assumes an attitude toward history that is so preoccupied with mediums that he seems unable to conceive of an experience of the past that is not finally the experience of its mediation. "If there is such a thing," he writes, as "the instant of archivization," it does not mark a moment of "so-called live or spontaneous memory," but instead the "prosthetic experience of the technical substrate" (25). From within the logic of such extreme technological determinism, which outdoes McLuhan or even Friedrich Kittler, the particular question that Gitelman poses about the historical status of media is all but impossible to ask: in much the same way that "archivization" encompasses and conflates (encompasses *to* conflate) discrete acts of selection, storage, preservation, indexing, searching, and retrieval, so too does the notion of "technique in general" result from Derrida's bleeding of specific mediums (printing, writing) into a "substrate" that itself dematerializes, almost immediately, into "an archivable concept of the archive" (36). What begins, then, as a version of a modernist aesthetic of historical representation—the recursive relay between form and content, medium and message, that we experience as their identity—becomes instead the image of a decidedly postmodernist and post-medium condition in which there is "hypomnesia" instead of memory, "technique in general" instead of technologies. There are neither mediums nor messages, but "traces" that do not represent the past, and in any case, cannot be read in the present.

The logic of the archive is Derrida's familiar logic of endless anticipation and deferral: "if we want to know what [the archive] will have meant, we will only know in times to come" (36). We wait for history's message but realize that it has arrived only when we understand that we have already missed its meaning. Once history itself is subjected to "technique in general," it is forever lost—or always "not yet" in Derrida's temporal map—in much the same manner that writing vanishes in the face of "writing in general." Described memorably in "Signature Event Context," this is what we are left with once we realize the "actual or empirical nonpresence of the signifier" in the experience of the sign itself. Thus while it might appear that Derrida's interest in "the general graphematic structure of every 'communication'" would involve renewed attention to the medium-specific properties of writing—the shapes of letters on the page, the differences between manuscript and print—he insists instead that none of these materialities speak to the effect of writing that he is after. Indeed, to even posit that such questions concerning technologies of writing are possible is mistakenly to presume that any "mark," in any medium, is something other than a "disruption" of its own presence. A materialist account of mediums as messages—one that wholly identifies their forms with their contents—must also, Derrida insists, understand that this equation goes both ways; if messages are always failures not just to communicate but to exist, then the mediums that are these messages are similarly disrupted at their inception, and can make no difference after all. As Derrida admits in 1977, this is a proposition to which McLuhan, with his relentlessly progressive teleology of media experience (from individual "typographic man" to interconnected "global village") would not abide. "We are witnessing not an end of writing," argues Derrida, "that would restore, in accord with McLuhan's ideological representation, a transparency or an immediacy to social relations; but rather the increasingly powerful historical expansion of a general writing, of which the system of speech, consciousness, meaning, presence, truth, etc., would be only an effect, and should be analyzed as such."[33] In other words, if there are no messages, then there are no mediums either. "Writing, if there is any, perhaps communicates, but certainly does not exist."[34] So why replace it? Which is to say that Derrida's model of "prosthetic experience," despite its superficial similarity to McLuhan's own prosthetics of media as "the extensions of man," is something else entirely. What makes experience "prosthetic" for Derrida is not that it is augmented and amplified by way of media technologies; "experience" is instead a prosthetic substitute or simulation for a direct experience of the medium that we simultaneously mourn and anticipate. All that mediums can communicate as mere trace, or "technical substrate"—their materiality, in other words—emerges most powerfully when we stop believing in them.

New media critics put their faith in other forms of materiality. Mark Hansen and Brian Massumi argue for a return to phenomenologies of affect and intensity that emphasize the physiology of perception over the physicality of the object. "The digital era and the phenomenon of digitization itself," Hansen writes, "can be understood as demarcating a shift in the correlation of two crucial terms: media and body. Simply put, as media lose their material specificity, the body takes on a more prominent function as a selective processor of information."[35] Though Massumi relies on an idiosyncratic language, he stresses much the same development when he suggests that contemporary culture has discovered "the autonomy of affect" by attending to "*virtually synthetic perspectives* anchored in (functionally limited by) the actually existing, particular things that embody them."[36] Hayles recalls the rhetoric of modernism when she directs us to "the physical attributes constituting any artifact" as the site where an understanding of its materiality must start.[37] But since computers confront us with a "potentially infinite" array of such attributes—"the polymers used to fabricate the case, the rare earth elements used to make the phosphors in the CRT screen, the palladium used for the power cord prongs"—most examples of new media expression, or "technotext," "will select a few to foreground and work into its thematic concerns" (32). This makes for a useful new release of modernist materiality—Greenberg 2.0?—but at the expense of all the existential drama that surrounds the way an art, to count as modernist, must "surrender" to its medium. The image of "selecting" from a menu of materialities has a technocratic ring to it that distinguishes this account of creativity from Greenberg's heady mix of confrontation and commitment; and this is in keeping with Hayles's care never to ontologize the materiality of electronic or digital art as a property that inheres within the object. Materiality depends as much "on the user's interactions with the work and the interpretive strategies she develops" (33). Its performative character is primary for Hayles because materiality can emerge only "from the dynamic interplay between the richness of a physically robust world and human intelligence as it crafts this physicality to create meaning."[38]

Yet any materiality at all, however pragmatically defined or operatively described, might still be too much—too archaic—for a culture that aspires to the model of "transcendental data" that Alan Liu ascribes to "discourse network 2000."[39] He adapts the latter term from Kittler, but draws on Derrida to characterize the desire on behalf of Web designers, media artists, and software engineers to fashion "technologies enforcing ever more immaculate separation of content from presentation" (62). "The very religion," Liu writes, "of text encoding and databases" today reflects an inflation of semiosis "in the manner of Derrida himself in his discussion of the transcendental signified": "According to its dogma, true content abides in a transcendental logic, reason, or noumen so completely structured and described that it is in and of itself inutterable in any mere material or instantiated form" (62). We see this spirit working in increasingly minimalist Web pages that rely on bare lists, or grids or other "simple geometries" so as better to "surrender their soul to data pours that throw transcendental information onto the page from database or XML sources reposed far in the background"; "records are poured automatically from the database onto the web page one at a time, but because the data pour is nested within a repeat statement . . . the operation generates a list or table containing all relevant items in the database even though the author may not know what is in the database or may have ceded control of the database to someone else" (60).

Networked servers and markup languages are vastly different technologies than fumigation chambers, but the "data pours" that Liu identifies as fetish objects for a contemporary ideology and aesthetics of information nonetheless evoke the same economies of scale that haunt the discourse of the National Archives in the 1930s. There we have a "ceaseless stream of records" pouring in, "reposed," as Liu might say, in storage facilities all over Washington, D.C., and beyond; who knows how many cartloads, how many linear feet of documents, how many times the two men in the photograph will execute the "repeat statement" to fill the vault and fumigate, to fill the vault and fumigate, to fill the vault and fumigate . . . A modernist aesthetic of materiality is a lousy principle of database design. This much was clear to Vannevar Bush, who writes, in his groundbreaking 1945 essay "As We May Think," that man "has built a civilization so complex that he needs to mechanize his record more fully if he is to push his experiment to its logical conclusion and not merely become bogged down part way there by overtaxing his limited memory. His excursion may be more enjoyable if he can reacquire the privilege of forgetting the manifold things he does not need to have immediately at hand, with some assurance that he can find them again if they prove important."[40] For Bush, the solution to this problem is his hypothetical "memex" machine, which imagined spools of indexed microfilm and multiple television screens providing for a precociously contemporary experience of information; only this maximalist, multimedia technology can match our own ability to "enormously extend the record," which grows so rapidly in its "present bulk," which grows so rapidly that "we can hardly consult it" (38).

An electrical engineer and dean at MIT, and later director of the Office of Scientific Research and Development during World War II, Bush is often credited for articulating much of the conceptual framework for what we know now as hypertext. It thus makes perfect sense that many of the virtues of his imagined "memex"—speed, adaptability, and efficiency—are precisely those that figure most importantly in the databases of "discourse network 2000." For transmission on the Internet, information must be as "as *transformable* as possible between varying technological and social conventions"; discourse must be rendered "*autonomously mobile*" so that even "atomistic parts of a file" possess enough "logical autonomy" to suggest the structure of the larger document; to achieve this on a scale that matters is necessarily to "*automate* such discourse so that a proliferating population of machinic servers, databases, and client programs can participate as cyborgian agents and concatenated web services facilitating the processing and reprocessing of knowledge."[41] This is what Liu means when he says that contemporary media culture's "govern-ing ideology" is *the separation of content from material instantiation or formal presentation* (58).

My concern, however, is less with Liu's suggestive account of how this set of imperatives is shaping computer culture in the twenty-first century than with his powerful explanation of just how this new ideology of digital discourse and expression emerges from and then transcends what should by now be a familiar model of modernist aesthetics. "Modern art and literature at the beginning of the twentieth century," writes Liu, "apprehended the spirit of industrialism in the formalist credo that form is integral with content or, transmuted into the new idiom of process, function. The avant-garde of the time could be famously perverse or obtuse in implementing that formula—offering up everything from art as a Duchamp ready-made to a New Critical verbal icon" (79). The incoher-ence of an aesthetic that would claim as exemplary both R. Mutt's *Fountain* and Eliot's *Four Quartets* is, for Liu, a symptom that the "modernist equation of form and content" was haunted from the start by "the implicit substrate" of materiality (80). This repressed materiality returns as noise and interference, as that which remains "perverse" or "obtuse" in the fantasy of perfect communica-tion between form and content—the communication of form *as* content—that modernism dreams of reproducing but never quite achieves.

American modernism in the 1930s is remembered for its many attempts to translate such formalist projects into fully operational, historical aesthet-ics. There are moments when anyone pretending to the avant-garde seems required to break as radically as possible with any sense of the past, and it is widely agreed that the 1930s were not such a moment.[42] For Alfred Kazin, the period was marked by a "new nationalism" that was at once a politics and an in-formatics: "to understand the spirit in which so many writers turned to recover America . . . is to appreciate how compelling was the drive toward national in-ventory which began by reporting the ravages of the depression and ended by reporting on the national inheritance."[43] There is, for Kazin, a necessary line of descent from impassioned social documentary to reverent historical recollec-tion that reflects the deeper influence of a single technological correlative for both aesthetics, each of which registers "the extent to which the camera *as an idea*" (the emphasis is his) shapes verbal representation in the period (495). Photography provides both the means of producing and a language for imagin-ing an aesthetic of direct confrontation with realities at hand, an "enforced sim-plicity" of manner and form exploiting the medium's own technical predisposi-tion toward mimetic fidelity, unfiltered accuracy, and, above all, a perspective of extreme objectivity. Enlisting a remark of James Agee's from *Let Us Now Praise Famous Men*, Kazin celebrates photography for revealing "the cruel radiance of what is" (495). Or, as Barthes would phrase much the same conviction some decades after: "In Photography, the presence of the thing (at a certain past moment) is never metaphoric."[44]

I want to suggest that photography's contribution to mediating a sense of "national inheritance," as Kazin terms it, involves a more equivocal and hesitant appreciation of how history can be made to look like information to be inventoried. Let me give a brief but remarkable example of how this experience of photography is registered in a work whose aspirations to Kazin's "enforced simplicity" could not be more dramatically apparent. Completed sometime between 1932 and 1934, the following George Oppen poem first appeared in *Discrete Series*; it is "Objectivist" in the extreme—the product of a rigorous, perhaps even exaggerated adherence to Pound's dictum for "direct treatment of the 'thing,' whether subjective or objective."[45] Little mystery as to which one Oppen elected:

> Civil war photo:
> Grass near the lens;
> Man in the field
> In silk hat. Daylight.
> The cannon of that day
> In our parks.[46]

Now *this*, with all due respect to Benjamin, is a "small history of photography."[47] I am not, of course, insinuating that hidden somewhere in these twenty-three words there is anything approaching a narrative of technical advance and stylistic innovation of the kind Benjamin produces in his 1931 essay, much less those found in the first full American accounts of the medium, which appear a few years later.[48] But Oppen's poem is, despite its honed and conspicuous brevity, surprisingly informative about a particular way that photography mediates our sense of the past. "Like the Western camera," Kenner writes, "the Objectivist poet is the geometer of minima."[49] Oppen's "Civil War Photo" is a poem that more than proves Kenner right; indeed, it is a poem that is determined to see just how small it can make the history that is made out of photography. As a drastic experiment in economies of scale, Oppen's poem suggests the appeal of translating the past into always smaller units of information. Yet his own aesthetic of intentionally diminishing returns reminds us that a medium's own materiality (photography or writing) is sometimes most intensely felt when it urges us to see through it.

We should give the poem's formidable sparseness its due: it consists, as I said, of just twenty-three words, nineteen of which have but one syllable, and one of the two-syllable words, "daylight," is revealed rather starkly in this context as two little words put together, while another polysyllabic, "photo," is itself an abbreviation. Oppen organizes these twenty-seven syllables in lines that sound either two or three heavy stresses, with what must be a calculated avoidance of any musicality; the first line has a particularly blunt rhythm to it—each word laying claim to a full initial stress—befitting a nominalization out of thin air, a statement whose sole purpose is to declare an object and convince the reader that this thing, above all, exists. To that end, "Civil war" seems not so much to modify "photo" as to allow for a more specific designating of this historical artifact; the poem's first line describes no scene whatsoever, but rather gives us genus and species, so to speak, as one semantic block. The next two lines are mirror images in both meter and syntax: stress falls on the first and last word, or put another way, on the nouns at either ends of prepositional phrases. The third line is the first in the poem that is anything but self-sufficient, though there is something inelegant about the grammar that pulls us from the line above—a flagrantly dangling prepositional phrase makes for shoddy enjambment, though it is obviously an effect of hesitation that Oppen is after, since the language makes better sense if we again place "man" at the beginning of the line. As if the poem's semantic units are not disconnected enough, Oppen invites us to break things down further, to see just what we can do with the miniature pieces of description. Two decisive periods—isolating "daylight" as a self-contained unit of meaning—reduce the poem's pace to a still slower movement in the final lines; lines that repeat, with slight variation, the syntactical arrangement of the third and fourth lines—noun followed by prepositional phrase, and then another prepositional phrase, without punctuation. There is not a verb to be had.

Another reader might take the poem apart differently, with more attention to punctuation in its first lines and less interest in the rhythm—or lack of it—that I would say Oppen's punctuation is serving here. The poem, it seems to me, reads amazingly slowly given its minimalist vocabulary and syntax. Writing of another poem from *Discrete Series*, Marjorie Perloff cites a journal entry in which Oppen describes syntax as "a deadening, to avoid destroying a word by its relationships"; syntax functions in much this way in this description of a "civil war photo," a description that is carefully calibrated so that each component of the scene remains insulated from every other.[50] Given that this text immediately announces itself as a work of ekphrasis ("the verbal representation of visual representation," as W. J. T. Mitchell defines this literary mode), it is frustrating—in a manner that speaks to crucial aspects of Oppen's agenda—to be provided with almost nothing of significance to "look at" in a poem about a photograph.[51] For Oppen, ekphrasis would appear to be a process not simply of translating pictures into words but also of reducing them to verbal data; what results, however, is an artifact of information so stripped bare that it has nothing left to communicate. Compare this "civil war photo" to a typical image taken from *The Photographic History of the Civil War*, a ten-volume compendium of pictures, attributed mainly to Mathew Brady or Alexander Gardner, which was assembled by Francis Trevelyan Miller and published in 1911, on the fiftieth anniversary of Fort Sumner (fig. 4.3).[52] Grass, man, field, hat, daylight, cannon—here we see all the nouns from Oppen's description, but we see also,

FIGURE 4.3.   Daguerreotype from *The Photographic History of the Civil War*, ed. Francis Trevelyan Miller (New York: The Review of Reviews Co., 1911).

FIGURE 4.4. "A Harvest of Death," Timothy O' Sullivan, photographer; printed by Alexander Gardner, negative 1863; print 1866.

I think, just how inscrutable Oppen's treatment of photography truly is. We could locate these nouns in almost any Civil War photo, from formal portraits, staged commemorations, casual snapshots, scenes of battle, or even more harrowing images, such as Timothy O'Sullivan's "Harvest of Death," taken shortly after the battle of Gettysburg (fig. 4.4). "Grass near the lens" could imply an image of a man not just "in the field," but his corpse laid out upon it, and the poem's reticence with visual information could itself figure as a display of disavowal, or a retreat from the traumatic sights of war to inconsequential details. But there is no evidence to support these speculations, nor nearly enough subjectivity of any kind, in these twenty-three little words, to assume any "speaker" at all, much less one on whom a reader may project a psychology. Oppen shows us a picture that neither transmits some information, nor symbolizes a range of culturally available meanings, nor signifies some "third meaning," to borrow from Barthes, that "intellection cannot succeed in absorbing, at once persistent and fleeting, smooth and elusive."[53] For even the fugitive pleasures of "obtuse" significance require some manner of engagement with the visual, whereas Oppen here is brutally insistent that a photograph is nothing to look at.

Yet this is not to say that Oppen's "photo" is without bearing on a range of questions we might pose about the experience of photography in the 1930s—the experience of photography in the decade of its centennial when the medium's own status as historical phenomenon and artifact was acutely recognized. Indeed, as Alan Trachtenberg reminds us, the Civil War photography of Brady in particular enjoyed something of a vogue in the 1930s as critics looked for an American "tradition" in a visual style that would provide artists like Walker Evans with a retrospective framework within which their innovations could be better valorized.[54] Evans himself contributed a glowing review of *The Photographic History of the Civil War* to Lincoln Kirstein's *Hound and Horn*, and Kirstein introduces Evans's *American Photographs* (1938) by first paying tribute to "the attitude of the early photographic master," which was "a simple but overwhelming interest in the *object* which was set before his machine. His single task was to render the object, face, group, house or battlefield airlessly clear in the isolation of its accidental circumstances . . . to create out of a fragmentary moment its own permanence."[55] Oppen certainly describes—to the extent that this poem is a description—an image constructed around an "overwhelming interest in the *object*"; there is no specific reference to any event or personality, to one side or the other, or to any patriotic sentiment or call for mourning. Still, if the poem's language is too rudimentary to support any memorializing affect, it manages nevertheless to hint at a surprisingly resonant criticism of photography's use-value as historical edifice or monument lending a mediated "permanence" to the past. This dimension of the text is implicit in the poem's interest in what amounts to an entirely generic Civil War scene—so generic that it renders a rhetoric of photography's transcendent specificity just slightly obsolete, or as Stein might put it, a photo is a photo is a photo. On a more careful reading, we realize that the cannon to which Oppen refers is likely not part of the "photo" he here reproduces; the relationship is in fact ambiguous in a way that seems calculated to trouble the historical stakes of the image in question. Recalling the famous machine-gun camera of Etienne-Jules Marey, we might wonder about the implicit likeness between two technologies that "shoot" and leave behind a lifeless scene where nothing moves; the camera that has made this image can do violence of its own, and as Barthes observes, with the invention of photography, "we enter into *flat Death*."[56] Oppen's poem does end rather flatly: from a battlefield scene of perhaps sublime intensity, or horrors the spectator must disavow by not looking at them too closely, we are removed to a much different scene at one of "our parks," where, if we were to snap a picture of some military relic on public display, there might again be "grass near the lens," but to no great loss. Oppen captures in his "Civil War Photo" an experience of historical mediation that is unavoidably experienced as one of "deadening" and distance.

More than that, the "Civil war photo" in Oppen's text feels oddly analogous to the "cannon," a relic in its own right, an object to be contemplated and analyzed with a measure of reserve. We get the sense that the "photo" represents less a specific "moment" of the American past preserved with idealized fidelity, and more a generic thing—an everyday material artifact—that may well be as mute and inoperative as any other piece of history. It is not merely that Oppen resists an easy romanticizing of photography, but that he reminds us that the camera's transaction with the material produces a mechanically precise image, yes, but also another example of the material, be it a plate, a tin, a card, a sheet of paper. A photograph of a cannon obviously takes up less space than a cannon, and is perhaps easier to maintain over time; this, at least, is what Baudelaire suggests in "The Modern Public and Photography" when, determined to delimit the medium's scope and prevent any untoward traffic between technology and art, he writes, "let [photography] save crumbling ruins from oblivion, books, engravings, and manuscripts, the prey of time, all those precious things, vowed to dissolution, which crave a place in the archives of our memories."[57] More compelling however, given my interests here, is another account of photography's ability to salvage and preserve the materials of history, from the same year as Baudelaire's brief essay, and that is Oliver Wendell Holmes's 1859 fantasy of an entirely photographed history, a visual archive that will not only represent things, but replace them with images and thus allow for a more permanent, more accessible record of practically everything. The paragraphs from "The Stereoscope and the Stereograph" are worth quoting at length:

> *Form is henceforth divorced from matter.* In fact, matter as a visible object is of no great use any longer, except as the mould on which form is shaped. Give us a few negatives of a thing worth seeing, taken from different points of view, and that is all we want of it. Pull it down or burn it up, if you please. . . .
> There is only one Coliseum or Pantheon; but how many millions of potential negatives have they shed,—representatives of billions of pictures,—since they were erected! Matter in large masses must always be fixed and dear; form is transportable. We have got the fruit of creation now, and need

not trouble ourselves with the core. Every conceivable object of Nature and Art will soon scale off its surface for us. Men will hunt all beautiful, grand objects, as they hunt the cattle in South America, for their *skins*, and leave the carcasses as of little worth.

The consequence of this will soon be such an enormous collection of forms that they will have to be classified and arranged in vast libraries, as books are now. The time will come when a man who wishes to see any object, natural or artificial, will go to the Imperial, National, or City Stereographic Library and call for its skin or form, as he would for a book at any common library. We do now distinctly propose the creation of a comprehensive and systematic stereographic library, where all men can find the special forms they particularly desire to see as artists, or as scholars, or as mechanics, or in any other capacity. . . .

Again, we must have special stereographic collections, just as we have professional and other special libraries. And as a means of facilitating the formation of public and private stereographic collections, there must be arranged a comprehensive system of exchanges, so that there may grow up something like a universal currency of these bank-notes, or promises to pay in solid substance, which the sun has engraved for the great Bank of Nature.[58]

Holmes's dream of a finally perfect technology of history is by turns marvelously prescient and appalling. What is most striking about the archive he imagines is its belligerent idealism—in both the technical sense, in that Holmes indulges a complete disregard for the material in favor of "form," and as part of a larger utopia of technological achievement, a fantasy couched in a rhetoric of democratic availability, and for a newly classless kind of history that no longer depends on the expense of seeing scarce objects, as I might put it with some caution, in the flesh. Holmes himself seems to relish a metaphorics that everywhere suggests "form" is rather messy and carnal in its own right—"fruit" that has been stripped from the "core," or "*skins*" off the "carcasses." The very materiality that a photographic archive renders obsolete returns with the photograph itself; Holmes's image of "vast libraries" filled with pictures offers the most bracing modernity in a familiar form, but it might be more accurately figured as a colossal menagerie of taxidermic representations. Perhaps Holmes makes much of this fantasmatic visceralness to distinguish the illusions of depth and dimension in "stereo" photography; but the gusto with which he disposes of the material world—"pull it down or burn it up, if you please"—and the fact that he does so without any discernible irony, suggests a representational violence that exceeds the mimetic.[59] All this throws a darker light too over Holmes's later insistence on the final "liquidation" of these archived forms into a "universal currency." What starts out as a distinctly populist project, one that multiplies "one Coliseum or Pantheon" into "billions of pictures," becomes a pay-as-you-go affair that relies on "a comprehensive system of exchanges" and ultimately, on a sort of gold standard measured in terms of actual material. If Cleveland's "Stereographic Library" borrows an image of a horse from New York, and then manages to lose it, the cost of a horse, or maybe just a horse itself is due in return. Holmes pursues his vision in intricate bureaucratic precision—well past the point where it makes any sense. But my concern is less that Holmes gets carried away by his own techno-enthusiasm and more how his dream of a better archive—no longer subject to decay and clutter, scarcity or distance—comes to founder on the need for material reckoning after all, some hard currency payable to the "Bank of Nature." The fervor behind this paradise of historical messages consumed entirely by their mediums founders on the need—at the level of metaphor and of what I can only call its business plan—for ever more raw material, more reality to reference, more "carcasses" to skin for their beautiful forms and surfaces.

History and Hygiene

In 1934 Lewis Mumford rehearses the central tenet of Holmes's techno-historicist fantasy, arguing that we now live in the age of the "New Permanent Record." The slogan is an oxymoron, though this is something that Mumford seems content to ignore. Or perhaps the dissonance is something that Mumford is willing to accept as part of a larger "orientation" in *Technics and Civilization* toward a "basic communism," as he terms it, a soft-core Marxism, which is also apparent in his kind words for "soviet courage and discipline" and for Stalin's Russia itself—the only nation whose "social apparatus" is not "antiquated" or, worse, merely "renovated in archaic forms," as in Fascist Germany and Italy.[60] I do not want to make too much of Mumford's politics in 1934—which have plenty of room for celebrations of American individualism as well—but I note them because they most certainly inform the narrative structure of *Technics and Civilization*. The book tells a doggedly Hegelian tale of thesis succumbing to antithesis, antithesis vanquished by synthesis: the eotechnic phase, which stretches from roughly the tenth to the eighteenth centuries, witnesses the invention of

"technics," which is Mumford's term for the "translation into appropriate, practical forms" of scientific advances, be they "implicit or formulated, anticipated
or discovered" (52). The eotechnic gives way to the paleotechnic phase in the
middle of the eighteenth century and persists throughout the nineteenth century; this is the age of the first industrial revolution, a horrid interregnum of
soot and exploitation that is most fully realized in Victorian Britain—in En-
gels's Britain, to be precise, as described in *The Condition of the Working Class
in England in 1844*. For Mumford, England in the 1800s is a landscape of death,
where nature is befouled and corrupted, quarters are cramped, and labor is in-
humane; Victorian industrialism is a "relapse into barbarism" (211) that pushes
civilization to "the ultimate abysses" (210). And then, thankfully, the page is
turned to the neotechnic phase, which signals the progressive course of technological empire simultaneously westward, to the United States, and eastward,
to Russia; more than that, the neotechnic is the miraculous culmination of the
two previous epistemes, differing from the "paleotechnic phase almost as white
differs from black," but also returning to the best of a more distant past, bearing
"the same relation to the eotechnic phase as the adult form does to the baby"
(212).

   Mumford describes the new permanent record as a coordinated assembly
of recording technologies and public institutions, and more, as a whole network of individual historical experiences—a new psychology of memory—
patterned on the formal textures of photographic and phonographic reproduction. "Man's culture," Mumford observes, "depends for its transmission in time
upon the permanent record: the building, the monument, the inscribed word"
(242), all of which constitute the *old* "permanent record," which conflates the
built environment and the written text as essentially related elements, both
geared toward memorializing the past. The *new* "permanent record" connects
the transformed "conceptual world" of modern media to a fantasy of cultural
tradition that is part Van Wyck Brooks, part Frederick Winslow Taylor; and so
these "new forms of permanent record," Mumford writes, "gave modern civilization a direct sense of the past and a more accurate perception of its memorials
than any other civilization had, in all probability. Not alone did they make the
past more immediate: they made the present more historic by narrowing the
lapse of time between the actual events themselves and their concrete record"
(244). It is this two-way communication of history—bringing the past forward
while pushing the present out of sync—that Mumford accomplishes by his
own past-tense narration of a modernity in which he is immersed. "Direct" and

"accurate" thus seem as much to describe a new aesthetics of historical representation as a new temporality of historical experience. But this "direct sense
of the past" depends on more than the sum of mimetic capacities possessed by
the photographic image or phonographic recording; it is also an effect of the
efficiency with which these media forms store away visual and auditory information, allowing the raw material of history to be maintained in an economical fashion, allowing the archive to be organized coherently and retrieved on
demand. "In a world of flux and change," Mumford argues, "the camera gave a
means of combating the ordinary processes of deterioration and decay, not by
'restoration' or 'reproduction' but by holding in convenient form the lean image
of men, places, buildings, landscapes: thus serving as an extension of the collective memory" (243).

Thus the emphasis of Mumford's new permanent record is at once economic and hygienic. Photography participates in an "extension of the collective
memory" that is above all "convenient." Stripped of its larger implications—
which is exactly what Mumford himself tries to do in the passage that follows—
the new permanent record promises more record, with less cleanup:

> Whatever the psychal [*sic*] reactions to the camera and the moving pic-
> ture and the phonograph may be, there is no doubt, I think, as to their
> contribution to the economic management of the social heritage. Before
> they appeared, sound could only be imperfectly represented in the conven-
> tions of writing. . . . Other than written and printed documents and paint-
> ings on paper, parchment, and canvas, nothing survived of a civilization
> except its rubbish heaps and its monuments, buildings, sculptures, works
> of engineering—all bulky, all interfering more or less with the free develop-
> ment of a different life in the same place.
>
> By means of the new devices this vast mass of physical impedimenta
> could be turned into paper leaves, metallic or rubber discs, or celluloid films
> which could be far more completely and far more economically preserved.
> It is no longer necessary to keep vast middens of material in order to have
> contact, in the mind, with the forms and expressions of the past. (244)

Here, technology becomes historically invaluable for all the ways it permits a
"direct sense" of the past that remains untouched by the suspect materiality
of the old and antiquated. Mumford in effect imagines a historical experience

that is "direct" to the degree to which it is thoroughly mediated. He describes a sort of circuit in which history registers as an idea or image only "in the mind," yet only after a series of exchanges from the "vast masses of physical impedimenta"—the detritus and waste of the past—to a "more economically" material range of media representations, which, though still material—"paper leaves, metallic or rubber discs, or celluloid films"—put us in closer "contact" with a perfectly "preserved" record of the past. Now we can get rid of the garbage that is "interfering" with the "free development" of the modern. This is historiography as waste management, using technology to dispose of the untreated "heaps" and "middens" that are mucking up "the same place" where we are trying to achieve a "different life." Without the "economic management of our social heritage," or so Mumford would have it, we have no choice but to eat where we shit.

"The industrial world produced during the nineteenth century," Mumford writes earlier in *Technics and Civilization*, "is either technologically obsolete or socially dead. But unfortunately its maggoty corpse produced organisms which in turn may debilitate or kill the new order that should take its place" (215). At these moments in the text—and there are many—it is difficult to overstate Mumford's loathing for Victorian industrialism and the environment, architecture, and world of objects he attributes to the by-products of this older modernity. In the book's opening pages, for example, Mumford wonders whether a better understanding of the coming "mechanical complex," indicated by the "telephone, the phonograph, the motion picture," can help us "remove the turbid residues left behind by our earlier forms of technology" (7). Later, we read that among the worst sins of the "paleotechnic" era in eighteenth- and nineteenth-century England was that it forced a "habituation to wreckage and debris as part of the normal human environment" (158). Even when Mumford notes a breakthrough of nineteenth-century technology—such as when he echoes Siegfried Gideon in celebrating iron construction as the precursor of the modern skyscraper—there is a focus on morbid excess: "Much of the iron that period boasted was dead weight" (167). The factories of Victorian England create an "atmospheric sewage" (168), and the productive energies of these factories yield goods and commodities in a useless abundance that Mumford characterizes as "the empire of muddle" (191). The narrative of *Technics and Civilization* charts the progress from a period whose way of life is "busy, congested, rubbish-strewn" to what Mumford hopes will be instead a period of "light and life" (245). Even when rhapsodizing about a new aesthetic patterned on "mathematical accuracy, physical economy, chemical purity, surgical cleanliness," though, he never tracks far from his concerns with the rudest needs to deal with the material. "The neotechnic phase produced important conservative changes," he observes; "one of them was the utilization once more of human excrement for fertilizers, in contrast with the reckless method of befouling stream and tidal water" (257). In much the same way that the technologies of the new permanent record convert the "impedimenta" of history into better "expressions of the past," here too a more modern modernity can redeem our "excrement" and make it work to "actually enrich" the world, to "help bring it to a higher state of cultivation" (257). The historiographical fantasy of the new permanent record is as much about waste management as media technology. It evokes what Michael North calls "the paradox of new media, which can preserve the present forever, but only as a dead thing whose persistence mocks the possibility of change."[61]

Mumford's history of technology is patterned on the pursuit of more sanitary realizations of modern life—not more "streamlined," to use the key term of Norman Bel Geddes's *Horizons* (1932), but also cleaner and purer for their avant-garde styling. There are distinctly technocratic leanings to some of Mumford's arguments that would subject historical representation to a cost-benefit analysis, and these are concerns that are widely shared. We hear echoes, for example, of Stuart Chase's 1927 Taylorist gospel, *The Tragedy of Waste*; several of Chase's books appear in Mumford's bibliography, where he revealingly characterizes them as "full of useful material on the perversions of modern commerce and industry" (453).[62] Gramsci cannot hide his disgust with the "viscous and parasitical sedimentations of tradition" in his writings on "Americanism and Fordism"; he is undeceived about the dehumanizing rigors of labor in Ford's "completely mechanized" factories, but still this purging of an anachronistic set of ideological forms is to be applauded.[63] I need not remark on Eliot's *The Waste Land* in this context, and variations on this theme are simply everywhere in the modernism of the 1920s and 1930s. The reek of "atmospheric sewage" surrounds the figure of Henry James in Pound's Canto 7, where the aging Master—an imposing predecessor for any American literary expatriate—is encountered within a murky interior "touched with imprecision": "The house too thick, the paintings too oiled."[64] And Pound is just getting warmed up. Cantos 14 and 15 tour us through the scatological, anti-Semitic landscape dominated by "USURA"—a gruesome creature incarnating several of Pound's sexual and economic rants in a "beast with a hundred legs" who revels amid "the petrifaction of putrefaction" (64). Pound shows a special gusto for describing what we might call, returning to Mumford, the "physical impedimenta" to the ideal of "free development":

> And Invidia,
> the corruptio, fœtor, fungus,
> liquid animals, melted ossifications,
> slow rot, fœtid combustion,
>   chewed cigar-butts, without dignity, without tragedy,
> .....m Episcopus, waving a condom full of black-beetles,
> monopolists, obstructors of knowledge,
>   obstructors of distribution. (63)

Like the new permanent record, this is a diagnosis of blockage, a constipated economy of material that will be cured with improved circulation. Though Pound perhaps strains a bit when he insists that all this is "without dignity, without tragedy—as if a reader might otherwise bathe "fœtor," "fungus," and "chewed cigar-butts" in a valorizing, memorial light—the blood and muck of these cantos is of particular use in helping to identify the stench that Mumford wants to cover in his relentless abstraction of historical materials.

◊

William Carlos Williams stresses a similar network of themes throughout this period—though employed with less political invective. Several of the "impro-visations" that make up *Kora in Hell* return to moments of renewal in the face of a ruined culture, and the "imperfections of the flesh."[65] Or take the well-known first poem of *Spring and All* (1923), which depicts a scene whose every detail is resonant with the historical aesthetic that Mumford imagines for the new permanent record. We start "by the road to the contagious hospital," an especially resonant play on words given Mumford's anxiety about the risks of architectural contamination; here we see only "the / waste of broad, muddy fields / brown with dried weeds."[66] And the poem's final intimations of spring suggest a fraught return of an organic vitality that is itself chastened in ways that evoke a sense of technical precision. Nature returns as "[o]ne by one objects are defined"; it is not an exuberant gush of the wild that Williams celebrates, but rather "the stark dignity of / entrance" as some isolated leaves and a few blades of grass "enter the new world naked, / cold, uncertain of all */ save that they enter" (183).

The first poem in *Spring and All* represents one of Williams's many rejoinders, lyric and otherwise, to Eliot. Williams wants to take us "beyond the waste" to a "new world" that retains the capacity for nascent life to the degree that it is "rooted" and knows to "grip down" in native soil. This is a commonplace reading of Williams's culturally nationalist response to Eliot's mix of erudition, technical proficiency, and expatriate despair; *Spring and All* confesses that its speaker cannot "say what is in [his] mind in Sanscrit or even Latin," that there is no greater danger today than the "TRADITIONALISTS OF PLAGIARISM," and that it is "fruitless for the academic tapeworm to hoard its excrementa in books" (179, 182, 215). Modernism, with Eliot as the negative example, tends to produce such "excrementa" in the form of historical allusion and arcane cultural reference—think of the "notes" that Eliot himself adds to *The Waste Land*, ignore their irony, and you get a picture of Williams's "academic tapeworm" in action—but the spare lyrics of *Spring and All* prove that a decade before Mumford's *Technics and Civilization*, the doctor was championing his own version of aesthetic hygiene.

Which makes two of Williams's lesser-known poems—"Poem" and "It Is a Living Coral," both written in 1924 and later published in little magazines— notable for their density of external reference; these are not just poems "containing history," to borrow from Pound's famous designation for *The Cantos*, but poems consisting of little more than nominal instances of historical material. Taking first the more extreme example, simply titled "Poem," the reader is confronted by a block of text that only the most intrepid tapeworm would find rewarding as a lyric:

> Daniel Boone, the father of Kentucky. Col. W. Crawford, the martyr to Indian revenge. Simon Gerty, the White Savage. Molly Finney, the beautiful Canadian Captive. Majors Samuel and John McCullough, patriots and frontiersmen. Lewis Wetzel, the Indian killer. Simon Kenton, the intrepid pioneer. Gen. George R. Clark, that heroic conqueror. Capt. Brady, the great Indian fighter. Davy Crockett, the hero of the Alamo. Gen. Sam Houston, the liberator of the Lone Star State. Kit Carson, the celebrated plainsman and explorer. Gen. Custer, the hero of Little Big Horn. Buffalo Bill, the

tireless rider, hunter and scout. Wild Bill, the lightning marksman. California Joe, the scout. Texas Jack, the government scout and hunter. Captain
Jack, the poet scout. Gen. Crook, the conqueror of the Apaches. (259)

This is "Poem" in full. An assemblage of names and epithets, like Oppen's
"Civil War Photo," there are no verbs here because this is history without either actions or events. Famous figures (Daniel Boone, Davy Crockett) are
jumbled alongside obscurities (Molly Finney, Simon Kenton); crucial players in the nation's politics (Sam Houston) are thrown in with popular icons
largely memorable for being famous (Buffalo Bill, Wild Bill). Williams places
the names in a rough chronology that charts the course of westward expansion
in the nineteenth century, from Boone's early explorations across the Appa-
lachians, to the annexation of Texas, and ultimately to the end of the Indian
wars in the Southwest. In contrast to many of the essays on American history
from *In the American Grain* (1925), which features a variety of racialist and
primitivist appreciations for the "dark life" of the New World, the perspective
of "Poem" is drastically one-sided in its terminology: Crawford is "the mar-
tyr to Indian revenge," and Custer is "the hero of Little Big Horn."[67] That said,
when "Poem" was published in the *Little Review* in 1926, I doubt that many of
its readers would have been concerned, well, to read against the grain of its
implicit politics; despite the arcana on display, "Poem" would have been understood quite easily as an expression of Williams's familiar mix of nationalist
enthusiasm and avant-garde poetics. Indeed, part of what seems behind the
gesture of "Poem"—or better, the gesture that *is* "Poem"—is the assertion of
the material itself as laying claim to an aesthetic effect even in this radically
shapeless form. We might think, then, of Williams's testing out the minimal
requirements for Whitman's bravura declaration, in the preface to the first edition of *Leaves of Grass*, that "[t]he United States themselves are essentially the
greatest poem."[68] Is a paragraph of prose with no discernible interest in sound,
rhythm, or symbolism still a "poem" by virtue of the content it relays? Whitman stresses that the Hegelian grandeur of America means that its particular
features need almost no embellishment to communicate as works of art ("Here
is action untied from strings necessarily blind to particulars and details magnificently moving in vast masses"). But Williams provides a litany of data that is
verbally lax and decidedly unmoving in every sense of the word. The westward
course of empire flows from the iconic Daniel Boone to a series of interchangeable "scouts" named Joe, Jack, and Jack.

My point, however, is less that Williams's "Poem" is maybe not very good and more that its particular failure to even *be* a poem speaks to the difficulties of a modernism that tries to operate as a medium for the transmission of raw information. Pure data, to return to the pungent invective from Pound's Canto 14, here takes it place alongside the fungus, beetles, and other "obstructors of knowledge" as a materiality that overwhelms the work of art to the precise degree that materiality itself marks the aesthetic limit that Williams's "Poem" would otherwise achieve. "Poem" functions as a precocious variation on Liu's "data pours," and thus marks a site where "an author in effect surrenders the act of writing to that of parameterization" (59). "In these topoi," Liu writes, "the author designates a zone where content of unknown quantity and quality . . . pours into the manifest work" minimally structured by the way it is "parameterized in such commands as 'twenty items at a time,' or 'only items containing "sick rose"'" (59). "Poem" is not a poem so much as it is the performance of some unknown parameter—the first twenty names in some volume of U.S. history Williams owned in 1926?—that occasioned this exercise in what is at once a display of semiotic excess and a conceit of semiotic emptiness. Bare chronology functions as the sole evidence that Williams has arranged these signifiers into a rudimentary story of a century of warfare between whites and Indians; but this does not so much translate these details into a coherent narrative as place them along a predetermined vector borrowed from the very mythology of manifest destiny that they embody, that they materialize. Or, as Lev Manovich's work on contemporary database design can help us see, the historical information in "Poem" finally takes the form of information as such: "database represents the world as a list of items and it refuses to order this list. In contrast, a narrative creates a cause-and-effect trajectory of seemingly unordered items. . . . Therefore, database and narrative are natural enemies. Competing for the same territory of human culture, each claims an exclusive right to make meaning out of the world."[69] Manovich's language is surprisingly apt insofar as "Poem" stages this particular territorial struggle between mediums—database and narrative—as it registers and records a history of conflict between whites and Indians in nineteenth-century America. Williams does not, I want to stress, allegorize this struggle in "Poem," but the text does depend on what might be called the implicit tension between its medium and the recalcitrance of its materials to transcend their "native" form.

Another Williams poem, one that similarly indulges an abundance of historical information, renders this tension more overt—though no less unresolved.

Written in 1925, "It Is a Living Coral" was not published by Williams until 1932, when it was featured in *An "Objectivists" Anthology*, edited by Louis Zukofsky. The poem is an impossibly allusive and ekphrastic description of the paintings, murals, and other artworks in the Capitol building, from the fresco in the canopy of the dome (*The Apotheosis of George Washington*), to John G. Chapman's 1837 image *The Baptism of Pocahontas*, to portraits of former House Speakers by Jonathan Trumbull, among others. Thus Williams's principal of "parameterization," borrowing from Liu, is immediately established by the poem's first sentence, which syntactically incorporates its title:

It is a living coral

a trouble

archaically fettered
to produce

E Pluribus Unum an
island

in the sea a Capital
surmounted

by Armed Liberty—
painting

sculpture straddled by
a dome

eight million pounds
in weight

iron plates constructed
to expand

and contract with
variations

of temperature
the folding

and unfolding of a lily. (255)

I venture nothing with the assertion that this is a far better poem than "Poem."
The involved and complex parataxis dramatically sustains the push-and-pull
that Williams makes central to his elaborately metaphorical imagining of the
Capitol dome as an ingenious feat of living engineering and design. So there is
no "like" or "as" to specify the simile between the building's architecture and
the organic, evolving structure of the coral; the description of the dome, with
its materiality evoked in two especially ponderous and heavily accented lines
("eight million pounds" and "iron plates constructed"), simply "straddles" the
image of the lily that ends the sentence. Williams's stanzas aspire to much the
same effect. The longer first lines, which for the most part feature two or three
stresses, both metrically and visually overlie the shorter second lines, many of
which are just a single word.

The poem proceeds with considerable speed as it references and accumulates an increasingly diverse array of historical material, which is drawn into the
momentum of the text with almost no regard for medium or narrative logic.
That is, "It Is a Living Coral" engages in what amounts to ekphrasis degree zero:
description of the visual gives way instead to its citation, and the speaker's experience of any individual works of art is lost to capture more effectively their
numerousness:

a sculptured group
Mars

in Roman mail placing
a wreath

of laurel on the brow
of Washington

Commerce Minerva
Thomas

Jefferson John Hancock
at

the table Mrs. Motte
presenting

Indian burning arrows
to Generals

Marion and Lee to fire
her mansion

and dislodge the British—
this scaleless

jumble is superb
and accurate in its
expression

of the thing they
would destroy—

Baptism of Poca-
hontas

with a little card
hanging

under it to tell
the persons

in the picture. (256–257)

It is technically possible to decode all of this encrypted visual information, but it hardly makes for an efficient history lesson in the way that Mumford might envision. However streamlined, Williams's poem signals an allegiance to an aesthetics of material disarray. He breaks from stanza form to isolate the line reminding us that a "jumble is superb"—particularly when it is "scaleless," and therefore "accurate," in suggesting just how difficult it is to contain all of this history within a single edifice. Nowhere does the poem work more sloppily than in its use of pronouns: apparently Marion and Lee are the "they" who are primed to destroy Mrs. Motte's mansion (to prevent British troops from seizing it as a barracks during the Revolution); but within the associative illogic of Williams's sentences, it is as grammatically correct to read the works of art themselves as threatening to destroy whatever it is that their "expression" would repress or "dislodge." If we take the dash to function as a colon, this "thing" literally becomes the painting *The Baptism of Pocahontas*. Of course, this painting itself commemorates an event that Williams seems to treat rather ironically as a conversion that, in its proximity to indiscriminate destruction, is more fateful than salvific. Support for such a reading is ample in sections of *In the American Grain* where Williams shows a decided sympathy for Native Americans, however primitivist, that is distinct from both the romantic triumphalism of the Capitol's art and the cold detachment of "Poem." "History begins for us with murder and enslavement," Williams writes, "not with discovery. No, we are not Indians but we are men of their world."[70] Or more viscerally, "We are the slaughterers. It is the tortured soul of our world."[71] "Doesn't it make you want to go out and lift dead Indians tenderly from their graves," asks Williams later, though his prose breaks down into ambiguous stammers before he gets around to finishing his question; still he manages to identify what he thinks we want to "steal" from them: "as if it must be clinging even to their corpses—some authenticity, that which—. Here not there."[72] Is this "it" the "it" that is a living coral? The "it" that "runs," "climbs," "wears / a beard," and "fetches naked / Indian / women from a river" in the lines that follow Williams's reference to Pocahontas? As a sign of some abiding "authenticity" that has survived not just its literal destruction but its transposition into this astonishing profusion of historical images, the "it" that patterns Williams's accelerated rendering of this national archive would seem the only hope for "life" under the weight of all this material. Ever the exemplary modernist, he does not want "it" to be "archaically fettered" so much as he wants to watch it move and run. Still "It Is a Living Coral" ends with a figure not of Liu's "transcendental data" but of morbidity and decay; for all the energy with which Williams has freed his history from any formal constraint that would obstruct its distribution, we find ourselves again, when the poem concludes, facing "the dead / among the wreckage / sickly green" (258). Not even Dr. Williams has a cure for history's inescapable decay.

"The most inevitably inaccurate of all mediums of record and communication"

Every civilization tends to overestimate the objective orientation
of its thought and this tendency is never absent.

—CLAUDE LÉVI-STRAUSS, *THE SAVAGE MIND*

American culture in the 1930s proves no exception to this pronouncement of Lévi-Strauss, though I think it safe to say that James Agee, whose words on the "inaccurate" medium of words we see above, should be set apart as someone who seemed never, in *Let Us Now Praise Famous Men* at least, to oversell his objectivity. Even when paying tribute to photography for its uncanny precision and inhuman rigor, he shows his striking tendency to emote with a profound disregard for clarity:

> One reason I care so deeply for the camera is just this. So far as it goes (which is, in its own realm, as absolute anyhow as the traveling distance of words or sound), and handled cleanly and literally in its own terms, as an ice-cold, some ways limited, some ways more capable, eye, it is, like the phonograph record and like scientific instruments and unlike any other leverage of art, incapable of recording anything but absolute, dry truth.[73]

It is hard to imagine a more hesitant and conditional declaration of the "absolute"—or rather, the absolute "anyhow," "so far as it goes"—significance of photography, and of the other media Agee mentions, than what we witness here. Agee's "one reason" for believing in photography is in truth a spliced together series of contrasts—the camera as a "more capable eye"—and similes—the photograph "like the phonograph record"—which build to nothing like a single argument, but echo off each other as Agee tries to specify what matters most about the medium. On this count, it does not help that his final point of emphasis is phrased in a tortured double negative that translates roughly as: photography, "unlike" other forms of art, records an "absolute, dry truth." Or does Agee like his truth "ice-cold"? His metaphoric abandon produces a picture of photography, as both medium and cultural practice, which does not look to have been "handled

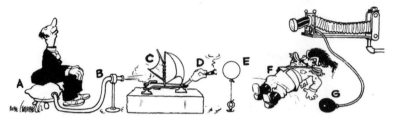

FIGURE 4.5.   Rube Goldberg, "Picture-Snapping Machine," circa 1932. Copyright © Rube Goldberg, Inc.

cleanly and literally," two adverbs we might well apply to Walker Evans's accompanying images, but possessing little relevance to the prose at hand. This passage seems of a piece with Agee's pained understanding of language as a medium in which distortion and misrepresentation are unavoidable; language, for Agee, communicates "by such a Rube Goldberg articulation of frauds, compromises, artful dodges and tenth removes as would fatten any other art into apoplexy if the art were not first shamed out of existence" (236). Again, his metaphors are flagrantly mixed—how does one "fatten" a Rube Goldberg machine?—and again, this misuse of the medium seeks to demonstrate Agee's message about the inherent drift of any use of language toward "falsification" on the one hand, and the "inability to communicate simultaneity with any immediacy" on the other (237). Goldberg's own design for a "Picture Snapping Machine" (fig. 4.5) wonderfully illustrates the rococo inefficiency that Agee wants to invoke as essential to the nature of his verbal medium. Here, we see a man sitting on a cushion; which then expels air to fill a sail that pushes an ice-boat outfitted with a hand holding a lighted cigar toward a balloon; which then pops, causing the Dictator to think that he's been shot; so that he falls over, landing on the bulb, which snaps the picture. While providing an ideal analog for Agee's wrought aesthetic, Goldberg's absurd dilation of photographic procedure travesties, returning to Cavell, the very "automatism" that so many critics and artists make into the signature and essence of the medium. Or as photographer Jeff Wall articulates the difference between writing and photography that seems especially to trouble Agee, "Photography constitutes a depiction not by the accumulation of individual marks, but by the instantaneous operation of an integrated mechanism. . . . Depiction is the only possible result of the camera system."[74]

The work of Walker Evans is rightly celebrated for representing what photography can achieve when it pursues the specific qualities of its material form instead of mimicking the painterly gestures that enthralled Stieglitz and other "art photographers" of the early twentieth century. This is a familiar argument about photography in the 1930s, and I will not rehearse it here.[75] Suffice it to say that Agee's emphasis on photography "handled cleanly and literally" is an echo of Lincoln Kirstein's more fulsome discussion of Evans's aesthetic in the afterword to *American Photographs*. Kirstein stresses that "the most characteristic single feature of Evans' work is its purity, or even its puritanism"—"It is 'straight' photography not only in technique but in the rigorous directness of its way of looking," Kirstein insists—and he goes on to describe it as a radical example of hygienic modernism in practice.[76] Evans's work shows "neither a baroque nor a decorative, but a purely protestant attitude: meager, stripped, cold, and, on occasion, humorous. It is also the naked, difficult, solitary attitude of a member revolting from his own class, who knows best what in it must be uncovered, cauterized and why. The view is clinical. Evans is visual doctor, diagnostician rather than specialist" (197). There can be little doubt that Agee knew the praise that Kirstein and others heaped on Evans in the 1930s; and perhaps it is even this account of Evans that Agee has in mind when he introduces him as "a counter-spy, traveling as a photographer" in *Let Us Now Praise Famous Men*, and thus a necessary complement to Agee, "a spy, traveling as a journalist."[77] Indeed, Agee seems more than willing to play the guilty, emotive, and liturgically ornate Catholic to Evans's Protestant; Agee's prose is indulgent and affected, whereas Evans's photographs are "meager, stripped, cold"; both may well be devoted to performances of class revolt, but Evans's politics show what should be negated ("cauterized"), whereas Agee's politics are relentlessly associative and additive, trying always to pursue more elaborate and self-involved connections. All this to suggest, borrowing from Peter Cosgrove, that *Let Us Now Praise Famous Men* "stands as a prime exhibit for equality of representational modes between the same covers" not because Agee and Evans aspire to the same aesthetic but because in "their collaboration word and picture seem to combine in a naturalized version of media mutuality."[78]

Agee offers his "Rube Goldberg" theory of language in a section of *Let Us Now Praise Famous Men* titled "(On the Porch: 2." The open parenthesis gives a small taste of Agee's punctuational eccentricity in the book, about which there is much to say. That this is the second part of an ongoing series of interludes is also important, because these three sections as a whole narrate, in often microscopic detail, the first night that Agee and Evans spend at the house of the Gudger family, the tenant farmers with whom they become most intimate in the course of their documentary project; within this narrative, "(On the Porch: 2" takes place just as Agee and Evans are lying down to sleep, but Agee's description of this moment soon expands into a theoretical discussion of how words and images respectively communicate, and how this difference is best understood as a variation on modernism's aesthetics of medium-specificity. I lapse into a language redolent of Greenberg because Agee's arguments on behalf of his own medium as a writer are either covertly indebted to—or precisely parallel with—some of the more doctrinaire positions first ventured by Greenberg in "Towards a Newer Laocoön" and its vision of modernism as what happens when the arts are "hunted back to their mediums," and thus "isolated, concentrated, and defined."[79] By the time *Let Us Now Praise Famous Men* was published in 1941, I think it likely that Agee would have read Greenberg's 1940 essay—but whether he incorporated its ideas into the final version of "(On the Porch: 2" is hard to know.[80] Agee's medium theories nonetheless seem to rehearse Greenberg's essential claims in an idiom of philosophical abstraction and homespun swagger that belongs entirely to *Let Us Now Praise Famous Men*. This, then, is Agee taking his shot at a "Laocoön" of his own:

> [W]ords like all else are limited by certain laws. To call their achievement crippled in relation to what they have tried to convey may be all very well: but to call them crippled in their completely healthy obedience to their own nature is again a mistake: the same mistake as the accusation of a cow for her unhorsiness. And if you here say: "But the cow words are trying to be a horse," the answer is: "That attempt is one of the strongest laws of language, just as it is no law at all so far as cows are concerned." In obeying this law words are not, then, at all necessarily accusable, any more than in disobeying it. The cleansing and rectification of language, the breakdown of the identification of word and object, is very important, and very possibly more important things will come of it than have ever come of the lingual desire of the cow for the horse: but it is nevertheless another matter whenever words start functioning in the command of the ancient cow-horse law. Human beings may be more and more aware of being awake, but they are still incapable of not dreaming; and a fish forswears water for air at his own peril. (209)

At first, Agee appears to grant that language pales in comparison to pictures. Following on his admission that words are defined by their "inability to communicate simultaneity with any immediacy," it certainly seems the case that not only are they "limited by certain laws" but these laws exact a higher cost than those which govern visual mediums like photography. Yet he also labors to make his case that when words are used "in their completely healthful obedience to their own nature," it is a mistake to find them wanting; thus his odd fable about cows and horses, "cow words" and "the lingual desire of the cow for the horse." In the end, Agee's loquacious cows have become human beings and finally fish, but all these animals are allegorical for the figure of the writer, which is to say, for Agee, who would forswear words for another medium "at his own peril."

Roughly translated out of Agee's convolutions, this makes for a spirited defense of a less powerful and efficient medium in the face of not just competition from, but replacement by, a new technology with an incomparable aesthetic all its own. What especially interests me about this crucial moment in "(On the Porch: 2" is that it champions, however inelegantly, a media aesthetic at odds with any "new permanent record" we might imagine. Indeed, a certain inelegance, or indirection, is central to Agee's method and the epistemology it assumes: "It seems likely at this stage that the truest way to treat a piece of the past is as such: as if it were no longer present. In other words, the 'truest' thing about the experience . . . is rather how it turns up in recall, in no such order, casting its lights and associations forward and backward upon the then past and the then future, across that expanse of experience" (215). Agee could not sound more like Henry James in his ardent belief in "associations," relations, and the categorical centrality of experience. Moreover, this Jamesian sensibility extends to Agee's sense of style and form, and presses him to radicalize his departure from the clean, "ice-cold" practice of photography. Because he is at once "interested in the actual and the telling of it," he is not just willing to accept, but is determined to produce, a text that is remarkable for its baroque disorder and confusion.[81] "The whole job may well seem messy to you," writes Agee in a gesture that is at once a confession and a challenge to the reader, "but a part of my point is that experience offers itself in richness and variety and in many more terms than one and that it may therefore be wise to record it no less variously" (216).

Thus even as Agee pays tribute to photography as the exemplary medium of modernist expression—and even as he does so in language fully in accord with the fantasies of hygiene and streamlined materiality that we see in Mumford, Kirstein, and other critics of photography in the 1930s—it should come as no surprise that his own prose is altogether profligate when he tries to communicate the "variety" of his visual experience. There are countless moments in *Let Us Now Praise Famous Men* when Agee attempts to reproduce a version of this total photographic recall; and the effect that he achieves does not read like ekphrasis, but rather like an exercise in the database aesthetics of Liu or Manovich. Here is one of Agee's more aggressive efforts to render what he sees as a material phenomenon of endless information:

> The Ricketts are much more actively fond of pretty things than the other families are, and have lived here longer than they have, and in obedience of these equations the fireplace wall is crusted deep with attractive pieces of paper into the intricate splendor of a wedding cake or the fan of a white peacock: calendars of snowbound and stag-hunting scenes pressed into bas-relief out of white pulp and glittering with a sand of red and blue and green and gold tinsel, and delicately tinted; other calendars and farm magazine covers or advertisements of dog-love; the blessèd fireside coziness or the poor; indian virgins watching their breasts in pools or padding up moon-lit aisles of foliage; fullblown blondes in luminous frocks leaning back in swings, or taking coca-cola through straws, or beneath evening palmleaves, accepting cigarettes from young men in white monkey-coats, happy young housewives at resplendent stoves in sunloved kitchens . . . three-quarter views of locomotives at full speed, young couples admiring newly acquired brown and brocade davenports: all such as these overlaid in complexes and textured with the names and numberings of days months years and phases of the moon and with words and phrases and names such as –'s Shoes; — Furniture, Hay, Grain and Feed, Yellow Stores, Gen'l Merchandise, Kelvinator, Compliments of, Wist ye not that I am about my Father's Business, Mazola, Railroad Age, Maxwell House, They Satisfy, Mexico, Mexico, The Pause that Refreshes . . . The Progressive Farmer, After Six, Congoleum, Farm and Fireside, Love's Gift Divine, You Can't Afford *NOT*, Soft, Lovely Hands, You Owe It to Her, You Owe it to Him, You Owe it to Them, Country Gentlemen, Daughters of Jerusalem, weep not for me but for your children, and your children's children, Energize, Save, At Last, Don't Be a Stick-in-the-Mud, et cetera. (174–176)

The complete passage is almost 450 words long, depending on how one counts all the hyphenated compounds, and I have quoted less than half of it. It ends with an "et cetera" that invites us to imagine that Agee is just warming

up, and that however exhausting the list of visual details, he has already condensed it to this more manageable scale. Although intentionally bewildering
as a description, the interior that Agee itemizes would have been immediately
recognizable to his readers. The newspaper-covered walls of shacks and cabins
in the South were a familiar subject for documentary photographers, as evi-
denced by this Margaret Bourke-White picture from *You Have Seen Their Faces*
(fig. 4.6). These were pictures that called attention to extreme poverty, and also
to the desperate human effort to ameliorate it, but it seems just as likely that
part of what attracted photographers in the period to this particular subject was
the way it exemplified, in a profoundly indigenous form, the collage aesthetics of synthetic cubism, or of dada practices of photomontage. And as Agee's
description devolves into a litany of advertising slogans, the homage to Evans's
own predilection for signs and other "wordy" material becomes especially apparent. The closest photographic analog in the images that open *Let Us Now
Praise Famous Men* feels positively spare by comparison (fig. 4.7)—but here
are Agee's calendars and dogs, as well as the cover of an issue of *The Progressive Farmer*, which registers with equivalent irony in both word and image. This
last detail would seem to establish this image as the text's first representation
of what Agee here identifies as "the Ricketts' fireplace"; and the astonishing
amount of information Agee pours onto the page, almost none of which we
are able to "read" in Evans's photograph, mounts an implicit, though far from
subtle, defense of his "Rube Goldberg articulation" of experience, even in the
face of the photography's genius for "absolute, dry truth."

Agee closes this long descriptive passage with a curious footnote. Anticipating that his reader will not believe that he has reproduced all these details
unaided, Agee confesses that "these are in part by memory, in part composited
out of other memory, in part improvised, but do not exceed what was there in
abundance, variety or kind" (176). I do not know what Agee means in his distinction between "memory" and "other memory." Has he mixed his own recol-
lections with those of Evans? Has he "composited" this spectacular display from
several different interiors? Still more questions are raised when he then admits
that this daunting scene of recall, however contrived or imagined, is "much better recorded in photographs for which there is no room in this volume" (176).
Agee shows this sort of cheek throughout *Let Us Now Praise Famous Men*, but
rarely does he refer to Evans's photographs; "the photographs are not illustrative," Agee writes in the preface, adding that "they, and the text, are coequal,
mutually independent, and fully collaborative" (xi). Moreover, Agee seems to

East Feliciana Parish, Louisiana
"Blackie ain't good for nothing, he's just an old hound dog."

FIGURE 4.6. Margaret Bourke-White, photograph from Erskine Caldwell's and Margaret Bourke-White's *You Have Seen Their Faces*, (New York: Modern Age Books, 1937).

FIGURE 4.7. Walker Evans, "Fireplace in Frank Tingle's home. Hale County, Alabama." Library of Congress, Prints & Photographs Division, FSA-OWI Collection, LC-USF342- 008152-A, 1941.

understand the full equality of Evans's photographs as flourishing, at least in part, exactly because of "their fewness," which is to say, the very principle of economy that puts all sixty-two of the book's images inside the front cover (xi). If there really was "no room" in the book, why not cut a few thousand words here or there in a text that can be admired on many grounds, but certainly not for its stylistic economy? Was the publisher unwilling to pay for illustrations

that Agee and Evans wanted to include? Did Agee hope that Evans would select different pictures than those he finally assembled? There are several likely
explanations, in other words, for why we have no recourse to the photographs
that Agee mentions, but answering such material questions about the making
of the text would not resolve the gamesmanship of Agee's own posturing at this
exemplary moment of "remediation," to borrow from Bolter and Grusin. They
use this term to capture not only the particular ways in which "media are continually commenting on, reproducing, and replacing each other" but also the
idea that "this process is integral to media," and therefore not a distinguishing
feature of the contemporary moment.[82] "*All* mediation is remediation," Bolter
and Grusin observe, since as a matter of practical necessity, "a medium in our
culture can never operate in isolation" and so "must enter into relationships of
respect and rivalry with other media" (65). Agee's *Let Us Now Praise Famous
Men* is a text that is, to put it mildly, obsessed with remediation at almost every
turn, and is, by design, a work determined to invoke, perform, and explicate the
relationship between writing and photography. And for the most part, Agee
understands this relationship to involve more gestures of respect than rivalry;
each medium has its limited domains of competence and technique, its own
aesthetic and materiality that the other cannot achieve. Recall his homespun
turn on medium specificity: "A fish forswears water for air at his own peril."
Thus even when Agee indulges in a dazzling and wearying catalog of visual information that appears calibrated not just to mimic but to exceed the capacity
of photography to record a rich and varied world of objects, he still technically
defers to the superiority of the "new permanent record"—particularly when it
is nowhere to be seen.

So while I do not doubt Agee's sincere appreciation of, and deference to,
Evans's photographs, I also think that it is obvious that he relishes his own medium for all the ways in which its inefficient, "crippled," and altogether messy
style gives him the opportunity to gratify his own desires and impulses to communicate on different, more mediated ground. The carnal overtones are essential here. Agee's account of language as a "Rube Goldberg" medium is followed
by a somewhat cryptic attempt to defend "'description'"—the scare quotes are
his—against the accusation that this is a fatally corrupted mode because "words
cannot embody; they can only describe" (210). Agee then suggests that "a certain kind of artist, whom we will distinguish from others as a poet rather than
a prose writer, despises this fact about words or his medium, and continually
brings words as near as he can to an illusion of embodiment. In doing so he

accepts a falsehood but makes, of a sort in any case, better art" (210). As the logical extension of Agee's belief that words are inevitably prone to "falsification" and the "inability to communicate" with immediacy, it makes sense that he again finds himself arguing from a relatively abject position for the "superiority" of his entirely indirect medium; indeed, he couches his argument as an apparent paradox that locates art "both nearer the truth and farther from it" than merely descriptive, or objective enterprises, such as "science" as Agee understands it, and the raw materials of the world "and those things which, like human beings . . . merely are, the truth" (210). All of which is characteristically overblown and scattershot, like much of Agee's self-conscious theorizing in *Let Us Now Praise Famous Men*. But in arguing on behalf of words in all their mediating inefficiency and "falsehood," Agee finally signals that his commitment to mere description is as much erotic as aesthetic—or better, erotic because it is aesthetic:

> Most young writers and artists roll around in description like honeymooners on a bed. It comes easier to them than anything else. In the course of years they grow or discipline themselves out of it. . . . But again I suspect that the lust for describing, and that lust in action, is not necessarily a vice. Plain objects and atmospheres have a sufficient intrinsic beauty and stature that it might be well if the describer became more rather than less shameless. (211)

Appearing as it does in close proximity to a strange and brief account of the "naturalist's regard for the 'real,'" Agee's defense of sheer description looks back to naturalism's "mechanical submission to the given." For Jennifer Fleissner, who argues convincingly that this "compulsion to describe" has long been associated with the genre's iterative obsessions and mania for the capture and reproduction of visual detail, "the notion of sexualizing the symptom" that is description—"inhabiting it too passionately"—allows for its recuperation as a literary technique.[83] Or as Agee puts it when he explains his own naturalistic tendency toward documentary redundancy, "one of your first anxieties, in advance of failure foreseen, is to make clear that a sin is a sin" (210). But Agee's "shameless" indulgence in description just as clearly manifests a "logic of hypermediacy," to return to Bolter and Grusin, that is pervasive in modernism's "hyperconscious recognition or acknowledgement of the medium" (38). This is, almost by definition, Greenberg's modernism; and Bolter and Grusin accordingly enlist his 1960 essay "Modernist Painting," which is perhaps

Greenberg's purest expression of modernism's recursive materiality, not only to invoke what they call an emergent "fascination with the reality of media" that flourishes in the first decades of the twentieth century but also to ascribe this phenomenon, in large measure, to artistic friction with "conventional photography" and its ascendant status as "a medium with such loud historical claims to transparency" (38). If their account of modernism's "hypermediacy" feels too condensed and perhaps even deterministic in its treatment of photography, Bolter and Grusin do offer a suggestive explanation for what we see in *Let Us Now Praise Famous Men* as Agee's fetishized attachment to photographic "truth" gives way to his even more sexualized "lust" for the medium of words. The very "desire for immediacy," Bolter and Grusin write, upon which such "transparent technologies" as straight photography depend for their authority and prestige, "cannot satisfy that desire because they do not succeed in fully denying mediation" (236). This is so, they argue, because every technology "ends up defining itself with reference to other technologies," which is of course their version of McLuhan's famous slogan from *Understanding Media* that "the 'content' of any medium is always another medium."[84] And thus it is as if the immediacy of photography, which Agee avows with almost as much abandon as Holmes or Mumford, inspires his own "shameless" desire to perform, and to embody with considerable drama the circuitousness and indirectness of language, which he renders equivalent to its most visceral, messy pleasures. His own "lust" for language is decidedly residual and retentive; it aims to communicate a sensual experience of words operating as an "old" record that refuses to relent when confronted by the promise of another medium's newer, faster, more efficient treatment of the same historical material.

After the Colon

"If I could do it, I'd do no writing at all here," Agee declares in his "Preamble" to *Let Us Now Praise Famous Men*, addressing himself to a reader preparing for the several hundreds pages that come next (10). He continues, "It would all be photographs; the rest would be fragments of cloth, bits of cotton, lumps of earth, records of speech, pieces of wood and iron, phials of odors, plates of food and of excrement. Booksellers would consider it quite a novelty; critics would murmur, yes, but is it art; and I could trust a majority of you to use it as you would a parlor game. A piece of the body torn out by the roots might be more to the point" (10). If followed to the letter, Agee's design for *Let Us Now*

Praise Famous Men might have produced a modernist artifact along the lines of a Joseph Cornell box, or Duchamp's *The Box in a Valise*.[85] And though at first it seems strange to compare Agee's passionate, even melodramatic sincerity to the wry tactics and intellection of Duchamp, this show of medium-specific aggression at the beginning of his book suggests that Agee too knew how to challenge the market category of art with an avant-garde commitment to materiality. Or from a slightly different vantage point, we might hear in Agee's pipe dream for a book composed entirely of things and objects aimed at the body and its senses—cloth and wood to touch, records to hear, odors to smell, food to taste—anticipations of the 1960s minimalism that Michael Fried, for one, describes as dependent on a "literalist" aesthetic for the ways in which it sought to confront its beholders with materials that "do not represent, signify, or allude to anything; they are what they are and nothing more."[86] Agee, with his intermittent claims to be a Communist and bitter self-incriminations about his job at Time, Inc., and securely bourgeois class status, makes this commitment to the raw materials of his project into a compensatory performance of his politics.[87] Since he cannot assault his reader with body parts and excrement, he knows in advance that "nothing [he] might write could make any difference whatever. It would only be a 'book' at the best" (11).

Given Agee's investment in the aesthetic possibilities of excrement, it is only fitting that his "book" is everywhere enamored with the colon. A chapter titled "Colon" separates part 1 of *Let Us Now Praise Famous Men* from part 2; here Agee abruptly stops his involved description of his and Evans's early days spent with the Gudger family and calls for "a sharp end and clean silence," and then "a new and more succinct beginning" (87). The preceding pages feature some of Agee's most notorious displays of narrative sympathy and projection—including his heartfelt conviction that Emma Ricketts, aged eighteen, has "intimately communicated," not with words but "in sudden and subtle but unmistakable expressions of the eyes" that she would like "having a gigantic good time in bed, with George [Gudger], a kind of man she is best used to, and with Walker and me, whom she is curious about and attracted to" (55). Seeming to understand that such fantasizing can hardly help his cause, Agee announces that "herein I must screen off all mysteries of our comminglings" and pursue instead a more objective and, strictly speaking, modernist perspective on the "sorry and brutal infuriate yet beautiful structures" of his sharecroppers' lives: "and this in the cleanest terms I can learn to specify: must mediate, must attempt to record" (87). Colons, as we see here in "Colon" and throughout the text, allow Agee to construct his sentences as elaborate accretions of material. And grammatically speaking, his colons do not produce the "cleanest" prose. Here is the first occurrence of what becomes the book's paradigmatic punctuation. I offer it not so much to be read as to be viewed as an illustration of the gaudy excess Agee dumps onto the page:

Why make this book, and set it at large, and by what right, and for what purpose, and to what good end, or none: the whole memory of the South in its six-thousand-mile parade and flowering outlay of the facades of cities, and of the eyes in the streets of towns, and of hotels, and of the trembling heat, and of the wide wild opening of the tragic land, wearing the trapped frail flowers of its garden of faces; the fleet flush and flower and fainting of the human crop it raises; the virulent, insolent, deceitful, pitying, infinitesimal and frenzied running and searching, on this colossal peasant map, of two angry futile and bottomless, botched and overcomplicated youthful intelligences in the service of an anger and of a love and of an undiscernible truth, and in the frightening vanity of their would-be purity; the sustaining, even now, and forward moving, lifted on the lifting of this day as ships on a wave, above whom, in a few hours, night once more will stand up in his stars, and they decline through lamplight and be dreaming statues, of those, each, whose lives we knew and whom we love and intend well toward, and of whose living we know little in some while now, save that quite steadily, in not much possible change for better or much worse, mute, innocent, helpless and incorporate among that small-moted and inestimable swarm and pollen stream and fleet of single, irreparable, unrepeatable existences, they are led, gently, quite steadily, quite without mercy, each a little farther toward the washing and the wailing, the Sunday suite and the prettiest dress, the pine box, and the closed clay room whose frailly decorated roof, until rain has taken it flat into oblivion, wears the shape of a ritual scar and of an inverted boat: curious, obscene, terrifying, beyond all search of dream unanswerable, those problems which stand thickly forth like light from all matter, triviality, chance, intention, record in the body, of being, of truth, of conscience, of hope, of hatred, of beauty, of indignation, of guilt, of betrayal, of innocence, of forgiveness, of vengeance, of guardship, of an indenominable fate, predicament, destination, and God.

(7–8)

This sentence is a travesty of economy on every level; Agee never stops at four adjectives when he can think of five; two semicolons and another colon only further distend this parody of parataxis, all of which is meant to answer Agee's own rhetorical questions. I could, without much difficulty, cite more than a dozen sentences where Agee uses colons with much the same abandon. In "Colon," appropriately enough, almost every paragraph includes long litanies that flow from Agee's favorite punctuation mark in shows of logorrhea that more than earn the scatological connotations of this term: a particularly manneristic sequence begins, "Of the five and twenty known human senses," followed by a colon; but after two pages spent describing how "swarms of immediacy" work to "push steep holes in the bowels of gliding heavens," the next four paragraphs are not only almost entirely structured by a series of colons but they also end with them, as if we are reading our way through an intestinal tract of prose (92–95). Then after a question mark, the next paragraph begins: "Here then he is, or here is she: here is this tender and helpless human life: subjected to its immediacy and to all the enlargÉd [*sic*] dread of its future:" and so on, for five more colons (95–97). After which, Agee informs us that the final pages of "Colon" are "all one colon" (97). The chapter, "(On the Porch: 1)" ends in a colon, as does the brief untitled chapter that introduces "A Country Letter" (19, 42). A colon ends each of the sections within "A Country Letter," making for an absurdly additive display of narrative accumulation, which is frequently punctuated by sentences like this: "the land, in its largeness: stretches: is stretched:" (76). The opening section of "Work" concludes with a colon—"But I must make a new beginning:"—but what it grammatically expels is excess material from earlier portions of the text that Agee seems otherwise unable to digest (283). This "(Selection from Part I:"—a heading that replays the punctuational idiosyncrasy of so many other subtitles in the book—devolves into a series of what Agee calls "a few crude sketches:" "A man: George Gudger, Thomas Woods, Fred Ricketts: his work is with the land . . . the training of his sons: A woman: Annie Mae Gudger, Ivy Woods, Sadie Ricketts: her work is in the keeping of the home . . . the training of her daughters: Children: all these children: their work is as it is told to them" (286). Colons become pervasive once again as a connective device between paragraphs in "Inductions" and other late chapters, but by this point, we are perhaps so inured to this particular technique that it no longer registers as unusual. Which is maybe why one of the final and most extreme displays of Agee's colon function operates in the absence of the punctuation mark itself. In a paragraph that Agee identifies as a "Note" to a bitter discussion of terminology (about why "sharecropper" is such a galling term, when misused for "tenant"), Agee looses a logorrheic torrent of well over four hundred words with no warning whatsoever: "Other anglosaxon monosyllables are god, love, loyalty, honor, beauty, duty . . . " (403). Some fifty words later, Agee starts listing racial slurs and epithets ("Negro, negro, Jew, jew, dinge, jig, boog, colored, jigaboo, nigger, darky, spade, eph, shine, smoke, hebe, kike . . .); he turns to sex around the one-hundred-twenty-word mark ("syphilis, wasserman, sex, sexual, sexuality, homosexual, heterosexual, bisexual, asexual, fairy, pansy, flit, headleigh, swish, les, lesbie, lesbian . . . "); a small flurry of "-isms" occurs a hundred words later, ending with a perhaps inevitable swerve back to a body fluid that sustains the sound pattern ("regionalism, nationalism, jingoism, patriotism, americanism, altruism, schism, jizzum . . . "); profane and sacred variations on the name of Christ appear just seventy words from the end ("Jesus, Jesus Christ, Jesus Christ, Jesus H. Christ, Jeez, jeez fellas, jeez fellas, The Nazarene . . . "); it all ends topically in some words that would have resonated powerfully in 1941 ("fifth-column, reactionary, demagogue, blitzkreig, defense") (403–405). Brilliant and childish in its excess, this iterative discharge—which riffs haphazardly on both the sound and the sense of words—provides the most telling performance of Agee's obsession with language at the very limit of its crude materiality. High colonic modernism?

In a book conceived as a collaboration between writing and photography, the colon is also Agee's most graphic technology of illustration. The colon allows Agee to suggest an even more radical mode of description, one in which the naturalist's "mechanical submission to the given" has become so thoroughly internalized that even the barest sign of grammatical connection or subordination would seem to be considered an imposition of some mediating "falsification" or perspectival "illusion" upon the material at hand, whether objects, words, people, experiences, or perceptions.[88] The colon, simply put, is Agee's formal analog for photography. He makes this explicit near the end of a long passage in the first section of "A Country Letter" when he describes "the two elder [*sic*] talking (and the child, the photographic plate, receiving: These are women, I am a woman, I am not a child any more" (64). A metaphor that modernizes Locke's famous figure of young consciousness as a tabula rasa, Agee's "photographic plate" also translates this "developmental" moment (the pun comes all too readily) into a visual register. These are passages that show how Agee's pervasive colons help communicate his desire to function as a kind of linguistic camera: "as if visual phenomena are captured and made present without the intervention of human maker."[89] I take this from Svetlana Alpers's discussion of seventeenth-century Dutch art, which further stresses that the use of cameras (camera obscuras, to be precise) by painters such as Vermeer was intended to embrace "the artifice of the image ... along with its immediacy" (33). Given the theatricality of Agee's reliance on colons in *Let Us Now Praise Famous Men*— and, too, his profligacy in reproducing all the details and information that come after them—we might also think of their illustrative value in slightly different terms. As legendary grammarian H. W. Fowler observes of the colon in *Modern English Usage* (1926), "It is not now a stop of a certain power in any situation demanding such a power, but has acquired a special function, that of delivering the goods that have been invoiced in the preceding words."[90] That Fowler sees the colon as mercantile is even better: Agee began working on the text that grew (and grew) into *Let Us Now Praise Famous Men* while on the staff at *Fortune*.

The most elaborately photographic section in the book is dedicated to the topic "Shelter," and it unfolds largely as a series of room-by-room anatomies or still-lifes of, it would certainly appear, everything that Agee possibly can see. Beginning with the Gudger house, and then proceeding to the two other tenant farmers' homes that he and Evans visited while on assignment, the text of "Shelter" offers an account of American things that is unsurpassed in its attention to material detail, as well as its flamboyant performances of identification, across class lines, at the level of the object. His inventory of artifacts revels in both physical detail and, like certain Evans photographs, in the accidental ironies and semiotic juxtapositions provoked by the fragments of various "modern" discourses—newspaper headlines, advertisements, magazine illustrations— that have found their way into these antiquated, underdeveloped interiors. In the following description of the Gudgers' mantel, for example, Agee's un-inflected notation of object and of surface detail turns rather sharply on the misplaced signs of luxury and abundance:

> On the mantel above this fireplace:
> A small round cardboard box:
> (on its front:)
>> Cashmere Bouquet Face Powder
>> Light Rachel
> (on its back:)
>> The Aristocrat of Face Powders.
>> Same quality as 50¢ size.

Inside the box, a small puff. The bottom of the box and the bottom face of the puff carry a light dust of fragrant softly tinted powder.

A jar of menthol salve, smallest size, two thirds gone.

A small spool of number 50 white cotton thread, about half gone and half unwound.

A cracked roseflowered china shaving mug, broken along the edge. A much worn, inchwide varnish brush stands in it. Also in the mug are eleven rusty nails, one blue composition button, one pearl headed pin (imitation), three dirty kitchen matches, a lump of toilet soap.

A pink crescent celluloid comb: twenty-seven teeth, of which three are missing; sixteen imitation diamonds.

A nailfile.

A small bright mirror in a wire stand. (152)

This display of observation would seem determined to ferret out visual information that even the sharpest photographic image might miss—the number of broken teeth on a comb, the pattern of wear on tiny cups and jars. Such details suggest either outright fabrication or tactile scrutiny, and I would not want to guess which is in evidence here. There is also an austerity and a finely wrought stillness in the first lines of this passage that recall Oppen's "Civil War Photo," or one of Williams's experiments in concrete poetry, such as typographic reproduction of a restaurant sign at the beginning of "Brilliant Sad Sun" or of an ad for "soda" in "The Attic Which Is Desire."[91] Yet Agee's descriptions do just as much to emphasize how unconventional Oppen's focal details are; there is a sense of visual coherence and again, of mobile, filmic perspective in which Oppen shows little interest. The irony Agee strives for is clear enough: neither "cashmere" nor anything of the "aristocrat" belongs amid this jumble of penny toiletries, broken housewares, and imitation jewelry. And it is this sometimes crude, sometimes elaborate irony that returns us in *Let Us Now Praise Famous Men* to the question of how the material artifact is lived and experienced in its habitat, how it signifies within its social space. Agee later emphasizes that the "classic" status of the objects he describes—their aesthetic shape and form, their resonant isolation from the world that he and the majority of his readers occupy—cannot be treated separately from the status of the people who live with and use these objects. "These classicisms," he argues, "are created of economic need . . . and in their purity they are the exclusive property and privilege of the people at the bottom of the world" (203). Most readers of *Let Us Now Praise Famous Men* no doubt hear their fill of this particular accusation long before the book is finished, as Agee recriminates his own narration constantly on this very charge. But his endless self-consciousness as a beholder of objects, persons, and their shared histories is worth remembering as we turn to the *Index of American Design* and the paintings of Charles Sheeler, two projects that attempt to provide Americans in the 1930s with variations on Mumford's "new permanent record" that are more than willing to efface and streamline, for a modern culture of information, all the materiality that Agee so completely and so viscerally communicates. The havoc that he wreaks between medium and message reveals a much wasteful and circuitous side of 1930s documentary culture, where a fascination with the technicalities of representation commands our attentions in ways that would seem a distraction from the imperative to treat documentary subjects "cleanly and literally."

Rendered Material: The Index of American Design

The Index of American Design, which was inaugurated in December 1935 under the direction of the Federal Arts Project of the WPA, treated the "literal" representation of objects as its aesthetic aim and bureaucratic mandate. Like other WPA programs, the Index aimed to generate employment for a particular class of worker—in this case, mainly commercial artists and illustrators—but at the same time, it had to articulate a political and cultural rationale above and beyond the economic crisis facing those whom it would help. A 1938 press release announces that the Index "will stimulate the artist, designer, and manufacturer of articles of everyday use to build upon our American tradition, and that it will offer an opportunity to the student, teacher, research worker and the general public to familiarize themselves with this important phase of the American culture pattern."[92] The language here is more than vaguely reminiscent of Van Wyck Brooks, Vernon Parrington, or Howard Mumford Jones; F. O. Matthiessen memorably figures his subject in *American Renaissance* (1941) as the nation's "coming to its first maturity and affirming its rightful heritage in the whole expanse of art and culture," and the Index in effect hypostasizes a corollary "renaissance" in the country's material—as opposed to literary—culture.[93] Put another way, the Index rests comfortably at the intersection of several crucial discourses of the period: it indicates, again, the appetite for "reporting on the national inheritance" that Kazin captures so well, but it also suggests how this documentary mode reached back expressly as a mode of historical recovery and recuperation—the mode of Matthiessen but also that of Perry Miller, Waldo Frank, and Williams himself in *In the American Grain*; and more, in that the Index refers to an "American tradition" that will be of particular use to interior designers and "manufacturers" of furniture, china, glassware, and the like, we are reminded of a thriving Colonial revival and emerging market for American antiques.

Another aspect of the Index's overt ideology is captured best in the image of an illustrator at work on a drawing of a drop-leaf table (fig. 4.8), produced as part of a promotional series entitled "The Making of an Index Drawing." In the photograph we see a woman finishing a sketch that looks to have been taken from one of two photographs laid out before her on her table; a larger, rougher sketch of the same table is also visible, along with various implements and drafting tools. It goes without saying that she is thoroughly "absorbed" in the act of drawing, and this image could readily be situated alongside many, many others that Michael Fried has described and celebrated.[94] At the same time, though the artist in this scene assuredly appears "wholly oblivious to being beheld," in Michael Fried's words, her pose of rapt contemplation is also quite theatrical, and perhaps even overdetermined, by the piece of soft-core propaganda

FIGURE 4.8. "Index artist making a drawing." Publicity photograph of Linnet Alward for the Index of American Design, 1939. National Gallery of Art, Washington, D.C., Gallery Archives.

squarely before her. Since a white curtain hangs just to her left, depriving her, as well as us, of anything else to look at, we might wonder if her rapt show of contemplation is also evidence that she is tired of reading that "the theory that art is a marginal activity has to be discarded." We might also wonder if what we see her doing—making at least a second version of a copy of a photograph—is an appropriate scene to demonstrate that the child's "imagination" develops "immeasurably" as the expression of "innate creative powers." A more studious image of the "creative arts" is hard to conceive: her copying seems especially mechanical as a remediation of photographs that are themselves extremely stark, "objective" close-ups stripped of almost any sign or inflection of original-ity. But making art look more like work—rather than the "marginal activity" it may remain—is precisely the point. The Index of American Design, as an article by Archibald MacLeish in *Fortune*, "Unemployed Arts," phrased it with a certain lack of tact, was one of the "means by which the Federal Arts Project made a virtue of necessity, put their less talented artists to work on useful rather than creative labors, and began the cultivation of the American audience."[95] An anonymous writer for the *New Yorker* is not quite so insulting in his apprecia-tion for the Index after seeing a gallery exhibition of some watercolor render-ings in 1936, but there is still a sense that what makes the project admirable is less its individual artistry and more the genius of its bureaucracy, the elegance of its database aesthetic. Though not "exciting" like some Federal Arts Project works, the Index, "which is making a documentary record of old American fur-niture, pottery, textiles, painting" and hopes to produce "an adequate folio of materials toward a cultural history of the country," nevertheless "gives one a queer shock; but it is hard to say whether one is more happily surprised by the aesthetic competence or by the administrative intelligence that has brought it into existence."[96]

The Index was a considerable administrative undertaking. By the time the project was suspended in 1942, hundreds of illustrators in more than thirty states had generated 18,257 watercolor renderings of American objects; many of these renderings were based on photographs, and most were accompanied by infor-mation on the original location, provenance, design history, and significance of the illustrated artifact. Dozens of researchers spent countless hours on all aspects of American material culture in preparation for the proposed series of portfolios that were eventually abandoned with the outbreak of World War II. But long before funding was suspended, Index administrators had begun to worry about the costs of publishing this vast archive of visual material in any usable form. Adolph Glassgold, the national coordinator for the Index, writes in 1939 that when the project "was initiated in the fall of 1935 it was impossible to foresee the vast accumulation of material which was to result."[97] Plans were ventured for filmstrips that would reproduce 2,500 to 3,000 drawings from the Index and allow for "visual lectures" on particular topics; estimates were assembled for color microfilming of Index materials, to be paid for by $1,475 grants from the American Council for Learned Societies; publishers submitted bids for folios of color plates sold by subscription to offset high production costs.[98] It was not until 1950 that the National Gallery released a two-volume version of the Index (*The Treasury of American Design and Antiques*). Clarence Hornung, one of the project's early administrators, writes in his preface to the *Treasury* that he contacted many, many publishers in the late thirties, hoping to find one willing to accept the Index as a book, or a series of books; every one, however, "felt disinclined to proceed because of the very magnitude of the project and the staggering costs involved. One publisher even pleaded for a Congressional subsidy."[99] This is not to suggest that the Index, however obscure its ultimate destination in the archives of the National Gallery, came and went without a trace. Several prominent magazines ran features on it—among them a seven-page color feature in *Fortune*—and newspapers covered many local and regional shows of Index materials, several of which were sponsored by the Associated Merchandising Corporation, and brought Index watercolors to the floors of Macy's, Marshall Field, Carson Pirie Scott, and Stix, Baer, and Fuller.

In both scope and method, the Index of American Design recalls any number of Orientalist endeavors to collect and catalog historical artifacts, perhaps most obviously in the fervor of its accumulative redundancy. (Index artists, in fact, were taught the so-called Egyptian method, named for techniques devised in early-nineteenth-century France to streamline the process of making watercolor drawings of the objects seized by Napoleonic conquests in the Middle East.) Consider two of the reproductions of Index materials, the first an array of jars and pitchers, the second a similarly profuse collection of chairs (figs. 4.9 and 4.10). There are identical presentations in *The Treasury of American Design and Antiques* of glass pitchers, cigar-store Indians, ship figureheads, whiskey flasks, highboys, grandfather clocks, lamps, stoves, chalkware figurines, tankards, teapots, pewter, chests, busts, gates, railings, weather vanes, pots, pans, coffee grinders, trivets, cookie cutters, hatboxes, rugs, quilts, carousel horses, dolls, puppets, piggy banks, stoveplates, santos, *bultos*, branding irons, Shaker boxes, and spurs. This list, culled from flipping through the *Treasury*'s pages, reflects an

FIGURE 4.9. Renderings and photographs of pottery from the Index of American Design as reproduced in Clarence Hornung, *The Treasury of American Design*, (New York: Abrams, 1997; originally published 1950).

FIGURE 4.10. Renderings and photographs of chairs from the Index of American Design as reproduced in Clarence Hornung, *The Treasury of American Design*, (New York: Abrams, 1997; originally published 1950).

organizational scheme that groups these objects into categories based largely on where they were used—"In the Home," "Around House and Garden"—and by whom—"Woman's World." But such categories were not part of the Index in the 1930s; its manual instead offers a more intriguing set of categories completely divorced from the object's social place and utility, and fixated on every aspect of the object's material form and visual presence. For the artists at work on the Index, furniture for which an "exact front view" is "inadvisable" includes chairs, chests, and tables; knives, boxes, and clocks "should be drawn as if resting on a table" (though of course there will be no table in the final image); mirrors and picture frames "may be drawn in front view" (12). Glass and ceramics are subdivided into "pieces with handles," which "are often shown best in profile," and "dishes, plates, bowls, etc.," which "should be drawn in full top view with a side view shown in shallow perspective" (12). Other phyla in this ecosystem of objects include "Metal," "Textiles," "Costume," and "Accessories," and each involves another set of instructions for how best to pose the artifact, how best to predict its shadows and contours, how best to reveal its structure, texture, and surface detail.

No large-scale project of the period comes closer to realizing Mumford's dream for a "new permanent record" that perfectly translated the materiality of history into an archival form. The Index was predicated on the dream of mass-producing images that reflected a precise attention to visual detail and that were essentially anonymous. These would seem like two aesthetics that photography could offer in abundance, which begs the question of why it was not used more extensively. A text devised to guide Federal Arts Project officials through a "Typical Ten-Minute Speech" on the Index even featured, as "Point 8," an argument about "advantages of artist's renderings over photographs."[100] Quick to insist that this "is not merely the result of an employment problem," the text instructs its speaker to inform a potential audience that "a photograph is not always an assurance of accuracy, and that, often, even when it is an accurate reproduction, it lacks the spark of life inherent in the original." Constance Rourke offers a technically specific corollary on this issue in a 1937 article on the Index in the *Magazine of Art*: "Photography is being used," she writes, "in some instances when color is immaterial, but emphasis upon color is dominant in the Index, and water color has proved the most efficient and practical medium."[101] This was undoubtedly the case before color film became widely available in the early 1940s, but when the "typical" Index speech suggests that photographs often fail to capture the "spark of life" that animates an object, the anticipations of Agee's qualified respect for the camera's "ice-cold" truth are hard to miss. Indeed, given that the Index aimed at illustrations of surpassing trompe l'oeil realism—"It is no exaggeration," Rourke boasts, "to say that observers have been able to satisfy themselves that the mounted plates were water color on paper rather than the actual ... only by the sense of touch"—the specter of photography deeply haunts the project. As Holger Cahill recalls in his introduction to the *Treasury* in 1950, though some dealers and curators "thought [the Index] might better be carried out by what they considered the cheaper and more expeditious method of photography," the vast majority of the project's originators argued fiercely for the advantages of live artists, stressing, as J. Carter Brown writes, that painters could "[compile] a visual archive of remarkable beauty in a form far less perishable and more sensitively interpretive that the color photograph." If these statements rehearse the folktale of John Henry—with humble commercial artists pitted against relentless machines of vision—this was, to be fair, a contest that few artists seemed interested in fighting. "Many artists felt that the Index was dead copying," Cahill admits, adding that "Index artists had to discipline themselves to meticulous rendering techniques and to the objects they recorded."[102]

The Index, then, stressed a practice of visual objectivity that was redolent of—indeed, medium-specific to—photography, even as artists and illustrators were imagined as essential for capturing the "spark" that no machine could reproduce. This imperative for objectivity, at least for Index administrators and contemporary reviewers, did not reduce the artists to mere instruments or technologies so much as it made them exemplary modernists: Index renderings were celebrated, according to MacLeish in *Fortune*, for "their impersonality" and "objective beauty"; they were "factual and precise," and this is because the artist, as an individual, "remains in shadow," subject to a "self-effacement [that] is practically complete."[103] Thus in this publicity photograph of Index artists, taken in 1939 (fig. 4.11), we see only faceless figures differentiated by the identity of the object—a bit of embroidery, a horse-and-rider miniature, a mechanical toy—that it is their job to render fully. We also see the way that Index drawings aspire to an extreme version of formalism, one in which historical artifacts are isolated and decontextualized, turned into icons of "American design" that float in a white ether where they cast no shadow and occupy no human space (fig. 4.12). This picture of "The First Talking Doll," encased in glass beside its Index rendering for a show in Pennsylvania, suggests the degree to which the Index could evoke an explicitly "uncanny" aesthetic, accentuated here, of course, because the object itself is a folk-art variation on Hoffmann's "Olympia," which

FIGURE 4.11. "Index artists group." Photograph from the Index of American Design promotional series, "From Garret to Gallery," New York City, 1939. National Gallery of Art, Washington D.C., Gallery Archives.

famously provides Freud with his model for the term. But any of the "truly magical portraits of artifacts and implements," suggests Virginia Tuttle Clayton in a catalog accompanying a 2002 exhibition of Index materials, permits us to "encounter the mundane objects in these renderings close-up . . . as if they had been transported to a timeless, airless realm," and finally in this mediated vacuum do we "at last discover the startling beauty of the all-too familiar."[104]

This is a magic that photography cannot do on its own, and so the Index develops an amazing "Rube Goldberg articulation" of procedures for its artists. The first Index manual features almost no direction on how best to make a suitable drawing. But in the second Index manual, published as a "W. P. A. Technical Series Art Circular," three pages are devoted to straightforward, itemized instructions for artists: "Objects should be drawn as if held with the top slightly below eye-level"; "Simplify highlights and shadows"; "Study manner in which different fabrics drape."[105] By the time a third Index manual appears in 1938, these instructions have flourished into a comprehensive catalog of how to experience the world of objects. Regarding the sheen and weave of fabrics, we are reminded that "texture is not only a matter of thread. The texture of a cloth is shown by the way it falls into folds; crisp, sharp folds like taffeta; clear smooth folds of silk; soft folds in wool; lightly buckled folds and creases of linen" (19). When looking at a metal artifact, artists were admonished to be sure to "observe all properties which are peculiarly its own, and ask, "Is it harsh or brittle?

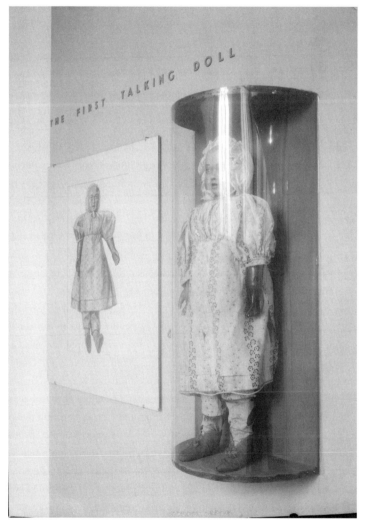

FIGURE 4.12.   "The First Talking Doll." Photograph of an Index of American Design exhibition in Philadelphia, Pennsylvania. National Gallery of Art, Washington, D.C., Gallery Archives.

Is it tough, elastic, malleable? Has it been cast, forged, drawn, turned, or rolled? Has it been filed, beaten, burnished?" (22–33). We rarely find such fetishized sensitivity in governmental prose or expect such lavishly aesthetic how-to advice, but what interests me about the Index manual is also the difficulty it seems to have in keeping to its objective—which is, above all else, an "objectivity" redolent of Mumford—as it instructs artists in ways of imaging that are both modeled on and deeply antagonistic to the photographic. The Index manual instructs its reader in a variety of tricks and methods that will yield renderings that perfectly capture those "physiognomic aspects of visual worlds," in Benjamin's memorable phrase, that the human eye may miss, and that are so often talked about as the special province of the camera.

Thus the Index manual finally asks us not just to see the object but to identify with it and to feel the history of its construction as we gaze upon its surfaces. Hidden, then, within the operating system that produced 18,527 renderings distinguished for their "impersonality," we discover, against all odds, the dream of a richly affected, even erotic contact with the materialities of both art and technology. "Do not regard the task as a picture," we are told. Instead, "[i]magine that by means of the drawing, a craftsman is to be shown . . . exactly what the finished job *is* like—not merely what it *looks* like" (23). A prospective artist of 1938 would then have read through an example that describes a "piece of iron casting" whose "raised surfaces have become polished by handling" and on whose "parts that have been generally unseen and neglected" might well be discovered "the unmistakable pitting and scaling of rust, with its accompanying zones of yellow-orange, dull reds and red-violets" (23). This is a sympathetic formalism, and as a dream of descriptive objectivity, it stands in contrast to the startling detachment of the perspective of, to cite a well-known example, the speaker in Williams's "The Raper from Passenack," or "Fine Work with Pitch and Copper," much less the "straight" photography of Evans or Edward Steichen. These are works that show an extreme "ethical detachment"—language that Robert von Hallberg draws from a 1937 Williams essay—of exactly the sort we might expect from a commercial artist doing a watercolor of a Tidewater drip pan, properly mounted on cardboard (two standard sizes to choose from), submitted with "the original and first copy of the DATA REPORT SHEET," and registered with classification number, so that the image will be correctly filed and stored somewhere in the basement of the National Gallery, perhaps, where it likely sits today.[106] The Index draws on two distinct inclinations toward the historical object: one traffics in a language that is patently "objective" in a familiar lexicon of 1930s modernism—"accuracy of drawing," "clarity of construction," "faithful rendition of the material"; the second, however, traffics in an observer's sympathetic, even fantasmatic identification with the object—our concern is "not merely what it *looks* like" but "what the finished job *is* like." The Index wants to show us a massive accumulation of material as only a machine could view it, and yet let us know each object as only a human being could tell its story. But "database and narrative are natural enemies," recalling Manovich, and the fact that we see the Index so powerfully conflicted between its informatics and its sympathies, is perhaps an indication that it was bound to fail.

Technical Difficulties

In 1938 Constance Rourke published *Charles Sheeler: Artist in the American Tradition*, one of the first monographs on a modern U.S. painter, and an entirely appropriate subject for a book by the national editor of the Index of American Design. Known widely in the 1930s for his photographs and paintings of Ford's River Rouge factory—including such iconic images as *American Landscape* (1930) and *Classic Landscape* (1931)—Sheeler was among the most successful artists of the period and a leading precisionist. He was also a prominent collector of Shaker furniture, and he permitted several of his pieces to be reproduced by Index artists; this reflected only a small measure of his interest in American arts and crafts, which took hold early in his career when he began to spend time in Bucks County, Pennsylvania, where he produced a series of brilliant photographs and paintings of an eighteenth-century barn at which he stayed from time to time. A friend of the prominent Philadelphia patron Walter Arensberg, Sheeler frequented a salon of artists that included Marcel Duchamp and Francis Picabia, and was a first-hand witness to the R. Mutt affair at the Armory Show of 1913, when Duchamp debuted his famous *Fountain* and helped to make a particular kind of "ready-made," material aesthetic into an international sensation. Through Arensberg, Sheeler met William Carlos Williams, who based several poems on his images. He also undertook numerous assignments as a commercial photographer, first for Condé Nast, and later for *Fortune*, and codirected, with Paul Strand, the pioneering avant-garde film *Manahatta* (1920), making him a true multi-media artist. His dealer was Edith Halpert, at whose Downtown Gallery, in 1937, a popular exhibition of Index renderings—paired in many cases with the original objects—attracted a great deal of attention. Wanda Corn notes that Sheeler's aesthetic—which stressed "a distinctly American tradition of plainness, simplicity, and functionalism"—was ascendant in the period; his subjects spoke to the abiding impulses that were said to shape a coherent, deeply resonant sense of national identity, even as his "high modernism . . . favored form over feelings, composition over biography."[107] Small wonder, then, that Rourke, Halpert, and Holger Cahill all looked to Sheeler's work "as the evidence that made their paradigm seem plausible," as Virginia Tuttle Clayton puts it.[108] Cahill believed that Sheeler would have been an ideal candidate to help start the Index in 1935: someone who "[knew] the field" of American arts and crafts, who was "deeply interested" and had "done a lot of work in this field."[109] But since Sheeler was among the most successful artists of the 1930s—with private commissions from Ford and John D. Rockefeller, features in *Vogue* and *Life*, and even a starring role, in 1939, in the first art telecast in the United States—he didn't need the WPA's money.[110]

There are many Sheeler images from the 1930s that seem to be in communication with the mission, visual style, and ideology of the Index, but none more than *Kitchen, Williamsburg, 1937* (fig. 4.13). At first glance, this painting looks like a composite of trompe l'oeil drawings from the Index of American Design: cast-iron skillet, copper mold, bread trough, kettle, pot, tongs, candle lamp. Yet the painting, on closer inspection, hardly treats these objects with the clarity and precision that the Index would have required. The painting shows little respect for those objects that just happen to be located at its edges: the candle lamp is decapitated, several copper utensils on the upper recessed shelf come to rather abrupt ends, a pot in the fireplace is left structurally incomplete, as is the cabinet cut off by both the left and the bottom of the frame. The image is cropped like a snapshot, and it should come as no surprise to learn that Sheeler based this painting on a photo taken while he was "on assignment" at Colonial Williamsburg, commemorating the restoration for its major patron, John D. Rockefeller. Sheeler spent three months in Williamsburg at the request—and, one imagines, the expense—of Rockefeller, to whom Sheeler later gave this painting. Thus this picture shares more than we might think with Sheeler's work at Ford's River Rouge complex in the late 1920s; here too a landmark of American corporate power is depicted in ways that simultaneously verify and question how that power would present itself.[111] What we see here, in other words, is a picture that at once visualizes Colonial Williamsburg and "Colonial Williamsburg, Incorporated." The painting also puts the historical and the historiographical in a relationship that is difficult to resolve; Sheeler represents these objects in their archaeologically exact surroundings, which themselves are testimony not to a past that has been miraculously preserved but to one

FIGURE 4.13.   Charles Sheeler, *Kitchen, Williamsburg*, 1937. Fine Arts Museums of San Francisco, Gift of Mr. and Mrs. John D. Rockefeller 3rd, 1993.35.24.

that has been convincingly simulated in the present—an illusionistic triumph of technical ingenuity and anachronism. "It would be impractical to restore the city to a specific date," writes the anonymous author of *The Williamsburg Restoration*, an official "Colonial Williamsburg, Inc." document of 1933 that is printed to resemble an eighteenth-century text, even as it describes how engineers shored up aging buildings, how architects reproduced structures long since gone, and how chemists sampled period paints and matched their formulas down to the molecule. The project strives not so much for authenticity as for its effect: Colonial Williamsburg "will provide a composite representation of the original forms of a number of buildings and areas known or, on good authority, believed to have existed in Williamsburg between the years 1699 and 1840."[112] We can only imagine what Sheeler thus intended to give Mr. Rockefeller: visual testimony that the historicist simulacra he helped to build was, according to design, thoroughly and seamlessly convincing; or, testimony to the bravura of such historicism, and to the improbable reassembly of *this* kitchen *in* 1937. At only 10" × 14", the painting is ideally sized to grace a wall without upstaging the decor, the perfect memento in return for all the collectibles that Rockefeller has so generously given to the public.

Though held privately by the Rockefeller estate from the time of its comple-
tion, *Kitchen, Williamsburg, 1937* enjoyed significant publicity thanks to a *Life*
profile of Sheeler that ran in 1938 and featured this painting among several others in a five-page article. "He works all day every day," *Life*'s brief bio concludes,
letting Sheeler himself have the last word, "'like any day laborer.'"[113] Thus the
domestic scene of *Kitchen, Williamsburg, 1937* captured during a pause in mid-
day chores, with carrots waiting to be chopped and dough rising in a bowl, is
suggestive of Sheeler's own gesture of self-definition—one "day laborer" recording the domestic workplace of another. On the final page of *Life*'s profile
we discover another picture of this same interior that casts such a comparison
in a different light: a Sheeler photograph shows an elderly African American
woman dressed in a servant's costume (period-specific), sitting in a Windsor
chair and looking directly at us from a table crowded with household objects
(fig. 4.14). The fireplace seen in *Kitchen, Williamsburg, 1937* is behind her, and
the same rack of spoons and ladles (hanging at the left edge of the painting)
is visible in the upper right. *Life*'s cheeky effort to make sure that we see the
parallel produces the title "Cook, Williamsburg" for this Sheeler photograph.

FIGURE 4.14. Charles Sheeler, "Cook, Williamsburg," Photograph taken at Colonial Williamsburg, circa 1936, as
published in *Life* (8 August 1938).

In addition to this strictly generic information, *Life* captions the photograph with some details about its subject and her relationship to Sheeler: "'Mr. Rockefeller has taken pictures of me, so I guess you might as well too,' Aunt Mary told Sheeler. Because she is strictly a stuffed shirt in a kitchen where nothing is cooked, Aunt Mary is an exception to the Sheeler fondness for functionalism" (45). Given that Sheeler puts these words in Aunt Mary's mouth for *Life*'s reporter to reproduce, we might wonder if we are being told that the artist, who takes his cues from Mr. Rockefeller, isn't also something of a "stuffed shirt." But we certainly learn that Sheeler, famous for his images of pristine artifacts, machines, and depopulated factories (none of the paintings in *Life* have any recognizable people in them), occasionally sees the value of a human subject, even if it violates the love of "function" that defines his painting.

As *Life* reminds us, "Cook, Williamsburg" is not a painting, and therefore speaks to another aspect of Sheeler's aesthetic: a headline just below the image reads, "Painter Sheeler's Second Love Is Photographing Plain Things"—a category, judging from the other pictures on the page, that includes the architectural details of eighteenth-century barns, the giant smelters of Ford's River Rouge plant, and an elderly black woman. If this is not a full-blown return to a discourse of racialized materiality we have seen before (the way James Weldon Johnson, for example, observes that black musicians are virtually the same things as phonographs), it is still a striking gesture of objectification. Aunt Mary becomes another artifact of American culture, a "plain thing" otherwise without a purpose ("a stuffed shirt in a kitchen where nothing is cooked") except to make history itself appear more resonant and affecting. Like the other props imagined to make Colonial Williamsburg seem more lifelike—carrots, rising dough—she communicates a sense of human presence in a scene where every other object has been thoroughly contrived or reproduced.

Sheeler gave *Kitchen, Williamsburg, 1937* to his patron; he gave "Cook, Williamsburg" to his friend: William Carlos Williams received a print of the photograph shortly after Sheeler returned from Virginia. More than evidence of Colonial Williamsburg's commitment to historical fidelity—the look of slavery must also be re-created—Aunt Mary might be viewed as literally embodying a modernist iconography that was fascinated with women of color through which white men, such as Williams, could access the idea of a more primal history that the twentieth century had obscured. There are figures of this "dark life," as we saw in Williams earlier, throughout *In the American Grain*: De Soto arrives in the New World and becomes enraptured with "Black Jasmine" ("vigilant, sagacious,

firm besides"); Daniel Boone realizes that there must be a "new wedding" between the white man and the Indian, "the flower of his world"; Aaron Burr meets
"Jacataqua, a girl scarce eighteen, in whom showed the best traits of her mixed
French and Indian blood"; and Williams himself pays tribute to his acquaintance
with "Dudu," who is "gentle as the dew or rain in April" and who is one of many
"colored women" that came to America with "the advent of the slaves."[114] Telling
examples of how deeply Williams's own historical imagination was shaped by
primitivist conventions, the accumulation of these figures—not just in *In the
American Grain* but elsewhere in his poetry—all but reduces them to versions of
each other. Each of them communicates the same fantasy of nature and sensuality that uses race—as Nicole does, with the help of phonograph, in *Tender Is the
Night*—as one of its essential mediums in U.S. modernism.

Writing of Richard Avedon's 1963 photograph "William Casby, Born a
Slave," Barthes attributes the power of the image—which shows an extremely
aged black figure turned squarely at the viewer—to its ability to lay bare "the
essence of slavery." We do not see a face in the photograph at all, according to
Barthes; instead we confront a mask of "pure meaning" that invokes both the
political tragedy of slavery (a mask as pure "as it was in the ancient theater")
and its incommunicability, since society cannot stand to confront the products
of its past so transparently and needs instead for the meaning of race "to be surrounded by a noise (as is said in cybernetics) which will make it less acute."[115]
Whether or not Aunt Mary, like William Casby, was born a slave, she certainly
appears old enough in Sheeler's photograph to achieve the same effect; and if
the "mask" she turns to the camera is a relic from a time when she herself was
technically more thing than person, then the demeanor that Sheeler amusingly
remembers ("Mr. Rockefeller has taken pictures of me, so I guess you might as
well too") becomes more cryptic, and perhaps even a refusal to communicate
that takes the very form of idle conversation. We can further appreciate the
signifying static of Aunt Mary's pose—a "meaning" delivered so directly that
it turns to cybernetic "noise"—by comparing Sheeler's photograph to an image
of a black illustrator working on a rendering for the Index (fig. 4.15). Here again
we do not see a face, but we do not see a mask either, and this helps to minimize
the impact of this otherwise outlandish remediation of racial identity. Showing
the illustrator absorbed in the finishing touches on his rendering of a toy that
features at least one figure that is marked as black, this photograph makes for
a tricky object lesson in the impersonality that the Index required to achieve a
sympathetic understanding of the material, but we are deprived of the potential

FIGURE 4.15. "An Early American Mechanical Toy." Publicity photograph from the series "From Garret to Gallery" of an artist from the Index of American Design at work on a drawing, New York City, 1939. National Gallery of Art, Washington D.C., Gallery Archives.

drama that surrounds this reproduction of an item that finally turns the damage done because of race in U.S. history into a game. Since we have practically been invited by the artist's pose to stand over his shoulder as he works—to share with him in his labors—any sign of conflict is suppressed.

The longer that we look at Aunt Mary, on the other hand, the more dissonance we experience. The spoons and ladles sparkle in the background and the candlestick near her left hand is polished to a glow; we start to realize that the reason why the hearth behind her is so clean and free of soot, every brick delineated, is that this is a kitchen "where nothing is cooked." Everything we see in Sheeler's photograph is an exception to his "fondness for functionalism," save, perhaps, Aunt Mary herself: the fact that Sheeler erases her from the painting that he bases, at least in part, on this photograph suggests that her presence does do something. Aunt Mary functions to communicate the resistance to communication that, as I have been arguing from the start, provided modernism with one of its most powerful aesthetics. She might be offered as a ready icon for a familiar primitivism, but in the context of the other artifacts on display, she is also a more unsettling reminder of the "absolute alterity of the black body" that, Mark Hansen argues, must interfere with any "mechanism of projection" that white people employ to imagine race as an "excess of embodiment."[116] These variations on a kitchen at Colonial Williamsburg thus suggest a messiness and margin for historical error that visions of technological precision and archival immediacy cannot afford. We are not really managing our "social heritage" more economically if every painting requires another photograph to understand it, if all our ruthless objectivity in the name of some machine-tooled version of the past leaves us only more entangled in the wreckage. Sheeler does give us a chance to see just how bright and new this wreckage can be made to look; there is an implicit cordon sanitaire between his painting and his photograph of Aunt Mary's kitchen; he tries to keep his beautifully salvaged objects at a distance from the other histories—those less easily disposed of—that could be imagined for the artifacts we behold. If these two pictures intimately communicate with each other, they suggest as well a potentially endless network of contexts and associations, iconographic resemblances, anecdotes, biographies, ideologies—all manner of historical data, in short, at which we could work for as long as it might take. "Like any day laborer," as Sheeler would say, whose material is the medium of information.

◊

"I think Sheeler is particularly valuable," writes William Carlos Williams in his introduction to the catalog of Sheeler's 1939 show at the Museum of Modern Art, "because of the bewildering directness of his vision, without blur, through the fantastic overlay with which our lives so vastly are concerned, 'the real,' as we say, contrasted with the artist's 'fabrications.'"[117] Although Williams's spare aesthetic shares little with Agee's more wrought manner, this praise for Sheeler sounds like one of the "Rube Goldberg" articulations about the value of photography from *Let Us Now Praise Famous Men*. We could borrow the idea of a "bewildering directness" and apply it to what Agee might have admired most in his own work, or in Henry James, but it feels odd coming from Williams, and odder still as praise for Sheeler's precisionism. It is impossible to decide whether the "fantastic overlay" is the "real" that we should want to see more clearly ("without blur") or the "fabrications" with which we "so vastly are concerned," and which are the only "real" that has any hope of communicating to us directly. Trying, perhaps, to clear things up himself, Williams falls back on a comfortingly strong and familiar proposition: "Pictures are made with paint and brush on canvas." This is a prescription for modernist medium specificity that could not be put with any more precision. For all the complexities of modernism—all the questions it might raise about what is "the real" or what "fabrications" blur our perceptions—we know the answers finally lie in the materialities of its technologies. "The fate of modernist art generally," notes Stanley Cavell, is that "its awareness and responsibility for the physical basis of its art compel it to assert and deny the control of its art by that basis."[118] And as if reading over Cavell's shoulder, Williams follows his assertion of materiality with a denial that is just as powerful. "A picture," Williams writes, "at its best is pure exchange, men flow in and out of it, it doesn't matter how."[119]

Both the painting *Kitchen, Williamsburg, 1937* and the photograph of Aunt Mary were included in Sheeler's show at MOMA, and if we don't care which one is the other's "fantastic overlay," it should be clear by now that there is little chance of any "pure exchange" between them. This is language speaking to a dream of communication that anticipates a digital sublime, that celebrates the convergence of all the mediums that modernism fetishized, and that channels our attention to other forms of information—to Liu's "transcendental data" or Hayles's "immaterial fluid." I am more attracted to the noise and friction that are inescapable effects of Sheeler's two images of history at Colonial Williamsburg. I would not have us "flow" from painting to photograph as if they offered the same content in different formats, but would rather recognize that Sheeler's uncanny sense of history rendered clean in *Kitchen, Williamsburg, 1937* feels empty without "Cook, Williamsburg," and that the untranslatable materiality of race in the photograph is what the elaborate technological mediation of the past, to which *Kitchen, Williamsburg, 1937* pays high tribute, has been after from the start. If "the content of any medium," to return to McLuhan, "is always another medium," we witness in these two images something of a feedback loop that produces race as the content of materiality as a medium but then returns to materiality as the content of race as a medium, and so on. The pictures circulate the same two-way analogies—between people who seem like things because things seem like people in the first place; between a past that looks better than brand-new because the technologies of modern life have made it so—but also fill in the other's blanks. The photograph captures the single moment that becomes the object of so much labor in the painting, which renders ladle, brick, and pan in meticulous detail. In *Kitchen, Williamsburg, 1937*, Aunt Mary's carrots are on the table, waiting for her to get back to work; but "Cook, Williamsburg" reminds us that in this "kitchen where nothing is cooked" the most revealing function she can perform is to make us look at history from the perspective that Williams seems to have in mind when he says Sheeler is master of "bewildering directness."

"Everything that enters awareness can be communicated in one way or another, even if only partly," Clement Greenberg insists in one of his later seminars on aesthetics, but it is the final concession, with its wavering "partly" suggesting at once failure and hope, that I find especially affecting.[120] As evidence of the "enterprise of self-criticism" that remains one of Greenberg's most enduring contributions to both the history and the theory of modernism, moments where communication "partly" succumbs to noise, distortion, or other forms of obdurate materiality are always doubly resonant.[121] This is also true when Agee describes one of his and Evans's few encounters with blacks in "Late Sunday Morning," an early section of *Let Us Now Praise Famous Men*. Having just arrived in town, a local landowner welcomes Agee and Evans with an uncomfortably forced performance of some spirituals—"to show us," Agee writes, "what nigger music is like" (26). When the men are asked to sing another number, Agee, already exquisitely self-conscious, proceeds from self-criticism to self-abuse without missing a beat. "Meanwhile, and during all this singing, I had been sick in the knowledge that they felt they were here at our demand," he worries, "and that I could communicate nothing otherwise; and now, in a perversion of self-torture, I played my part through . . . trying at the same time, through my eyes, to communicate much more, and said I was sorry we had held them up and that I hoped they would not be late; and he thanked me for them in a dead voice, not looking me in the eye, and they went away" (28). The profound insufficiency of the communication that Agee fantasizes speaks to the experience of "connectibility" that animates so much of James's late fiction. Agee's flowery shows of intimacy with his subjects and their material surroundings—the erotics of attention he can indulge as if he were a kind of human medium for relaying visual information—require him to keep his eye trained on white people alone, because his scrutiny, however objective and mechanical it tries to be, will otherwise meet with nothing but interference.

Williams too, despite his easy language of "pure exchange," knew that modernism was made of moments where communication partly fails, and thus means even more. In 1938 he wrote a short poem that confirms this point, and again reminds us why we might hesitate to pattern our historical memories on media technologies. This is, as if responding to Mumford's fantasy with a bitter flourish, "The Defective Record":

> Cut the bank for the fill
> Dump sand
> pumped out of the river
> into the old swale
>
> killing whatever was
> there before—including
> even the muskrats. Who did it?
> There's the guy.
>
> Him in the blue shirt and
> Turquoise skull cap.
> Level it down
> For him to build a house
>
> on to build a
> house on to build a house on
> to build a house
> on to build a house on to . . . [122]

The poem displays an instantly recognizable catalog of Williams's signature techniques: diction and syntax are austere, especially in the first stanza, where it is hard at first to pick out a complete sentence from the guttural harmonies ("cut," "dump," and "pumped" almost, but not quite, rhyme) and the imperative grammar, which is so minimal that we can't know whether we are reading a description or taking orders. There are no signs of the speaker's relationship to this scene, no sense of a participant observer through which we might better understand on what details we are supposed to focus. I would not say that this is one of Williams's more subtle poems; the "objectivity" is too affected in the hard-boiled lines that introduce us to the poem's only human figure: "Who did it? / There's the guy. / Him in the blue shirt and / Turquoise skull cap." This dialogue brings to mind the stylized efforts at communication we associate with detective fiction or film noir. Yet if any popular genre is evoked by "The Defective Record," I would suggest it is the western. For what is skipping and repeating in the ostentatious sound effects that end the poem if not a story of the American frontier? Aren't we being told, and told again, the story of the solitary man—the "American Adam," we might say—establishing his domain over nature ("killing whatever was / there before") and conquering the "Virgin Land"?[123] This is the story of the Turner thesis, of the originary "errand into the wilderness" at the heart of an American mythology of impossibly unceasing progress, and it enjoyed a resurgence with the opening of the so-called electronic frontier in the 1990s, though here "progress" looks—or rather sounds— like something else entirely, like the mindless iteration of the poem's own technical difficulties. "A poem," according to a famous Williams pronouncement of 1944, "is a small (or large) machine made of words," which, for this broken "record" at least, means that a poem is subject to the same malfunctions and mechanical disruptions, and to becoming, without any sign of trouble, utterly inoperative. Almost a decade before writing "The Defective Record," Williams had warned that "to stop before any machine is to make of it a fetish." "As soon as we make it," he argues, "we must at once plan to escape—and escape." Modernism is itself a version of this fetish, which has Greenberg, in "Towards a Newer Laocoön," sounding supremely satisfied that the modern arts have at last attained "a more radical purity" because, "like the machine, they *look* what they *do*."[124] Given that this is no easy trick, we might expect the mediums that are our messages on occasion to break down, and inevitably to appear the worse for wear. And after a long twentieth century of new technologies that seem unending, it is easy to feel the rush and the allure of digital media that promise to deliver on what modernism, for all its fascination with mediums and their materiality, could never quite accomplish: "pure exchange, men flow in and out of it, it doesn't matter how." If this is modernism pushed beyond its limits, this is also "cyberspace" in its first breath: "A consensual hallucination experienced daily by billions of legitimate operators," William Gibson writes. "Unthinkable complexity. Lines of light ranged in the nonspace of the mind, clusters and constellations of data. Like city lights, receding."[125] But the technologies of the present will also leave us with their histories, and whatever forms they take, there is a good chance that they will look to many like a defective record that is better left behind. I hope that someone saves them anyway.

EPILOGUE
Looking Back at Mediums

I suffer from a nostalgia for the future. I am one of those people who works with computers, a ubiquitous trade within the information economy. I find myself missing systems, software, tools, and products before they are even gone. I miss them because I know that the ever-redoubling speed of digital technologies will render them obsolete in the blink of my too human eye. If I do not prepare myself emotionally for their absence even before the moment of their release, I will be less able to adjust to the immediate future that will regard them either as detritus or charming anachronisms. Only nostalgia for the future allows me the mental space to confront the convergence of digital technologies and cultural production.

PETER LUNENFELD, *SNAP TO GRID*

Before Walker Evans went to work for the U.S. government in the 1930s, he negotiated a higher salary and was given a new title to go with it, Information Specialist.[1] At the time, this job designation was no doubt the easiest way to explain to New Deal bureaucrats why the Department of Agriculture needed so many photographers on its payroll. It is also possible to imagine that the term appealed to Evans—the $400 raise notwithstanding—because it marked another way in which his straight photography and its modernist aesthetic could be distinguished from the late Victorian artistry of a previous generation, many of whom made pretty pictures with their gauze-draped lenses but never would be taken for producers of information. Recalling Alan Trachtenberg, we might say that Evans's tricky relationship to the dialectic between Alfred Stieglitz's "camera work" and Lewis Hine's "social work" is powerfully resolved by his time as an information specialist in the 1930s; Evans ended the decade having shot hundreds of pictures for the Farm Security Administration, but also having published *American Photographs* (1938), a "remarkable achievement," as Trachtenberg rightfully describes it, that demonstrated "a political art of the photograph" predicated on "social observation and critical intelligence."[2] Evans did not deploy photography on behalf of any overt "program of reform," but this affiliated his modernism more deeply with that of Eliot and Williams insofar as *American Photographs* "serves to recover a world of matter shaped by culture to human use—a fallen world of unredeemed . . . objects scattered in a fragmented landscape" (277).

The global economy of the twenty-first century is full of countless "information specialists," and it at once expects much less of them and much more. I, too, after all, may be described accurately—if not so flatteringly—as one of the "symbolic analysts" whom former secretary of labor Robert Reich places at the center of an American economy increasingly reliant on "people who manipulate information to solve problems."[3] Like other specialists in the information that is literary history, broadly construed, I also sometimes wonder just what problems I am supposed to solve by analyzing the systems that I do. No one has written more eloquently on these issues than Alan Liu, who points out that one thing "knowledge workers" in the humanities can do is "impose a 'lag' or 'slack' upon the just-in-time norms of postindustrialism," and so give more people a chance to realize how the "raw process of historicity" might better be acknowledged and assessed. If history feels like it is going faster—due in no small measure to the "frantic sequence of artistic modernisms, postmodernisms, and post-postmodernisms" that patterned culture in the twentieth century—the least that we can do is use the information at our disposal to slow it down and consider it more closely.[4] New media critic Peter Lunenfeld's idea of a "nostalgia for the future" makes for a suggestive parallel to Liu's desire for some "slack" in culture based on speed. Lunenfeld already can anticipate the obsolescence of the new technologies that surround him; to guard himself against the loss, he sees the latest computers or software as anachronisms, or worse, as garbage, "even before the moment of their release." Technology now moves so fast that we must imaginatively project ourselves ahead in time to have any chance of keeping up with innovations that are outdated as they are produced. Lunenfeld can indulge this fantasy of materialist fascination and retention only by discovering a different temporality of technological experience at the very core of our relationship to systems, software, and tools that the modern world demands we leave remorselessly behind.[5] As someone holding on to all the computers I have ever owned—my first Mac Plus is in the closet, along with all its subsequent replacements—I respond to his confession with sympathy and self-projection, or maybe just relief at finally having a condition to identify my symptom. This unwillingness to give up on our old mediums marks yet another way that "communications now are love," to return one last time to Karl Shapiro, and in just the manner he most feared.

That said, Lunenfeld's "nostalgia for the future" sounds too much like Fredric Jameson's "nostalgia for the present" to indulge it unselfconsciously.[6] I still have my Mac Plus, but I no longer use it (nor even know if it still works). Even such canny historical aesthetics as Lunenfeld's are prone to devolving into a far less compelling nostalgia for the past, which is to say, nostalgia plain and simple. For all Evans's genius as an information specialist, we can see this in an August 1953 photo-essay he published in *Fortune*, "Vintage Office Furniture." Devoted to what survives of "the grand old office trappings" of "commercial life through the nineteenth century," Evans's accompanying prose tries to be mordant but settles for melancholy: "Contemporary designers are perhaps the most triumphant group of professionals operating in the land today. They may alter the entire face of business in a matter of years now. When this happens, a photographic record like the collection on these pages will be wanted by historians."[7] Worn wooden filing cabinets, rolltop desks, disheveled papers, clocks with brass pendulums: the objects in these photographs are pictured because they depart from "the reasoned perfection" of modern office furniture (127). In this series, Evans also departs from the "perfection" of his familiar visual style and treatment of his medium. The focus is far softer than in any of his iconic images from the 1930s; the pictures have a warm, burnished glow, as if evoking the sepia tone of antique daguerreotypes. In one image, Evans lets the swinging pendulum of a clock blur with motion in a gesture that recalls Stieglitz at his most painterly. In another (fig. E.1), Evans captures a room in a Boston law firm as a virtual memory theater, or, as he puts it, "an accretion of atmosphere" (127). The walls are covered with old prints, none of which are clearly rendered. A military bust presides over a corner of the space, the only presence of a human figure save for the abandoned homburg sitting on a small desk near the door. It appears that we enjoy the view from a desk of our own— a picture frame, its image smudged to a white square, faces out to us, and the pens are angled for whoever occupies the large desk cropped by the near edge of the photo. This is also where Evans and his camera must be, which makes the artist himself into a version of this office's sad occupant: "Are there men in hiding who *like* their old desks: who think and work extremely well behind them (127)?" A picture of Evans from sometime in the 1950s (fig. E.2) situates him even nearer to the trash heap; curved and hunched over his camera, he is a weird mirror image of the rounded cylinder of the garbage can, and his posture as he looks into his viewfinder would be just as appropriate if he were peeking to see what rubbish has been "put here." By 1962 he is taking untitled

FIGURE E.1. Walker Evans, "An accretion of atmosphere in Boston: the law firm of Tyler & Reynolds." From the *Fortune* portfolio, "Vintage Office Furniture," August 1953. The Metropolitan Museum of Art, New York, Walker Evans Archive.

FIGURE E.2. Unknown Artist, "Walker Evans Photographing Trash Can," circa 1950. The Metropolitan Museum of Art, New York, Walker Evans Archive.

pictures of "street debris," which remains a favorite subject in his photographs from the early 1970s, when he also photographs the pull tabs from beer cans as they accumulate in his sink.

All this is to suggest that for exemplary modernists such as Walker Evans, there may have been a sense that something happened in the 1960s and 1970s that antiquated not only the constellation of aesthetics that had defined the most forward-looking artistic experiments of the first decades of the twentieth century but also the very mediums whose technical capacities were tested, provoked, and often beautifully confirmed by modernism as it was enshrined by artists and critics alike. This is a familiar story that needs no rehearsal here: suffice it to say that challenges to Clement Greenberg's modernism were already emerging at the moment when his prestige was greatest, and even as he was offering some of his most pugnacious delimitations of what should count as "Modernist" art (capitalized by Greenberg for the first time in 1960), there was ample evidence that many figures were determined to change the direction of Greenberg's emphasis on medium specificity and "self-criticism," and thus "subvert" the arts that he wanted to see entrenched "more firmly in [their areas] of competence."[8] Pop and minimalism inaugurate a nearly continuous "subversion" of modernist aesthetics in the visual arts, and there are parallels between their stylistic innovations and the postmodern literary sensibility that patterns the work of Thomas Pynchon, William Gaddis, John Barth, or Donald Barthelme, or that of Language poets such as Bruce Andrews and Charles Bernstein. These allusions are not meant to constitute an argument, but they do point toward a different way that artists and writers after the 1960s confronted their immersion in a world of media that the mediums of modernism seemed no longer able to accommodate. If modernism attempted to exploit the visceral immediacy it associated with high technologies and cutting-edge experiences of communication, the "information specialists" of Evans's artistic generation had every reason to feel anxious about a world that had so thoroughly incorporated a media aesthetic that it felt like common sense to treat art as just more data for delivery and distribution. In 1970 the Museum of Modern Art named its first major show of conceptual art "Information," which not only announced yet another network of styles and methods deeply antagonistic to the rhetoric of modernist medium-specificity but also rendered modernism's medium fetish just another subroutine for "symbolic analysts" to run and repeat.

Ed Ruscha presents an especially intriguing case for charting what happens to mediums within the information economy of art after modernism. Consider

Ruscha's artist's book *Records* from 1971. Consisting of thirty photographs of LPs and their covers—all from Ruscha's personal collection but photographed by a friend—we see each album cover on the left side of the page, matched to the black vinyl object it holds on the right (fig. E.3). The music itemized is a mix of soul, blues, jazz, rock, and country that is presented in no discernible order and hints at no encrypted narrative. Some of the sequencing invites more scrutiny, and the fact that this display of American popular culture begins with a compilation titled *18 King Size Rhythm and Blues Hits* and then proceeds directly to the Velvet Underground's *White Light/White Heat*, allows us to wonder whether Ruscha is suggesting that the influence of black music in America is indeed originary and "King Size"—even for such avant-gardists as Lou Reed and company. But following the Velvet Underground with Ray Price, Leon Russell, and a selection of Satie does not provide much leverage to extend his phantom logic further. The Rolling Stones' *Beggars Banquet* gives way to Otis Redding and Carla Thomas's *King and Queen*; Chuck Berry's *Concerto in B-Goode* comes just before Lesley Gore's *I'll Cry If I Want To*, but by this point, the alternation between black music and white seems little more than a brute binary opposition, as if 1s and 0s in a pure display of information that is itself a version of the book's minimalist fascination with alternating shapes—square then circle, square then circle. The effect is less to "remediate," as Bolter and Grusin would say, the sensuality that made music a modernist ideal than to call our attention to the randomness of Ruscha's exercise in bookkeeping. At only seven inches high and five inches wide, the pages bound behind the plain red cover reading *Records* are scaled for taking notes or tracking account balances, and the photographs cut these artifacts down to size in order to remind us how thoroughly they have been silenced. It is as if Ruscha's only interest in his "Records" is as examples of mass culture now re-produced as the expression of some invisible or arbitrary parameter that we can never know. In this respect, two of the most telling "records" in Ruscha's collection are Mason Williams's *Hand Made* and Linda Ronstadt's *Hand Sown*, which is the last LP in the book. But we look in vain to find some signature of the artist's direct or bodily engagement with the materials of a medium—Ruscha has not even taken these photos—and so come to understand instead that while we may admire the symbolic analysis, there is little "handiwork" left to praise.

Ruscha's next artist's book was titled *Colored People* (1972), and here the conceptual gamesmanship of *Records* becomes more overt. The photographs of *Colored People* depict cacti and other succulents native to Southern California. Though obviously predicated on a play of racial signifiers, Ruscha insisted

FIGURE E.3. Ed Ruscha, from *Records*. Photographs by Jerry McMillan. Heavy Industry Publications, 1971. Copyright © Ed Ruscha. Courtesy of Gagosian Gallery.

that the title reflected a growing interest in meaningless words, or was just a "dispassionate" designation that "the enclosed photographs [were] 'colored.'"⁹ Or as he put it in a 1973 interview, "the term 'Colored People,' the two words together, and the photographs of the cactus . . . my amusement with the whole project was being able to use them together thinking that they weren't really too similar."¹⁰ Just a few years after the Watts riots—which are perhaps sardonically invoked by Ruscha's painting *Los Angeles County Museum on Fire* (1965–68)— and near the height of the Black Power movement, it is hard to take Ruscha at his word that the "colored" in *Colored People* refers only to photography. With its anthropomorphizing title, we are asked to wonder why these figures are so prickly, and to realize that if we were to touch them without care, at least a little blood may spill. Of course, the politics of Ruscha's book might be far more straightforward: one should not judge a book by its cover, because "colored people," according to Ruscha, are never quite what one expects.

If we saw in Fitzgerald, Agee, or Sheeler that modernists were more than willing to think through the materiality of their mediums by what they imagined as the materiality of race, Ruscha offers instead a far more literal experiment with the everyday meanings of racial signifiers. Cacti are *not* colored people until they are labeled by Ruscha's assertive misrepresentation, which formally operates as metonymy—the artifice of juxtaposition is primary, and the relationship between the title words and the photos is aggressively contiguous— even as it conspires to suggest an absurdly metaphorical resemblance. We are close, then, to seeing language become what Derrida describes as "written syntagma," or sequential forms whose meaning is irreducibly indeterminate as they are reproduced in their "essential iterability" and "lose all possibility of function."¹¹ Ruscha's *Colored People* depends primarily on two mediums—language and photography—to confound the way that each would communicate something else entirely if left alone. "The medium itself is no longer identifiable as such," writes Jean Baudrillard in *Simulations*, in an idiom at once clichéd in its familiar postmodern posturing and yet still vital, I think, in the context of Ruscha: "it is now intangible, diffuse and diffracted in the real, and it can no longer even be said that the latter is distorted by it."¹²

A sense of both medium and race is so distorted and confused in Ruscha's 1972 pastel *Three Hanging Books* that their respective materialities—which modernism could imagine as powerfully analogous—are rendered as intellectual abstractions, or even empty variables in an equation that perhaps could only be contrived for us by an artist who imagined for himself an alter ego

FIGURE E.4.   Ed Ruscha, *Three Hanging Books*, 1972. Copyright © Ed Ruscha. Courtesy of Gagosian Gallery.

named "the Information Man" (fig. E.4). Or put more plainly, *Three Hanging Books* is an image that trades on the transmission of content from form to form as if the material were irrelevant. Commemorating his most concentrated period spent making artists' books, *Records* floats on a barely visible strand of monofilament, with a copy of *Colored People* on the right, and the back cover of 1971's *A Few Palm Trees* on the left. Ruscha had grown restless at the thought of further books, and the image announces, as a knowing joke, that he is ready to do what artists should—that is, produce flat objects that hang on walls for viewers to look at. But if at one level *Three Hanging Books* is a sophisticated play on "remediation"—a pastel drawing of books of photographs, and in the case of *Records*, of photographs of records and of the photographs on their covers—Ruscha also frames this radical diffusion of medium specificity within a more harrowing context. It is one thing, after all, to string up the "records" of your own artistic practice to show that a particular aesthetic has maybe run its course; but it is something else entirely to hang "colored people," and the nameless black thing suspended at the far left only makes for a more uneasy feeling that we are witness to a lynching, if only in the most impossible and mediated terms. The resemblance of *Three Hanging Books* to photographs depicting "colored people" as victims of white aggression is both absurd and irresistible: by piercing his subjects in their upper-left-hand corners, Ruscha renders their shapes elongated and more anthropomorphic; with their insides exposed and coming out for us to gaze at, they have been stripped of all their dignity; these books are as good as dead to Ruscha, and he wants us to know it. Yet even though I see all this in *Three Hanging Books*, I do not entirely believe it either. Race is as much attenuated as invoked, and rather than registering with the unlikely resonance of Nicole Diver's communicated blackness in *Tender Is the Night*, or with the startling directness of Sheeler's Aunt Mary, it is hard to say that Ruscha wants race to matter here at all. I see "colored people" hanging, violently transformed to things. Ruscha, if I were to guess, sees only floating signifiers. "You don't necessarily learn anything from my books," he stresses in an early interview. "I want absolutely neutral material."[13] Ruscha does not appeal to race to register his desire for a more visceral experience of his medium or because he needs to invoke the history of race to record the tensions within his own identity as an artist. Ruscha appeals to race because like any other "neutral material" that an artist after modernism uses, it does not mean anything at all.

"Is it natural that one medium should appropriate and exploit another?"[14] When Marshall McLuhan asks this question in 1967, it is not just rhetorical, but formulated to affirm the logic of the phenomena it observes. We have known the answer to it for almost half a century: "the 'content' of any medium is always another medium." But this first principle of media ecology, as McLuhan and others come to name this school of thought later in the 1970s, figures processes of translation and transposition that, even at their most structurally involved, cannot always account for all the ways in which "content" returns in the form of material that asks us to consider other messages that are just as certainly the mediums of history. Modernism, as this book has pursued its practices and implications, thus reminds us that surrendering to a medium does not necessarily mean a self-containing formalism that resists communication; indeed, modernism becomes more historically communicative the more completely it surrenders to its mediums and their particular aesthetics. The medium aesthetic of modernism is obviously no longer new, and perhaps no longer even operative in our contemporary culture of digital technologies and the computer, whose claim to be at last our "universal media machine," to invoke Lev Manovich, seems only to be getting stronger.[15] But if this is the case, it is just as true that modernism itself remains among the "accumulated media material" that digital culture, as Manovich observes, is "now busy reworking, recombining, and analyzing."[16] Which is also to say that while digital technologies, according to Kittler, may someday "carry off so-called humanity," and in so doing "render their own description impossible"—as printed words and pictures, voice and writing, sound and sense all give way to "data streams" and "unreadable rows of numbers"—we might remember, in the meantime, that "operating at their limits, even antiquated media become sensitive enough to register the signs and indices of a situation."[17] Here is one way of registering our own (fig. E.5).

Between 2003 and 2005, photographer Chris Jordan produced a series of images titled *Intolerable Beauty: Portraits of American Mass Consumption*, and this photograph, "Circuit Boards #2," is one of several devoted to the detritus of high technology, or "e-waste," as another picture describes the accumulation of wires, cables, keyboards, and other far more mysterious computer parts. This is not the only type of material that Jordan documents in its extreme profusion; there are photographs of cigarette butts, glass, lumber, shredded steel, oil drums, and crushed cars. But I am, for obvious reasons, drawn to his pictures of cell phones, diodes, circuit boards, and other bits of media, many of which he captures as they wait to be salvaged or recycled. A different media ecology, to be sure, but also one McLuhan anticipated in *Understanding Media*: "Technological media are staples or natural resources, exactly as are coal and cotton and oil" (161). Of course, what McLuhan is worried about here is the possibility that a society might run out of media technology, not that it will have so much that its raw materiality—tonnage, cubic volume, chemical composition—will inspire an anxiety and aesthetic all its own. "Nearly 250 million computers will become obsolete between 2004 and 2009," writes Elizabeth Royte, "or 136,000 *a day*."[18] Royte cites grisly statistics—it finally takes 1.8 tons of fossil fuels, water, and metal ores, for example, to make a desktop PC and monitor—and describes how "African and Asian nations are tearing up their lands" to supply copper, gold, silver, and palladium to computer manufacturers. She argues that there are inherent difficulties in recycling old electronics, many of which emit toxins that are prohibitively expensive to contain given the uncertain market for what can be eventually recovered.[19] After surveying the electronic wreckage, she wonders, "Maybe shoving the stuff in the basement or attic isn't such a bad idea after all."[20] Fredric Jameson once cautioned us that "history is what hurts";

FIGURE E.5. Chris Jordan, *Circuit Boards #2*, New Orleans, 2005. Copyright © Chris Jordan.

technology may be what accumulates—and just because we are always getting more and better versions of it, that doesn't mean the old has anywhere to go.[21]

The aesthetics that Jordan himself recycles in his work are appropriate for the materials at hand. He has acknowledged that Andreas Gursky's large-format color photographs—densely detailed images of repetitious forms (traders at the Chicago Mercantile Exchange, or rows of items at a 99 Cent store)—are an influence on his work, and we might consider Jordan's work as drawing also on Gursky's own teachers, Bernd and Hilla Becher, whose career-long photographic enterprise produced a series of famous books featuring relentlessly similar pictures of water towers, gas tanks, blast furnaces, and other artifacts of the industrial landscape of modernity.[22] On page after page in the Bechers' books, we see almost the same anonymous object or icon of technology, in straight black and white, facing the camera. Jordan's photography could hardly be said to show what one admiring critic of the Bechers' project describes as "the way in which it engages in the play of signification with diminished concern for its attachment to some properly material reality."[23] This language lets us see the Bechers and their books in the same cool light as Ruscha's *Records*, and guided by a similar detachment from the drama of the medium of photography (its essential dependence, as we saw in chapter 4, on "material reality") in favor of a more detached aesthetic of information. Jordan's work may function on this same post-industrial scale, but it also expresses an avowed environmental politics, and at times recalls a mode of impassioned documentary practice that is all but specific to photography. Like Evans himself in the 1930s, Jordan captures what is at once a "world of matter shaped by human use" and "objects scattered" across a wasteland of salvage yards, recycling centers, and landfills. And Evans is not the only modernist whom Jordan cannily evokes to help remind us—despite the already aging promises of a digital culture and its inclinations toward the fantastic immateriality of information—that we remain attached to "some properly material reality," whether we want to be or not.

Thus in their imposing size and scale—"Circuit Boards #2" is roughly four feet high and five feet wide, and other Jordan prints are positively cinematic— as well as in their density of visual information and all-over attention to the optical field within the frame, Jordan's photographs might also be considered inheritors of the modernism that Greenberg championed most loudly: abstract expressionism. Many of the photographs in Jordan's *Intolerable Beauty* sequence evoke, in their thickets and swirls of surface action and their layered, complex geometries and lines, Jackson Pollock's drip paintings of the late 1940s and 1950s—the ultimate achievement, for Greenberg, of modernism in America. It is not just that Jordan's photographs capture the all-over aesthetic of Pollock's abstraction by filling up the visual field with information to the limit of its capacity; Jordan's imagery also reminds us that Pollock himself was fond of making pictures that were full of garbage—nails, pennies, matches, the caps of paint tubes, and other pieces of "the debris of everyday life," as T. J. Clark observes. These raw materials, Clark points out, vanish when we view the paintings at a distance, and Jordan's photographs achieve a similar effect by operating, so to speak, at several different resolutions: if we look too closely, we might see nothing but visual noise and random detail; as we move farther away, the material itself comes into focus; but at still greater distances, the excess of it all becomes again a mystery of pattern and form. "Circuit Boards #2" is striking for its wealth of intricate detail; but if we step back and survey the wreckage, we see another force at work in the circling vortex that emerges from all these cast-off parts. To focus on the fact that there is too much information is perhaps to miss that we are already in the eye of the storm. Recalling Pollock's own erratic Freudianism and its broad influence in the period, one could even offer Jordan's photographs as re-imaginings of the primal, unconscious forces that abstract expressionism, according to its popular mythology, promised to both materialize and release—these are, after all, motherboards, from which flow all the information on our computer screens.

If this is, perhaps, a flighty parallel, let me point out another that is more tangible. Pollock often used industrial enamels and house paints—hardly innocent technologies in the postwar years of America's manufacturing supremacy and rapid suburban growth, and so there is a way in which, even as his canvases largely defer from representing anything directly, their materiality and historical location as artifacts remain encoded in the properties of their medium. Jordan's cell phone chargers, diodes, circuit boards, and e-waste are far more explicitly in communication with the economy that has produced them in such extreme abundance, charmed us with their effects, and then, inevitably, convinced us to get rid of them so that we can repeat the process. "The task of the modernist artist," Stanley Cavell once suggested, "is to find what it is his art finally depends upon." If "Circuit Boards #2" is taken as evidence, Jordan's art finally depends on finding ways to salvage both modernism and what comes after modernism with equally intense conviction; his photography may be processed and printed by computers, distributed on DVDs and posted on the Web, but it also recycles some of the twentieth-century aesthetics whose technologies have been this book's concern. Modernism as we knew it is not going to return. But the digital technologies that are the future also look a lot like history, and maybe there is still modernism enough to hunt us back to mediums that we have left behind. What we do with them next is another matter.

Notes

INTRODUCTION: "COMMUNICATIONS NOW ARE LOVE"

1. Karl Shapiro, *The Bourgeois Poet* (New York: Random House, 1964), 15–16. The prose poem I am quoting here is the fourteenth in the book's originally untitled sequence of poems. Shapiro gives it the title "The Funeral of Poetry" in later selections, and later anthologists have reproduced it with this title.

2. Walter Ong, S.J., *The Presence of the Word: Some Prolegomena for Culture and Religious History* (New Haven, Conn.: Yale University Press, 1967), 324.

3. Ibid., 11, 205. Marshall McLuhan, *Understanding Media: The Extensions of Man*, 2nd ed. (New York: Signet, 1964), 148, 146.

4. I discuss below the influence of McLuhan on contemporary media theorists such as Friedrich Kittler, Jay David Bolter, and Richard Grusin. As I also mention below, the fact that McLuhan was listed as a "patron saint" by *Wired* magazine testifies to his continuing appeal outside academic circles. McLuhan directed Ong's thesis at Saint Louis University, where McLuhan taught from 1937 to 1944. He spent the majority of his academic career at Catholic institutions.

5. Marshall McLuhan, *The Letters of Marshall McLuhan*, ed. Matie Molinaro, Corinne McLuhan, and William Toye (New York: Oxford University Press, 1987), 99, 280–281.

6. Ibid., 236.

7. Marshall McLuhan and Quentin Fiore, *The Medium Is the Massage: An Inventory of Effects* (New York: Bantam, 1967), 26.

8. Hugh Kenner, *The Poetry of Ezra Pound* (Norfolk, Conn.: New Directions, 1951), 10.

9. Ibid., 146, 51. Kenner's interests in technology, and especially design, also pay tribute to R. Buckminster Fuller. Fuller is cited throughout the book, and near the end Kenner describes a meeting between Pound and Fuller, shortly before Pound's death (559–560).

10. Ibid., 15. Kenner was not always this doctrinaire in his disregard for mass culture; if anything, he managed to find a great deal of popular culture that he admired. This early remark, then, is perhaps more indicative of modernist discourse generally than of Kenner and his own writings.

11. John Durham Peters, *Speaking Into the Air: A History of the Idea of Communication*, (Chicago: University of Chicago Press, 1999), 7.

12. "Marshall McLuhan—A Candid Conversation with the High Priest of Popcult and Metaphysician of Media," *Playboy* interview, in Eric McLuhan and Frank Zingrone, eds., *The Essential McLuhan*, 234 (New York: Basic Books, 1995).

13. McLuhan, *Understanding Media*, 162.

14. Peters, *Speaking Into the Air*, 22.

15. T. S. Eliot, "Tradition and the Individual Talent," in Frank Kermode, ed., *Selected Prose of T. S. Eliot*, 26–27 (San Diego: Harcourt Brace, 1975).

16. Ibid., 40.

17. Mark Wollaeger, *Modernism, Media, and Propaganda: British Narrative from 1900 to 1945* (Princeton, N.J.: Princeton University Press, 2006), 30. While concerned primarily with British figures, Wollaeger offers a compelling account of modernism's media ecology in respect to various forms of propaganda in the period that has been very helpful to me throughout this project.

18. Norbert Weiner, *Cybernetics: or Control and Communication in the Animal and the Machine*, 2nd ed. (Cambridge, Mass.: MIT Press, 1961), 161.

19. Claude E. Shannon and Warren Weaver, *The Mathematical Theory of Communication* (Urbana: University of Illinois Press, 1949), 95.

20. Katherine Hayles, *How We Became Posthuman: Virtual Bodies in Cybernetics, Literature, and Informatics* (Chicago: University of Chicago Press, 1999). See especially her illuminating chapter "Contesting for the Body of Information: The Macy Conferences on Cybernetics," 50–83.

21. Jurgen Ruesch and Gregory Bateson, *Communication: The Social Matrix of Psychiatry* (New York: Norton, 1951), 3.

22. James W. Carey, *Communication as Culture: Essays on Media and Society* (New York: Routledge, 1989), 201–204.

23. Henry David Thoreau, *Walden* (1854; Boston: Houghton Mifflin, 1960), 36.

24. Clement Greenberg, "Avant Garde and Kitsch," in *Critical Essays* (Boston: Beacon, 1961), 15.

25. Andreas Huyssen, *After the Great Divide: Modernism, Mass Culture, Postmodernism* (Bloomington: Indiana University Press, 1986), 53–55.

26. In addition to the aforementioned Hayles, see also Hayles, *Writing Machine*, designer Anne Burdick (Cambridge, Mass.: Mediawork/MIT Press, 2002); and Hayles, *My Mother Was a Computer: Digital Subjects and Literary Texts* (Chicago: University of Chicago Press, 2005). Both Mark B. N. Hansen and Brian Massumi have explored new media art and culture in theoretical frameworks drawn from Henri Bergson, Giles Deleuze, and Maurice Merleau-Ponty; their arguments implicitly and at times explicitly call into question the modernist aesthetic of medium specificity championed by Greenberg and other figures of interest here. See Hansen, *New Philosophy for New Media* (Cambridge, Mass.: MIT Press, 2004), and Massumi, *Parables for the Virtual* (Durham, N.C.: Duke University Press, 2002). Lev Manovich argues for a strong continuity between particular modernist projects—mainly Russian constructivism and experimental cinema—and contemporary digital culture. But he suggests that the influence of modernism is perceptible mainly in the way computers have rendered traditional distinctions between media irrelevant, thus achieving the dream of Dziga Vertov and other early-twentieth-century figures who tried to develop a cinematic style that pushed beyond the limits of the medium and toward a viewing experience more like what we would now call an "interface." See Manovich, *The Language of New Media* (Cambridge, Mass.: MIT Press, 2001).

27. McLuhan, *The Letters of Marshall McLuhan*, 504.

28. Clement Greenberg, "Modernist Painting," in John O'Brien, ed., *The Collected Essays and Criticism*, vol. 4, *Modernism with a Vengeance, 1957–1969*, 86 (Chicago: University of Chicago Press, 1993).

29. Rosalind Krauss, *"A Voyage on the North Sea": Art in the Age of the Post-Medium Condition* (New York: Thames and Hudson, 1999), 6.

30. Hansen, *New Philosophy for New Media*, 22, 21.

31. Friedrich A. Kittler, *Gramophone, Film, Typewriter*, trans. Geoffrey Winthrop-Young and Michael Wutz (Stanford, Calif.: Stanford University Press, 1999), 1.

32. Lev Manovich, *The Language of New Media* (Cambridge, Mass.: MIT Press, 2001), 47.

33. Jay David Bolter and Richard Grusin, *Remediation: Understanding New Media* (Cambridge, Mass.: MIT Press, 1999), 15.

34. McLuhan, *Understanding Media*, 23.

35. David Minter, "A Cultural History of the Modern American Novel, in Sacvan Bercovitch, gen. ed., *The Cambridge History of American Literature*, vol. 6, *Prose Writing, 1910–1950*, 120 (Cambridge, Eng.: Cambridge University Press, 2002).

36. Michael North, *Camera Works: Photography and the Twentieth-Century Word* (New York: Oxford University Press, 2005), v.

37. Marjorie Perloff, *Radical Artifice: Writing Poetry in the Age of Media* (Chicago: University of Chicago Press, 1991), 202.

38. Werner Sollors, "Ethnic Modernism," in Sacvan Bercovitch, gen. ed., *The Cambridge History of American Literature*, vol. 6, *Prose Writing, 1910–1950*, 551 (Cambridge, Eng.: Cambridge University Press, 2002).

39. Douglas Mao and Rebecca L. Walkowitz, "Introduction: Modernisms Bad and New," in Douglas Mao and Rebecca L. Walkowitz, eds., *Bad Modernisms*, 1–2 (Durham, N.C.: Duke University Press, 2006).

40. Kevin Kelly, "What Will Happen to Books?" *New York Times Magazine,* May 14, 2006, 44–49, 64, 71. Caleb Crain, "Twilight of the Books: What Will Life Be Like If People Stop Reading?" *New Yorker,* December 24, 2007.

41. Sven Birkerts, *The Gutenberg Elegies: The Fate of Reading in an Electronic Age* (Boston: Faber and Faber, 1994), 190.

42. Alan Liu, *The Laws of Cool: Knowledge Work and the Culture of Information* (Chicago: University of Chicago Press, 2004), 236.

43. Thomas Foster, *The Souls of Cyberfolk: Posthumanism as Vernacular Theory* (Minneapolis: University of Minnesota Press, 2005), 82.

44. Cory Doctorow, "Two-Person Teledildonic Rig," http://www.boingboing.net/2007/01/15/ twoperson-teledildon.html. "Teledildonics Advanced Again," http://gizmodo.com/ gadgets/gadgets/teledildonics-advanced-again-the-hug-shirt-220846.php.

45. Roland Barthes, *The Pleasure of the Text*, trans. Richard Miller (New York: Hill and Wang, 1975), 27.

46. Roland Barthes, *S/Z: An Essay*, trans. Richard Miller (New York: Hill and Wang, 1974), 132.

47. Adam Greenfield, *Everyware: The Dawning Age of Ubiquitous Computing* (Berkeley, Calif.: New Riders, 2006), 1.

48. Lisa Gitelman, *Always Already New: Media, History, and the Data of Culture* (Cambridge, Mass.: MIT Press, 2006), 11.

49. McLuhan, *Understanding Media*, 185.

50. Ibid., 23.

51. McLuhan, *Essential McLuhan*, 61.

52. In addition to the above-mentioned Cavell, see also his essay "A Matter of Meaning It," in *Must We Mean What We Say?* updated ed. (Cambridge, Eng.: Cambridge University Press, 2002), 213–237. Cavell here approaches the question of the medium in modernism by way of Michael Fried, whose most influential engagements with Greenberg's vocabulary of modernism in the late 1960s include "Shape as Form: Frank Stella's New Paintings" and "Art and Objecthood." These essays appear in Fried's *Art and Objecthood: Essays and Reviews* (Chicago: University of Chicago Press, 1998). See also T. J. Clark's "Clement Greenberg's Theory of Art," Fried's "How

Modernism Works: A Response to T. J. Clark," and Clark's "Arguments About Modernism: A Reply to Michael Fried," in Francis Frascina, ed., *Pollack and After: The Critical Debate*, 2nd ed. (New York: Routledge, 2000). This volume also features Rosalind Krauss's essay "Greenberg on Pollock" from her important book *The Optical Unconscious* (Cambridge, Mass.: An October Book/MIT Press, 1993). Thierry de Duve has also powerfully engaged with Greenberg's legacy; see his *Clement Greenberg Between the Lines*, trans. Brian Holmes (Paris: Éditions Dis Voir, 1996), and *Kant After Duchamp* (Cambridge, Mass.: An October Book/MIT Press, 1997). In her highly illuminating treatment of Greenberg, Caroline A. Jones examines Greenberg's stress on vision within a broader context of how his art criticism constitutes an examination of modern subjectivity; see *Eyesight Alone: Clement Greenberg's Modernism and the Bureaucratization of the Senses* (Chicago: University of Chicago Press, 2005).

53. Mark McGurl provides an insightful account of the novel's aspirations to artistic status in the modernist period; see *The Novel Art: Elevations of American Fiction After Henry James* (Princeton, N.J.: Princeton University Press, 2001).

54. Fredric Jameson, *Postmodernism, or, The Cultural Logic of Late Capitalism* (Durham, N.C.: Duke University Press, 1991), 162.

55. Fredric Jameson, *A Singular Modernity: Essay on the Ontology of the Present* (London: Verso, 2002), 154.

56. de Duve, *Clement Greenberg Between the Lines*, 53.

57. Hugh Kenner, *The Mechanic Muse* (New York: Oxford University Press, 1987), 10.

58. Kenneth Burke, *Language as Symbolic Action: Essays on Life, Literature, and Method* (Berkeley: University of California Press, 1966), 416.

59. Kittler, *Gramophone, Film, Typewriter*, xl.

60. For more on the "conduit metaphor" see Michael Reddy, "The Conduit Metaphor," in A. Ortony, ed., *Metaphor and Thought* (Oxford, Eng.: Oxford University Press, 1979).

61. McLuhan, *The Essential McLuhan*, 187.

62. Kittler, *Gramophone, Film, Typewriter*, xxxix.

63. Kenner, *The Mechanic Muse*, 9.

64. Rosalind Krauss, "'. . . And Then Turn Away?': An Essay on James Coleman," *October* (Summer 1997), 8.

65. J. M. Bernstein, *Against Voluptuous Bodies: Late Modernism and the Meaning of Painting* (Stanford, Calif.: Stanford University Press, 2006), 108.

66. McLuhan, *Understanding Media*, 238.

67. Ibid.

68. Henry James, "The American," in *Literary Criticism: French Writers, Other European Writers, The Prefaces to the New York Edition* (New York: Library of America, 1984), 1067. Subsequent citations internal.

69. William James, *Essays in Radical Empiricism* (Lincoln: University of Nebraska Press, 1996), 42.

70. Charles Horton Cooley, *Social Organization: A Study of the Larger Mind* (New York: Charles Scribner's Sons, 1927), 65. Subsequent citations internal.

71. Jameson, *A Singular Modernity*, 34.

72. Fredric Jameson, *The Geopolitical Aesthetic: Cinema and Space in the World System* (Bloomington: Indiana University Press, 1995), 11.

1. PLEASURE AT A DISTANCE IN HENRY JAMES AND OTHERS

1. This term is of course taken from the title of the second volume of Leon Edel's biography of James. See Edel, *Henry James: The Conquest of London: 1870–1881* (New York: Avon Books, 1962).

2. Henry James, *The Middle Years*, 1917, in Frederick W. Dupee, ed., *Henry James: Autobiography*, 548 (New York: Criterion Books, 1956). I will be drawing on passages found in pages 548–551 for the discussion immediately following. Subsequent internal citations to this text will be abbreviated as *MY*.

3. Though common enough in Jamesian criticism to go without citation, the "major phase" is a locution I am taking from F. O. Matthiessen, *Henry James: The Major Phase* (New York: Oxford University Press, 1944). For the full flowering of this periodization as a paradigm for understanding James—with "understanding" here meaning something more like "exalting"— see the last volume of Leon Edel's biography of James (*The Master: 1901–1916* [New York: Avon Books, 1972]). And though Edel and other earlier critics credit James's dictating with a radicalization of his style, it has been only in recent years that this shift in James's mode of composition has formed the basis of a categorical refiguring of his relationship to various phenomena of modernity. See in particular Sharon Cameron, *Thinking in Henry James* (Chicago: University of Chicago Press, 1989), and Mark Seltzer, *Bodies and Machines* (New York: Routledge, 1992), 47–90, 195–197, and "The Postal Unconscious," *Henry James Review* 21 (2000): 197–206. Also important to my arguments here is a growing body of work centering on James's "In the Cage," a story that has for obvious reasons—it tells of the romance, of sorts, between a telegraph operator and one of her upper-class customers—become central for questions concerning technology in Henry James. Excellent discussions of this story and its larger implications include: Pamela Thurschwell, "Henry James and Theodora Bosanquet: On the Typewriter, *In the Cage*, at the Ouija Board," *Textual Practice* 13, no.1 (Fall 1999): 5–23; and Richard Menke, "Telegraphic Realism: Henry James's *In the Cage*," *PMLA* 155, no. 5 (October 2000): 975–990. Other accounts of this story have also proven valuable to me given my concerns in this chapter, though these are less crucially interested in matters of technology: Dale M. Bauer and Andrew Lakritz, "Language, Class, and Sexuality in Henry James's 'In the

Cage,'" *New Orleans Review* 14, no. 3 (Fall 1987): 61–69; Jennifer Wicke, "Henry James's Second Wave," *Henry James Review* 10, no. 2 (Spring 1989): 146–151; Eric Savoy, "'In the Cage' and the Queer Effects of Gay History," *Novel: A Forum on Fiction* 28, no. 3 (Spring 1995): 284–307; Andrew J. Moody, "'The Harmless Pleasure of Knowing': Privacy in the Telegraph Office and Henry James's 'In the Cage,'" *Henry James Review* 16 (1995): 53–65; Jay Clayton, "The Voice of the Machine: Hazlitt, Hardy, James," in Jeffrey Masten, Peter Stallybrass, and Nancy Vickers, eds., *Language Machines: Technologies of Literary and Cultural Production* (New York: Routledge, 1997); Hugh Stevens, "Queer Henry in the Cage," in Jonathan Freedman, ed., *The Cambridge Companion to Henry James* (Cambridge, Eng.: Cambridge University Press, 1998); John Carlos Rowe, "Spectral Mechanics: Gender, Sexuality, and Work in *In the Cage*," in *The Other Henry James* (Durham, N.C.: Duke University Press, 1998), 155–180; Nicola Nixon, "The Reading Gaol of Henry James's *In the Cage*," *ELH* 66, no.1 (Spring 1999): 179–201.

4. See Bernhard Siegert, *Relays: Literature as an Epoch of the Postal System* (Stanford, Calif.: Stanford University Press, 1999), 207–264. I am indebted to David Halliburton for bringing this text to my attention while it was still in press.

5. Henry James, "In the Cage," 1898, in *Complete Stories, 1892–1898* (New York: Library of America, 1996), 844. Subsequent internal citations to stories from this volume will be abbreviated as *CS*.

6. Katherine Hayles, *My Mother Was a Computer* (Chicago: University of Chicago Press, 2005), 71.

7. Richard Menke, *Telegraphic Realism: Victorian Literature and Other Information Systems* (Stanford, Calif.: Stanford University Press, 2008), 198. I am greatly indebted to Menke's work for complicating and clarifying my own thinking about the James and media technologies. The James cited here is from "In the Cage," in *Complete Stories*, 847.

8. Marshall McLuhan, *Understanding Media*, 2nd ed. (New York: Signet, 1964), 219.

9. These figures are available from the University of Nebraska Press's "Calendar of the Letters of Henry James and Biographical Register of Henry James's Correspondents," http://james-calendar.unl.edu.

10. See Leon Edel, *The Treacherous Years: 1895–1901* (New York: Avon Books, 1969), 174–182; and also Edel, *The Master*, 90–95, 360–367.

11. Claude E. Shannon and Warren Weaver, *The Mathematical Theory of Communication* (Urbana: University of Illinois Press, 1949), 34–48.

12. *The Letters of Henry James*, vol. 4, *1895–1916*, ed. Leon Edel (Cambridge, Mass.: Belknap Press of Harvard University Press, 1984), 302. Subsequent internal citations to correspondence from Edel's edition will be abbreviated as *HJL*.

13. James's remarks here bring to mind Gerard Genette's discussion of narrative "duration" in his *Narrative Discourse: An Essay on Method*, trans. Jane E. Lewin (Ithaca, N.Y.: Cornell

University Press, 1980), 86–112. "No one can measure the duration of a narrative," Genette argues, because "[w]hat we spontaneously call such can be nothing more . . . than the time needed for reading; but it is too obvious that reading time varies according to particular circumstances, and that, unlike what happens in movies, or even in music, nothing here allows us to determine a 'normal' speed of execution" (86).

14. Richard Menke offers a powerful account of James's interest in the narrative figure of the thread in respect to his reading of Eliot's *Daniel Deronda*. Menke, *Telegraphic Realism*, 61.

15. Two critics demand special mention on the thematics of communication in James: Sharon Cameron and Mark Seltzer. See Cameron, *Thinking in Henry James*, and Seltzer, "The Postal Unconscious" and *Bodies and Machines*, 47–90, 195–197.

16. Henry James, *The Wings of the Dove* (1902; London: Penguin, 1986), 497; *The Golden Bowl* (1904; Oxford, Eng.: Oxford University Press, 1983), 452; *The Ambassadors* (1903; London: Penguin, 1986), 302–303. I am alluding to scenes no doubt familiar to many. In *The Wings of the Dove*, Merton brings Milly's last letter to Kate in book 10, chapters 4 and 5; at the end of chapter 5, Kate throws the letter, still sealed, into the fire. This is a scene I will discuss in greater detail in sections to come. Also worth noting here is Milly's grand mute gesture— "She had turned her face to the wall," Merton reports—upon his final, failed attempt to see her in Venice (456). Maggie's famous scene of negative accusation takes place in chapter 36 of *The Golden Bowl*, during an evening at Fawns including Adam Verver, Prince Amerigo, and the Assinghams. The gamesmanship of Maggie's rhetorical turn is emphasized by being situated within an evening given over to cards. Her actual statement to Charlotte is "I accuse you—I accuse you of nothing." And finally, Strether comes to this realization at the end of book 7 in *The Ambassadors*, soon after receiving a telegram informing him that Sarah, Jim, and Mamie have been dispatched to return both him and Chad to Woollett. As I will be making frequent reference to these texts, subsequent internal citations will be abbreviated as *WD*, *GB*, and *AM*, respectively. Also, while I am using the text of the first English edition of *The Golden Bowl*, from 1905, for *The Wings of the Dove* and *The Ambassadors*, I am referring to the New York Edition versions (1907) of these novels.

17. *Henry James: A Life in Letters*, ed. Philip Horne (New York: Viking, 1999), 211–213. Subsequent internal citations of correspondence from Horne's edition will be abbreviated as *LL*.

18. This is exactly the sort of language that made James ripe for the new historicist picking in the 1980s. I am thinking of Mark Seltzer's *Henry James and the Art of Power*, which offers *The Golden Bowl* as a primary example of how James's aesthetic subscribes entirely to forms of managerial discipline and control that thrive on the obscurity of authority itself. See "'The Vigilance of Care': Love and Power in *The Golden Bowl*," in *Henry James and the Art of Power* (Ithaca, N.Y.: Cornell University Press, 1982), 59–95. Interestingly enough, James then singles

out *The Golden Bowl* for marking a rare occasion when this style of narration is avoided. "I catch myself again shaking it off," he writes of his usual "manner" that relies on a personified observer, "and disavowing the pretence of it while I get down into the area and do my best to live and breathe and rub shoulders and converse with the persons engaged in the struggle" (*GB*, xlii). But a different form of mediation remains the objective: the preface ends by identifying "communication" as the objective of the work of art, and more, recommends reading out loud as the operative way of experiencing the text (*GB*, lix–lx).

19. Percy Lubbock, *The Craft of Fiction* (1921; New York: Viking, 1957), 149. All quotations from Lubbock are from a discussion found on 149–150 of this edition.

20. Henry James, *The American* (1876–1877; New York: Penguin Books, 1981), 114, 58.

21. Henry James, *The Tragic Muse* (1890; New York: Penguin Books, 1995), 167.

22. I discuss "ubiquitous computing" in the introduction as a model for the modernist experience of communication. For a thorough and illuminating treatment of this emerging field, see Adam Greenfield's *Everyware: The Dawning Age of Ubiquitous Computing* (Berkeley, Calif.: New Riders, 2006).

23. Jonathan Freedman, *Professions of Taste: Henry James, British Aestheticism, and Commodity Culture* (Stanford, Calif.: Stanford University Press, 1990). Freedman considers the three major novels in light of aestheticist discourse in his final chapter, 202–257; an especially valuable overview of James's career in this context is found in Freedman's first chapter. Also necessary to consider on this topic is Michael Moon's *A Small Boy and Others: Imitation and Initiation in American Culture from Henry James to Andy Warhol* (Durham, N.C.: Duke University Press, 1998). Moon reconstructs how both James's personal and literary styles were inflected by more flamboyant patterns of homosexual culture in England, and more, how many Americans who made the pilgrimage to meet the Master were struck immediately by the insinuations of his style and manners.

24. Maxwell Geismar, *Henry James and the Jacobites* (Boston: Houghton Mifflin, 1963), 221. Geismar's biographical verdict on James is as familiar as it is questionable: "the later James was obsessed by sex," but so frustrated by his latent homosexuality that his erotic energies were ever more displaced into the mannerisms of his style (238). That this claim is dubious, unprovable, and formally incoherent goes without saying, but Geismar does, I fear, deserve a measure of the credit for the current visibility of queer approaches to James. Geismar's phobic unleashing of James's homosexuality was perhaps the only way the topic could have been broached in 1963, and it has provided later critics an easy foil for infinitely more nuanced accounts of James's sexuality. At the same time, the strongly psychoanalytic work of Sedgwick and others often boils down to the same understanding of James's style as an artifact of sublimation and displacement.

25. Ibid., 202.

26. Roger Gard, ed., *Henry James: The Critical Heritage* (London: Routledge and Kegan Paul, 1968), 322.

27. Ibid., 340.

28. Ibid., 337.

29. An excellent overview of this topic is to be found in the compilation of essays *Cybersexualities: A Reader on Feminist Theory, Cyborgs, and Cyberspace*, ed. Jenny Wolmark (Edinburgh: Edinburgh University Press, 1999). Especially useful in this anthology is a reprint of Claudia Springer's "The Pleasure of the Interface," originally published in *Screen* (32, no. 3 [Autumn 1991]: 303–323). See also Allucquère Rosanne Stone, *The War of Desire and Technology at the Close of the Mechanical Age* (Cambridge, Mass.: MIT Press, 1995), and Sherry Turkle, *Life on the Screen: Identity in the Age of the Internet* (New York: Simon and Schuster, 1995). Of interest as well is Howard Rheingold, "Teledildonics and Beyond," in *Virtual Reality* (New York: Summit Books, 1991), 345–377. Two articles by Ellis Hanson have also been of immense help in clarifying certain issues relating to the "technologization" of sexuality and vice versa; see "The Telephone and Its Queerness," in Sue-Ellen Case, Philip Brett, and Susan Leigh Foster, eds., *Cruising the Performative: Interventions into the Representation of Ethnicity, Nationality, and Sexuality* (Bloomington: Indiana University Press, 1995), 34–58, and "Technology, Paranoia, and the Queer Voice," *Screen* 34, no. 2 (Summer 1993): 137–161.

30. Springer, "The Pleasure of the Interface," 307.

31. *Lightning Flashes and Electric Dashes: A Volume of Choice Telegraphic Literature, Humor, Fun, Wit & Wisdom* (New York: W. J. Johnston, Publisher, 1877). Subsequent internal citations to this text will be abbreviated as *LF*. There are two editions of this text, however, both published in 1877. The first, which I will be using for the most part, is shorter and, according to its preface, was aimed at a professional audience of telegraph operators and others in the industry. (W. J. Johnston published several trade journals in the field.) The second, which does add some material that will be of interest, was, according to its "Introductory," "intended for the general reading public—for people who have no knowledge whatever of the art or business of telegraphy."

32. The specific works I'm drawing on in the discussion that follows include: Mark Twain, "The Loves of Alonzo Fitz Clarence and Rosannah Ethelton" (1878), in *The Complete Short Stories of Mark Twain*, ed. Charles Neider (New York: Bantam Books, 1957), 127–143; Brander Matthews, "By Telephone," *The Century* 36, no. 2 (June 1888): 305–309; "The Careless Word," *Harper's New Monthly Magazine* 6, no. 34 (March 1853): 510–519; Charles Barnard, "————————[Kate]: An Electro-Mechanical Romance," *Scribner's Monthly Magazine* 10, no. 1 (May 1875): 37–46; (Capt.) Jack Crawford, "Carrie the Telegraph Girl: A Romance of the Cherokee Strip," *The Sentinel*, June 20, 1901; "The Thorsdale Telegraphs," *Harper's Monthly Magazine* (October 1876): 400–417. From the first edition of the anthology *Lightning Flashes*

and Electric Dashes: "Wives for Two; of Joe's Little Joke"; "Dangerous Christmas Courtship"; "Playing with Fire"; "A Slight Mistake"; "What Came of Being Caught in a Snow-Storm." From the second edition of this anthology: "Wooing by Wire." From Walter Polk Phillips, *Oakum Pickings: A Collection of Stories, Sketches, and Paragraphs Contributed from Time to Time to the Telegraphic and General Press* (New York: W. J. Johnston, Publisher, 1876): "Love and Lightning"; "Departed Days"; "Yank." From *Telegraphic Tales and Telegraphic History: A Popular Account of the Electric Telegraph—Its Uses, Extent, and Outgrowth* (New York: W. J. Johnston, Publisher, 1880): "Misplaced (Telegraphic) Affection"; "Married by Telegraph." And also, Charles Barnard, "Applied Science: A Love Story," in Charles Barnard, ed., *Knights of To-Day*, 120–208 (New York: Charles Scribner's Sons, 1881). As the inclusion of some of these titles might disclose, I do not see a strong distinction between stories centered on the telephone as opposed to the telegraph, although questions of voice are crucial in Twain and "By Telephone." A useful discussion of some later stories incorporating wireless and radio is found in Jeffrey Sconce, *Haunted Media: Electronic Presence from Telegraphy to Television* (Durham, N.C.: Duke University Press, 2000). Some of these later fictions include: Rudyard Kipling, "Wireless," in *Traffics and Discoveries* (London: Macmillan and Co, 1904), 213–239; Walter S. Hiatt, "Sparks of the Wireless," *Scribner's* (April 1914): 502–511; John Fleming Wilson, "Sparks," *McClure's Magazine* (May 1911): 140–154.

33. Roland Barthes, *S/Z: An Essay*, trans. Richard Miller (1970; New York: Hill and Wang, 1974), 78–79.

34. Taking the term also in its older sense of physical conveyance as well as information transfer, it is possible to enumerate: (1) Summerville preparing to mail a letter; (2) Eva reading a love letter; (3) the hearts of "love" moving through the telegraph wires; (4) Summerville signaling with his mustache; (5) Eva keying Morse on the windowsill; (6) the man behind Summerville reading a newspaper; (7) Eva's parents nonverbally "communicating" their displeasure through their worried observation; (8) the telegraphic Cupid; (9) Summerville handing a note to Eva as she walks through the turnstile; (10) the "communication" of all these railway passengers; (11) the riverboat in the bottom left vignette also "communicating" passengers and cargo.

35. This is the subtitle of the aforementioned *Relays*.

36. "A Centennial-Telegraphic Romance," 101.

37. Charles Barnard, "——— ——— ——: An Electro-Mechanical Romance," *Scribner's Monthly Magazine* 10, no. 1 (May 1875): 37–46.

38. For questions of embodiment and physicality in telegraphic fictions of the nineteenth century, see Katherine Stubbs, "Telegraphy's Corporeal Fictions," in Lisa Gitelman and Geoffrey B. Pingree, eds., *New Media, 1740–1915*, 91–111 (Cambridge, Mass.: MIT Press, 2003).

39. Ella Cheever Thayer, *Wired Love: A Romance of Dots and Dashes* (New York: W. J. Johnston, Publisher, 1880), 255–256. Subsequent internal citations will be abbreviated as *WL*.

40. The alphabetic play that patterns the relationship between Nattie and Clem brings to mind two other texts that are well worth considering in this context. In Goethe's *Elective Affinities*, a work that marks perhaps the first attempt to scientifically represent the technologies of love and desire, the dominant metaphors are drawn from the discourse of chemistry, botany, and architecture. Chemistry, for Goethe, involves a range of electromagnetic phenomena, and the Captain and Eduard, in trying to schematize the possible "affinities" within a closed system of desire, offer the following model for Charlotte in hopes of convincing her to summon (her niece) Ottilie from school:

> "Provided it does not seem pedantic," the Captain said, "I think I can briefly sum up in the language of signs. Imagine an A intimately united with a B, so that no force is able to sunder them; imagine a C likewise related to a D; now bring the two couples into contact: A will throw itself at D, C at B, without our being able to say which first deserted its partner, which first embraced the other's partner."

> "Now then!" Eduard interposed: "until we see all this with our own eyes, let us look on this formula as a metaphor from which we may extract a lesson we can apply immediately to ourselves. You, Charlotte, represent the A, and I represent your B; for in fact I do depend altogether on you and follow you as A follows B. The C is quite obviously the Captain, who for the moment is to some extent drawing me away from you. Now it is only fair that, if you are not to vanish into the limitless air, you must be provided with a D, and this D is unquestionably the charming little lady Ottilie, whose approaching presence you may no longer resist." (56)

This attempt to capture the symbolic essence of attraction and sexual connection is oddly echoed—I should say formally echoed—by the opening paragraphs of Alan Turing's seminal essay in cybernetic theory, "Computing Machinery and Intelligence." The first stages in the "Turing test," as we now know it, involve not the attempt to discriminate human from machine, but to discriminate man from woman. Turing describes a scenario that could provide the initial conditions for an experiment in "elective affinities," or for a melodrama of "wired love":

> The new form of the problem can be described in terms of a game which we call the "imitation game". It is played with three people, a man (A), a woman (B), and an interrogator

(C) who may be of either sex. The interrogator stays in a room apart from the other two. The object of the game for the interrogator is to determine which of the other two is the man and which is the woman. He knows them by labels X and Y, and at the end of the game he says either "X is A and Y is B" or "X is B and Y is A." (433)

Wired Love might be said to occupy a middle ground between these two dramas of love and information; but it will remain for some other occasion to pursue a full-fledged "cybernetics of romance." See Johann Wolfgang von Goethe, *Elective Affinities*, trans. R. J. Hollingdale (London: Penguin Books, 1971); Alan M. Turing, "Computing Machinery and Intelligence," *Mind: A Quarterly Review of Psychology and Philosophy* 59, no. 236 (October 1950): 433–460.

41. Stubbs, "Telegraphy's Corporeal Fictions," 102.

42. This passage in *Wired Love* anticipates a sequence in Abbott and Costello's *Who Done It?* Frustrated by a telephone operator who can't complete a call that might win several thousands in prize money, Costello aims a seltzer bottle at the mouthpiece and lets fly. We cut to the switchboard, where the operator is sprayed first in the face and then directly in her mouth. There is a charge of sexual violence to this moment, which is of course not apparent in *Wired Love*, but a similar fantasy of visceral communication is the ultimate effect.

43. For more on the emergence and development of female secretarial labor, see Margaret W. Davies, *Woman's Place Is at the Typewriter* (Philadelphia: Temple University Press, 1982); and Sharon Hartman, *Beyond the Typewriter: Gender, Class, and the Origins of Modern American Office Work* (Urbana: University of Illinois Press, 1992). Both of these works provide excellent overviews of the historical context in which the discussion could be placed. In drawing attention to an admittedly perverse set of meanings, I do not intend to slight the importance of this historical context nor to overlook the lack of agency that is strikingly apparent in these illustrations. Closer to my interests here, Pamela Thurschwell, in "Henry James and Theodora Bosanquet: On the Typewriter, *In the Cage*, at the Ouija Board," makes a series of brilliant arguments about the secretarial implications and workplace dynamics of James's "scene of writing" that have inspired me. More generally, this illustration serves as a wonderful example of the "discourse network" of 1900, as described by Friedrich Kittler. See especially *Discourse Networks, 1800/1900*, trans. Michael Metteer, with Chris Cullens (Stanford, Calif.: Stanford University Press, 1990), 347–368.

44. Niklas Luhmann, *Love as Passion: The Codification of Intimacy*, trans. Jeremy Gaines and Doris L. Jones (Stanford, Calif.: Stanford University Press, 1998), 136.

45. Ross Posnock, *The Trial of Curiosity* (Oxford, Eng.: Oxford University Press, 1991), 246.

46. *AM*, 37. For more on the implications of this comparison, see Ken Warren, *Black and White Strangers* (Chicago: University of Chicago Press, 1993).

47. See Mark Seltzer's aforementioned *Henry James and the Art of Power* and also Jennifer Wicke, *Advertising Fictions: Literature, Advertisement, and Social Reading* (New York: Columbia University Press, 1988).

48. Laurence Bedwell Holland, *The Expense of Vision: Essays on the Craft of Henry James* (Princeton, N.J.: Princeton University Press, 1964), 272, 230.

49. Kaja Silverman, *Male Subjectivity at the Margins* (New York: Routledge, 1992), 163, 167.

50. I take particular inspiration on these matters from Wendy Graham, whose work has illuminated the world of erotic options—as opposed to prohibitions—in which James seems to have lived. This is not to say that James's sexuality, and more importantly, the representation of sexuality in his work, is not a matter of occasionally tortuous displacements and occlusions. But it is also clearly the case that James was fluent in several dialects of sexual representation, and, as Graham argues, we are rewarded if we start with these, and their historical contexts, as opposed to feeling that James must first be extracted or saved from his own carefully wrought self-fashionings before we may say anything of substance about what, and how, sex signifies in his career. See Wendy Graham, *Henry James's Thwarted Love* (Stanford, Calif.: Stanford University Press, 1999).

51. See Harry Levin's introduction to *AM*, 12–13.

52. See Graham, *Henry James's Thwarted Love*, 8–51, and Freedman, *Professions of Taste*, 202–257.

53. In the New York Edition, some fifty pages separate the delivery of this telegram from the scene in which it is revealed to the reader—a span from book 2, chapter 7 to book 3, chapter 5.

54. Henry James, *The American*, 391. This language closes chapter 22 of the novel, in which Mrs. Bread tells Christopher Newman how Madame de Bellegarde killed her husband—information that provides Newman with the power he needs to overcome Mme. de Bellegarde's opposition to his marrying Claire. Mrs. Bread specifically gives him a letter, written by the dying Bellegarde, which operates at a high pitch of melodrama in its every rhetorical turn: "My wife has tried to kill me, and she has done it; I am dying, dying horribly. It is to marry my dear daughter to M. de Cintré. With all my soul I protest—I forbid it. I am not insane—ask the doctors, ask Mrs. B—. It was alone with me here, to-night; she attacked me and put me to death. It is murder, if murder ever was. Ask the doctors" (391). Of course Newman elects not to use the letter against the Bellegarde family, marking a certain resistance to conventional plots of communication even in this early and patently melodramatic narrative. For more on James and popular forms of melodrama, see Peter Brooks, *The Melodramatic Imagination: Balzac, Henry James, Melodrama, and the Mode of Excess* (New Haven, Conn.: Yale University Press, 1976), and also William Veeder, *Henry James: The Lessons of the Master: Popular Fictions and Personal Style in the Nineteenth Century* (Chicago: University of Chicago Press, 1975).

55. James R. Beniger, *The Control Revolution: Technological and Economic Origins of the Information Society* (Cambridge, Mass.: Harvard University Press, 1986).

56. Henry James, *The Portrait of a Lady* (1881; New York: Oxford University Press, 1981), 460.

57. Tom Gunning, *The Films of Fritz Lang: Allegories of Vision and Modernity* (London: BFI Publishing, 2000), 88.

58. *The Complete Notebooks of Henry James*, ed. Leon Edel and Lyall H. Powers (New York: Oxford University Press, 1987), 583–584.

59. Friedrich Kittler, *Gramophone, Film, Typewriter*, trans. Geoffrey Winthrop-Young and Michael Wutz (Stanford, Calif.: Stanford University Press, 1999), 216.

60. As Wendy Graham notes, the tenor of James's correspondence changes with the death of Andersen's brother, becoming more overtly erotic and suggestive. See *Henry James's Thwarted Love*, 47–49.

61. Edel cites Wharton's account, found in her *A Backward Glance*, of James's late fondness for Whitman and speculates that an affinity with the homoerotic elements of *Leaves of Grass* is to be partially credited for this change in James's tastes. See Edel, *The Master*, 255.

62. Graham, *Henry James's Thwarted Love*, 26.

2. LOVE AND NOISE

1. Herman Melville, *Pierre, Or, The Ambiguities*, in *Herman Melville: Pierre, Israel Potter, The Piazza Tales, ...*, ed. G. Thomas Tanselle (New York: Library of America, 1984), 103. The quotation I use in my first epigraph appears on pp. 297–298 of this edition. Subsequent citations to this text will be internal. My second epigraph is found on p. 173 of *Everybody's Autobiography* (Cambridge, Mass.: Exact Change, 1993; originally published by Random House in 1937). Subsequent internal citations to this text will be abbreviated as *EA*. I will also be making frequent reference to the following Stein texts: *The Autobiography of Alice B. Toklas*, in *The Selected Writings of Gertrude Stein*, ed. Carl Van Vechten (New York: Vintage Books, 1962), 1–237, internal citations abbreviated as *ABT*; *Lectures in America* (Boston: Beacon Press, 1985; originally published by Random House in 1935), internal citations abbreviated as *LA*.

2. Melville, *Pierre, Or, The Ambiguities*, 297.

3. Leo Braudy, *The Frenzy of Renown: Fame and its History* (New York: Oxford University Press, 1986), 506. Braudy describes the whole period of modernity, from the seventeenth century to the present, as participating in "the democratization of fame," a phrase with a special relevance for Melville in that his satire on celebrity is tied closely to his *political* satire at the expense of "Young America," a loose affiliation of expansionists and nationalists centered around the Democratic Party and active in the 1840s and 1850s. Melville thus excoriates a certain mode of the (print) culture industry by way of attacking a mode of radical democracy that also fell short of its advertising.

4. For more on how Stein's fame has engendered a fundamentally split critical response, see Catherine R. Stimpson, "Humanism and Its Freaks," *boundary 2*, nos. 12/3–13/1 (Spring/ Fall 1984): 301–319. Stimpson argues that most critics have focused on Stein's output either before *The Autobiography* or after; and more importantly, they have articulated absolute preferences for either an avant-garde or a popular Stein, with a popular Stein coming in a distant second.

5. Gertrude Stein. *Lectures in America* (Boston: Beacon Press, 1985; reprint of 1935 Modern Library edition), 177. A number of critics have done valuable work on the problem of "series production" in Stein, which is in part why I have slighted this topic here. See especially Friedrich A. Kittler, *Discourse Networks, 1800/1900*, trans. Michael Metteer with Chris Cullens (Stanford, Calif.: Stanford University Press, 1990), 225–229, and also Mark Seltzer, *Bodies and Machines* (New York: Routledge, 1992), for a general discussion of writing and its psycho-mechanics in American culture. From a much different perspective on Stein and mechanical reproduction, see Michael Davidson, "The Romance of Materiality: Gertrude Stein and the Aesthetic," in *Ghostlier Demarcations: Modern Poetry and the Material Word* (Berkeley, Calif.: University of California Press, 1997), 35–63. Davidson's account draws on classic discussions in Benjamin; Kittler and Seltzer both attend from a theoretical matrix of Lacan and Foucault, among others, and so push toward conclusions far removed from the latent (albeit negative) romanticism of the Frankfurt School. For a perspective on these issues that operates within a more traditional literary-historical framework, see Cecelia Tichi, *Shifting Gears: Technology, Literature, Culture in Modernist America* (Chapel Hill: University of North Carolina Press, 1987).

6. Marshall McLuhan, *Understanding Media*, 2nd ed. (New York: Signet, 1964), 259.

7. Garrett Stewart, *Between Film and Screen: Modernism's Photo Synthesis* (Chicago: University of Chicago Press, 1999), 266.

8. Clement Greenberg, "Towards a Newer Laocoön," in John O'Brien, ed., *The Collected Essays and Criticism*, vol. 1, *Perceptions and Judgements, 1939–1944)*, 86 (Chicago: University of Chicago Press, 1988). While Stewart does not refer to Greenberg, his engagement with Stanley Cavell's *The World Viewed* provides one possible explanation for how this particular strain of modernist medium specificity comes to reverberate in his work on film and photography.

9. Hugh Kenner, *The Pound Era* (Berkeley: University of California Press, 1971), 385.

10. Kittler, *Discourse Networks*, 229.

11. Ibid.

12. Important discussions that address the interrelation of form and gender in Gertrude Stein include Marianne DeKoven, *A Different Language: Gertrude Stein's Experimental Writing* (Madison: University of Wisconsin Press, 1983), and Lisa Ruddick, *Reading Gertrude Stein:*

Body, Text, Gnosis (Ithaca, N.Y.: Cornell University Press, 1990). Recent work by Priscilla Wald reads Gertrude Stein against the discourse and ideology of "Americanization" and marks a significant turn in Stein criticism, sustaining a concern for form and language within a self-consciously "new" historicist project and politics. See especially her "A 'Losing-Self Sense': *The Making of Americans* and the Anxiety of Identity," in *Constituting Americans: Cultural Anxiety and Narrative Form* (Durham, N.C.: Duke University Press, 1995), 237–298. A special issue of *Modern Fiction Studies* devoted to Gertrude Stein (vol. 42, no. 3, Fall 1996) also features a number of articles that offer revisionist interpretations of Stein and her cultural status; the category of "race" in Stein's work merits the most attention in this issue, which includes striking pieces from Charles Bernstein, Julie Abraham, and others.

13. Peter Nicholls, *Modernisms: A Literary Guide* (Berkeley: University of California Press, 1995), 202.

14. Susan McCabe, "'Delight in Dislocation': The Cinematic Modernism of Stein, Chaplin, and Man Ray," *Modernism/Modernity* 8, no. 3 (Fall 2001): 429, 430, 442.

15. Stanley Cavell, "A Matter of Meaning It," in *Must We Mean What We Say?* (1969; updated ed. Cambridge, Eng.: Cambridge University Press, 2002), 219.

16. Rem Koolhaas, *Delirious New York: A Retroactive Manifesto for Manhattan* (New York: Monacelli Press, 1994), 148.

17. Peter Applebome, "You Ought to Be in Pictures. Everyone Else Is These Days," *New York Times*, February 2, 1999.

18. I owe the phrase "operational aesthetic" to Neil Harris, from his classic discussion of P. T. Barnum in *Humbug: The Art of P. T. Barnum* (Boston: Little, Brown, 1973). And I use the term "attraction" here with particular reference to the work of Tom Gunning. In the most general sense, a "cinema of attractions" represents the sheer "harnessing of visibility" that narrative cinema modifies, represses, and otherwise enlists in the service of its various agendas—articulated most forcefully in film studies by psychoanalytic and feminist accounts of voyeurship. Two articles provide an excellent introduction to Gunning's groundbreaking work: "The Cinema of Attraction: Early Film, Its Spectator and the Avant-Garde," *Wide Angle* 8, no. 3–4 (1986): 63–70, and "'Now You See It, Now You Don't': The Temporality of the Cinema of Attractions," *Velvet Light Trap* 32 (Fall 1993): 3–12. Writing in the earlier piece, Gunning describes the cinema of attraction as a historical mode that savors "its ability to *show* something": "This is a cinema that displays its visibility, willing to rupture a self-enclosed fictional world for a chance to solicit the attention of the spectator" (64). And while cameo appearances are rarely put to avant-garde ends, they certainly represent what Gunning would call a "tamed attraction," a moment that recalls the sheer visuality of early film within the containment of narrative structure. See also Richard deCordova, *Picture Personalities: The Emergence of the Star System in America* (Urbana: University of Illinois Press, 1990), 1–21,

98–116; see also Miriam Hansen, *Babel and Babylon: Spectatorship in American Silent Film* (Cambridge, Mass.: Harvard University Press, 1991), 245–294.

19. Cameos date back to antiquity as a form of portraiture and visual representation. By the nineteenth century, however, the hand carving of cameos from precious or semiprecious stones had largely vanished, replaced in popularity by miniatures and then, of course, by photography. Generic cameos remained fashionable as jewelry throughout the nineteenth century, however, and to some extent, remain so to this very day. *The Oxford English Dictionary* dates the first use of "cameo" in the context of the theater to the middle of the nineteenth century, and it is this sense that expands in the twentieth to cover similar brief performances in film and on television.

20. Claude Lévi-Strauss, *The Savage Mind* (Chicago: University of Chicago Press, 1966), 23–24.

21. Tom Gunning, "The Cinema of Attraction: Early Film, Its Spectator and the Avant-Garde," *Wide Angle* 8, no. 3–4 (1986): 65. I discuss Gunning's notion of a "tamed" attraction in a previous footnote.

22. I am indebted to Scott Bukatman for pointing out that special subcategory of personality that seems to exist only to star as who they in fact are: Zsa Zsa Gabor, Charles Nelson Riley, etc. It is at this tawdriest level of celebrity that the strange "reality effect" of the cameo appearance becomes most apparent.

23. Susan Stewart, *On Longing: Narratives of the Miniature, the Gigantic, the Souvenir, the Collection* (Durham, N.C.: Duke University Press, 1993), 69.

24. Ibid., 68.

25. "Metro-Goldwyn-Mayer," *Fortune*, December 1932, 51.

26. Ibid., 114; Tino Ballio, *Grand Design: Hollywood as a Modern Business Enterprise, 1930–1939*, vol. 5 of *History of the American Cinema*, general ed. Charles Harpole (New York: Charles Scribner's Sons, 1993), 13–15; Thomas Schatz, *The Genius of the System: Hollywood Filmmaking in the Studio Era* (New York: Pantheon Books, 1988), 159.

27. Rudolph Arnheim, "Film Report (1933)," in *Film Essays and Criticism*, trans. Brenda Benthien (Madison: University of Wisconsin Press, 1997), 194.

28. See Walter Benn Michaels, *The Gold Standard and the Logic of Naturalism: American Literature at the Turn of the Century* (Berkeley: University of California Press), 1–28, 115–139, and Seltzer, *Bodies and Machines*, 80–90, and esp. 198–201.

29. Sara Blair, "Home Truths: Gertrude Stein, 27 Rue de Fleurus, and the Place of the Avant-Garde," *American Literary History* 12, no. 3 (Fall 2000): 420.

30. Bob Perelman, "Seeing What Gertrude Stein Means," in *The Trouble with Genius: Reading Pound, Joyce, Stein, and Zukofsky* (Berkeley: University of California Press, 1994), 45.

31. I am thinking in particular of the critical debates discussed by Stimpson in the aforementioned article on shifts in Stein's reputation. When, for example, a writer like Marianne

DeKoven, in *A Different Language*, suggests that Stein's productions of the thirties and forties were "conventionally written," a much larger dialectic between avant-garde and popular representation is invoked, and in the case of Stein, this dialectic has often been phrased as a narrative of declension—from experimentalist to co-opted "modern" author. Some of the best work on *The Autobiography* has concentrated on the matter of the genre itself as reformulated by Stein. See especially James Breslin, "Gertrude Stein and the Problems of Autobiography," in Michael J. Hoffman, ed., *Critical Essays on Gertrude Stein*, 149–159 (Boston: G. K. Hall). I am greatly indebted to Breslin's work on the text's first edition, as well as to his effort to engage with questions of what might be called the social poetics of Stein's writing and her perpetual inventiveness at the level of social representation, even when the linguistic surface of her late texts takes on a more comfortably conforming look.

32. Blair, "Home Truths," 433.

33. Mikhail Bakhtin, "Forms of Time and of the Chronotope in the Novel: Notes Toward a Historical Poetics," in *The Dialogic Imagination*, ed. Michael Holquist, trans. Caryl Emerson and Michael Holquist (Austin: University of Texas Press, 1981), 135.

34. Jennifer Ashton, "'Rose Is a Rose': Gertrude Stein and the Critique of Indeterminacy," *Modernism/Modernity* 9, no. 4 (Winter 2002): 582. Ashton makes a strong case against critics of Stein who argue that her poetics pave the way for contemporary Language writing; for Ashton, Stein's emphasis on intentionality and meaning is finally at odds with a poststructuralist understanding of language that stresses materiality as a limiting condition upon interpretation itself.

35. F. Scott Fitzgerald, *The Great Gatsby* (New York: Collier Books, 1991), 65–68.

36. For more on the relationship between Fitzgerald and Stein, see James R. Mellow, *Charmed Circle: Gertrude Stein and Company* (New York: Praeger), 275–276.

37. Marjorie Perloff, "'Grammar in Use': Wittgenstein/Gertrude Stein/Marinetti," in *Wittgenstein's Ladder: Poetic Language and the Strangeness of the Ordinary* (Chicago: University of Chicago Press, 1996), 98–99.

38. See Stephen Greenblatt, *Marvellous Possessions: The Wonder of the New World* (Chicago: University of Chicago Press, 1991), 5–7. See also his essay "Towards a Poetics of Culture," in H. Aram Veeser, ed., *The New Historicism*, 1–14 (New York: Routledge, 1989). For a useful discussion of these now "classical" statements of historicist method, see Alan Liu, "Local Transcendence: Cultural Criticism, Postmodernism, and the Romanticism of Detail," *Representations* 32 (Fall 1990): 75–113. Liu employs a language that is highly suggestive in considering the implicitly "technological" status of the text and of the archive in current critical theory.

39. David Shenk, *Data Smog: Surviving the Information Glut* (San Francisco: HarperSanFrancisco, 1998).

40. Michael Fried, "Art and Objecthood," in *Art and Objecthood: Essays and Reviews* (Chicago: University of Chicago Press, 1998), 155.

41. Joseph Frank, *The Widening Gyre: Crisis and Mastery in Modern Literature* (New Brunswick, N.J.: Rutgers University Press, 1963), 57.

42. Katherine Hayles, *Writing Machines* (Cambridge, Mass.: MIT Press, 2002), 22.

43. Kittler, *Discourse Networks*, 357.

44. See Breslin, "Gertrude Stein and the Problems of Autobiography," for a powerful explication of *The Autobiography*'s authorial gamesmanship and how the first edition's photographs are enlisted in this deep play. But to what extent this play was "real"—i.e., designed to convince a reader of Toklas's authorship—is another matter. Excerpts of *The Autobiography* appeared under Stein's name in the *Atlantic*, for example. It seems safe to say that the text was no *Primary Colors*, and that Stein's displaced authorship was often presented as just another performative dimension of her public personality, another way her "eccentricity" manifested itself.

45. Coburn had recently completed his work with Henry James on the photographic frontispieces for the complete "New York Edition" of James's writings. Coburn also made famous photographs of George Bernard Shaw and Ezra Pound, among others. His presence here marks a strategic insistence on Stein's part that her true status was visible long before the mere accident of a breakthrough public success.

46. Alex Woloch, *The One vs. the Many: Minor Characters and the Space of the Protagonist in the Novel* (Princeton, N.J.: Princeton University Press, 2003), 42. For calling this phrase to my attention, I am indebted to Alexander Nemerov's *Icons of Grief: Val Lewton's Home Front Pictures* (Berkeley: University of California Press, 2005).

47. Norman Bel Geddes, *Horizons* (New York: Little, Brown, 1932), 126–127. These remarks recall the famous declarations of Le Corbusier, "A house is a machine for living in," made in *Towards a New Architecture* (New York: Payson and Clarke, 1927).

48. Sigmund Freud. *Civilization and Its Discontents*, trans. James Strachey (New York: W. W. Norton, 1961), 38. I am indebted to Avital Ronell's *The Telephone Books* for bringing this passage to my attention.

49. Bell Telephone System advertisement, *Saturday Evening Post*, January 19, 1935, 43.

50. Stein herself gives an account of her unexpected writer's block in *Everybody's Autobiography*, 65–67. Many Stein biographies, including Mellow's, make reference to this period as a time of crisis in her writing; some critics, such as those Stimpson describes in aforementioned articles, believe this to be a crisis from which her writing never recovers, especially as an experimental project.

51. Upon the film's release, John Mosher in the *New Yorker* writes, "In spite of the brevity of her appearance, against what many a star would call ground odds, Garbo dominates the picture

entirely." Quoted in Michael Conway, Dion McGregor, and Mark Ricci, *The Complete Films of Greta Garbo* (New York: Citadel Press, 1991), 112.

52. The plot of *Der Letze Mann* involves an aging doorman (Emil Jennings) who is removed from his position of prominence when a manager comes to the mistaken conclusion that he can no longer manage the physical demands of the job. The loss of the stature associated with such an important role in the workings of a "grand hotel," here called the Atlantic, signals a widespread crisis in the man's family life as well. But in a staggering and arbitrary reversal—mandated by UFA—the doorman, now working in the washroom, is left a small fortune in return for a gesture of kindness, and at the end of the film he is seen enjoying a life of almost decadent privilege and indulgence.

53. *Der Letze Mann*, dirrected by F. W. Murnau. UFA, 1924.

54. The famous phrase from Marx is the starting point for Marshall Berman's *All That Is Solid Melts Into Air* (London: Verso, 1983).

55. The film ends with all of its main characters, with the exception of Crawford's Flaemmchen, facing some sort of implicit or explicit mortality: Preysing leaves under arrest for murder, perhaps to be executed for killing the Baron; Kringelein accompanies Flaemmchen for one last whirl of pleasure and spending before his illness takes its inevitable course; and though Grusinskaya remains unaware of the Baron's death at the film's conclusion, the viewer might well recall her earlier talk of suicide and wonder just what awaits her when she learns the truth. Thus the film's melodramatic architecture is securely structured.

56. Henry James. *The American Scene* (New York: Penguin, 1994), 78–81. Originally published in 1907, James's account of the Waldorf-Astoria remains of interest, especially in light of Koolhaas's cybernetic account of the "grand hotel." For James as well, the hotel offers a scene of information-in-motion, a representational environment in which the spectators' attempt to make sense is implicated in the space's attempt to make its impression.

57. James's experience of the Waldorf-Astoria is powerfully discussed by Ross Posnock in *The Trial of Curiosity: Henry James, William James, and the Challenge of Modernity* (New York: Oxford University Press, 1991), 250–284.

58. For a compelling discussion of *The American Scene*, see Mark Seltzer. *Henry James and the Art of Power* (Ithaca, N.Y.: Cornell University Press, 1984).

59. Donald Albrecht, *Designing Dreams: Modern Architecture in the Movies* (New York: Harper and Row in collaboration with the Museum of Modern Art, 1986), 138–142.

60. Northrop Frye, *Anatomy of Criticism* (Princeton, N.J.: Princeton University Press, 1957), 43. I should add that the aforementioned critical discussions of the telephone—Hanson, Gunning, Ronell—tend to emphasize the more "tragic" or "ironic" aspects of the technology.

61. Malcolm Willey and Stuart Rice, *Communication Agencies and Social Life* (New York: McGraw-Hill, 1933), 153.

62. For more on the role of the telephone in modernist Hollywood set design, see Albrecht's discussion of "Offices" on film in *Designing Dreams*, 123–133. I am indebted to this discussion for bringing this image from *Reaching for the Moon* to my attention.

63. Jean Baudrillard, *The Ecstasy of Communication*, trans. Bernard Schutze and Caroline Schutze (New York: Semiotext(e), 1987), 12.

64. The opening sequence of telephone calls establishes not just an array of character types but also a balance sheet of who has money and who needs money, and who has money but needs something else, i.e., Grusinskaya, represented by her secretary in this sequence. The various alignments between characters we witness as the narrative proceeds always refer back to the underlying economics established at the beginning of the film. But I would not enforce upon the film a strict materialist reading. Rather, I would say that the film imagines a particular zero-sum game of human pleasure and happiness, and tropes this game by constant references to the having and spending of money.

65. The *Oxford English Dictionary* entry for "network" acknowledges no use of this word as a verb until its 2nd edition; it there traces "network" as a verb back to the 1880s.

66. Terry Castle, *The Apparitional Lesbian: Female Homosexuality and Modern Culture* (New York: Columbia University Press, 1993), 9. The etymological evidence for this usage is somewhat slight; in the larger context of Stein's depiction in U.S. newspapers in 1934 and 1935, amid constant references to her "mannish" attire and to her "companion," Toklas, whom one reporter notes she calls "Pussy," I do think it more than possible that inciting curiosity about Stein's sexuality was accomplished by such reporting, whether intentional or not. In this, the press still lagged far behind *The Autobiography* itself. See also "Gertrude Stein Arrives and Baffles Reporters by Making Herself Clear," *New York Times*, October 25, 1934, and "Gertrude Stein, Home, Upholds Her Simplicity," *New York Herald Tribune*, October 25, 1934.

67. B. F. Skinner, "Has Gertrude Stein a Secret?" *Atlantic*, January 1934, 50–57. My favorite instance of a sexual suggestion about Stein in the press, however, is a sheer coincidence from 1969. On the same page as a *New York Times* article concerning the MOMA's acquisition of Stein's art collection (January 10, 1969), there is also an ad for Radley Metzger's *Therese and Isabelle*: "The Most Whispered About, The Most Talked About Motion Picture Of The Year." A blurb from *Cosmo* reads: "When the two girls get down to business, it is riveting." The ad makes explicit—in a classic soft-core sort of way—everything that isn't said when Toklas is referred to as Stein's "longtime companion" just a column to the left.

68. The conversation I'm imagining would involve the aforementioned texts by Terry Castle, D. A. Miller, and Eve Sedgwick, among others.

69. Stein elsewhere writes of the "peaceful penetration of the 'Oriental,'" signaling a shift to a modernity marked by the "Oriental mixing with the European" (22).

70. See my discussion of Ella Wilcox's *Wired Love* in chapter 1.

71. Alexander Walker, *Garbo: A Portrait, Authorized by Metro-Goldwyn-Mayer* (New York: Macmillan, 1980), 129.

72. For more on the sometimes odd sexuality of the telephone, see Ellis Hanson, "The Telephone and Its Queerness," in Sue-Ellen Case, Philip Brett, and Susan Leigh Foster, eds., *Cruising the Performative: Interventions Into the Representation of Ethnicity, Nationality, and Sexuality*, 34–58 (Bloomington: Indiana University Press, 1995), and also Avital Ronell, *The Telephone Book: Technology, Schizophrenia, Electric Speech* (Lincoln: University of Nebraska Press, 1989).

73. Michael Taussig, *Mimesis and Alterity: A Particular History of the Senses* (New York: Routledge, 1993), 213.

74. This formulation also patterns the text "Identity a Poem," which is constructed from different passages of *The Geographical History*. This text may be found in *A Stein Reader*, ed. Ulla E. Dydo (Evanston, Ill.: Northwestern University Press, 1993), 588–595. For more on this piece, see Charles Bernstein, "Stein's Identity," *Modern Fiction Studies* 42, no. 3 (Fall 1993): 485–488. For more on Stein and the way she uses the dog as a figure to express the paradox of identity, see Michael Trask, *Cruising Modernism: Class and Sexuality in American Literature and Social Thought* (Ithaca, N.Y.: Cornell University Press, 2003).

75. Bernstein. "Stein's Identity." 485.

76. Ibid., 488.

77. This is not a claim that I can make with full certainty, but it is a verifiable impression one gets from a recent pictorial biography of Stein assembled from various archival sources by Renate Stendhal (*Gertrude Stein in Words and Pictures* [London: Thames and Hudson, 1995]). For more on an American iconography of dogs, see Marjorie Garber, *Dog Love* (New York: Simon and Schuster, 1996).

78. See Catharine Stimpson, "Gertrude Stein and the Lesbian Lie," in Margo Culley, ed., *American Women's Autobiography: Fea(s)ts of Memory*, 152–166 (Madison, University of Wisconsin Press, 1992).

79. This passage from *A Long Gay Book* is found in Stein's lecture "The Gradual Making of *The Making of Americans*," (*LA*, 155–157).

80. I am thinking of the aforementioned essay "The Beast in the Jungle," by Eve Sedgwick, as well as a later essay, mainly on James's *The Wings of the Dove*, where she argues for a much more explicit reading of several passages in James as allegories of anal sex (see *Tendencies* (Durham, N.C.: Duke University Press, 1993). I say "allegories" in the technical sense: Sedgwick insists on a direct correspondence between a manner of syntax and an imagined bodily act.

81. Walter Benjamin, "The Work of Art in the Age of Mechanical Reproduction," in *Illuminations*, trans. Harry Zohn (New York: Schocken Books, 1968), 250. See also "On Some Motifs in

Baudelaire," 163–165. One might also compare this passage in Stein to related moments in George Simmel's famous essay "The Metropolis and Mental Life," in *On Individuality and Social Forms*, ed. Donald N. Levine (Chicago: University of Chicago Press, 1971), 324–339, for while Stein makes few remarks that address urban experience as such, she describes a modern psychology that has much in common with that posited by Simmel.

82. "Photograph, A Play in Five Acts," in *A Stein Reader*, 344.

83. *The Letters of Gertrude Stein and Carl Van Vechten, 1913–1946*, vol. 2, ed. Edward Burns (New York: Columbia University Press, 1986), 667.

84. The wartime activities of Faÿ continue to be a subject of debate, and while there is evidence, discussed in Mellow, *Charmed Circle*, of his intervention on behalf of Stein throughout the war, there is less evidence about what Stein herself knew of her protector's actions on her behalf.

3. SOUNDTRACKS: MODERNISM, FIDELITY, RACE

1. Pound's interest in music has been extensively discussed, especially since the publication of R. Murray Schafer, ed., *Ezra Pound and Music: The Complete Criticism* (New York: New Directions, 1977). More recently, Margaret Fisher's *Ezra Pound's Radio Operas* (Cambridge, Mass.: MIT Press, 2002) offers a fascinating and detailed account of Pound's *The Testament of François Villon* and *Calvacanti*. Pound returns to his famous trinity of poetic types (Melopoeia, Phanopoeia, Logopoeia) throughout his career; but his arguments in "How to Read" are particularly fascinating in this context. Here, Pound contends that "*melopoeia* can be appreciated by a foreigner with a sensitive ear, even though he be ignorant of the language in which the poem is written" (*The Literary Essays of Ezra Pound*, ed. T. S. Eliot [New York: New Directions, 1935], 15). One can hardly imagine a more extreme assertion of the sensuous, non-semantic experience of language. See "How to Read," in *The Literary Essays*, 15–40. Pound also rehearses his three Imagist dicta at various times after their initial formulation in 1913. Their appearance in 1916's *Gaudier-Brzeska* (New York: New Directions, 1970) is telling, given my interests, as here they allow Pound to describe an aesthetic of medium specificity that is evocative of Greenberg. Thus after returning to the Imagist stress on "the musical phrase," and conceding that "the arts have indeed 'some sort of common bond, some inter-recognition,'" Pound proceeds immediately to insist that works of the "first intensity" are those that, on the contrary, reveal that "certain emotions or subjects find their most appropriate expression in some one particular art" (83–84).

2. T. S. Eliot, "The Music of Poetry," in *The Selected Prose of T. S. Eliot*, ed. Frank Kermode (San Diego: Harcourt Brace, 1975), 109. For more on the pervasive fascination with black music and its influence on Harlem Renaissance writing, see Houston Baker, *Blues, Ideology, and Afro-American Literature: A Vernacular Theory* (Chicago: University of Chicago Press, 1984).

The continuing relevance of Baker's work can be tracked in many of the essays in the more recent collection *Music and the Racial Imagination*, ed. Ronald Radano and Philip V. Bohlman (Chicago: University of Chicago Press, 2000).

3. James Weldon Johnson, *God's Trombones: Seven Negro Sermons in Verse* (New York: Penguin, 1927), 8.

4. Walter Pater, *The Renaissance* (Oxford, Eng.: Oxford University Press, 1986), 86. For a highly instructive and valuable discussion of Pater's relationship to modernism, see Brad Bucknell, *Literary Modernism and Musical Aesthetics: Pater, Pound, Joyce, and Stein* (Cambridge, Eng.: Cambridge University Press, 2001). I have also learned much from the work of Daniel Albright, especially from *Untwisting the Serpent: Modernism in Music, Literature, and Other Arts* (Chicago: University of Chicago Press, 2000).

5. Clement Greenberg, "Towards Newer Laocoön," in John O'Brien, ed., *Clement Greenberg: The Collected Essays and Criticism*, vol. 1, *Perceptions and Judgments, 1939–1944*, 23–37, phrase quoted, 37 (Chicago: University of Chicago Press, 1986). Subsequent citations internal.

6. For another account of how late-nineteenth-century aestheticism shapes one version of early modernism in the novels of Henry James, see Jonathan Freedman, *Professions of Taste: Henry James, British Aestheticism, and Commodity Culture* (Stanford, Calif.: Stanford University Press, 1990).

7. Ellington is among the figures on whom Adorno heaps abuse in "On Jazz," which has rightly earned its reputation as a scabrous critique of popular music that reveals much about Adorno's tin ear for jazz. That said, Adorno's usefulness as a whipping boy for modernist elitism has, I think, run its course, and I am more interested in the ways in which his hostility to certain forms of sexual provocation in modern culture seems also to pay tribute to the appeal of affect and sensation, albeit reluctantly. Theodor Adorno, "On Jazz," in *Essays on Music*, ed. Richard Leppert, trans. Susan H. Gillespie et al. (Berkeley: University of California Press, 2002), 470–495. The translation of "On Jazz" in this collection is by Jamie Own Daniel, as modified by Richard Leppert. I have learned much from useful discussions of Adorno's writings on popular music and recorded sound by Thomas Y. Levin. See "For the Record: Adorno on Music in the Age of Its Technological Reproducibility," *October* 55 (Winter 1990): 23–47.

8. T. J. Clark, *Farewell to an Idea: Episodes from a History of Modernism* (New Haven, Conn.: Yale University Press, 1999), 158.

9. Gilbert Seldes, *The 7 Lively Arts* (Mineola, N.Y.: Dover, 2001), 57.

10. Constant Lambert, *Music Ho!: A Study of Music in Decline* (New York: Charles Scribner's Sons, 1934), 239.

11. Michael Fried, *Absorption and Theatricality: Painting and Beholder in the Age of Diderot* (Chicago: University of Chicago Press, 1980), 92.

12. In this regard, see Fried's discussion of such paintings as Gustave Courbet's *The Cellist* in *Courbet's Realism* (Chicago: University of Chicago Press, 1990), 83–84; or his account of Eakin's many images of music from *Realism, Writing, Disfiguration* (Chicago: University of Chicago Press, 1987), 3–89. Richard Lepperts treats the art-historical tradition of musical scenes in *The Sight of Sound: Music, Representation, and the History of the Body* (Berkeley: University of California Press, 1993). For more on the long tradition of associating music and its materiality with sexuality, see Judith A. Peraino, *Listening to the Sirens: Musical Technologies of Queer Identity from Homer to Hedwig* (Berkeley: University of California Press, 2006).

13. Theodor Adorno, "On the Fetish-Character in Music and the Regression of Listening," in *Essays on Music*, 295.

14. Ian Whitcomb, *Irving Berlin and Ragtime America* (London: Century, 1987), 81.

15. Edward A. Berlin, *King of Ragtime: Scott Joplin and His Era* (Oxford, Eng.: Oxford University Press, 1994), 210–212.

16. Seldes, *The 7 Lively Arts*, 73.

17. Theodor Adorno, "The Form of the Phonograph Record," trans. Thomas Y. Levin, in *Essays on Music*, 280.

18. Ralph Ellison, *Invisible Man* (New York: Vintage, 1952), 8. Subsequent citations internal.

19. Count Du Moncel, *The Telephone, the Microphone, and the Phonograph* (New York: Harper & Brothers, 1879), 242–243.

20. Mladen Dolar, *A Voice and Nothing More* (Cambridge, Mass.: MIT Press, 2006), 60.

21. Michel Chion, *The Voice in Cinema*, trans. Claudia Gorbman (New York: Columbia University Press, 1999), 18.

22. Ralph Ellison, *Living with Music: Ralph Ellison's Jazz Writings*, ed. Robert G. O'Meally (New York: Modern Library, 2002), 4.

23. These expressions of anxiety about an all-consuming passion for stereo technology are taken from Kier Keightley, "'"Turn it down!" she shrieked': Gender, Domestic Space, and High Fidelity, 1948–1959," *Popular Music* 15, no. 2 (1996): 162–163.

24. Jonathan Sterne, *The Audible Past: Cultural Origins of Sound Reproduction* (Durham, N.C.: Duke University Press, 2003), 225.

25. "Living with music today," Ellison writes in the last paragraph of the essay, "we find Mozart and Ellington, Kirsten Flagstad and Chippie Hill, William L. Dawson and Carl Orff all forming part of our regular fare. For all exalt life in rhythm and melody; all add to its significance" (14). This passage invokes something of the sentiment and style of Du Bois's famous assertion in *The Souls of Black Folk* that he sits "with Shakespeare and he winces not. Across the color line I move arm in arm with Balzac and Dumas, where smiling men and welcoming women glide in gilded halls." See Du Bois, *The Souls of Black Folk*, ed. Henry Louis Gates, Jr.,

and Terri Hulme Oliver (New York: Norton, 1999), 74. For both Ellison and Du Bois, culture emerges as a distinct domain of interracial accommodation and fellowship.

26. Alexander Weheliye, *Phonographies: Grooves in Sonic Afro-Modernity* (Durham, N.C.: Duke University Press, 2005), 122.

27. Sigmund Freud, "A Note Upon the 'Mystic Writing-Pad,'" in *General Psychological Theory* (New York: Collier, 1963), 207.

28. Theodor Adorno, "The Curves of the Needle," in *Essays on Music*, 273.

29. Christian Metz, "The Imaginary Signifier," in Philip Rosen, ed., *Narrative, Apparatus, Ideology*, 271–272 (New York: Columbia University Press, 1986).

30. Jürgen Habermas, "Reflections on Communicative Pathology," in *On the Pragmatics of Social Interaction: Preliminary Studies in the Theory of Communicative Action*, trans. Barbara Fuller (Cambridge, Mass.: MIT Press, 2001), 149.

31. Sigmund Spaeth, *At Home with Music* (Garden City, N.Y.: Doubleday, 1946), vii. This illustration is found facing page 270 in the text.

32. Isaac Goldberg, *George Gershwin: A Study in American Music*, supplemented by Edith Garson (New York: Frederick Ungar, 1958), 56. Goldberg published the first version of this work in 1931 and was planning a revised edition when he died in 1938. The majority of the 1958 text remains Goldberg's unchanged text of 1931, with Garson adding chapters that continue the narrative at the point where Goldberg had originally ended his account.

33. Juan Antonio Suárez, "T. S. Eliot's *The Waste Land*, the Gramophone, and the Modernist Discourse Network," *New Literary History* 32, no. 3 (Summer 2001): 757.

34. I take this phrase from Katherine Hayles; it provides the title for chapter 8 in her *How We Became Posthuman: Virtual Bodies in Cybernetics, Literature, and Informatics* (Chicago: University of Chicago Press, 1999), 192–221.

35. Arthur W. J. G. Ord-Hume provides an impressively detailed description of the player piano or pianola's technological development after the introduction of electrical recording mechanisms in *Pianola: The History of the Self-Playing Piano* (London: George Allen and Unwin, 1984), 155–172.

36. David Ewen, *The Story of George Gershwin* (New York: Henry Holt and Company, 1943).

37. Jeffrey Melnick, *A Right to Sing the Blues: African Americans, Jews, and American Popular Song* (Cambridge, Mass.: Harvard University Press, 1999); Michael Rogin, *Blackface, White Noise: Jewish Immigrants in the Hollywood Melting Pot* (Berkeley: University of California Press, 1996).

38. Bill Brown, "Reification, Reanimation, and the American Uncanny," *Critical Inquiry* 32 (Winter 2006): 183.

39. Stephen M. Best, *The Fugitive's Properties: Law and the Poetics of Possession* (Chicago: University of Chicago Press, 2004), 38.

40. As cited in Joel Dinerstein. *Swinging the Machine: Modernity, Technology, and African American Culture Between the World Wars* (Amherst: University of Massachusetts Press, 2003), 3.

41. Ibid., 53.

42. As cited in Rogin, *Blackface, White Noise*, 138.

43. Samuel Taylor Coleridge, *Poetical Works*, ed. Ernest Hartley Coleridge (New York: Oxford University Press, 1969), 100–101.

44. Willa Cather, *My Ántonia* (Boston: Houghton Mifflin, 1977), 116. Subsequent citations internal.

45. Brian Massumi, *Parables for the Virtual: Movement, Affect, Sensation* (Durham, N.C.: Duke University Press, 2002), 60.

46. Mark Seltzer, *Bodies and Machines* (New York: Routledge, 1992), 12–13.

47. As quoted in Geneva Handy Southall, *Blind Tom, the Black Pianist-Composer: Continually Enslaved* (Lanham, Md.: Scarecrow Press, 1999), 80–81. Southall is also the author of *Blind Tom: The Post–Civil War Enslavement of a Black Musical Genius* (Minneapolis: Challenge Productions, Inc., 1979). The latter details the several decades of legal wrangling that took place over the control of, and proceeds from, Tom's career once he was emancipated. The former reconstructs a great deal of the popular response to Blind Tom's performances and shows in particular how his status as a serious musician involved considerable traffic with highly theatrical displays of his abilities—displays that generated a certain amount of "Barnumesque" rhetoric and stylizing. Southall herself credits Richard Giannone for first tracing the character of Blind d'Arnault to Blind Tom. See his *Music in Willa Cather's Fiction* (Lincoln: University of Nebraska Press, 1968).

48. As quoted in Southall, *Blind Tom*, 81.

49. Best, *The Fugitive's Properties*, 59.

50. Michael Taussig, *Mimesis and Alterity: A Particular History of the Senses* (New York: Routledge, 1993), 208.

51. My thinking on Johnson has been aided greatly by the work of Katherine Biers. See her article "Syncope Fever: James Weldon Johnson and the Black Phonographic Voice," *Representations* 96 (Fall 2006): 99–125.

52. I borrow this phrase from Bruno Latour's *Laboratory Life: The Social Construction of Scientific Facts* (London: Sage, 1979).

53. James Weldon Johnson, *The Autobiography of an Ex-Coloured Man* (New York: Vintage Books, 1989), 99–100.

54. Hughes Panassié, *Hot Jazz: The Guide to Swing Music*, trans. Lyle and Eleanor Dowling (New York: M. Witmark and Sons, 1936), 20.

55. Cristina L. Ruotolo, "James Weldon Johnson and the Autobiography of an Ex-Colored Musician," *American Literature* 72, no. 2 (June 2000): 250.

56. Paul de Man, "Autobiography as De-Facement," in *The Rhetoric of Romanticism* (New York: Columbia University Press, 1984), 81.

57. Walter Benn Michaels, "Autobiography of an Ex-White Man: Why Race Is Not a Social Construction," *Transition* 7, no. 1, 127–128.

58. In *Along This Way* (New York: Penguin, 1990), Johnson recalls reading *Music and Some Highly Musical People* while still a boy, and the only names he singles out are Blind Tom and the Black Swan (51).

59. Michael North has a powerful reading of Johnson's own claims as a ragtime "originator" in *Camera Work: Photography and the Twentieth-Century Word* (New York: Oxford University Press, 2005), 180–181.

60. Tom Fletcher, *The Tom Fletcher Story: 100 Years of the Negro in Show Business* (New York: Burdge, 1954), 141, as cited in Edward A. Berlin, *Ragtime: A Musical and Cultural History* (Berkeley: University of California Press, 1980), 24; Whitcomb, *Irving Berlin and Ragtime America*, 100.

61. Berlin, *Ragtime*, 24.

62. Isidore Witmark and Isaac Goldberg, *From Ragtime to Swingtime: The Story of the House of Witmark* (New York: Lee Furman, 1939), 152.

63. LeRoi Jones (Amiri Baraka), *Blues People: Negro Music in White America* (New York: William Morrow, 1963), 110–111.

64. Ibid., 111.

65. Irene Castle, *Castles in the Air* (Garden City, N.Y.: Doubleday, 1958), 92.

66. My understanding of how Johnson gives us a version of Hegel's master-slave dialectic is informed by Richard Godden's powerful recasting of this formation in his *Fictions of Labor: William Faulkner and the South's Long Revolution* (Cambridge, Eng.: Cambridge University Press, 1997).

67. Jacques Attali, *Noise: The Political Economy of Music*, trans. Brian Massumi (Minneapolis: University of Minnesota Press, 1985), 32.

68. Cheryl Clarke, "Race, Homosocial Desire, and 'Mammon' in *Autobiography of an Ex-Coloured Man*," in George E. Haggerty and Bonnie Zimmerman, eds., *Professions of Desire: Lesbian and Gay Studies in Literature*, 93–94 (New York: Modern Language Association of America, 1995).

69. Arthur Loesser, *Men, Women, and Pianos: A Social History* (New York: Simon and Schuster, 1954), 607.

70. Cristina L. Ruotolo, "James Weldon Johnson and the Autobiography of an Ex-Colored Musician," *American Literature* 72, no. 2 (June 2000): 267.

71. My understanding of this scene has been informed by Michael North's aforementioned argument about Johnson. For North, the "final twist" of the ending underscores that the

narrator's "regret at having neglected his musical pursuits in favor of a life passed for white ignores the fact that the great subject of the musical theater of the time was in fact the very act of passing, literally and visually, or, in the borrowing of musical motifs, implictly and aurally." See *Camera Work*, 184.

72. Fredric Jameson, *A Singular Modernity: Essay on the Ontology of the Present* (London: Verso, 2002), 154.

73. F. Scott Fitzgerald, *The Beautiful and the Damned*, in *Novels and Stories, 1920–1922* (New York: Library of America, 2000), 441. Subsequent citations internal.

74. I am drawing here on two highly suggestive and imaginative essays on *The Great Gatsby* by Mitchell Breitwieser. The passages I cite are, respectively, taken from "Jazz Fractures: F. Scott Fitzgerald and Epochal Representation," *American Literary History* 12, no. 2 (Fall 2000): 368, and "*The Great Gatsby*: Grief, Jazz, and the Eye-Witness," *Arizona Quarterly* 47, no. 3 (Autumn 1991): 46.

75. Breitwieser, "*The Great Gatsby*: Grief, Jazz, and the Eye-Witness," 43; North, *Camera Work*, 43.

76. Walter Benjamin, *One Way Street and Other Writings*, trans. Edmund Jephcott (London: Verso, 1979), 349.

77. Rick Altman, *Silent Film Sound* (New York: Columbia University Press, 2004), 361–362.

78. I am thinking here of famous debates about orality and writing that are exemplified by such works as Walter Ong, *Orality and Literacy: The Technologizing of the Word* (New York: Methuen, 1988), and Jacques Derrida, *Of Grammatology*, trans. Gayatri Spivak (Baltimore: John Hopkins University Press, 1974). See also Garrett Stewart, *Reading Voices: Literature and the Phonotext* (Berkeley: University of California Press, 1990).

79. F. Scott Fitzgerald, "The Offshore Pirate," in *Novels and Stories, 1920–1922* (New York: Library of America, 2000), 72. Subsequent citations internal. I am indebted to Mark McGurl for calling this story to my attention.

80. F. Scott Fitzgerald, *Tender Is the Night* (New York: Scribner Paperback Fiction, 1985), 315. Subsequent citations internal.

81. Richard Dyer, *The Matter of Images: Essays on Representation* (London: Routledge, 1993), 160.

82. Matthew J. Bruccoli with Judith S. Baughman, *Reader's Companion to F. Scott Fitzgerald's Tender Is the Night* (Columbia: University of South Carolina Press, 1996), 108.

83. Niklas Luhmann, *Love as Passion: The Codification of Intimacy*, trans. Jeremy Gaines and Doris L. Jones (Stanford, Calif.: Stanford University Press, 1998), 124.

84. F. Scott Fitzgerald, *The Great Gatsby* (New York: Scribner, 1925), 12–13. In other words, I see Fitzgerald here associating the desperate romanticism that Gatsby represented *against* Tom Buchanan's nativism, with a version of that same nativism as shown by Dick.

85. Bruccoli and Baughman, *Reader's Companion to F. Scott Fitzgerald's Tender Is the Night*, 149.

86. See especially North's chapter on Fitzgerald in the aforementioned *Camera Works*.

87. Bruccoli and Baughman, *Reader's Companion to F. Scott Fitzgerald's Tender Is the Night*, 190–195. Bruccoli and Baughman compile a complete chronology of the novel's plot, starting with the birth of Dick Diver in 1889 and ending with the July 1929 conclusion.

88. Ibid., 137.

89. Arthur Freed and Nacio Herb Brown, "The Wedding of the Painted Doll" (San Francisco: Sherman, Clay and Co., 1929).

90. Donald Crafton, *The Talkies: American Cinema's Transition to Sound, 1926–1931*, vol. 4 of *History of American Cinema* (Berkeley: University of California Press, 1999), 236.

91. Ibid., 168.

92. For a fascinating discussion of the Steinach operation and its implications for modernist expression, see Tim Armstrong, *Modernism, Technology, and the Body: A Cultural Study* (Cambridge, Eng.: Cambridge University Press, 1998), 133–158. Widely discussed in the popular press of the period, many Steinach operations were little more than glorified vasectomies.

93. Greenberg, "Towards Newer Laocoön," 23, 31.

94. Richard Wright, *Uncle Tom's Children* (New York: Harper and Row, 1938), 106. Subsequent citations internal.

95. Sterne, *The Audible Past*, 251.

4. THE NEW PERMANENT RECORD

1. United States National Archives, *Second Annual Report of the Archivist of the United States, for the Fiscal Year Ending June 30, 1936* (Washington, D.C.: U.S. Government Printing Office, 1936), 40. Subsequent citations internal, abbreviated as "*Second.*"

2. United States National Archives, *Seventh Annual Report of the Archivist of the United States, for the Fiscal Year Ending June 30, 1941* (Washington, D.C.: U.S. Government Printing Office, 1941), 1. Subsequent citations internal, abbreviated as "*Seventh.*"

3. Lewis Hine, *Men at Work: Photographic Studies of Modern Men and Machines* (1932; New York: Dover Publications, 1977). For an exemplary reading of Hine's labor photography and its transformations over the course of his career, see Alan Trachtenberg, "Camera Work / Social Work," in *Reading American Photographs: Images as History, Mathew Brady to Walker Evans* (New York: Hill and Wang, 1989), 164–230.

4. Terry Smith, *Making the Modern: Industry, Art, and Design in America* (Chicago: University of Chicago Press, 1993), 283–328.

5. Ibid., 285.

6. Philip Johnson, foreword to *Machine Art*, 60th anniversary ed. (New York: Museum of Modern Art, 1994).

7. Ibid.

8. Katherine Hayles, *How We Became Posthuman: Virtual Bodies in Cybernetics, Literature, and Informatics* (Chicago: University of Chicago Press, 1999), 246.

9. William Carlos Williams, "Paterson," in *The Collected Poems of William Carlos Williams*, vol. 1, *1909–1939*, ed. A. Walton Litz and Christopher MacGowan (New York: New Directions, 1986). Subsequent citations internal, abbreviated as *CEP*.

10. Bill Brown, *A Sense of Things: The Object Matter of American Literature* (Chicago: University of Chicago Press, 2003), 8.

11. I am referring to Stewart's highly suggestive work *On Longing: Narratives of the Miniature, the Gigantic, the Souvenir, the Collection* (Durham, N.C.: Duke University Press, 1993). See especially "The Collection, Paradise of Consumption," 151–165.

12. United States National Archives, *Third Annual Report of the Archivist of the United States, for the Fiscal Year Ending June 30, 1937* (Washington, D.C.: U.S. Government Printing Office, 1937), 27.

13. Walter Benjamin, *Illuminations*, trans. Harry Zohn (New York: Schocken, 1968), 257–258.

14. For a comprehensive account of precisionism and its relationship to American culture, see *Precisionism in America, 1915–1941: Reordering Reality* (Montclair, N.J.: Montclair Art Museum, 1994).

15. Hugh Kenner, *A Homemade World: The American Modernist Writers* (New York: Knopf, 1975), 171, 83.

16. Marianne Moore, "Bowls," in *The Poems of Marianne Moore*, ed. Grace Schulman (New York: Viking, 2003), 154. Subsequent citations internal; abbreviated as *MM*.

17. Lisa M. Steinman, "The Precisionists and the Poets," in *Precisionism in America, 1915–1941*, 69.

18. Ellen Handy, "The Idea and the Fact: Painting, Photography, Film, Precisionists, and the Real World," in *Precisionism in America, 1915–1941*, 50.

19. Stanley Cavell, *The World Viewed: Reflections on the Ontology of Film,* enlarged ed. (Cambridge, Mass.: Harvard University Press, 1979), 102.

20. Beaumont Newhall, *The History of Photography, from 1839 to the Present*, rev. ed. (New York: Museum of Modern Art, 1982), 9.

21. Susan Sontag, *On Photography* (New York: Delta, 1977, 4; Roland Barthes, *Camera Lucida: Reflections on Photography*, trans. Richard Howard (New York: Hill and Wang, 1981), 80; Patrick Maynard, *The Engine of Visualization: Thinking Through Photography* (Ithaca, N.Y.: Cornell University Press, 1997), 3.

22. Barthes, *Camera Lucida*, 80.

23. Michael North, *Camera Work: Photography and the Twentieth-Century Word* (New York: Oxford University Press, 2005), 8.

24. Constance Rourke, *Charles Sheeler: Artist in the American Tradition* (New York: Harcourt, Brace, 1938), 85. Subsequent citations internal.

25. Louis Zukofsky, "Sincerity and Objectification, with Special Reference to the Work of Charles Reznikoff," *Poetry: A Magazine of Verse* 37, no. 5 (February 1931): 274.

26. Bill Viola, "The Porcupine and the Car," in Bill Viola and Robert Violette, eds., *Reasons for Knocking at an Empty House*, 59 (Cambridge, Mass.: MIT Press, 1995).

27. Van Wyck Brooks, "On Creating a Usable Past," 1918, in *Van Wyck Brooks: The Early Years*, ed. Claire Sprague (Boston: Northeastern University Press, 1993), 219–226.

28. Hayles, *How We Became Posthuman*, 193.

29. Lisa Gitelman, *Always Already New: Media, History, and the Data Culture* (Cambridge, Mass.: MIT Press, 2006), 127.

30. Katherine Hayles makes her call for "medium-specific analysis" in *Writing Machines* (Cambridge, Mass.: MIT Press, 2002), 18–29.

31. Benjamin, *Illuminations*, 255.

32. Jacques Derrida, *Archive Fever: A Freudian Impression*, trans. Eric Prenowitz (Chicago: University of Chicago Press, 1996), 16–17.

33. Jacques Derrida, *Limited Inc*, ed. Gerald Graff, trans. Jeffery Mehlman and Samuel Weber (Evanston, Ill.: Northwestern University Press, 1988), 20.

34. Ibid., 21.

35. Mark B. N. Hansen, *New Philosophy for New Media* (Cambridge, Mass.: MIT Press, 2004), 22.

36. Brian Massumi, *Parables for the Virtual: Movement, Affect, Sensation* (Durham, N.C.: Duke University Press, 2002), 35.

37. Hayles, *Writing Machines*, 33.

38. Ibid.

39. Alan Liu, "Transcendental Data: Toward a Cultural History and Aesthetics of the New Encoded Discourse," *Critical Inquiry* 31 (Autumn 2004): 62.

40. Vannevar Bush, "As We May Think," in Timothy Druckery, ed., *Electronic Culture: Technology and Visual Representation*, 45 (New York: Aperture, 1996). Bush's article originally appeared in the July 1945 issue of *Atlantic Monthly*.

41. Liu, "Transcendental Data," 58.

42. See Kenner, *A Homemade World*; Albert Gelpi, *A Coherent Splendor: The American Poetic Renaissance, 1910–1950* (New York: Cambridge University Press, 1987); Smith, *Making the Modern*; Wanda Corn, *The Great American Thing: Modern Art and National Identity, 1915–1935* (Berkeley: University of California Press, 1999).

43. Alfred Kazin, "America! America!" in *On Native Grounds: An Interpretation of Modern American Prose Literature* (1942; New York: Harcourt Brace, 1985), 487. Subsequent citations internal.

44. Barthes, *Camera Lucida*, 78. The literature on the ontology of the photographic image is both extensive and familiar; in addition to Barthes, see Sontag, *On Photography*, 153–156. An excellent survey of documents speaking to the historical and philosophical implications of photography is to be found in Alan Trachtenberg, ed., *Classic Essays on Photography* (New Haven, Conn.: Leete's Island Books, 1980).

45. Ezra Pound, *The Literary Essays of Ezra Pound*, ed. T. S. Eliot, as cited in the aforementioned Albert Gelpi, *A Coherent Splendor*, 176. As Gelpi points out, Pound conceived of these principles in collaboration with Richard Aldington and H.D. and had long since abandoned the "Imagist" tag by the 1930s.

46. George Oppen, *Collected Poems* (New York: New Directions, 1975), 9.

47. I am alluding here to Benjamin's essay "A Small History of Photography," from 1931. This is the title in its translation for *One Way Street and Other Writings*, trans. Kingsley Shorter (London: Verso, 1979), 240–257. This piece also appears quite often as "A Short History of Photography" or "A Brief History of Photography," depending on the translator.

48. This is the aforementioned Newhall, *The History of Photography*, 1982, the latest edition of Newhall's *History of Photography*, which was first issued as the catalog to the Museum of Modern Art's 1937 exhibition "Photography 1839–1937." Robert Taft's *Photography and the American Scene* (New York: Macmillan, 1938) also commemorates the centennial of the medium.

49. Kenner, *A Homemade World*, 171.

50. Marjorie Perloff, *Radical Artifice: Writing Poetry in the Age of Media* (Chicago: University of Chicago Press, 1991), 82.

51. W. J. T. Mitchell, *Picture Theory: Essays on Verbal and Visual Representation* (Chicago: University of Chicago Press, 1994). See especially his chapter "Ekphrasis and the Other," 151–181.

52. See Trachtenberg, *Reading American Photographs*, 79–80.

53. Roland Barthes, "The Third Meaning," in *Image-Music-Text*, trans. Stephen Heath (New York: Hill and Wang, 1977), 54.

54. Trachtenberg, *Reading American Photographs*, 230–232.

55. Lincoln Kirstein, "Photographs of America: Walker Evans," in Walker Evans, *American Photographs*, 190 (New York: Museum of Modern Art, 1938).

56. For more on Etienne-Jules Marey and his machine-gun camera, see Marta Braun, *Picturing Time: The Work of Etienne-Jules Marey (1830–1904)* (Chicago: University of Chicago Press, 1992). The Barthes quotation is from *Camera Lucida*, 92.

57. Charles Baudelaire, "The Modern Public and Photography," 1859, in Trachtenberg, *Classic Essays on Photography*, 88.

58. Oliver Wendell Holmes, "The Stereoscope and the Stereograph," *Atlantic Monthly*, June 1859, 747–748.

59. It is not for nothing that the "replicants" in Ridley Scott's *Blade Runner*, adapted from Philip K. Dick's novel *Do Androids Dream of Electric Sheep?*, are called "skin-jobs"; the film's androids are described as "more human than human," and it is this mimetic perfection that lies at the core of what makes "us" anxious about our status as persons.

60. Lewis Mumford, *Technics and Civilization* (San Diego: Harcourt, Brace, Jovanovich, 1934), 403, 417. Subsequent citations internal.

61. North, *Camera Work*, 31.

62. For more on Chase, and the modernist culture of efficiency captured in his writings, see Cecelia Tichi, *Shifting Gears: Technology, Literature, Culture in Modernist America* (Chapel Hill: University of North Carolina Press, 1987), particularly her chapter "Instability, Waste, Efficiency," 41–96. The striking word here is of course "perversions," which suggests the degree to which "waste," for Chase, figures as not just a problem of industrial engineering or labor economics but also one of misshapen and morally unsound desires. See his chapter "Wastes in Consumption, or Illth" in *The Tragedy of Waste*.

63. Antonio Gramsci, *Selections from the Prison Notebooks*, ed. and trans. Quintin Hoare and Geoffrey Nowell Smith (New York: International Publishers, 1971), 279–318.

64. Ezra Pound, *The Cantos* (New York: New Directions, 1973), 24. Subsequent citations internal.

65. William Carlos Williams, *Kora in Hell: Improvisations, Imaginations*, ed. Webster Schott (New York: New Directions, 1970), 46.

66. William Carlos Williams, *The Collected Poems of William Carlos Williams*, vol. 1, *1909–1939*, ed. A Walton Litz and Christopher MacGowan (New York: New Directions, 1986), 183.

67. William Carlos Williams, *In the American Grain* (New York: New Directions, 1925), 7. Williams is especially sympathetic—in a vein of sympathy marked everywhere by a deep Romantic racialism—to the plight of indigenous peoples who faced the Spanish conquistadors in the New World. See his chapter on Ponce de Leon, "The Fountain of Eternal Youth," 39–44.

68. Walt Whitman, *Leaves of Grass and Other Writings* (New York: Norton, 2002), 616.

69. Lev Manovich, "Database as a Genre of New Media," *AI & Society*, retrieved December 19, 2006, <http://time.arts.ucla.edu/AI_Society/manovich.html>.

70. Williams, *In the American Grain*, 39.

71. Ibid., 41.

72. Ibid., 74.

73. James Agee and Walker Evans, *Let Us Now Praise Famous Men* (1941; Boston: Houghton Mifflin, 1988), 234. Excellent readings of this landmark photo-text collaboration are found in Carol Schloss, *In Visible Light: Photography and the American Writer, 1840–1940* (New York: Oxford University Press, 1987), and also in Mitchell, *Picture Theory*.

74. Jeff Wall, "'Marks of Indifference': Aspects of Photography in, or as, Conceptual Art," in Douglas Fogle, ed., *The Last Picture Show: Artists Using Photography, 1960–1982*, 40 (Minneapolis: Walker Art Center, 2003).

75. For a very illuminating discussion of the ways in which photography was variously practiced as "art" or "social work," see Trachtenberg, *Reading American Photographs*. See especially his chapter on Alfred Stieglitz and Lewis Hine, "Camera Work / Social Work," 164–230.

76. Lincoln Kirstein, "Photographs of America: Walker Evans," in Walker Evans, *American Photographs*, 50th anniversary ed. (New York: Metropolitan Museum of Art, 1988), 196.

77. Agee and Evans, *Let Us Now Praise Famous Men*, xvi. Subsequent citations internal.

78. Peter Cosgrove, "Snapshots of the Absolute: Mediamachia in *Let Us Now Praise Famous Men*," *American Literature* 67, no. 2 (June 1995): 329.

79. Clement Greenberg, "Towards Newer Laocoön," in *Clement Greenberg: The Collected Essays and Criticism*, vol. 1, *Perceptions and Judgments, 1939–1944*, ed. John O'Brian (Chicago: University of Chicago Press, 1986), 32.

80. The complicated composition history of *Let Us Now Praise Famous Men* makes it hard to venture a more specific claim of influence; Agee began work on the text in the summer of 1936, and according a footnote in "(On the Porch: 2," this three-part sequence was written in 1937. But a later section of the text, "Intermission: *Conversation in the Lobby*," is a scabrous response to questions about the politics of writing posed by the *Partisan Review* in the summer of 1939. Greenberg's seminal essay "Avant-Garde and Kitsch" appeared in the next issue, and it is all but inconceivable that Agee would have missed it.

81. This passage may even be a nod to James insofar as it faintly echoes the New York edition preface to *The Ambassadors*: "There is the story of one's hero, and, thanks to the intimate connexion of things, the story of one's story itself." I discuss this dimension of James's style more fully in chapter 1.

82. Jay David Bolter and Richard Grusin, *Remediation: Understanding New Media* (Cambridge, Mass.: MIT Press, 1999), 55.

83. I am quoting Agee's remarks on naturalism from *Let Us Now Praise Famous Men*, 210; Jennifer L. Fleissner, *Women, Compulsion, Modernity: The Moment of American Naturalism* (Chicago: University of Chicago Press, 2004), 68, 72. Fleissner offers a powerful account of how problems of description pattern naturalism as both a literary mode and a discourse of gender in U.S. culture.

84. Bolter and Grusin, *Remediation*, 236; I have previously discussed this moment in McLuhan's *Understanding Media* in chapter 3.

85. For an excellent discussion of how the example of Duchamp complicates the model of modernism pursued by Greenberg, see Thierry de Duve's *Kant After Duchamp* (Cambridge,

Mass.: MIT Press, 1997); see especially his chapter, "The Monochrome and the Blank Canvas," 199–279.

86. Michael Fried, "Art and Objecthood," in *Art and Objecthood: Essays and Reviews* (Chicago: University of Chicago Press, 1998), 165.

87. For more on how Agee's professional status and political sentiments pattern his particular modernism in *Let Us Now Praise Famous Men*, see Michael Szalay, *New Deal Modernism: American Literature and the Invention of the Welfare State* (Durham, N.C.: Duke University Press, 2000), 24–27.

88. Fleissner, *Women, Compulsion, Modernity*, 68; Agee, *Let Us Now Praise Famous Men*, 210, 211.

89. Svetlana Alpers, *The Art of Describing: Dutch Art in the Seventeenth Century* (Chicago: University of Chicago Press, 1983), 30.

90. H. W. Fowler, *A Dictionary of Modern English Usage* (Oxford, Eng.: Oxford University Press, 1926), 569.

91. Williams, *Collected Poems, 1909–1939*, 269, 325.

92. Works Progress Administration, "Sample Press Release," *Index of American Design Manual, W. P. A. Technical Series, Art Circular No. 3* (Washington, D.C.: Federal Art Project, 1938).

93. F. O. Matthiessen, *American Renaissance: Art and Expression in the Age of Emerson and Whitman* (New York: Oxford University Press, 1941), vii.

94. Michael Fried first addressed the implications of such scenes in his *Absorption and Theatricality: Painting and the Beholder in the Age of Diderot* (Chicago: University of Chicago Press, 1980). He has frequently returned to this topic in subsequent works, most recently in a provocative article on photography, "Barthes's *Punctum*," *Critical Inquiry* 31 (Spring 2005): 539–574. Among the images he discusses, Jeff Wall's *Adrian Walker, Artist, Drawing from a Specimen in a Laboratory in the Dept. of Anatomy at the University of British Columbia, Vancouver* provides an especially suggestive analog to this Index photograph.

95. Archibald MacLeish, "Unemployed Arts," *Fortune* (May 1937). No page numbers available; clipping found in Index of American Design Archives, National Gallery, Washington, D.C.

96. Untitled item from the *New Yorker*, September 23, 1936. Clipping found in Index of American Design Archives, National Gallery, Washington, D.C.

97. Albert J. Glassgold, "Color Microfilm Studies of the Index of American Design," memo, April 7, 1939, Index of American Design Archives, National Gallery, Washington, D.C.

98. *Index of American Design Manual*, W. P. A. Technical Series Art Circular No. 2 (October 15, 1937), 24–25.

99. Clarence Hornung, preface to *Treasury of American Design and Antiques* (New York: Harry N. Abrams, 1997), xiii.

100. "Summary of Typical Ten-Minute Speech for Index of American Design," typescript, Index of American Design Archives, National Gallery, Washington, D.C.

101. Constance Rourke, "Index of American Design," *Magazine of Art* 30, no. 4 (April 1937). Clipping found in Index of American Design Archives, National Gallery, Washington, D.C.

102. Clarence Hornung, preface to *Treasury of American Design and Antiques*, xxiii, xvii, xxiii.

103. MacLeish, "Unemployed Arts."

104. Virginia Tuttle Clayton, "Picturing a 'Usable Past,'" in Virginia Tuttle Clayton, Elizabeth Stillinger, Erika Doss, and Deborah Chotner, *Drawing on America's Past: Folk Art, Modernism, and the Index of American Design*, 1(Washington, D.C.: National Gallery of Art, 2002).

105. *Index of American Design Manual*, W. P. A. Technical Series Art Circular No. 2 (October 15, 1937), 26–28.

106. See Robert von Hallberg, "The Politics of Description: W. C. Williams in the Thirties," *ELH* 45 (1978): 131–151.

107. Corn, *The Great American Thing*, 334, 337.

108. Clayton, "Picturing a 'Usable Past,'" 22–23.

109. Erika Doss, "American Folk Art's 'Distinctive Character': The Index of American Design and New Deal Notions of Cultural Nationalism," in *Drawing on America's Past: Folk Art, Modernism, and the Index of American Design* (Washington, D.C.: National Gallery of Art, 2002), 71.

110. Sheeler was featured in an NBC program titled "Art in Our Time" that was broadcast at the Museum of Modern Art on October 6, 1939. For information on this program, I am indebted to Charles Brock, *Charles Sheeler: Across Media* (Washington, D.C.: National Gallery of Art, 2006), 173.

111. For more on Sheeler's work at Ford, see Smith, *Making the Modern*, 93–136.

112. *The Williamsburg Restoration: A Brief Review of the Plan, Purpose, and Policy of the Williamsburg Restoration . . .* , (Colonial Williamsburg, Inc., 1933), 5–6.

113. "Sheeler Finds Beauty in the Commonplace: Classic Form and Function Interest This Artist Most," *Life*, August 8, 1938, 42.

114. Williams, *In the American Grain*, 45, 138, 187, 211. We might also think of the figure of Elsie in Williams's poem, "The pure products of America . . . ," as well as many more instances in the canon of U.S. modernism, including Faulkner's Dilsey in *The Sound and the Fury*.

115. Barthes, *Camera Lucida*, 35–36. I am indebted to the Michael Fried article cited above for helping to clarify the connection between race and form in Sheeler's photograph of Aunt Mary.

116. Mark B. N. Hansen, "Digitizing the Racialized Body, or, the Politics of Common Impropriety," in *Bodies in Code: Interfaces with Digital Media* (New York: Routledge, 2006), 155–156. I am drawing here on Hansen's useful discussion of Frantz Fanon in the context of new media art projects concerned with race.

117. William Carlos Williams, introduction to *Charles Sheeler* (New York: Metropolitan Museum of Modern Art, 1939), 6.

118. Cavell, *The World Viewed*, 105.

119. William Carlos Williams, introduction to *Charles Sheeler* (New York: Metropolitan Museum of Modern Art, 1939), 9.

120. Clement Greenberg, "Seminar Six," as quoted in Thierry de Duve, *Clement Greenberg Between the Lines* (Paris: Éditions Dis Voir, 1996), 106.

121. Clement Greenberg, "Modernist Painting," in *The Collected Essays and Criticism*, vol. 4, *Modernism with a Vengeance*, ed. John O'Brian (Chicago: University of Chicago Press, 1993), 86.

122. Williams, *The Collected Poems*, vol. 1, *1909–1939*, 455.

123. I am thinking in particular of the work of R. W. B. Lewis (*American Adam*) and Henry Nash Smith (*Virgin Land*).

124. Greenberg, "Towards Newer Laocoön," 34.

125. This is William Gibson's famous image of the "matrix" of cyberspace from *Neuromancer* (New York: Ace, 1984), 51.

EPILOGUE: LOOKING BACK AT MEDIUMS

1. Maria Morris Hambourg, "A Portrait of the Artist," in Jeff L. Rosenheim, Maria Morris Hambourg, Douglas Eklund, and Mia Fineman, *Walker Evans* (New York: Metropolitan Museum of Art, 2000), 73–74.

2. Alan Trachtenberg, *Reading American Photographs: Images as History, Mathew Brady to Walker Evans* (New York: Hill and Wang, 1989), 235, 285.

3. Tony Bingham and Pat Galagan, "Preparing the Work Force: An Interview with Robert B. Reich," *CareerJournal.com*, retrieved April 4, 2007, from http://www.careerjournal.com/hrcenter/astd/features/20060926-astd.html.

4. Alan Liu, *The Laws of Cool: Knowledge Work and the Culture of Information* (Chicago: University of Chicago Press, 2004), 381.

5. Peter Lunenfeld, *Snap to Grid: A User's Guide to Digital Arts, Media, and Cultures* (Cambridge, Mass.: MIT Press, 2000), 27.

6. Fredric Jameson, *Postmodernism or, The Cultural Logic of Late Capitalism* (Durham, N.C.: Duke University Press, 1991), 279. This resonant phrase is the title for Jameson's chapter on film.

7. This *Fortune* feature is reproduced in Walker Evans, *Unclassified: A Walker Evans Anthology* (New York: Metropolitan Museum of Art, 2000), 127.

8. Clement Greenberg, "Modernist Painting," in *The Collected Essays and Criticism*, vol. 4, *Modernism with a Vengeance*, ed. John O'Brian (Chicago: University of Chicago Press, 1993), 85.

9. Richard D. Marshall, *Ed Ruscha* (London: Phaidon Press, 2003), 62.

10. This is Ruscha in an interview with Howardena Pindell, titled "Words with Ruscha," *Print Collector's Newsletter*, January/February, 1973; as quoted in Marshall, *Ed Ruscha*, 62.

11. Jacques Derrida, "Signature Event Context," in *Limited Inc* (Evanston, Ill.: Northwestern University Press, 1988), 9.

12. Jean Baudrillard, *Simulations*, trans. Paul Foss, Paul Patton, and Philip Beitchman (New York: Semiotext(e), 1983), 54.

13. This is Ruscha in an interview with John Copplans, titled "'Concerning Various Small Fires': Edward Ruscha Discusses His Perplexing Publications," *Artforum*, February 1965; as quoted in Marshall, *Ed Ruscha*, 62.

14. Marshall McLuhan, "Is It Natural That One Medium Should Appropriate and Exploit Another?" in *Essential McLuhan*, ed. Eric McLuhan and Frank Zingrone (New York: Basic Books, 1995), 180.

15. Lev Manovich, *The Language of New Media* (Cambridge, Mass.: MIT Press, 2001), 47.

16. Ibid., 131.

17. Friedrich Kittler, preface to *Gramophone, Film, Typewriter*, reprinted in John Johnston, ed., *Literature, Media, Information Systems* (Amsterdam: OPA/G+B Arts International, 1997), 29.

18. Elizabeth Royte, "E-Gad!" *Smithsonian Magazine*, August 2005, retrieved April 2, 2007, from http://www.smithsonianmagazine.com/issues/2005/august/egad.html.

19. Ibid.

20. Ibid.

21. Fredric Jameson, *The Political Unconscious: Narrative as a Socially Symbolic Act* (Ithaca, N.Y.: Cornell University Press, 1981), 102.

22. For an especially illuminating discussion of the Bechers' career, see Blake Stimson, "The Photographic Comportment of Bernd and Hilla Becher, in *The Pivot of the World: Photography and Its Nation* (Cambridge, Mass.: MIT Press, 2006), 137–175.

23. Ibid., 160.

Index